4/10/95

To Win:

With thanks for the periodic "Constructive dialectic".

Cordially,

[signature]

International Technology Transfers

International Technology Transfers

Editor and Contributing Author
Harry Rubin

Graham & Trotman/Martinus Nijhoff
Members of the Kluwer Academic Publishers Group
LONDON/DORDRECHT/BOSTON

Graham & Trotman Ltd
Sterling House
66 Wilton Road
London SW1V 1DE
UK

Kluwer Academic Publishers Group
101 Philip Drive
Assinippi Park
Norwell, MA 02061
USA

© Graham & Trotman, 1995
First published 1995

ISBN 1-85966-175-0

British Library Cataloguing in Publication Data and Library of Congress Cataloging-in-Publication Data is available

This publication is protected by international copyright law. All rights reserved. No part of this publication may be reproduced, stored in a retrieval system, or transmitted in any form or by any means, electronic, mechanical, photocopying, recording or otherwise without the prior permission of the publishers.

Printed and bound in Great Britain by Hartnolls Ltd., Bodmin, Cornwall.

Contents

Acknowledgment	xvii
Why and How to Use this Book	xix
Chapter One: Intellectual Property Aspects of Technology Transfers	1
I. INTRODUCTION	1
II. CONFIDENTIAL INFORMATION AND TRADE SECRETS	3
A. Advantages of Confidential Information	4
B. Disadvantages of Confidential Information	4
C. Confidentiality Agreements	5
Supranational Regimes	7
Country Focus	8
III. PATENTS FOR INVENTIONS	11
A. What is a Patent?	12
B. Advantages of Patents	14
C. Disadvantages of Patents	14
D. How to Apply for a Patent	15
E. Alternatives to Patents	16
Supranational Regimes	16
Country Focus	21
IV. COPYRIGHT	26
A. What is a Copyright?	26
B. Advantages of Copyright	28
C. Disadvantages of Copyright	28
Supranational Regimes	29
Country Focus	30
V. DESIGNS	35
A. What is a Design?	35
Supranational Regimes	35
Country Focus	38
VI. SEMICONDUCTOR CHIP PROTECTION – TOPOGRAPHY RIGHTS	39
VII. TRADEMARKS AND UNFAIR COMPETITION	39
A. What is a Trademark?	40
Supranational Regimes	41
Country Focus	44

D. Deciding Where and for Which Marks to Register	48
VIII. PRACTICAL ISSUES FOR INTELLECTUAL PROPERTY TRANSFEREES	50
IX. CONCLUSION	52

Chapter Two: Structuring Alternatives for International Technology Transfers — 69

I. FOUR BASIC FORMS OF TECHNOLOGY TRANSFERS	70
A. Direct Sale and Assignment	70
B. Direct End-use Licensing	71
C. Strategic Alliance with Third Party	71
1. Contractual Alliances	72
a. Agents	72
b. Distributors	73
c. Representatives	74
d. Franchising	74
Supranational Regimes	77
Country Focus	78
2. Joint Ventures via Separate Entity	83
a. Joint Venture as a Corporation	84
b. Joint Venture as a Partnership	85
Supranational Regimes	86
Country Focus	87
D. Merger and Acquisition	96
II. KEY CONSIDERATIONS AND RATIONALES DETERMINING THE SELECTION OF THE APPROPRIATE TECHNOLOGY TRANSFER STRUCTURE	97
A. Business Factors	97
1. Technology, Know-how, and R&D	97
2. Capital	98
3. Market Access	98
4. Market Size	98
5. Materials and Supplies	99
6. Allocation of Risk	99
7. Cost Differentials, Expenses and Financing	99
8. Personnel	100
9. Business Cultures	101
10. Time Constraints	101
11. Term	102
12. Proprietary Information – the Business Aspects	102

13. Strategy	103
14. Goals	103
15. Competitive Environment	104
16. Managerial Control	104
17. Nature of Technology to be Transferred	105
18. Political Environment	106
B. Legal Factors	106
1. Ownership of Technology	106
2. Control of Operations and Equity Ownership	108
Country Focus	109
3. Competition Law	113
Supranational Regimes	113
Country Focus	119
4. Competition Between the Parties	126
5. Payment, Repatriation and Convertibility	127
Country Focus	127
6. Liability	130
Supranational Regimes	131
Country Focus	132
7. Local Content	135
Supranational Regimes	136
Country Focus	137
8. Regional Blocks	137
Supranational Regimes	137
9. Export Controls	139
Supranational Regimes	140
Country Focus	141
10. Exit Mechanisms	148
III. CONCLUSION	152

Chapter Three: Contractual Allocation of Rights and Obligations in Technology Transfers — 153

I. GOVERNMENT APPROVALS AND REGULATORY SCHEMES	154
Supranational Regimes	154
Country Focus	156
II. COMPETITION LAW	161
Supranational Regimes	161
Country Focus	163
III. DEFINITION OF TECHNOLOGY TO BE PROVIDED	165

IV. OWNERSHIP	166
Country Focus	168
V. LICENSE GRANT AND RESTRICTIONS	172
A. Purpose	172
B. Territorial Restrictions	172
Supranational Regimes	173
Country Focus	175
C. Exclusivity	177
Supranational Regimes	178
Country Focus	179
D. Use Restrictions	179
Supranational Regimes	180
Country Focus	181
E. Subsequent Transfer of Technology	183
Supranational Regimes	183
Country Focus	183
F. Resale Price Maintenance	184
Supranational Regimes	184
Country Focus	184
G. Tying and Quality Control	185
Supranational Regimes	186
Country Focus	186
H. Assignment of Agreement	187
Country Focus	187
I. Grant-Back and Cross License	188
Supranational Regimes	188
Country Focus	188
J. No Challenge Clauses	189
Supranational Regimes	189
Country Focus	190
VI. CONFIDENTIALITY	190
A. Scope	190
B. Procedures	191
C. Exceptions and Reciprocity	191
Country Focus	192
VII. WARRANTIES AND DISCLAIMERS	194
A. Non-infringement	194
B. Performance – Use, Operation and Results	195
C. Conformity to Laws and Regulations	195
Country Focus	195

CONTENTS

VIII. REMEDIES; INDEMNIFICATION; LIMITATION ON LIABILITY	198
Supranational Regimes	200
Country Focus	200
IX. REVENUES	201
A. Forms of Payment	202
Country Focus	202
B. Minimum Performance Requirements	204
Supranational Regimes	204
C. Royalty Structure	205
Supranational Regimes	205
Country Focus	206
D. Records and Audit Right	206
X. MAINTENANCE AND TRAINING	207
Country Focus	207
XI. NON-COMPETITION	208
Supranational Regimes	208
Country Focus	208
XII. TERM AND TERMINATION	210
A. Duration and Renewal	210
Supranational Regimes	211
Country Focus	211
B. Termination Reasons	213
Country Focus	214
C. Post-termination Rights and Obligations	215
Supranational Regimes	215
Country Focus	216
XIII. CERTAIN MISCELLANEOUS PROVISIONS	216
A. Payment of Fees	217
Country Focus	217
B. Relationship of the Parties – Independent Contractor; Labor Laws	217
Country Focus	217
C. Export Controls	218
D. Most Favored Nations Clause	218

Chapter Four: International Tax Aspects of Technology Transfers — 219

I. TAX DIMENSIONS OF DIFFERENT TRANSFER STRUCTURES — 220
   A. Sale vs. License — 221
   B. Cross Licenses — 225
   C. Contributions to Capital and Transfers for Stock — 226
   D. Distributions — 227

II. TAX IMPLICATIONS FOR DIFFERENT TECHNOLOGY OWNERSHIP AND DEVELOPMENT STRUCTURES — 228
   A. Arrangements within Foreign Multinational Groups — 231
      1. Research and Licensing Contracts within a Foreign Multinational Group — 231
      2. Cost Sharing Arrangements within a Non-U.S. Multinational Group — 234
   B. Arrangements within a U.S. Multinational Group — 236
      1. Contract Research Arrangements within a U.S. Multinational Group — 236
         a. Foreign Ownership — 236
         b. U.S. Ownership — 238
      2. Cost Sharing Arrangements within a U.S. Multinational Group — 239

III. SPECIAL ISSUES IN JOINT VENTURES WITH A UNITED STATES PARTY — 240
   A. Contribution of Technology — 241
   B. Sale or License of Technology — 242
   C. Domestic or Foreign Partnership — 243
      1. Use of U.S. Partner's Foreign Subsidiary — 244
      2. Use of U.S. Partnership with Foreign Subsidiary — 245

Chapter Five: Assignment and Protection of Rights in Technology: Security Interests and Insolvency — 251

PART ONE – SECURED TRANSACTIONS — 252

I. UNITED STATES — 252
   A. Applicable Legal Framework — 253
      1. Copyrights — 255
      2. Patents — 256
      3. Trademarks — 256
      4. Mask Works — 257
   B. Creation and Perfection of Security Interests — 257

CONTENTS

1. Copyrights	258
2. Patents	260
3. Trademarks	260
4. Mask Works	262
5. Technology not Subject to Federal Law – Uniform Commercial Code Article 9	262
C. Documentation Issues	263
D. Covenants Protecting the Intellectual Property Rights Taken as Collateral	265
E. Remedies	266
F. Source Code Escrow	268
G. Due Diligence – Debtor's Rights in the Collateral	268
1. General	269
2. Lien Searches	269
3. "Look-back" Periods	270
H. Contractual Relationships	271
II. CANADA	271
III. GERMANY	273
A. Applicable Legal Framework	274
1. Patents	274
2. Utility Models	275
3. Designs	275
4. Trademarks	275
5. Copyrights	276
6. Licenses	277
7. Software	277
B. Documentation Issues	279
1. Definition of Collateral	279
2. Use by the Debtor	279
3. Communication with the Patent Office	279
4. Third Party Infringement	280
5. Exploitation Rights	280
IV. RUSSIAN FEDERATION	280
V. CZECH REPUBLIC	281
VI. THE NETHERLANDS	282
PART TWO – INSOLVENCY LAWS	283
I. UNITED STATES	283
A. Invalidation of *Ipso Facto* Clauses (Bankruptcy Code Section 365(e)(1) and 541(c) (1)(B))	284

B. Rejection, Assumption and Assignment of Executory Contracts, Including Special Provisions Relating to Intellectual Property Licenses (Bankruptcy Code Section 365)	285
C. Right of Bankruptcy Trustee to Use, Sell or Lease Property (Bankruptcy Code Section 363)	289
D. Automatic Stay (Bankruptcy Code Section 362)	291
E. Avoiding Powers of the Bankruptcy Trustee (Bankruptcy Code Sections 544, 547 and 548)	292
F. Bankruptcy Code Provisions Affecting Security Interests	294
1. Preferential Transfers (Bankruptcy Code Section 547)	294
2. Avoiding Powers (Bankruptcy Code Section 544)	294
3. Fraudulent Transfers (Bankruptcy Code Section 548)	294
4. Cut Off of Security Interests (Bankruptcy Code Section 522)	295
5. Sale of Property Free of Liens (Bankruptcy Code Section 363(f))	295
6. Automatic Stay (Bankruptcy Code Section 362)	295
II. GERMANY	296
A. Patents	296
1. German Patents	296
2. Foreign Patents	297
3. European Union Patents	297
B. Utility Models	297
C. Licenses	298
D. Employee Inventions	298
E. Trade Secrets and Know-how	299
F. Designs	299
G. Trademarks	299
H. Copyrights	299
III. FRANCE	300
IV. CZECH REPUBLIC	301
V. THE NETHERLANDS	302
VI. SPAIN	303

Chapter Six: Applicable Law and Resolution of Technology Transfer Disputes — 305

I. APPLICABLE LAW	305
A. Determination of Applicable Law	306
1. Failure to Designate Express Choice of Law	306
a. The Rome Convention	307

CONTENTS

b. *General Choice of Law Principles*	309
2. Express Choice of Law	310
a. *Non-national Law*	312
b. *International Regimes*	313
c. *Severability*	316
3. Implied Choice of Law	316
B. Limitations on the Freedom to Select the Applicable Law	317
1. Superseding Public Policy Laws	318
a. *Competition Law*	318
b. *Trade Regulation*	320
2. Application of Supplementary and Extra-contractual Laws	322
II. DISPUTE RESOLUTION IN INTERNATIONAL TECHNOLOGY TRANSACTIONS	323
A. Litigation	324
1. The Litigation Forum	324
2. The Pretrial and Trial Process	329
3. Enforcement of Judgments	330
B. Arbitration	332
1. Enforcement	337
C. Other Alternative Dispute Resolution Mechanisms	338

Chapter Seven: Convergence of Technologies and Complex Transfer Structures — 341

I. STRUCTURING UNCERTAINTY IN COMPLEX TECHNOLOGY TRANSFERS	343
A. Types of Collaboration	343
1. Contract Research	343
2. Industrial Sponsorship	344
3. Industrial Collaboration	344
4. Case Study: Cooperative Research Ventures	345
a. *European Union and EFTA*	346
b. *United States*	349
5. Governmental Support	352
6. Case Study: Incubators in Israel	353
7. Strategic Outsourcing	355
8. Case Study: Certain Practical Issues in Structuring a Strategic Outsourcing	356
B. Selection of Partners	360
1. University or Research Institutes	360
2. Competitors	360
3. Other Industries	360

4. Nationality	361
C. Financing Issues	362
1. Monitoring Expenditures	362
2. Payment Against Milestones	362
3. Unforeseen Additional Expenditure	362
D. Implementing the Collaboration	363
1. Research Facilities	363
2. Equipment	363
3. Support Services	364
4. Personnel and Management Resources	364
5. Background Intellectual Property Rights	365
II. STRUCTURING UNCERTAINTY IN COMPLEX TECHNOLOGY TRANSFERS	365
A. Building Uncertainty Into the Collaboration	365
1. Minoxidil	365
2. Aspirin	366
3. Computer Imaging Sperm Selection	366
B. Ownership of Research Results	366
C. Exploitation of Unexpected Results	367
D. Unexpected Territorial Opportunities	368
E. Non-competition Clauses and Conflicts of Interest	368
III. MONITORING UNCERTAINTY IN COMPLEX TECHNOLOGY TRANSFERS	368
A. Cultural Differences Between the Parties	369
B. Monitoring Technological Development	370
C. Monitoring the Exploitation of the Technology	371
D. Establishing Management Controls	371
1. Key Personnel	371
2. Control over Functionality	372
3. Control over the Method of Performance	372
IV. UNWINDING COMPLEX TECHNOLOGY TRANSFERS	373
A. Term of the Agreement and Renewal	373
1. Limiting Access to Information	373
2. Grant of Rights	374
3. Financial Compensation	374
B. Unwinding the Collaboration	375
1. Allocation of Use and Ownership	375
2. Contracts with Outsiders	375
3. Personnel	375
4. Non-competition Obligations	376

V. THE CHALLENGE OF COMPLEX TECHNOLOGY 376
   TRANSFER

Appendix One: The Editor and Contributing Author 379

Appendix Two: The Contributing Authors 381

Index 387

Acknowledgment

I am grateful to Shaw, Pittman, Potts & Trowbridge for its support of this project and would like to express my appreciation to all contributing authors for their outstanding work: my colleagues at Shaw Pittman's Washington office, Trevor W. Nagel, Ralph A. Taylor, Jr., Lynn A. Soukup, Thomas E. Crocker, Jr., Constantine J. Zepos, and Daniela P. Feldhausen, who has also provided me with invaluable assistance in editing Chapter Five; Christopher Millard, Mark Owen and Deborah Ishihara of Clifford Chance in London; D. Kevin Dolan of Weil, Gotshal & Manges in Washington and Kevin McMahon of Weil, Gotshal & Manges in New York; Pierre Lenoir and Nathalie Meyer Fabre of Jeantet & Associés in Paris; Dr. Klaus Günther of Oppenhoff & Rädler in Cologne; and Mark M. Turner of Denton Hall in London.

My special thanks go to Steven L. Meltzer, Chairman of Shaw Pittman's Corporate Department, for his business acumen and practical insight into many of the matters discussed in this book.

Harry Rubin
Coordinator, International Practice Group
Shaw, Pittman, Potts & Trowbridge
Washington, D.C.
March 1995

Why And How To Use This Book

Harry Rubin
Shaw, Pittman, Potts & Trowbridge, Washington, D.C.

The purpose of this book is to provide businesspersons and legal practitioners with a conceptual framework for the analysis and implementation of cross-border technology transactions, and alert parties to technology transfers – the "transferors" and "transferees" – to the salient issues they should systematically resolve as they structure and implement their transaction. The authors have devoted particular attention to the identification of traps, both ominous and innocent, that lurk in the path of successful international technology transfers. The authors use the term "technology" in its broadest possible sense, including what in some countries is referred to as "industrial property" and encompassing all legal categories of intellectual property, such as copyrights, trademarks, patents, know-how and trade secrets.

The impetus for writing this book is the phenomenal growth, globalization and rapidly evolving nature of technology use and technology related transactions. Paradoxically, while technology justifiable has been called the "engine of economic growth,"[1] the transfer of technology from one country to another is perhaps the least appreciated element of economic development.[2]

Technological improvements provide nations with military and economic advantages, thereby shaping international relations. A nation's competitiveness depends on the capacity of its industry to innovate and upgrade products and services. As the world becomes increasingly technologically interdependent, the transfer of technology from one country to another is playing a key role in global development. The transfer of Western technologies to Japan, for example, was extremely successful and has been a predominant factor in securing Japan's current position in the world economy. Likewise, Korea,

---

1. J. Davidson Frame, International Business and Global Technology 7 (1983).
2. Sherman Gee, Technology Transfer, Innovation, and International Competitiveness 27 (1981).

Taiwan, Hong Kong, and Singapore are developing high-tech industries principally based on technology transfers from the industrialized world.

Various factors account for the rapid growth of international technology transfers.[3] One factor is the acceleration of technological development which itself is dependent upon technology transfer and absorption. Second, the "convergence of international capital and factor markets"[4] has permitted multinational corporations to access capital and labor at competitive rates, thereby providing them with needed investment capital for overseas projects irrespective of plant location."[5] Third, the advances in international communications and transportation, whether exemplified by satellite transmission, overnight delivery, or aviation, have contributed significantly to the rapid implementation of technology transfers across borders. Finally, and perhaps most importantly, the competitive reality and evolution of the global market have compelled businesses to keep up with, if not exceed, the prevailing technological state of the art.

As businesses compete in a global environment where trade and non-trade barriers are becoming increasingly transparent, they find that acquiring a technological competitive advantage is a necessary condition for success.[6] Current managerial thinking is beating the drums for firms to envision their "competitive space" if they are to survive. Indeed, in order to sustain and increase market share, many companies not only have stretched their core competencies, re-engineered their work processes and gone global, but also have been seeking ways to re-create their industries and develop new ones in which they could take centre stage.[7] Thus, businesses have adopted a more aggressive approach to technology and one that places the management of technology at the heart of corporate strategy.[8] This is not only true for high-technology industries, such as biotechnology, computers, telecommunications, and microelectronics, but also for other industries whose good fortune depends on their use and absorption of advanced technologies, such as office automation or communications, and for

---

3. See Denis Simon, *International Business and the Transborder Movement of Technology: A Dialectic Perspective, in* TECHNOLOGY TRANSFER IN INTERNATIONAL BUSINESS 11-12 (Tamir Agmon & Mary A. Von Glinow eds., 1991).
4. *Id.* at 11.
5. *Id.* at 12.
6. *See* Amir A. Sternhell, Transnational Movement of High-Tech Goods, at 1 (Sep. 1994) (unpublished manuscript, on file with Shaw, Pittman, Potts & Trowbridge).
7. *Id.*
8. Simon, *supra* note 3, at 13.

which technology-based strategies and operations remain paramount for achieving competitive success.[9]

The thesis of this book is that *different transfer structures impose correspondingly different substantive parameters on technology transfers.* Parties to technology transfers frequently are tempted to negotiate and resolve the operative terms of the transaction before settling the legal and business structure through which the transfer is to be effected. This is the wrong approach.

The parties should first determine their main business objectives. The transferor and, sometimes, transferee must subsequently decide *where* and *how* to protect the intellectual property embodiments of the transferred technology. The primary focus should then be on identifying and selecting the appropriate *structure* for accomplishing the transfer. Failure to do so may hamper and often altogether frustrate the parties' ability to achieve their business objectives. The parties should adopt the structure that is most likely to facilitate the achievement of their long-term and short-term business objectives throughout the life of the transaction. Thus, this book will seek to persuade its readers that clarity of vision and purpose, as well as a detailed appreciation of the intrinsic limits and possibilities presented by each transfer structure, are essential prerequisites for successful technology transfers.

The authors apply an interdisciplinary approach to a complex and interdisciplinary subject matter and seek to harmonize the frequently divergent perspectives that businesspersons and attorneys bring to technology transactions. Inevitably, therefore, it was not possible to treat with the same level of detail all the myriad issues discussed. However, the authors made a conscious effort to focus on those fields of law and business that are particularly germane to international technology transfers and, most importantly, discuss the manner in which they interact with one another.

A glance at the international high-technology arena reveals a predictably stable yet evolving picture. The United States remains the leading producer of high-technology products and is responsible for over one-third of total high-technology production of the membership of the Organization for Economic Cooperation and Development (OECD).

---

9. *See id.*

Table A Region/Country Share of Global High-Tech Market

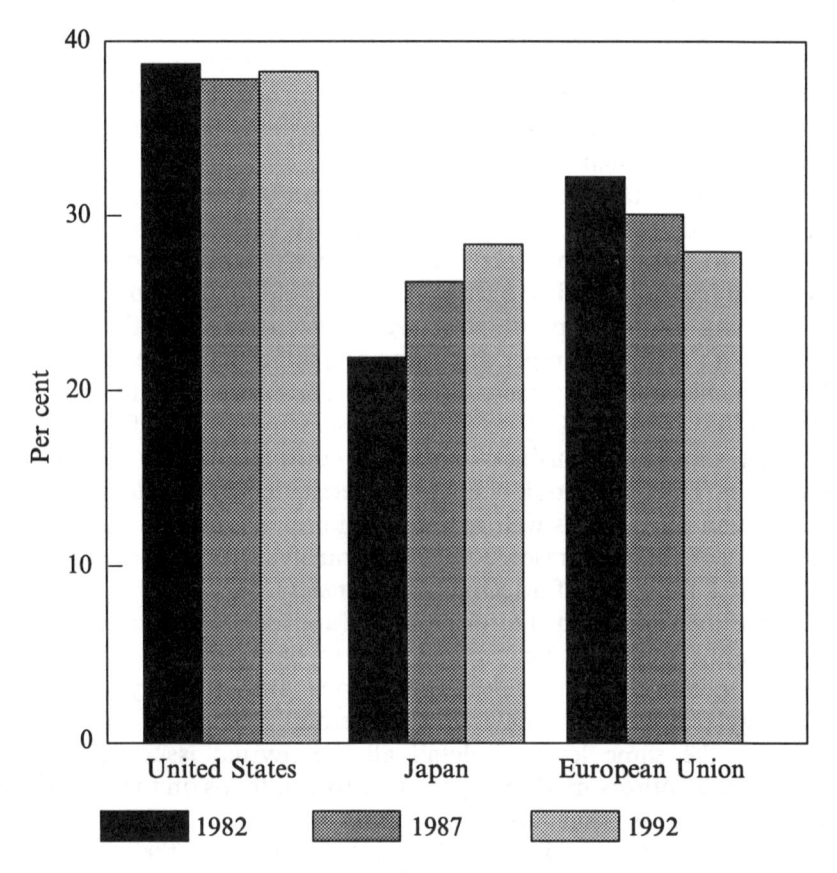

SOURCE: National Science Board, Science & Engineering Indicators – 1993, at 169 (1993).

Data for Table A

	United States	*Japan*	*European Union*
1982	37.5	22.3	33
1987	36.3	26	31
1992	37.2	27.9	29.1

The U.S. leadership position, however, is being challenged by Japan, which since 1983, has surpassed the United States in overall high-technology exports. The growth of Japanese high-technology production is attributable primarily to Japanese businesses investing twice as much of their gross domestic product in plants and equipment as do U.S. businesses.[10] The competitiveness of individual U.S. high-technology industries varies, moreover. Of the six industries that form the OECD high-technology group[11] – drugs and medicines, office and computing devices, electrical machinery, communication equipment, aircraft, and scientific instruments – three U.S. industries (those producing scientific instruments, drugs and medicines, and aircraft) gained global market share during the eighties and maintained their market share into the early nineties. The U.S. computer and office industry experienced the sharpest drop in global share of the six OECD high-technology sectors during the eighties, but also rebounded with the greatest gain in market share in the early nineties. As of the close of 1992, the United States remains the world's leading producer and exporter in aircraft (accounting for 60 per cent of the OECD production), but only the leading producer – not exporter – in scientific instruments (48 per cent), computers and office equipment (43 per cent), and pharmaceuticals (30 per cent).[12]

---

10. Sternhell, *supra* note 6, at 4.
11. The OECD's standard definition of high-technology industries identifies six industries with high R&D intensities (ratio of R&D performed by industry to the value of gross output).
12. NATIONAL SCIENCE BOARD, SCIENCE & ENGINEERING INDICATORS – 1993, at 89 (1993); *see also* Sternhell, *supra* note 6, at 5.

Table B Global Exports of High-Tech Products of Selected OECD Countries as a Percentage of Total OECD Exports (1992)

Drugs and Medicines	Office and Computing Machinery	Electrical Machinery	Communication Equipment	Aircraft	Scientific Instruments
W. Germany 17%	Japan 26%	Japan 22%	Japan 35%	US 41%	Japan 18%
UK 14%	US 19%	W. Germany 19%	UK 9%	France 16%	US 17%
France 12%	UK 12%	US 15%	W. Germany and US 8% each	W. Germany 16%	W. Germany 17%
US 11%	W. Germany 9%	France 8%	France	UK 6%	UK 11%

Source: National Science Board, Science & Engineering Indicators – 1993, at 440–45 (1993).

Parties to international technology transfers must inform themselves of the relevant provisions in at least four overlapping legal systems: the domestic laws of the transferor; the domestic laws of the transferee; supranational regimes, such as the North American Free Trade Agreement (NAFTA) and the European Union (EU); and applicable international regimes, conventions and treaties. Therefore, and in recognition of those countries that figure most prominently in the world's high-technology markets, most Chapters offer a comparative exposition in varying degrees of detail of the manner in which certain issues are treated in different jurisdictions. Inevitably, of course, the different backgrounds, practices and expertise of the contributing authors are reflected in the geographic foci of the Chapters.

Moreover, this book is neither intended to be, nor should it be used as, the definitive resource for effecting technology transactions with or in the reported countries. Rather, the country foci seek to illustrate the different or similar approaches of those jurisdictions to important technology transfer issues and to provide the reader with a flavor of what to expect when transferring technology out of or into those jurisdictions. Thus, while the authors do not purport to proffer the penultimate discussion of each country's law, the reader will find that a number of important legal issues in the key technology jurisdictions have received fairly extensive treatment, thereby providing more than merely a basic introduction into the applicable laws of those countries. This book should *not* be used as a substitute for local counsel, however. On the contrary, one of the main purposes of the country foci is precisely to underscore the need to seek expert local guidance and highlight those matters for which local counsel is particularly important.

Chapter One discusses intellectual property regimes and how to safeguard one's proprietary rights in technology. Transferors should understand the extent and nature of the proprietary rights' protections they may seek for their technology in their home country and in the target country. Whether or not intellectual property rights have been secured in a particular technology is of paramount importance both to transferor and transferee and often is the subject of an intellectual property audit that takes place before the transfer is effected.

With the globalization and specialization of markets, increased competition and high development costs, businesses have found that collaborating with other entities through any variation of strategic alliance forms makes good sense. Evidencing this trend, for example, is the number of reported international multi-firm research and development alliances which grew from about 250 in the 1970s to almost 1,500 in the 1980s.[13] The many business rationales underlying this trend are discussed in detail in Chapter Two. Of particular significance in this context are the time lags associated with technology development and marketing. New financial products, for example, reach the market within nine months after conceptualization. Upgrades of existing technologies usually are driven by specific

---

13. SCIENCE & ENGINEERING INDICATORS, *supra* note 12, at 161-162.

consumer exigencies and are marketed in extremely short time frames. Personal computer companies currently introduce upgraded models based on the 486 and Pentium chips in half-year intervals.[14] To achieve this pace of product development and marketing, even while maintaining vigorous quality controls, businesses necessarily must team up with, or in the rarer case, acquire, appropriate parties.[15]

Chapter Two, therefore, discusses in detail the various structural alternatives that are available for technology transfers, with a particular focus on the different strategic alliance forms, and analyzes the salient business and legal implications of the selection of each structure. Chapter Two seeks to elucidate the relationship between each transfer structure and numerous important legal and business factors in order to provide the reader with practical guidance on how to select the appropriate transfer vehicle for a contemplated transaction.

Chapter Three focuses on contractual provisions typically found in technology transfer agreements whose common denominator is that they invariably arise in the context of a licensing framework; for, as will be explained, the overwhelming majority of technology transfers rightly are constituted as licenses or at least include licensing elements in different permutations.

Chapter Four discusses tax structures and tax implications of technology transfer transactions. While this discussion primarily emanates from a U.S. perspective, it is generally applicable to most technology transfer transactions, and the conceptual principles discussed in this Chapter usually apply to transactions involving non-U.S. parties.

Chapter Five focuses on the rights in technology *after* it is transferred and elucidates the increasingly prevalent phenomenon of taking security interests in transferred technology. This Chapter also analyzes the rights of parties to technology transactions in the event of the bankruptcy of one of the parties.

Chapter Six focuses on conflicts of law, choice of law and dispute resolution in the international technology transfer context. The importance of those matters cannot be overstated, and the purpose of

---

14. Sternhell, *supra* note 6, at 1.
15. Many recent cases demonstrate the success of cooperative frameworks for the development and marketing of technologies. The European Airbus is a result of an alliance between various European enterprises. The SITA telecommunication project encompasses various European telecommunications carriers. The Sematech project in the United States has pooled different semiconductor manufacturers to develop leadership in the field so as to reduce U.S. dependency on Japanese suppliers. The General Magic project has teamed Apple and Motorola together with the software developer, Magic, in order to create tomorrow's personal communication devices. *Id.* at 2.

this Chapter, among other things, is to persuade the reader that they should be given ample consideration and weight at the outset of the transaction.

Chapter Seven focuses on two key themes increasingly characterizing the evolution of technology – *complexity* and *uncertainty* – and explores the implications of these themes for properly structuring, negotiating, and implementing technology transfers. This Chapter also describes several structures often used for complex technology transfers, including cooperative research ventures and "incubators" for developing early-stage research and strategic outsourcings for achieving optimal applications and performance for technology end-users.

Thus, the authors hope to proffer a conceptual road map for approaching, analyzing and most effectively implementing cross-border technology transactions while developing strategies for successfully maximizing the rewards and coping with the challenges and evolving landscape presented by international technology transfers.

Chapter One

Intellectual Property Aspects of Technology Transfers

Christopher Millard, Mark Owen and Deborah Ishihara
Clifford Chance, London

I. INTRODUCTION

The intellectual property rights embodied in technology constitute the core of technology businesses. The intangible nature of intellectual property assets and their significant value pose special problems and require particular sensitivities. Like other assets, the value of intellectual property rights can quickly depreciate or disappear completely if they are not properly protected and maintained. To avoid this, a business needs to be aware of both what intellectual property rights it has and how it may protect and exploit those rights. This Chapter will elucidate the different types of intellectual property rights and offer methods for identifying what rights a potential technology transferor or transferee should seek in a particular technology and how and to what extent those rights should be protected.

An intellectual property right is unlike a right to real estate or a security. The intangible nature of the right and the portability of ideas mean that a business has to consider not only how to protect its intellectual property in the place where it was first developed or, if different, in the transferor's home country, but also in the transferee's jurisdiction and elsewhere. Unfortunately, while there is a large number of international intellectual property treaties, there is no single worldwide system. Intellectual property rights have arisen in a piecemeal and inconsistent fashion around the world, thereby reflecting the varying priorities of different nations.[1] It is beyond the scope of this book to provide a definitive account of all the different intellectual property rights in every country. Instead, the various ways intellectual property rights are treated around the world are discussed by reference to a representative sample of countries. Significantly, due to the variety of ways in which rights may be acquired and protected in different countries, a business must seek appropriate advice on applicable local laws.

In order to understand intellectual property rights, the best place to start is probably not with an overview of the law but rather with an assessment of what a business may wish to protect and how it may go about doing so. We therefore explain the different types of intellectual property protection in the order in which a business should consider them when it makes a new invention or discovery, or develops a new technology for future domestic or international commercialization.

While "technology," as used in this book, has a broad meaning and covers many different fields, the inherent value of technology can, in general, only be protected by the enforcement of intellectual property rights. In determining what the applicable intellectual property rights are, one must first examine what it is about the particular technology invention, design or idea that the business should seek to protect because it is new or clever or the result of much hard work and which another business should not be able to use without payment or permission. The types of intellectual property rights that may be applicable here are confidential information, trade secrets, know-how, patents, copyright and design rights. There is a second tier of intellectual property rights which relate not to the innovation, but to the reputation of a business and are an important means by which a business can protect and secure the competitive advantage the innovation has given it. The applicable type of intellectual property right here is generally the subject of trademark law and, to a lesser extent, copyright law.

---

1. There may, one day, be a worldwide system of intellectual property rights and it is the area of law where international comity is perhaps closest. Discussion on intellectual property issues formed a large part of the Uruguay round of the talks on the General Agreement on Trade and Tariffs (GATT) and encouraging countries to establish strong systems of intellectual property forms a major part of many countries' (particularly the U.S.') foreign policy. As the world's use and reliance upon new technologies (for example in the biotechnology and computer fields) grows, such rights will become increasingly important.

II. CONFIDENTIAL INFORMATION AND TRADE SECRETS

An innovation generally begins with an idea or concept. An engineer, scientist or programmer (or indeed anyone) conceives of a new way of producing, depicting or doing something. With many inventions, the idea is the only potentially protectible feature. However, the intellectual property in an idea is fragile and can easily be compromised. The natural inclination when struck by such an idea may be to shout "Eureka!," jump out of the bath tub and tell everyone about it. However, while the inventor may be fleetingly rewarded with the admiration of others, control over the idea will have been lost. If someone who hears the inventor describe the idea then proceeds to use the idea, the inventor will have no right to sue that person. This places the inventor in something of a quandary. If he tells no one about the idea, it is unlikely he will be able to exploit it in any way because he will be unable to share it with a manufacturer or transfer the idea to anyone. The way around this dilemma is to ensure that those whom the inventor wants to tell about the idea are subject to restrictions of confidentiality which prevent them from disclosing the idea to others or using it for their own ends without the inventor's permission. There are some relationships (such as the relationship between employer and employee) where a duty of confidentiality will often be implied by law. However, as a general rule, an express agreement of confidentiality is a wise precaution (see below), as is marking any documents relating to the idea "confidential," leaving them only in secure places, and otherwise restricting access to such documents.

There are many ideas which a business will only protect as confidential information and for which it will not seek any other form of protection or for which no other form of intellectual property protection is available. This will depend upon the nature of the idea. For example, if the idea relates to a new design for a particular part of a machine, the idea will become known to anyone who buys the machine. They merely have to dismantle (or reverse engineer) the machine and look at the design of the particular part, and the idea will no longer be confidential. For this type of idea, the business may choose to rely on another form of protection, such as a copyright or a patent. However, an idea for a process of manufacture, the details of which are not apparent from the finished article, may only be discoverable by a competitor going inside the business' factory and seeing the process at work. For this type of information, the protection offered by the law of confidence may be the best protection available to ensure the business' exclusive rights to the idea for as long as possible. If the business decided to patent the process instead, the invention would be published in a patent application which would be available to competitors for study. If they were unable to find a way of designing around the patent within the term of the patent (up to 20 years in some countries), they would be able to use it as soon as the patent expired. With confidential information, the business can maintain control of the idea until such time as it enters the public domain. This may be many years away if the business takes appropriate precautions. An often-cited example of a piece of confidential information or trade secret that successfully has been kept secret for many years is the Coca Cola formulation which is said to be known only to a handful of people in the world.

A. Advantages of Confidential Information

One of the principal advantages of keeping an idea confidential (as opposed to, for example, applying for a patent in respect of a particular invention) is that it is a relatively cheap form of protection. A well-run business will, as a matter of course, keep its premises secure, not allow unauthorized visitors, place its employees under obligations of confidentiality, and not disclose its trade secrets and confidential information to outsiders. The other great advantage is that the protection offered by keeping an idea confidential is potentially infinite and will only be lost once the idea enters the public domain. Other rights, such as patents and copyright, are the subject of a limited term.

B. Disadvantages of Confidential Information

The principal disadvantage of the law of confidence as a method of protecting an idea is the ephemeral nature of the protection. The longer an idea has been protected as confidential information, the larger the number of people (such as employees) who will have become familiar with the idea. This increases the chances of the idea being made public and the protection being lost. In many jurisdictions, employers are unable – whether legally or as a practical matter – to prevent their ex-employees from later using for a new employer the skill and knowledge they have acquired as part of their trade. Such knowledge may include elements of the employer's confidential information, which thereby ceases to be confidential. In addition, the law of confidence does not offer a monopoly right over an idea. If other people come by the idea independently they are free to do with it as they will.

In practice, it can be very difficult to sue successfully for misappropriation of confidential information because the protection is so ephemeral and because of the wide-ranging defenses available for an infringer. If the infringer can establish that the information has been published anywhere in the world, the information has become public knowledge and cannot be protected. Even if the information has been disclosed illegally, once it has been disclosed, there usually is nothing that can be done to make it confidential again. A good example of how even governments are powerless to keep such information confidential is the *Spycatcher* case in the United Kingdom. An ex-member of the U.K. security services published an account of his activities. The U.K. government successfully prevented publication of the book in the United Kingdom relying on his continuing duty of confidentiality about his work.[2] However, the book was freely published in other countries and soon became readily available in the United Kingdom. Eventually the U.K. government had no alternative but to permit publication in the United Kingdom as well. A business should always, therefore, attempt to rely on other forms of intellectual property protection, such as copyright, in tandem with confidential information. This is the approach adopted by, for example, software publishers.

C. Confidentiality Agreements

Before revealing know-how, trade secrets or any other information about a new invention or work to another party, a business must consider first making that party subject to a non-disclosure or confidentiality agreement. If any information is revealed without a suitable agreement in place, the value of the information may be lost completely. The importance of this cannot be over-emphasized because the protection may be lost so easily.

Owners of confidential information are particularly vulnerable when providing the information to a potential customer or strategic ally for evaluation or trial purposes. All too often, a business will casually reveal the information to another in such contexts. This may devalue the information for both parties by rendering it non-confidential. The receiving party may no longer be interested in the information if it may also be freely used by its competitors. To protect the value of the information, the disclosing party must insist on an evaluation agreement that only allows the other party to inspect and assess the

---

2. *Attorney General v. The Guardian Newspapers Ltd.*, [1987] 1 W.L.R. 1248.

information but not to use that information for any other purpose, whether for the receiving party's own benefit or the benefit of any third party. Ideally, the agreement should enumerate all legitimate uses of the confidential information and impose strict time limits on the performance of the evaluation. The owner of the confidential information should require the recipient to return the information at any time the owner deems appropriate; at the end of the agreed-upon evaluation period; or on a certain date – whichever of the foregoing occurs first. The recipient should be required irrevocably to waive and renounce any claims to the information and undertake not to develop a competitive product within, for example, one year after the end of the evaluation. The agreement should also specify concrete steps to be taken by the recipient to protect the information. These should include keeping the information in a safe place; limiting access on a "need to know basis"; and having all employees, agents or contractors of the recipient, who have access to the information, acknowledge the disclosing party's ownership of the information and its confidential nature.

Confidentiality agreements must be carefully drafted. Antitrust and restraint of trade laws in many countries prevent parties from claiming rights over certain categories of information and an agreement which purports to do so may be unenforceable.[3] The information which the disclosing party considers to be confidential should be carefully identified as such. However, recipients of confidential information often insist that information which falls within one of the following categories not be considered confidential:

- information which at the time of the disclosure was in the public domain;
- information which, after the disclosure, entered the public domain other than through the fault of the receiving party;
- information which, at the time of disclosure, the receiving party already had in its possession or which the receiving party acquired from someone else;
- information which is or was independently developed by the receiving party;
- information which the disclosing party had disclosed to another party without restriction; or
- information which is disclosed as required, by law, or governmental rules or regulations.

3. *See* Chapter Three, Section VI.

Supranational Regimes

When transferring confidential information and know-how in the **European Union (EU)** countries, EU competition law must be considered, especially the Know-how Block Exemption[4] (which in due course will be replaced by the Technology Transfer Block Exemption[5]). This exemption allows parties to enter into know-how licenses provided those licenses do not include terms perceived as being anti-competitive. Objectionable clauses include restrictions on the licensee's use of the know-how once the information has entered the public domain and obligations on the licensee to grant the licensor exclusive licenses over improvements developed by the licensee.

The protection afforded to confidential information varies by country and there has been no general international agreement on its protection. One exception is **GATT TRIPs**[6] which requires member states to protect undisclosed confidential information against disclosure or use by others without the owner's consent in a manner contrary to honest commercial practices, including breach of contract or a breach of other obligations of confidentiality. This protection extends to data required to be disclosed to government bodies, for example, for product approvals. No unfair commercial use may be made of such data.

NAFTA[7] states that each party shall provide the legal means for any person to prevent trade secrets from being disclosed to, acquired by, or used by others without the consent of the person lawfully in control of the information in a manner contrary to honest commercial practices.[8] To be regarded as secret, the information must not generally be known; it must have actual or potential commercial value; and the person lawfully in control of it must have taken reasonable steps to keep it secret.[9] NAFTA further states that no party may discourage or impede the voluntary licensing of trade secrets by imposing excessive or discriminatory conditions on such licenses or conditions that dilute the value of the trade secrets.[10]

---

4. Commission Regulation 556/89 on the Application of Article 85(3) of the Treaty of Rome to certain categories of know-how licensing agreements, 1986 O.J. (L 61) 1.
5. Preliminary Draft Commission Regulation of September 30, 1994 on certain categories of technology transfer agreements, 1994 O.J. (C 178).
6. The Agreement on Trade Related Aspects of Intellectual Property Rights (TRIPs) which forms part of the General Agreement on Tariffs and Trade (GATT).
7. North American Free Trade Agreement which came into effect on January 1, 1994.
8. *Id.* art. 1711(1).
9. *Id.*
10. *Id.* art. 1711(4).

Country Focus

In **China,** prior to the new Unfair Competition Law,[11] trade secrets could only be protected by contract. Under the new law, trade secrets are defined as meaning technical and business information not in the public domain, which brings economic benefits to the party entitled thereto, is of practical use, and is kept confidential by the party entitled thereto.[12] When disclosing confidential information it is important to make sure that confidentiality be maintained, preferably by means of a confidentiality agreement. Under the new law business operators are prohibited from:

(i) obtaining trade secrets from their owner by means of stealing, luring by promises of gain, coercing or other improper means;
(ii) disclosing, using or permitting the use of a trade secret so obtained; or
(iii) acting in breach of an agreement or in breach of conditions imposed by the owner of the trade secret or disclosing, using or permitting the use of a trade secret without the owner's knowledge.[13]

Foreign know-how licensors are mainly protected by the obligation on the licensee to keep secret know-how and related technical data within the scope and term stipulated in the licensing contract.[14] The binding term of the obligation is usually not longer than the contract itself.

In **France,** Title II of Book VI of the French Intellectual Property Code covers trade secrets and know-how.[15] Its application is limited to the unauthorized use or disclosure of trade secrets by a director or salaried person of the enterprise in which he is employed.[16] Thus, most confidential information requires protection in contract.

Trade secrets in **Japan** can be protected under an amendment to the Unfair Competition Prevention Law.[17] In order to obtain protection under the law, a licensor must establish reasonable controls on confidentiality under agreement with the licensee. Provisions restricting

---

11. With effect from December 1993.
12. Unfair Competition Law of 1993, art. 10(3).
13. *Id.* art. 10(1)-(3).
14. Implementing Rules of the People's Republic of China's Regulations for the Administration of Technology Importation Contracts, art. 13.
15. This provision of the Code is reflected in art. 418 of the Penal Code.
16. Intellectual Property Code of 1992, art. L621-1.
17. Fred M. Greguras, *Software Licensing in Japan: 1991 Checklist for United States Licensors*, E. ASIAN EXEC. REP., May 1991, at 8.

the use and disclosure of trade secrets must be drawn up so as to survive the termination or expiration of the license agreement. The obligation to maintain confidentiality can be expressed to continue indefinitely, or be for a specified period, or subsist until the information has entered the public domain. Typically, a period of three to five years after expiration of the license agreement is provided for in agreements.

Prior to the new Law for the Development and Protection of Industrial Property,[18] there was virtually no legal protection of trade secrets in **Mexico**. The new law states that trade secrets comprise

> all information having industrial application kept confidentially by an individual or corporate entity. The information of a trade secret shall necessarily refer to the nature, the characteristics or purposes of the products; to the production methods or processes; or to the means or manner of distributing or marketing products or rendering services.[19]

Information will not be considered to be a trade secret if it is in the public domain or if it is obvious.[20] To be considered a trade secret, the secret must comprise information contained in documents, electronic or magnetic means, optical disks, microfilms, films, or any other similar instruments.[21] Despite the lengths to which the law goes to define trade secrets, as there is no injunctive relief available for unauthorized disclosures, it is uncertain how effectively they will be protected under it. Confidential information may be assigned or licensed, and confidentiality clauses may be included in agreements to protect such information.[22]

The law protecting confidential information in the **United Kingdom** is not statutory but is contained in the common law. Trade secrets and other confidential information may be protected. To qualify as confidential information, the information must have "the necessary quality of confidence"[23] and must have been imparted in circumstances importing an obligation of confidence on the recipient.[24] It is generally held that if a reasonable man standing in the shoes of the recipient of the information would have realized upon reasonable grounds that the information was being given to him in confidence, then this should

---

18. Law for the Development and Protection of Industrial Property of 1991.
19. *Id.*, art. 82.
20. *Id.*
21. *Id.*, art. 83.
22. *Id.*, art. 84.
23. *Saltman Engineering Co. v. Campbell Engineering Co. Ltd.*, [1963] R.P.C. 65.
24. *Coco v. Clark (AN) (Engineers) Ltd.*, [1969] R.P.C. 41.

suffice to impose upon him an equitable obligation of confidence.[25] In addition there must be an unauthorized use of the information to the detriment of the disclosing party.[26]

Know-how may be assigned or licensed, but it is essential to ensure the continued secrecy of the information. The owner should therefore obtain undertakings from anyone with whom he shares the information, preventing future use of the know-how or disclosure of the know-how to any third party. In addition, it is wise to impose express confidentiality obligations on employees even if they are also likely to be subject to an implied duty of confidentiality. Another frequently relevant legal doctrine is restraint of trade. The law accepts that there is a public interest in allowing individuals to carry on their trade freely, even where this may be based on the skills they have acquired working for a particular employer.[27] However, the law does allow an employer to restrict his employees from using business secrets acquired during his employment.

There is no federal trade secret law in the **United States**. Although a Uniform Trade Secret law has been proposed and a Uniform Trade Secret Act[28] adopted by over 35 states, there remain significant areas of the country where trade secret law is based upon the case law of that particular state. In addition, those states that have adopted the Uniform Trade Secrets Act have not done so uniformly. For example, it is procedurally more onerous for a trade secret owner to enforce its rights against a defendant in California than in some other states. However, apart from this, there are in practice few significant differences between state laws.

Application of trade secret law in the United States involves a balancing of competing interests. On the one hand, the law is concerned to protect the owner of trade secrets against misappropriation and to encourage innovation. On the other hand, it seeks to protect the rights of an employee to change employment and use any acquired knowledge, experience, skill, and expertise for a new employer. Generally, it seeks to promote the public interest in competition and a "full and free use of ideas in the public domain."[29] The most commonly used definition of a "trade secret" states that:

---

25. *Id.*
26. *Id.*
27. *See, e.g., Nordenfelt v. Maxim Nordenfeld Guns & Ammunition Co.,* [1894] A.C. 535.
28. Uniform Trade Secrets Act, 14 U.L.A. 433 (1990). In addition, an approach to trade secrets has been proposed in the Restatement (Second) of Torts.
29. *Lear, Inc. v. Adkins,* 395 U.S. 653, 668 (1969).

A trade secret may consist of any formula, pattern, device or compilation of information which is used in one's business, and which gives one an opportunity to obtain an advantage over competitors who do not know or use it. It may be a formula for a chemical compound, a process of manufacturing, treating or preserving materials, a patent for a machine or other device, or a list of customers.... The subject matter of the trade secret must be secret.[30]

An alternative and also widely used definition is that contained in the Uniform Trade Secrets Act:

Information including a formula, pattern, compilation, program, device, method, technique or process, that (i) derives independent economic value, present or potential, from not being generally known to, and not being readily ascertainable by proper means by, other persons who can obtain economic value from its disclosure or use, and (ii) is the subject of efforts that are reasonable under the circumstances to maintain its secrecy.[31]

A trade secret claimant in the United States must show that the claimed secret provides a demonstrable competitive advantage over alternatives. It is not sufficient for a claimant to show merely that the information is of some commercial value to him.[32] As in other jurisdictions, trade secret status can be lost easily by disclosing the secret in publications, such as patents.[33]

III. PATENTS FOR INVENTIONS

Once the business has had the idea and has put in place appropriate measures to ensure it is kept confidential, the business should next consider what other intellectual property protection may be available and appropriate. Certain intellectual property rights such as copyright,[34] will generally arise automatically. There are certain other rights, however, such as patents, which require a formal application to an appropriate government agency in each jurisdiction before they are granted. In many jurisdictions, the right to apply for a patent in respect of an invention will be lost if the application is not made within a certain

---

30. RESTATEMENT (SECOND) OF TORTS § 757, cmt. b (1939).
31. Uniform Trade Secrets Act, *supra* note 28, § 1.
32. *Pressure Science, Inc. v. Kramer,* 413 F. Supp. 618, 629 (D. Conn.), *aff'd without opinion,* 551 F.2d 301 (2d Cir. 1976).
33. *See Ruckelshaus v. Monsanto Co.,* 467 U.S. 986, 1002 (1984).
34. *See infra* Section IV.

period of time after the invention has been used. A patent attorney should be consulted at an early stage if the invention is one for which patent protection may be appropriate.

Patent law offers some similar protections to the law of confidence. Apart from total secrecy protection, a patent is the nearest form of intellectual property protection to a right over ideas. Significantly, however, it does not protect the basic idea behind the invention but rather the invention itself, as described in the patent specification.

A. What is a Patent?

A patent is a registered right which confers on its owner a monopoly for whatever is claimed in that patent. The claimed monopoly may be in respect of a product, such as an electronic component or a chemical, or in respect of a process, such as a method of manufacture. The monopoly is enforced by suing persons who use the invention without the consent of the patent holder for patent infringement. If another business comes by the same idea and develops its own invention similar to that contained in the patent, it will infringe the patent regardless of whether it actually copied the first business' idea. The rationale behind the patent system is that invention and innovation should be encouraged by providing inventors and innovators with monopoly rights for the *exploitation* of their invention or innovation for a limited period of time. Society benefits by the *disclosure* of the idea to it in the form of the patent specification from which others may learn and benefit. If the patentee[35] were allowed too broad or too long a monopoly, however, this could become counter-productive and could be abused by the patentee to stifle development and free competition. In order to strike a balance between incentive and restriction, therefore, the monopoly granted to the patentee is limited so that after a certain number of years the invention is available for anyone to use free of charge.

So long as the relevant fees are paid, and provided the patent is not revoked, a granted patent lasts for a set period of years from the date when the application giving rise to the patent was first filed.[36] After the expiration of that period, the invention is available for all to use. Some countries also give extended patent protection in respect of certain products. A common example is pharmaceuticals which, by the time

---

35. The owner of a patent is called "the patentee." Formally, the owner has received a grant of letters patent.
36. In the **United Kingdom** and most other European countries this period is 20 years. In the **United States** it is 17 years.

they have been through all necessary regulatory testing and experimentation, may have very little of the basic patent term left.[37]

Patents will generally be granted only for inventions which were not previously known (the "prior art") and which were not an obvious step in the light of what was previously known. If details of an invention are published before a patent application is filed, they become part of the prior art and the inventor will be unable to obtain a patent. It is important, therefore, for an inventor not to disclose an invention, for example, in a journal or at a trade show, before applying for a patent. The inventor will need to describe the invention to a patent attorney who will prepare an application for a patent. This should, however, only be done where the patent attorney is under an obligation to keep the invention confidential. The relevant date determining whether the alleged invention is new or not obvious is called the "priority date." That date will either be a date upon which the application for the patent was made in the particular country, or, within the previous 12 months, the date upon which another application was made either in the same country or elsewhere in respect of the same subject matter.

There is no unified patent system in force throughout the world. There are, however, a number of conventions between nations which ensure some degree of uniformity between different systems. The most significant country that does not yet adhere to the approach generally adopted elsewhere is the United States, though the differences are mainly procedural and their practical impact is limited. An example of the differences between the systems is the way each decides which of two or more competing inventors should be granted patent rights over an invention. In most countries, a "first to file" system is operated. This means that if two inventors come to the same invention independently of each other, the first inventor to file the patent application will be granted the patent. In the United States, however, there is a "first to invent" system. This means that where two inventors independently apply for a patent for the same invention, it will not be the first to file the patent application who is granted the patent but the first to have made the invention. For example, on March 1, inventor A invents a method for producing batteries that never need recharging. On March 2, inventor B independently also invents the same method for producing lifelong batteries. On March 3, inventor B files patent applications in the United States and the United Kingdom. On March 4, inventor A also files patent applications in the United States and United Kingdom. Faced with the two identical applications the United States would

---

37. An example of this, the European Union's Supplementary Protection Certificate Regulation, is discussed below.

award a patent to inventor A, who was first to invent the battery but not to B. The United Kingdom would award a patent to B who was first to file the patent application but not to A. The United States plans to come into line with the rest of the world and adopt a first-to-file system but as yet a date for this change has not been set.

Ethical issues have recently begun to arise in the field of patent law. In some jurisdictions, inventions which encourage immoral behavior are excluded from patent protection. Ethics have become particularly important in the context of bio-technological inventions where there has been considerable debate over whether a company can obtain a monopoly right to a particular life form.[38] A celebrated example was the application in Europe by The President and Fellows of Harvard College for a patent in respect of a mouse, the "Oncomouse," into which a gene had been incorporated to render it particularly susceptible to cancer. The application was granted by the European Patent Office (EPO), despite arguments that the invention was immoral.[39] The patent currently is the subject of further proceedings before the EPO in which various parties are seeking to have the patent revoked on the same grounds.

B. Advantages of Patents

A patent grants a monopoly right for the exploitation of a particular invention. If the patentee has sufficient resources, he can obtain equivalent patents in most countries around the world. In addition, having a patent over an invention makes it easier to license or assign rights in the invention. Companies tend to be wary of acquiring rights to confidential information in this way from an inventor because it is so difficult to know whether the inventor has any enforceable rights or whether the information is already publicly known. A patent, however, indicates that, at least in the opinion of the relevant patent examiner, the invention is not owned by any other party and is not in the public domain.

C. Disadvantages of Patents

Patents are expensive to obtain and maintain. There is the initial cost of drafting the patent application and the later costs of paying renewal

---

38. For example, sequences of recombinant DNA.
39. Decision of Technical Board of Appeal 3.3.2 (October 3, 1990).

fees. If renewal fees are not paid, the patent may be revoked. In addition, even where a patent is granted, it may be revoked at the suit of another party if, for example, the other party is able to show that the invention covered had been made known to the public before the patent application was made. Further, the patentee is generally under an obligation to describe the invention in sufficient detail in the patent specification for it to be understood by a person skilled in the relevant art. This means that the idea behind the invention is available to competitors who can then seek to design around the invention and the invention can be used freely in other countries where there is no patent protection.

If a patentee fails to exploit or "work" the invention protected by the patent, he may be *forced* to license the patent to others by means of a compulsory license. Many countries allow other parties to apply to the national authority for a license when the invention has not been worked for a period of time (often three years). Although the license granted may provide for royalties to be paid to the patentee under the compulsory license, the patentee has in effect lost much of the control over the invention that he would have had if he had worked the patent and licensed others on his own terms.

D. How to Apply for a Patent

The first step in applying for a patent is to describe in writing the invention that is to be made. This document is known as the "patent specification" and is commonly drafted by a skilled patent draftsman such as a patent agent or patent attorney. A patent specification comprises two major portions: the description and the claims. The claims of the patent define the scope of the monopoly sought by the applicant. The description describes the technology used before the invention was made and how the invention represents an improvement over that technology. It also describes at least one specific embodiment of the invention and there may be drawings or formulae appended to the specification to assist the reader in understanding the description of the specific embodiments. The description must be sufficiently clear to enable a person skilled in the relevant technology to carry out the invention.

The patent application is made to the appropriate national or international regulatory authority. Deciding to which authority to apply is not as straightforward as it sounds. Most countries permit an application to be made to a government agency in that country for a patent over the invention in that country. To acquire patent rights in other countries, the patent applicant will need to apply separately in each of those countries. Moreover, patent applications in the different countries have to be made nearly simultaneously[40] with the first application or the applicant will lose the right to obtain a patent in those other countries. This is because the disclosure of the invention in the patent application (and subsequent patent) in one country may amount to a publication of the invention worldwide. The invention will enter the prior art and the inventor will be unable to obtain further patents.

For an inventor to gain maximum patent protection for an invention, he is faced with applying for a patent in each country where he wishes to exploit the invention or wishes to stop others from exploiting it. Such duplication is extremely expensive and, given the differences in the priorities of national patent offices, introduces uncertainty into whether the patentee will be able to obtain the desired protection. In an attempt to reduce such duplication and harmonize practices, various international systems have arisen in recent years, allowing for a single patent application to an international authority which then grants a patent for the countries nominated by the applicant. Unfortunately, as discussed below, there are several different and overlapping systems, and the applicant is still faced with the difficult decision of what patent filings to make to protect the invention as effectively as possible.

E. Alternatives to Patents

Some jurisdictions have an alternative to a patent called a "petty patent" or "utility model." These are easier and cheaper to obtain but generally give the owner an even narrower monopoly than a patent and often are valid for fewer years. In addition, utility models only cover particular articles or products, not processes of manufacture.

Supranational Regimes

The **Patent Co-operation Treaty (PCT)** provides for a single application which can designate countries on a large international scale. The PCT signatory countries include most European countries, Japan and the United States.[41] The advantages of a PCT application are primarily cost and convenience. Under the PCT, the applicant applies

---

40. Under the Paris Convention there is a one-year grace period from the first application for a patent in one country for the patentee to make applications in other countries which are parties to that Convention.
41. The member countries are listed in the Comparative Table of Supranational Regimes.

for a patent to the applicant's national patent office specifying the other PCT countries in which he seeks a patent. The national office carries out an international search to determine, on a non-binding basis, whether the invention is novel, non-obvious and capable of industrial application. If the applicant still wants to proceed at this stage, the search and non-binding opinion are sent to each relevant national patent office for processing.

The advantage of a PCT patent application is that it makes it easier for an applicant who wishes to apply in a number of countries at the same time. The applicant need only complete one application, and the date on which that application is filed is used as the filing date for all the countries named in the application.

The **European Patent Convention (EPC)** provides for a centralized method of applying for national patents.[42] It allows for the submission of a single patent application to the EPO which can confer patent protection in one or more of the European signatory countries. These countries currently are **Austria, Belgium, Denmark, France, Germany, Greece, Ireland, Italy, Liechtenstein, Luxembourg, Monaco, The Netherlands, Portugal, Spain, Sweden, Switzerland** and the **United Kingdom**. On the grant of a European Patent, the patentee acquires the same rights in each of the countries he has designated in his application as if he had directly applied to the individual national patent offices.

The EPC application can be submitted either to any of the designated national patent offices or the EPO. If filed at the national office, the application will be forwarded to the EPO. The application must be filed in either French, German or English. If an application to revoke the European Patent is made at the EPO in the 12-month period following grant, the EPO can revoke that patent in all countries for which the European patent was granted. Such an application is called an opposition. It takes two to three years for a decision on an opposition to be reached. Further, the decision can be appealed and it can take another two to three years before that appeal is concluded.

On grant, the European Patent is treated in each country designated by the applicant as a national patent provided the applicant completes the necessary formalities for that country. Local agents and translations of the specification into the local language will be needed for each of the designated countries for which the applicant wishes to keep the patent (he does not have to keep all the countries originally designated).

National patent offices offering national patents still exist, although it is likely that some signatories to the EPC will decide that such offices are no longer viable. For the time being, national patents are cheaper if

---

42. The EPC came into force on October 7, 1977.

one simply requires local protection, but a European Patent is generally more cost-effective if protection is sought in three or more countries. Most local patent laws in EPC signatory countries have already been harmonized so that they broadly follow the EPC. Issues of infringement and validity, therefore, should theoretically be dealt with in a similar way.

The **Community Patent Convention** (CPC) is intended to produce a single EU-wide patent rather than the bundle of national patents provided for by the EPC. The CPC, originally signed in December 1975, will only come into force once all member states have ratified it. To date **Denmark** and **Ireland** still have not ratified the Convention. It is uncertain when these two countries will do so, if at all. In the opinion of some patent professionals, the CPC will probably never come into force.

The aim of the CPC is that any European patent application which designates an EU member state will automatically (unless a contrary intention is expressed) become a Community Patent Application and, when granted, will result in a patent valid in every member state. Once again, translations will be required into the languages of the individual EU member state. Questions of invalidity of the patent will be handled centrally in the EPO, but with infringement actions dealt with by local national courts at the first instance. It will be possible for a member state to decide that, in respect of actions for infringement relating to that territory, their courts can decide on both infringement and validity for that country.

Under the CPC, the patent can only be transferred, revoked (except in exceptional circumstances) or allowed to lapse in respect of the whole of the EU. It will, however, be possible to license the patent for any part of the EU and indeed to obtain national compulsory licenses in some circumstances (although patentees must be aware of the principle of exhaustion of rights).[43] There will be one Common Appeal Court (COPAC) which will hear all appeals from National Courts and the EPO on matters involving the infringement or validity of patents granted under the CPC.

A patent granted under the CPC will have several advantages for patentees. It will mean that a patentee's administration of its patent portfolio will be made substantially cheaper and simpler. For example, only one set of renewal fees will be payable. The initial cost

---

43. Under EU law, products sold by a patent owner in one EU country can circulate freely in the other member states. The patent owner cannot use his patent rights in the other member states to prevent sale of the products. This is known as the "exhaustion of rights" doctrine.

of obtaining and maintaining patent protection should decrease as the costs of a patent granted under the CPC should be less than the bundle of national patents which can be obtained under the EPC. It will become possible to take action against infringers which will have EU-wide effect, and only one revocation action (in the EPO) need be brought which will also have EU-wide effect. However, there are some disadvantages to a single patent system such as the CPC. The most obvious is that a non-specialist court in one country could make a decision which would have serious ramifications across the whole of the EU, thereby encouraging forum shopping. However, in time, this should mean that the levels of expertise in courts across the EU would approximate.

An important supranational regime in the pharmaceutical field is that of **Supplementary Protection Certificates (SPC).** Under the applicable EU regulation,[44] owners of patents in respect of pharmaceutical inventions have the option of obtaining an extension for their monopoly for a maximum period of five years after the expiration of the basic patents. This SPC extension is a national (rather than a European-wide) right. The rationale behind this extension facility is that it often takes many years for a formulation containing a new drug to receive marketing approval from the regulatory authorities. As it is necessary to apply for patent protection when the invention is first realized, it may take as long as 12 years from the original filing of a patent application to the receipt of such marketing approval. The **United States**[45] and **Japan**[46] had previously addressed this issue, granting further protection for pharmaceuticals and, in the case of Japan, agro-chemical products. The EU regulation addresses the same issue in respect of pharmaceuticals for human or veterinary use.

The EU regulation distinguishes between a medicinal product and a "product." A medicinal product is the actual preparation, including excipients, administered. A product, on the other hand, comprises the "active ingredients" of such a medicinal product. However, the EU regulation does not define what is meant by "active ingredients." An

---

44. EU Regulation 1768/92, concerning the creation of a supplementary protection certification for medicinal products is in force in all EU countries other than Spain, Portugal and Greece, which are exempted until January 1998.
45. The Drug Price Competition and Patent Term Restoration Act, 35 U.S.C. § 156 (1984).
46. The Patent, Utility, Model, Design and Trademarks Law of 1987.

SPC can be granted in respect of a product if the following conditions are met:[47]

(i) the product (*i.e.*, active ingredient) is the subject of a patent which is still in force;
(ii) marketing authorization for a medicinal product has been granted[48] in a country where the SPC is sought, pursuant to one of the relevant European Directives.[49] Consequently, there is a requirement that the marketing authorization (*i.e.*, product license) be lodged with the application for the SPC;
(iii) an SPC has not already been granted in respect of the same product (*i.e.*, active ingredients);
(iv) the marketing authorization for the medicinal product was the first authorization in respect of that product in the country where protection is being sought.

The application must be made to the relevant National Patent Office.

An SPC will be granted in respect of a particular active ingredient or combination of active ingredients (*i.e.*, the product). In applying for an SPC, consideration needs to be given as to what is, in fact, the active ingredient. Clearly the active ingredient will not include the excipients in the preparation. However, consideration should be given as to whether an application should be limited to particular drug derivatives, such as particular salts, or should be drawn more widely.

An SPC will be infringed by a third party who, for example, manufactures or sells a preparation containing the product identified in the SPC. It is not yet clear if the manufacture/sale of another derivative infringes the SPC if an SPC has been granted in respect of a particular derivative only.

Wherever the inventor decides to apply for a patent, he will then have to wait until the patent is granted. The time it takes for an application to be considered by the relevant authority will vary country by country. On filing, the patent application will be examined to check that it conforms to all the relevant rules (including formalities such as detailed requirements concerning the presentation of any drawings). Additionally, in many countries, a search will be carried out to see what

---

47. EU Regulation 1768/92, *supra* note 44, art. 3.
48. In most EU states, the authorization must have been granted after January 1, 1985. In Denmark and Germany the date is January 1, 1988, in Belgium and Italy it is January 1, 1982.
49. Directive 65/65 in respect of drugs for human use and Directive 81/851 in respect of drugs for pharmaceutical use.

published information (usually patents and patent applications) there is bearing upon the novelty or obviousness of the invention.

There are also plans to harmonize patent protection in some countries for biotechnological inventions. For example, the European Commission has proposed a directive to harmonize patent protection for biotechnological inventions across all member states of the EU.[50] It is proposed that all living matter (except plant and animal varieties) be patentable as well as processes for the production and use of plant and animal varieties. The draft directive is intended to allow European companies to compete on an equal footing with their United States and Japanese counterparts.

NAFTA provides that each party shall make patents available for any inventions in all fields of technology provided they are new, inventive and capable of industrial application.[51] The term of protection is at least 20 years from the date of filing or 17 years from the date of grant. Each NAFTA signatory is required to permit patent owners to assign and transfer their patents by succession and to conclude licensing contracts.[52]

Country Focus

The Patent Law of the **People's Republic of China**[53] came into force in April 1985 and certain amendments to it came into effect on January 1, 1993, as a result of a Memorandum of Understanding between China and the United States. The Patent Law covers not only the granting of patent rights but also the registration of utility models and designs. The Patent Law also extends the term of patent protection to 20 years.[54] Utility models and designs are protected for a ten-year period.[55] The Patent Law extends the grounds on which compulsory licenses may be granted. Previously, such licenses were only available for non-exploitation and in relation to dependent patents. The Patent Office may now grant compulsory licenses under the Patent Law if any third party, which is qualified to exploit an invention or utility model, has made a request for authorization for the patentee or registrant to exploit

---

50. Proposal for a Council Directive on the legal protection of biotechnological inventions, 1989 O.J. (C 10) 3.
51. NAFTA Treaty, *supra* note 7, art. 1709(1).
52. *Id.* art. 1709(9).
53. Patent Law of the People's Republic of China, March 12, 1984, as amended on September 4, 1992.
54. *Id.* art. 45.
55. *Id.*

the patent or utility model on reasonable terms and such efforts have not been successful within a reasonable period of time.[56] In addition, a compulsory license may be granted if the patented invention or utility model blocks the exploitation of a later invention or utility model.[57]

Patent protection in **France** is governed by Book VI, Title I of the Intellectual Property Code of 1992 which covers both the elements of French law relating to patents and the obligations under the various international conventions and agreements to which France is a party.[58] Patents are available, on a first-to-file basis, for products, processes or uses or any combinations of these, provided they meet the requirements of novelty, inventive activity and industrial feasibility.[59] It is also possible to obtain a certificate of utility for inventions that may quickly become obsolete. The term of protection of a patent is 20 years from the date of filing.[60] Certificates of utility are granted for a term of six years from the date of filing.[61] If a patent has not been exploited for a period of three years from grant, or if the patented product has not been produced in quantities sufficient to satisfy the French market for the product, a compulsory license may be granted.[62] Assignments and exclusive and non-exclusive licenses must be in writing.[63] If they are to be effective against third parties, they must by entered in the National Patent Register.[64]

Protection for inventions in **Japan** is available through the granting of patents and registration of utility models and design rights. Utility models are distinct from patents in that they apply only to articles and products, whereas patents can also encompass processes or methods.[65] "Design" is defined as the shape, pattern or color of an article or a combination thereof which produces an aesthetic impression on the sense of sight.[66] This is in contrast to patents and utility models, which

---

56. *Id.* art. 51.
57. *Id.* art. 53.
58. The Paris Convention, the Patent Cooperation Treaty, the Munich Agreement and the Luxembourg Convention for EC Patents.
59. Intellectual Property Code, *supra* note 16, art. L611-10(1).
60. *Id.* art. L611-2(1).
61. *Id.* art. L611-2(2).
62. *Id.* art. L613-11.
63. *Id.* art. L613-8.
64. *Id.* art. L613-9.
65. Utility Model Law of 1959, as amended, art. 3(1).
66. Design Law of 1959, as amended, ch. I, art. 2(1).

protect the creation of a technical idea utilizing natural law.[67] A design cannot, however, be purely aesthetic, but must have some industrial application. The three types of protection do, however, overlap to some extent and an application for any one can be converted into either one of the other two.[68] The term of validity of a patent is 15 years from its date of publication or not more than 20 years from the date of application,[69] whereas that of a utility model right is ten years from its publication date and that of a design is 15 years from the date of registration.[70] Patent, utility model and design rights give their respective owners the right to manufacture, use, assign, lease, exhibit for assigning or leasing, or import products protected by the relevant right for business purposes.[71]

If proper working[72] of the invention has not taken place without good reason, for more than three consecutive years in Japan, or if another owner or exclusive licensee of a patent, utility model or design is unable to work out his invention unless he utilizes another party's prior filed invention, a person wishing to use the invention may seek the permission of the Commissioner of the Patent Office to request the owner or exclusive licensee to enter into negotiations for obtaining a non-exclusive license. If negotiations fail, he may further request the Commissioner of the Patent Office for authorization to work the invention,[73] although such requests are rare.

The transfer of the ownership of a patent, utility model or design must be recorded with the Patent Office.[74] Similarly, unless registered, an exclusive license will be ineffective and a non-exclusive license cannot be enforced against a third party.[75] It should be noted that an assignment of a patent, utility model or design owned by a non-Japanese party to a Japanese party constitutes a technical assistance contract under the Law concerning Foreign Investment, and the parties concerned will need to obtain the approval of the Japanese government for the contract before recording. The same applies to the licensing of a

---

67. Patent Law of 1959, as amended, ch. I, art. 2(1).
68. Design Law of 1959, as amended, arts. 12 and 13.
69. Patent Law of 1959, as amended, art. 67(1).
70. Design Law of 1959, as amended, art. 21.
71. Patent Law of 1959, as amended, art. 68.
72. Meaning use, assignment, lease, exhibition for assignment or leasing, or importing.
73. Patent Law of 1959, as amended, art. 83.
74. *Id.* art. 98.
75. *Id.* art. 99(3).

patent, utility model or design by a non-Japanese party to a Japanese party.

Patent protection in **Mexico** now extends to products, second uses of compounds[76] and biotechnology.[77] The duration of patents is 20 years from the date of filing of the application.[78] Utility models may be granted for inventions lacking the degree of inventiveness necessary to obtain a patent.[79] These have a duration of ten years from the date of filing.[80] Similarly, it is possible to register industrial designs[81] and the duration of these is 15 years from the date of filing.[82] The exploitation of patents is no longer compulsory, but non-exclusive compulsory licenses may be obtained for patents that have not been exploited for three years after grant.[83] Licensees in such cases must have the technical and economical capacity to exploit the patented invention efficiently.[84] The patent holder will be given an additional year in which to exploit the patent before any compulsory license is granted.[85] Compulsory licenses will not be granted if there has been importation of the patented goods into Mexico. Patents, utility models and designs may be assigned under the same regulations as any other personal property but neither assignments nor licenses will be effective as against third parties unless recorded at the newly established Mexican Institute of Industrial Property (IMPI).[86] The IMPI can only refuse to record an assignment or license of a patent if the patent or registration has lapsed or if its duration is longer than the term of the patent or registration.[87]

The governing legislation in the **United Kingdom** is the Patents Act 1977, as amended by the Copyright Designs and Patents Act 1988 and, in relation to patents granted before June 1, 1978, the Patents Act 1949. Patents are valid for a period of 20 years from the filing date.[88]

76. Law for the Development and Protection of Industrial Property, *supra* note 18, art. 16 (1991).
77. *Id.*, art. 20.
78. *Id.*, art. 23.
79. *Id.*, art. 27.
80. *Id.*, art. 29.
81. *Id.*, art. 31.
82. *Id.*, art. 36.
83. *Id.*, art. 70.
84. *Id.*, art. 71.
85. *Id.*, art. 72.
86. *Id.*, art. 62.
87. *Id.*, art. 65.
88. Patents Act 1977, s. 25(1).

Any patent or patent application may be assigned.[89] An assignment will, however, be void unless in writing and signed by or on behalf of the parties to the transaction.[90] A patentee may grant exclusive and non-exclusive licenses. An exclusive license confers rights in respect of the invention on the licensee to the exclusion of all others including the proprietor. Assignments and licenses should be recorded on the Register of Patents. If they are not, a later assignee/licensee with conflicting rights without knowledge of the earlier assignment/license will take precedence.[91] A patentee can be forced to grant a compulsory license for the patent to others if the patent had not been sufficiently exploited within three years from the grant of the patent.[92] There is also a provision that if a patent was originally granted under the Patents Act 1949 for 16 years, it becomes the subject of a compulsory license for four further years. As time has passed, this provision has ceased to be of much, if any, relevance.

In all **European Union** countries consideration needs to be given to EU competition law which often has a bearing on exclusive licensing arrangements. Article 85 of the Treaty of Rome may come into operation if the license in question has a significant effect on trade between member states.[93] In addition, licenses should be reviewed in the light of the Patents Block Exemption (due to be replaced by the Technology Transfer Block Exemption in July 1995), which may save them from the consequences of Article 85.[94]

United States federal law in relation to patents is governed by the Patent Act of 1952 which came into effect on January 1, 1953.[95] Patents are available for new and useful processes, machines, manufacture or composition of matter, or any new and useful improvement thereof.[96] To obtain a patent, an application must be made to the United States Patent and Trademark Office (the PTO). The types of patent that are

---

89. *Id.* s. 30(2).
90. *Id.* s. 30(6)(a).
91. *Id.* s. 33(1).
92. *Id.* s. 48.
93. EU competition law may have an impact on technology transfer arrangements even where neither the transferor nor the transferee is located in an EU country but where, for example, the products to be produced using the technology are to be manufactured within the EU. *See* Chapter Two, Section II.B.3 and Chapter Three, Section V for a detailed discussion on these issues.
94. *See* Chapters Two and Three.
95. Act of July 19, 1952, ch. 950, 66 Stat. 792 (codified as amended at 35 U.S.C. §§ 1-376 (1988)).
96. *Id.* § 101.

registrable are utility patents, plant patents and design patents. Utility and plant patents are granted for a term of 17 years from the date of issue of the patent.[97] Design patents have a duration of 14 years. Patents are treated in the same way as any item of personal property and can be assigned or licensed.[98] An assignment will be void as against any subsequent purchaser or mortgagee for value without notice of the assignment unless it is recorded with the PTO within three months from the date of such assignment or before any subsequent purchase.[99] There are no exploitation requirements in the Patents Act and no provisions relating to the grant of compulsory licenses.

IV. COPYRIGHT

If an idea relates not to an invention but to an improved way of describing or expressing something, the appropriate form of intellectual property protection is more likely to be copyright, perhaps backed-up with protection as confidential information.

A. What is a Copyright?

Copyright is a right which attaches to various categories of expression of human endeavor such as literary, artistic or musical works. Copyright does not protect ideas. It only protects the *expressions* of ideas. It is not a monopoly right but protects against copying of the original work. Indeed, the creation of an identical work without reference to the original work will not amount to an infringement of copyright in the original work.

In the high-technology field, the principal areas in which copyright law is implicated are in the protection of computer software and, in some countries, design drawings. Typically, computer software is created by a programmer writing instructions for a computer to execute. These instructions are known as "source code." This source code is then compiled or translated into a binary format, consisting of ones and zeros, on which the computer can operate directly. This is known as "object code." In most jurisdictions, copyright subsists both in the source code for a program as written by the programmer and in

---

97. *Id.* § 154.
98. *Id.* § 261.
99. *See also* Chapter Five, Part One.

the object code as compiled or translated. If a competitor were to obtain access to the source code version of a particular program (which would be unusual since software companies tend to keep their source code extremely secure) he would be prevented from copying the source code by the law of copyright. He could, however, examine what the source code did and then write his own source code with the same effect.[100]

Unlike patents and registered trademarks, copyright is not generally dependent on registration.[101] The absence of a registration procedure in many jurisdictions means that ownership has to be proven when the copyright is to be enforced. Given the long term of copyright which is well in excess of the author's life, it is better to secure this right at the outset. Authors of copyright works should therefore sign, date and keep all drafts. Particular care is needed on commissioning works to be clear, preferably in a written agreement, about who will own the copyright and who will have a license to use it.[102] Where the commissioner of the work is only to get a license, it may also be wise to specify whether the licensee can sue third parties for infringement and whether he can look to the author for assistance in proving ownership.[103] It is also wise to identify copyrighted works with a copyright notice typically with a "c" in a circle (©), the owner's name and the date. Although this is now not required in order to establish a copyright, it may help later in proving copyright ownership and that an infringer knew the work was the subject of copyright.

The owner of the copyright in a work will generally be the author. If, however, the work is made by an employee in the course of employment or is commissioned, then the copyright may be owned by the employer or commissioner. In the United States such works are referred to as "works for hire." A business should be careful to include as an express term in any employment contract a provision that the business will own

---

100. Depending upon the level of the concepts drawn from the source code, this may in some jurisdictions still amount to copyright infringement. It may also amount to a misappropriation of confidential information if the necessary circumstances existed such as the information being truly confidential and disclosed in circumstances imparting an obligation of confidence.

101. In the **United States**, there is still provision for registration of domestic (*i.e.*, owned by U.S. nationals) copyright works which is used, in particular, with software programs. It is not a requirement which must be fulfilled before a work can attract copyright but in an action for infringement of copyright certain remedies, including attorneys' fees and statutory damages, may not be available against an infringer if the work has not been registered by the copyright owner.

102. *See* Chapter Three, Section IV.

103. Terms which may be included in technology transfer agreements are discussed in more detail in Chapter Three.

the copyright in works made by the employee as part of his or her job. While this will happen automatically in many countries, the principle is not universal. Even where the copyright does become the employer's, the employee still may have moral rights which can limit the ways in which the business can exploit the copyright. Such rights are found, in particular, in civil law countries and are explained below.

B. Advantages of Copyright

Because copyright generally arises automatically, it has the advantage over both confidential information and patents of not involving expensive security measures or filing fees. The work must be the product of skill and labor, but in practice this requirement is generally not difficult to meet. Copyright lasts for a long period of time, commonly 50 or 70 years after the death of the author of the work. It is also the easiest right in which to obtain virtually worldwide rights and the international copyright system is perhaps the most developed of all those relating to intellectual property rights.[104]

C. Disadvantages of Copyright

It is important to remember that a copyright only extends to the expression of an idea and not the idea itself. Where the essence of an innovation is the idea itself, a business would be unwise to rely on copyright alone as an indirect means to protect that idea since it is often very easy to design around the particular way in which one business has expressed an idea in a design. However, in the technological fields where copyright has flourished, such as computer software, the substantial amount of effort involved in writing a copyright work often makes it impractical for a potential infringer to design around the particular way that ideas have been expressed by the copyright owner.

Copyright does not protect against another person independently creating the same work. In infringement cases there can often be difficult questions of proof as to how a similar work was created and, in the absence of evidence that the person who created it had access to the first work before doing so, courts are often reluctant to conclude that there has been copyright infringement. It can also be difficult to prove infringement, especially where the infringing work is close, but not identical, to the original work. In most jurisdictions an infringing work

---

104. *See infra* Supranational Regimes and Country Focus.

must be "substantially similar" to the original work for there to be a finding of infringement. This is often a question of fact and degree and the outcome of copyright litigation is difficult to predict with certainty. A number of defenses are available even if the works are similar. These include fair use (often argued, for example, by software developers who have decompiled a competitors' product to discern its structure[105]), parody[106] and, if the defendant is merely an importer of infringing works, ignorance of the fact that the works were infringing.[107]

Supranational Regimes

The **Berne Convention** establishes basic categories of "work" to be protected by copyright and sets forth a framework within which Berne member states are required to protect copyright works originating from other Berne countries in the same way as they protect domestically originating works. This concept is known as "national treatment." The Convention establishes minimum copyright terms (generally, the life of the author plus 50 years) and the basic set of acts restricted by copyright. It also introduces certain "moral" rights, including the right of the author of the work to be identified as such.[108]

The **Universal Copyright Convention** establishes a second international framework, conceptionally similar to the Berne Convention, but which, for example, permits non-Berne members to retain national restrictions relating to registration and the use of copyright notices as a precondition to registration.[109] The **Rome** and **Geneva Conventions** deal with protection of the rights of performers, producers of records and broadcasters. The systems they establish are similar to those established under the Berne Convention.[110]

There have been a number of **European Union** copyright initiatives. In contrast to the position in relation to registered rights, there is a great deal of diversity amongst EU member states concerning copyright protection. Although some EU-wide initiatives have been made, these

105. *See Sega Enterprises Ltd. v. Accolade Inc.*, 977 F.2d 1510 (9th Cir. 1992).
106. *Campbell v. Acuff-Rose Music, Inc.*, 113 S.Ct. 1642 (1993).
107. This is a good reason to place copyright notices on any copyright works because the defence of innocent infringement is then more difficult to sustain.
108. The current members of the Berne Convention are set out in the Comparative Table of Supranational Regimes.
109. The current members of the Universal Copyright Convention are set out in the Comparative Table of Supranational Regimes.
110. The current members of the Rome and Geneva Conventions are set out in the Comparative Table of Supranational Regimes.

cover relatively narrow fields such as software, rental and lending rights, and satellite and cable broadcasting.

Parties to **NAFTA** are required to protect the works covered by Article 2 of the Berne Convention.[111] NAFTA states that this should include protecting computer programs as literary works and compilations of data as intellectual creations.[112] Sound recordings[113] and encrypted program-carrying satellite signals[114] are also protected. Protection is provided in most cases for the life of the author plus 50 years.[115]

NAFTA provides that for copyright and related rights any person acquiring or holding economic rights may freely and separately transfer such rights by contract for purposes of their exploitation and enjoyment by the transferee;[116] and any person acquiring or holding such economic rights by virtue of a contract, including contracts of employment underlying the creation of works and sound recordings, shall be able to exercise those rights in his own name and enjoy fully the benefits derived from those rights.[117]

Country Focus

China's copyright law is contained in the Copyright Law of the People's Republic of China,[118] the Implementing Regulations of the Copyright Law of the People's Republic of China, the Regulations for the Implementation of International Treaties and two separate laws for the protection of computer software.[119] Copyright protection is given to works of Chinese citizens, legal persons and "non-legal persons," *i.e.*, those without the status of legal persons of China, whether published or not.[120] Works by foreign persons are not protected by the Copyright Law of the People's Republic of China as such, but the Regulations for the Implementation of International Treaties make it clear that copyright works of foreigners covered by international copyright

111. NAFTA Treaty, *supra* note 7, art. 1705(1).

112. *Id.* art. 1705(1)(a) and (b).

113. *Id.* art. 1706.

114. *Id.* art. 1707.

115. *Id.* art. 1705(4).

116. *Id.* art. 1705(3)(a).

117. *Id.* art. 1705(3)(b).

118. Passed September 7, 1990.

119. The Regulations for the Protection of Computer Software, effective from September 30, 1992 and Measures for the Registration of Computer Software, effective from April 18, 1992.

120. Copyright Law of the People's Republic of China of 1990, art. 11.

treaties and bilateral agreements to which China is a signatory (*e.g.*, the Berne Convention and the Universal Copyright Convention) will be protected in China. Protection is available for works which are not covered by such treaties, provided that the work is first published in China.

Most types of copyright work are protected under Chinese copyright law for the life of the author plus 50 years.[121] Copyright owners have the right to authorize others to exploit their work and to receive remuneration therefor.[122] In addition, in certain circumstances it is possible for anyone to use a work if he pays certain fees fixed by the Chinese government.[123] This is possible where the work is for commercial performance and put on by a performer (*i.e.*, an individual performer or a performing group);[124] previously published musical works for new sound recordings;[125] and previously published works for use in the creation of a new work by a television or radio station[126] excluding cinematographic works, television films and video recordings.[127]

French copyright law[128] stresses the "moral rights" of an author as well as the economic rights to the proceeds of works emphasized in common law jurisdictions. There are four perpetual, inalienable moral rights that attach to the author of a work.[129] These are:

(i) the right of disclosure – that is to say, the right of the author to allow or prevent the disclosure of the work to the public;
(ii) the right of paternity – that is, the right of the author to have his name indicated when his work is published (and indeed, his right to withhold his name);
(iii) the right to respect for the integrity of the work; and[130]
(iv) the right of repentance – that is to say, the right to terminate the exploitation of the work, subject to indemnification.

---

121. *Id.* art. 21.
122. *Id.* art. 10.
123. *Id.* arts. 23 and 27.
124. *Id.* art. 35.
125. *Id.* art. 37.
126. *Id.* art. 40.
127. *Id.* art. 44.
128. Intellectual Property Code, *supra* note 16, Book 1.
129. *Id.* art. L121-1.
130. The right to respect is deemed to complement the right of disclosure, so that the author alone may decide whether and when to disclose his work to the public.

French law identifies two economic rights, the right of reproduction[131] and the right of performance.[132] The Intellectual Property Code sets out a broad spectrum of works, including scientific, literary and artistic writings, theatrical works, maps, architectural plans and fashion creations. In general the length of protection afforded to works is the life of the author plus 50 years. The transfer of works is permitted as long as it is remunerated proportionally, that is to say, remuneration must be proportional to the revenues resulting from the sale or commercial exploitation of the work.[133]

Japan is a signatory to the Berne Convention and the Copyright Law of Japan 1986 provides that the enjoyment of a copyright shall not be subject to any formality.[134] Thus, copyright is automatically conferred upon creation and copyright notices and registration are not required to enjoy those rights. Under Japanese law the author of a copyright work may be a natural or legal person.[135] Generally, copyright comes into being at the moment of the work's creation and endures for 50 years after the death of the author.[136] Compulsory licenses may be issued by the Commissioner of the Agency for Cultural Affairs for the broadcasting by a broadcasting organization of a work already made available to the public,[137] where negotiations have failed or could not take place,[138] and for the recording of musical works three years after a commercial recording was first put on sale in Japan.[139] Compensation is fixed by the Commissioner of the Agency for Cultural Affairs in consultation with the Copyright Council.[140]

Copyright law in **Mexico** is not contained within the Law for the Development and Protection of Industrial Property but in a companion

---

131. *Id.* art. L122-3 provides that "reproduction shall consist of a material fixation of the work by any and all methods that allow it to be communicated to the public in an indirect fashion."
132. *Id.* art. L122-2 provides that "performances shall consist in communication of a work to the public by any means."
133. *Id.* art. L131-4.
134. Copyright Law of Japan of 1986, art. 17.
135. *Id.* art. 6.
136. *Id.* art. 51.
137. *Id.* art. 67.
138. *Id.* art. 68.
139. *Id.* art. 69.
140. *Id.* art. 71.

piece of legislation passed on July 17, 1991, reforming the Copyright Law.[141] Computer software and sound recordings, in particular, are much better protected than previously. Software can now be protected for a term of at least 50 years. A software owner may now identify itself as the sole legitimate source of the software and take action against anyone effecting changes in the software. Sound recordings can also be granted copyright protection for at least 50 years. Moral rights remain unassignable under the new law. However, the author may assign the right to publish, reproduce, perform, exhibit, adapt or in any other way exploit a copyrighted work, through any acceptable legal instrument. Such an assignment does not include the right to alter or change the title, form or contents of the work.

Copyright and unregistered designs are protected in the **United Kingdom** under the Copyright, Designs and Patents Act 1988 (CDPA). Registered designs are protected by the Registered Designs Act 1949 (RDA 1949) as amended by the CDPA. Copyright may be assigned or licensed in whole or in part.[142] Assignments must be in writing and signed by or on behalf of the assignor.[143] A license granted by a copyright owner is binding on every successor in title to his interest in the copyright, other than a *bona fide* purchaser for value without notice of the license or a person deriving title from such a person.[144] Compulsory licenses may be granted by the Monopolies and Mergers Commission on terms settled in default of agreement by the Copyright Tribunal where it is considered to be against the public interest for a copyright owner to refuse to grant a license on reasonable terms.[145]

There are provisions in the CDPA relating to the assignment and licensing of unregistered designs which are similar to those described above in relation to copyright.[146] Compulsory licensing of designs is available as of right during the last five years of the design right term.[147] A registered design may also be assigned or licensed, and any such assignment or license should be recorded on the Register of Designs.[148] A compulsory license may be granted by the Registrar in respect of a registered design on the

---

141. John B. McKnight & Carlo Muggenburg, *Mexico's Industrial Property and Copyright Laws: Another Step Toward Linkage with a Global Economy*, 20 INT'L BUS. LAW. 573 (1992).
142. Copyright, Designs and Patents Act 1988, s. 90(1) and (2).
143. *Id.* s. 90(3).
144. *Id.* s. 90(4).
145. *Id.* s. 144.
146. *Id.* s. 222.
147. *Id.* s. 237.
148. Registered Designs Act 1949, s. 19.

grounds that the design is not being applied sufficiently in the United Kingdom.[149] A compulsory license may also be granted where the Monopolies and Mergers Commission considers it against the public interest that the owner of a registered design has refused to grant a license on reasonable terms.[150]

The law of copyright in the **United States** is governed by the Copyright Act of 1976, which became effective on January 1, 1978, as amended by the Berne Convention Implementation Act of 1988 and a series of additional amendments contained in a number of statutes, including the Computer Software Copyright Act of 1980;[151] the Satellite Home Viewer Act of 1988; the Computer Software Rental Amendments Act of 1990; and the Audio Home Recording Act of 1992. Copyright protection under the Copyright Act lasts for the life of the author plus 50 years.[152] Title to copyright may be transferred in whole or in part by means of a conveyance.[153] Transfer includes assignment and exclusive licenses.[154] Both must be in writing and signed by the owner of the rights conveyed or his duly authorized agent.[155] Such transfers should be recorded at the Copyright Office, for if not the transfer will not prevail over subsequent transfers to third parties.[156] It is also possible to grant non-exclusive licenses and these need not be in writing.[157] The United States is unusual in providing a mechanism for registering copyrights. Since the United States acceded to the Berne Convention in 1988, the registration of copyright is no longer a prerequisite for securing ownership in copyrights. The significant advantage of registration, however, remains that in copyright infringement proceedings, a copyright owner may be awarded attorney's fees and statutory damages only if the copyright is registered.

---

149. *Id.* s. 10.
150. *Id.*, s. 11A.
151. This confirmed the application of the Copyright Act to computer software.
152. Copyright Act, § 302 (1976).
153. *Id.* § 201(d)(1).
154. *Id.* § 201.
155. *Id.* § 204(a).
156. *Id.* § 205. *See also* Chapter Five.
157. 3 NIMMER ON COPYRIGHT, 10.03[A], 10-38 (1994).

V. DESIGNS

A. What is a Design?

In this context, a design means the shape of a product or a pattern applied to its surface. Product shapes will be dictated to a greater or lesser extent by aesthetic and functional considerations depending upon the nature of the product (for example the design of an engine component may be dictated entirely by function, whereas a wallpaper design would be dictated by aesthetic considerations only). Greater protection tends to be given to those designs which are not solely dependent on function.

The protection of designs varies considerably from country to country in terms of both nature and period of protection. Common law countries, such as the **United Kingdom** and **Ireland** historically have protected designs through copyright law whereas in civil law jurisdictions, such as **Italy** and **Germany**, designs are often protected through the laws relating to unfair competition. All European Union member states, except for **Greece**, also provide a registration system for designs, each with varying requirements and periods of protection.

Supranational Regimes

The **Paris Convention** extends the principles of national treatment and convention priority to protection of industrial designs and requires industrial designs to be protected in all Paris Convention member states. It also includes certain other provisions in relation to protection of industrial designs. The **Berne Convention** leaves its member states the choice of protecting industrial works on applied art and industrial designs by way of copyright or specific legislation or both.

The **Hague Union** is an arrangement for the international deposit of industrial designs which has been in effect since 1928. Any national, resident or commercial enterprise from a Union country may apply for registration of a qualifying design by depositing the design at the international bureau of the World Intellectual Property Organization in Geneva (WIPO).[158] The effect of deposit is the same as if a design had been deposited directly in each of the Union countries specified in the application. The design will be registered in each of those countries unless that country provides for examination of design applications (for example, for novelty) or for opposition by third parties. In either of these cases,

---

158. WIPO is an organization established under the auspices of the United Nations with the task of harmonizing worldwide intellectual property laws. As such, it drafts and proposes legislation and acts as the central office and registry for various harmonization initiatives.

refusal of an application must be communicated to WIPO by the relevant national office within six months of the national office's receipt of notification of the international registration.

The effectiveness of the Hague Union is impaired by the limited number of signatories and by complex amendments to the original arrangement, each of which applies only to some of the signatories. The **United States**, **Japan** and the **United Kingdom** have all remained outside the Union. There are approximately 20 signatories of which the most significant are **Germany**, **France** and the **Benelux** countries.[159] Proposals are being considered to revise the Hague agreements so as to render the system more flexible and attractive to applicants in an effort to encourage more countries to join.

A Proposed **European Union** Harmonization Directive, which was presented by the European Commission in December 1993,[160] applies only to registered design rights (though it does not preclude those member states which wish to do so from protecting unregistered designs). It defines a design as the appearance of the whole or part of the product resulting from the specific features of the lines, contours, colors, shape and/or materials of the product or its ornamentation. To qualify for registration, a design must be novel and have individual character, such as to produce a significantly different impression on the informed user from that produced by any prior design.

Designs dictated by technical function would be excluded from protection. A controversial second exclusion is that of designs which necessarily must be reproduced in their exact form and dimensions in order to permit the relevant products to be mechanically assembled or connected with another product. The European Commission's stated intention is to enhance interoperability of products of different origin and to prevent manufacturers from securing captive markets in peripherals and replacement parts. The "must fit" provision does not cover modular products, such as fittings, which enable chairs to be stacked together, or interconnecting toys. A further controversial limitation on the scope of protection relates to features of designs that are dependent on the appearance of another product of which they are intended to form an integral part. The present form of the proposals contains a limited exception to infringement in respect of necessary repairs where the product "must match." The proposed directive would enable registration for up to 25 years, with a 12-month grace period within which to decide whether or not to file an application for registration.

---

159. The members of the Hague Union are set out in the Comparative Table of Supranational Regimes.
160. Proposal for a European Parliament and Council Directive on the legal protection of designs, COM (93) 344 final, COD 464.

The Proposed EU Design Registration right[161] would create a single EU-wide right. The proposal deals with both registered and unregistered design rights. The substantive law relating to registered EU designs would be essentially the same as that under the proposed design harmonization directive. An application for a registered EU design would have to be filed at the Community Designs Office (CDO) (or, if the law of an EU member state so permits, at the central industrial property office of that member state which will then forward it to the CDO). The CDO would then examine an application as to formal requirements. It is intended that the registration procedure will be simple, inexpensive and quick. It is anticipated that an application, if accepted, should proceed to registration within six months of filing.

The protection offered by a registered design would last five years and be renewable up to a maximum total period of 25 years. Registered designs could be challenged on invalidity grounds. These are that:

(i) the design lacked novelty or individual character;
(ii) the design was purely functional or fell within the "must fit" exception;
(iii) the design exploitation or publication was contrary to public policy or to accepted principles of morality; or
(iv) the right holder was not entitled to ownership of the design.

The unregistered Community design would be subject to essentially the same rules under which rejected designs are protected, but ownership would only be granted for a maximum period of three years from the date on which the design was first made available to the public.

In deciding whether to opt for registered or unregistered design protection, the benefit of the extended period would have to be weighed against the cost of applying for registration. Certain designs (for example, fashion items) whose commercial life is relatively short might obtain adequate protection from the three years afforded by the unregistered Community design. There would also be differences in the rights against infringement. An unregistered Community design would be infringed by anyone who, without the owner's consent, copied the design or made, offered, put on the market, imported, exported or used products incorporating it, but it would be necessary to prove copying in order to establish infringement. In contrast, a registered Community design would confer a monopoly right, and infringement would occur even where there had been no copying.

---

161. Proposal for a European Parliament and Council Regulation on community design, 94/C 29/02, and Proposal for a European Parliament and Council Directive on the legal protection of designs, COM (93) 344 final, COD 464.

The right to a Community design would belong to the designer, *i.e.*, the person who created the design. If a design were developed by an employee in the execution of his or her duties or following instructions given by the employer, the right to the Community design would belong to the employer.

GATT TRIPs requires member states to protect novel or original industrial designs, but permits the exclusion of designs dictated essentially by technical or functional considerations. It includes special provisions relating to textile designs. It describes the acts that should be restricted by the right and restricts exceptions to those rights. It requires a minimum term of ten years' protection.

NAFTA provides for the protection of independently created industrial designs that are new or original.[162] The term of protection shall not be for less than ten years.[163] The layout designs of semiconductor integrated circuits are protected for a similar period.[164]

Country Focus

China's design law formally forms part of its Patent Law.[165] Under that law designs and utility models are granted protection for ten years.

Book V of the **French** Intellectual Property Code covers two dimensional designs, and three dimensional models. It applies to

> any new design, any three-dimensional shape, any industrial article that differs from similar articles, either by a distinctive and recognizable configuration affording it novelty or by one or more external effects giving it an individual and new appearance.[166]

Protection as a design or model can often overlap with patent and copyright protection. However, a design or model cannot be simultaneously protected by the law of designs and the law of patents. A design or model is protected for 25 years from the date of filing and is renewable for the same period.[167] Assignments and licenses may be granted, but will only be effective against third parties if recorded with the National Register of Designs.

---

162. NAFTA Treaty, *supra* note 7, art. 1713(1).
163. *Id.* art. 1713(5).
164. *Id.* art. 1710.
165. *See* Section III.
166. Intellectual Property Code, *supra* note 16, art. L511-3.
167. *Id.* art. L513-1.

In **Japan, Mexico** and the **United States** design law forms part of the patent laws, previously discussed.[168] **United Kingdom** design law is discussed together with copyright law.[169]

VI. SEMICONDUCTOR CHIP PROTECTION – TOPOGRAPHY RIGHTS

Some countries have separate intellectual property rights protecting the topography of semiconductor chips. The protection is of the design of the circuits on the chip, *i.e.*, the way they are laid out, rather than of the inventiveness of the chip. The right is therefore more akin to copyright than patent. The right was first introduced by the **United States**[170] which granted a period of protection of ten years from the date of registration of a "mask work" or its first commercial exploitation. In an effort to encourage other nations to adopt similar protection, the benefit of the United States legislation is only available to overseas nationals in the United States where that national's home country has entered into a bilateral chip protection treaty with the United States.[171]

VII. TRADEMARKS AND UNFAIR COMPETITION

Trademark protection cannot protect an innovation or idea from being copied or used by another business. However, it can be used to protect the reputation, name recognition and goodwill that the business has acquired as a result, or prior to the making, of the innovation. For example, pharmaceutical manufacturers commonly market their drugs by reference to a certain trademarked name and in a particular trade dress (or "get up") such as the color scheme on the tablet. If another pharmaceutical manufacturer marketing the same drug attempts to sell its drugs by reference to the same name and using the same trade dress it may infringe the first company's trademark rights. Another example of the importance of trademark protection is in the computer software field. In many parts of the world it is possible to purchase pirated copies of software programs

---

168. *See* Section III.
169. *See* Section IV.
170. Semi-Conductor Chip Protection Act, 17 U.S.C. § 914 (1984).
171. The European Union has adopted a similar measure to the United States.

which simply have been copied from disks of well-known software programs under the same trademarks as those programs. Faced with such infringement, the software publisher may sue the pirates for copyright infringement but may find it easier to sue them for trademark infringement based on its registered trademark. If it does this, it would not have to, for example, prove that it owned the copyright in the software.[172]

A. What is a Trademark?[173]

A trademark is a sign used by a business to distinguish its goods and services from the same or similar goods or services coming from another source. Significantly, it may also act as an indicator of the origin of goods or services and as a guarantee of quality to consumers. As part of a technology transfer arrangement, the transferor will often permit, and indeed may require, the transferee to use one or more marks associated with the transferred technology.

The rights a business may have in a trademark may vary according to whether the trademark is registered or unregistered. Rights in a trademark and, in particular, the right to prevent others from using it, are acquired by registration and/or through use. These rights can be of great value, not least because they are not limited in duration as are other intellectual property rights. They can last indefinitely so long as the trademark continues to be used and (in case of registration) the appropriate renewal fees are paid when required.

In many countries a trademark becomes the property of the person first using it, and exclusive rights are acquired in the mark from the moment of that first use. In most other countries the first to register a mark obtains the rights in it, sometimes regardless of any prior use. In any event, registration invariably confers stronger rights than mere use rights and is highly recommended for any party contemplating technology transfer transactions that also involve trademark licensing or acquisition.

Trademarks most commonly consist of names or other words, but many devices, logos, numbers, symbols, distinctive shapes or patterning and other distinctive features of products or their packaging or appearance are capable of being trademarks. This does not, however, mean that all signs which traders may use in their businesses will be

---

172. Commonly, in such a situation, the software publisher will bring proceedings for **both** copyright infringement and trademark infringement.
173. The term "trademark" is used here to refer to two similar rights, trademarks (which are applied to goods) and service marks (which are applied to services). There is also a category called "trade names," the names used by a business to describe itself.

registrable. Trademarks are registered in respect of specific categories of goods or services and the monopoly granted to the registered trademark owner will be limited to its use in respect of such or confusingly similar marks for those goods and services.

Supranational Regimes

A number of international conventions cover trademark law and allow trademark owners to register their rights in many different countries relatively simply. Those trademark rights usually are only available in respect of the type of goods to which the trademark is applied. There is also an international agreement on the classification of goods and services for trademark registration purposes.[174]

The **European Union** is near to establishing an EU-wide Community Trademark (CTM) which will enable a trademark owner to make a single application for a registered trademark which would be effective in all EU countries. This will be the first EU-wide intellectual property right.

The main features of the CTM are as follows:

- Unitary character – a CTM may only be registered, assigned or cancelled in respect of the whole of the European Union.
- Permitted Applicants – nationals of EU member states, nationals of Paris Convention signatories, companies with a real and effective commercial presence in a member state, and nationals of those countries exercising reciprocal agreements with member states may apply.
- Registered items – any sign capable of distinguishing the goods or services of one undertaking from those of other undertakings (including words, names, designs, shapes, packaging) may be registered.
- Registration period – registration is for ten years, renewable indefinitely.
- Rights – to prevent unauthorized use of the mark or a confusingly similar mark on identical or similar goods/services, or on any goods/services where such use is taking unfair advantage of the CTM or is detrimental to its distinctive character or reputation.
- Assignment – a CTM may be assigned, but only for the whole of the EU and to those whose nationality or business would have entitled them to file the CTM application themselves.

174. Nice Agreement on the International Classification of Goods and Services, June 15, 1957, revised at Stockholm on July 14, 1967 and at Geneva on May 13, 1977 and amended at Geneva on October 2, 1979.

- Licensing – a CTM may be licensed exclusively or non-exclusively for some or all of the goods or services for which it is registered for all or part of the EU. A CTM may not be used to prevent the use of a mark in relation to goods put on the market in the EU by the proprietor of the CTM.
- Security interests – a CTM may be given as security and security interests may be recorded and published.[175]
- Courts – each member state shall designate a number of Community Trademark Courts of first and second instance for the hearing of infringement and invalidity actions. Usually, proceedings will be brought in the court in whose jurisdiction the defendant is domiciled. Infringement actions, if successful, may result in an injunction, but damages and other remedies will be awarded in accordance with the national law of the CTM court in question. On any issue not specifically covered by the CTM Regulation, the national law of the court in question will be applied. Appeal is to the court of second instance in that member state and further appeal will only be possible if that member state so provides.
- Conversion into a national application – a CTM application or registration may be converted into separate national applications to the extent that it is refused, withdrawn or cancelled, except where cancellation is due to non-use. Payment of the national fee will be required.

The **Madrid Arrangement** is an international treaty which was set up in an attempt to overcome some of the administrative inconvenience and costs associated with multiple national applications for registration of trademarks.[176] Under the Arrangement, a national or resident of one contracting state who has registered a trademark in that state may, by a single application to WIPO, apply for an international registration. The application is, in effect, a bundle of national trademark applications covering those contracting states designated by the applicant. WIPO passes on details of the application to the relevant national trademark registries and the trademark will automatically acquire protection in the designated countries with the exception of any which notify WIPO within one year that the trademark is not entitled to protection under their laws. However, one disadvantage of an international registration is

---

175. *See also* Chapter Five.
176. The signatories to the Madrid Arrangement are set out in the Comparative Table of Supranational Regimes.

that it will be cancelled if, within five years, that national registration upon which it is based is cancelled.

While the system is widely used in member countries of the Madrid Arrangement, its membership has remained limited, largely because of features which make it incompatible with national systems with extensive search and examination procedures prior to registration. In an attempt to widen the scope of international registrations, a Protocol to the Madrid Arrangement has been adopted by 28 countries including **France, Germany, Italy** and the **United Kingdom** and there is a possibility that **Japan** will join as well. The **United States** has publicly announced its intention to join.

The main features of the Madrid Protocol (the "Protocol") are as follows:

- Federal character – an international registration operates as a series of separate national rights other than for administrative purposes (*e.g.*, renewal and assignment).
- Permitted Applicants – any national of a Protocol country or party with a real and effective business presence in such a country may apply to extend a national *application* (including a CTM application) from any Protocol country to any other Protocol countries, whereas only a *registration* may be extended under the Madrid Protocol.
- Registered items – only marks which would be registered if applied for under a national application in the country in question.
- Duration – ten years from application date, renewable indefinitely.
- Rights – after registration a mark acquires the same rights and effects as a national registration in that country, except that international registrations may only be assigned to a party capable of applying for a Protocol registration itself.
- Courts – all proceedings relating to international registrations must be brought in the appropriate domestic court where infringement has arisen or cancellation is sought. However, it is possible to attack the validity of a trademark in all the countries in which it is registered by attacking it in one country where it is registered.
- Membership – the Protocol becomes effective when ratified by four countries. So far only Spain has formally ratified it, but the following countries have all commenced the ratification process: **Austria, Belgium, Bulgaria, Cuba, Denmark, Egypt, Finland,**

France, Germany, Greece, Hungary, Ireland, Italy, Korea, Luxembourg, Monaco, Sweden, Switzerland, United Kingdom and **United States**.

NAFTA states that each party is to provide a specified system for the registration of trademarks.[177] While it allows each party to determine conditions for the licensing and assignment of trademarks, the compulsory licensing of trademarks shall not be permitted and the owner of a registered trademark must have the right to assign its trademark with or without the transfer of the business to which the trademark belongs.[178]

Country Focus

The Trademark Law of the **People's Republic of China** 1982 and Implementing Regulations[179] provide that the first applicant to file an application for registration of a mark will pre-empt all later applicants irrespective of prior use of the mark.[180] Registered trademarks have a validity period of ten years from the date of registration[181] and may thereafter be renewed.[182] Since 1 July 1993 there has been an extension of the Trademark Law to encompass the registration of service marks.[183] All trademark licenses must be recorded with the Trademark Office[184] and failure to record may result in the license being cancelled. Goods which are the subject of licenses must bear the name of the licensee and the place of manufacture.[185] Assignments can only be made if a joint application has been submitted to the Trademark Office.[186] No assignment will become effective until approved by the Trademark Office.[187]

China is under an obligation imposed by the Paris Convention, to which it is a signatory, to protect foreign companies against passing off and other forms of unfair competition. In consequence, China recently

177. NAFTA Treaty, *supra* note 7, art. 1708(4).
178. *Id*. art. 1708(11).
179. Both updated with effect from July 1993.
180. Trademark Law of 1982, s. 18.
181. *Id*. s. 23.
182. *Id*. s. 24.
183. Implementing Regulations under the Trademark Law of 1993, s. 2.
184. Trademark Law of 1982, s. 26.
185. *Id*. s. 26.
186. *Id*. s. 25.
187. *Id*. s. 30.

enacted the Unfair Competition Law, which came into effect on December 1, 1993. The law covers a number of areas including the counterfeiting of registered trademarks; the making of false statements about competitors' products; the making of false trade descriptions, including by way of misleading advertising; and predatory price cutting. A series of laws was passed at a provincial level before the Unfair Competition Law had been enacted. These laws were largely aimed at the protection of consumers rather than commercial competitors. For this reason and because of the past ethos of the country, it is uncertain how the Unfair Competition Law will be enforced, though the new law is certainly a significant step for China in fulfilling its obligations under the Convention.

In **France**, the law on trademarks was substantially revised by a statute in 1991[188] repealing the law of 1964 and reflecting EU requirements. This statute was restated in the Intellectual Property Code the following year.[189] Both trademarks and service marks are registrable.[190] Rights in both types of mark last for a period of ten years from the date of filing.[191] Registration may be renewed an unlimited number of times for additional periods of ten years.[192] Trademarks and service marks can be assigned in whole or in part.[193] Transfers and modifications of rights must be in writing[194] and recorded in the National Register of Marks. Assignments will not be effective against third parties unless recorded.[195]

In **Japan**, trademarks are protected by registration with the Japanese Patent Agency in accordance with the provisions of the Trademark Law 1959 as amended. The owner of a registered trademark is entitled to exclusive use of the trademark on the goods designated in the registration for a period of ten years,[196] renewable for further ten-year periods.[197] Since April 1, 1992, service marks have also become registrable under the new Service Mark Registration System. Trade-

---

188. Law No. 91-7, January 4, 1991.

189. Intellectual Property Code, *supra* note 16, Book VII.

190. *Id.* art. L711-1.

191. *Id.* art. L712-1.

192. *Id.*

193. *Id.* art. L714-1.

194. *Id.*

195. *Id.* art. L714-7.

196. Trademark Law of 1959, as amended, arts. 19(1) and 25.

197. *Id.* art. 19(2).

marks may be licensed on an exclusive or non-exclusive basis.[198] Exclusive licenses must be registered at the Patent Office to be effective against third parties.[199] Non-exclusive licenses may be registered. Trademarks may be assigned with or without an assignment of underlying goodwill. Trademarks may be jointly owned in Japan.[200]

Under **Mexican** law, three-dimensional shapes, trademarks,[201] slogans,[202] company names[203] and service marks may be registered. In addition, collective marks may be registered by, for example, associations of producers.[204] Trademarks are protected for ten years from the date of filing.[205] They must be used within three years of the registration date, or may be cancelled.[206] There is now no system of compulsory licenses relating to trademarks, though this is a change from the old law. In order to be enforceable, trademark licenses must be registered before the Mexican Institute of Industrial Property (IMPI).[207] Failure to do so will render any license unenforceable against third parties. The IMPI is obliged to record the license agreement unless by its terms the applicability of the Industrial Property Law is excluded, or unless the IMPI finds it to be "in the public interest" to refuse.[208] It is not clear from the face of the Law what constitutes the public interest. The assignment of trademarks, trade names and service marks is permitted in the same way as the assignment of any other personal property, but any assignment must be recorded at IMPI for it to be valid as against third parties.[209]

The law concerning trademarks in the **United Kingdom** is contained in the new Trademarks Act 1994, which came into effect on October 31, 1994. A trademark registration will normally last for ten years, but may be renewed thereafter for further periods of ten years on payment of the

---

198. *Id.* arts. 30 and 31.
199. *Id.* art. 35, *cross-referring to* Patents Law 1959, art. 98.
200. Trademark Law of 1959, art. 24.
201. Law for the Development and Protection of Industrial Property, *supra* note 18, art. 89.
202. *Id.* art. 99.
203. *Id.* art. 105.
204. *Id.* art. 96.
205. *Id.* art. 95.
206. *Id.* art. 130.
207. *Id.* art. 136.
208. *Id.* art. 150.
209. *Id.* art. 143.

necessary fees.[210] A trademark may be assigned either in connection with the goodwill of a business or independently of it.[211] It will only be effective if in writing and signed by or on behalf of the assignor.[212] The new Trademarks Act relaxes requirements relating to the recording of trademark licenses and the inclusion of terms as to quality control of the licensee's product. However, it is important to ensure that the licensee's use of a trademark will be subject to control from the licensor. In the absence of such controls the validity of the registration of the mark may be attacked.

Trademarks in the **United States** are governed by the Trademark Law Revision Act of 1988, which came into effect on November 16, 1989. A United States trademark registration covers all 50 states. In addition there are laws for the registration of trademarks in individual states but those apply only to trade within a state. State trademark laws may not interfere with the effectiveness of federal trademarks. Federal trademarks are applicable to interstate and foreign business. Federal law covers the registration of trademarks, service marks, certification marks and collective marks.[213] The registration of all of these marks lasts for ten years from the date of entry in the Register.[214] Registrations made prior to the Trademark Law Revision Act were granted a duration of 20 years. As a transitional measure, such registrations will automatically be renewed after ten years for a further period of ten years.[215] Marks and applications for marks are assignable with the goodwill of the business with which the mark is used or with that part of the goodwill of the business connected with the use of and symbolized by the mark.[216] An assignment is void against a subsequent purchaser for value without notice of the mark unless it is recorded in the Patent and Trademark Office within three months from the date of execution, or in any case prior to any subsequent purchase.[217] It is similarly possible to license marks but there is no recording requirement. Licenses must be in writing.

---

210. Trademarks Act 1994, s. 42.
211. *Id.* s. 24(1).
212. *Id.* s. 24(3).
213. Trademark Law Revision Act of 1988, §§ 2, 3, 4 and 45.
214. *Id.* § 8(a).
215. *Id.* § 9.
216. *Id.* § 10.
217. *Id.*

D. Deciding Where and for Which Marks to Register

In order to protect a trademark, a business should consider registering the mark at the earliest possible opportunity. A trademark owner will face considerable difficulties suing another party for use of the mark where that party's use of the mark pre-dates the owner's registration. There is also a considerable risk that in those circumstances the "infringer" will apply for the mark to be cancelled, thus depriving the mark of value. However, registering trademarks requires expenditures at the outset, and many businesses will not have sufficient funds to do so until the business has become established. A business needs therefore to prioritize its trademark application process in order to obtain the best protection at the lowest cost.

In developing a trademark registration strategy, a business will need to take various factors into account and decide where and for what products or services it should register as a first priority. These factors include for what classes of products the mark will be used; where the new product to which the mark is to be applied will first be marketed; when and in which other countries it will be marketed; whether it is the type of product that is likely to be counterfeited; and the costs of obtaining registrations in each country. Trademark registrations should probably be obtained in the countries where the product is launched and, initially, in other countries where the product will be launched shortly thereafter, or where counterfeit copies of the product are likely to appear.[218] Another important factor is the likelihood that the trademark might be pre-empted by others or registered by those who simply will seek to extort payment for relinquishing registrations for marks which they never really intended to use in a *bona fide* manner.

Faced with the number of different trademark systems, particularly in Europe, a potential transferor should consider carefully which system is the most appropriate for its needs. In an effort to assist in negotiating this maze, set out below are a number of commonly asked questions with suggested answers.

1. Will There Ever Be a Need to File Separate National Applications Again?

International filing programs vary in extent and purpose, and not every program will warrant or suit either the CTM or Madrid Protocol.

---

218. The Paris Convention allows some flexibility as to when applications are made by allowing a six-month grace period from the first application within which the later application can claim the date of the first application as its priority date.

The best method of filing will depend on the number of countries to be covered, the geographic spread of the countries, the "life expectancy" of the mark, and the urgency of obtaining registration. The structure of the CTM system means that it is likely to be a slow process in most cases.

2. Which System is Most Appropriate to Protect Marks in a Small Number of Countries?

The unitary nature of the CTM together with the added risk of encountering opposition make it likely that separate national applications will remain preferable for marks to be used in only a small number of countries. Additionally, a CTM application could be delayed by the opposition of a small trader in a part of the EU where the applicant does not even trade, thereby preventing registration in the parts of the EU of relevance to the applicant. Although the cost structure of the CTM is not yet established, a CTM will undoubtedly be more expensive than a small number of national applications. Protocol applications are unlikely to prove significantly cheaper than separate national applications, but there should be reduced costs in the early stages of the process by reason of the single filing (and the 18-month deadline for national examination may be useful in certain countries). Searching costs will not, however, be reduced.

3. Which System is Most Appropriate to Protect Marks in a Large Number of Countries?

The risk of opposition in one state resulting in having to convert the registration in all other states to national registrations, after considerable delay, makes the CTM an uncertain, slow, and potentially unnecessarily expensive route. The Madrid Protocol on the other hand offers administrative savings in the original filing and on renewals, assignments and licensing as well as the 18-month national examination. Accordingly, a Madrid application will be more cost-effective and administratively more straightforward than separate national applications, and with greater certainty than a CTM.

4. Will It Be Possible to Enforce Trademark Rights in Several Countries Through One Action?

The Madrid Protocol makes no provision for multi-jurisdictional infringement actions and, since Madrid registrations lead to national registrations, separate national actions for infringement probably will be required. International conflicts of law principles, and Article 16 of the 1968 Brussels Convention on Jurisdiction and the Enforcement of Judgments in Civil and Commercial Matters, as amended ("the Brussels Convention"), reserve to the jurisdiction of the contracting states proceedings concerning the validity of registered trademark rights. The Brussels Convention makes no special provision for infringement actions which may, therefore, fall under the general rules of the Convention, with the possibility of multi-state relief in appropriate cases. This raises various difficult issues, however. It is certainly not the case that multi-country injunctions are now common in trademark or other intellectual property infringement actions in the signatory countries to the Brussels Convention. The CTM offers the prospect of obtaining EU-wide relief, although the detailed jurisdictional aspects will only be clarified once the CTM Regulation has been ratified and appropriate implementing measures have been put in place.

VIII. PRACTICAL ISSUES FOR INTELLECTUAL PROPERTY TRANSFEREES

This Chapter has attempted to explain the type of intellectual property rights a technology transferor may secure for its technology. The following Chapters show how intellectual property can be exploited through the different types of structures under which intellectual property may be transferred and the ways in which a transferor and transferee may protect themselves in the course of technology transfer transactions. In order to best exploit its intellectual property, a transferor should do what it can to ensure that it has secured the strongest possible intellectual property rights. Securing the relevant protections should not be postponed until such time as the transferor is considering exploiting the rights, but should be undertaken when it first *acquires* these rights.

A party often obtains certain intellectual property rights – usually by license and more rarely by way of conveyance and acquisition – from another party. When acquiring title or only obtaining certain well-defined use or exploitation rights to the intellectual property in a product, process or invention, the transferee should conduct a due diligence exercise and ascertain that the transferor is, in fact, legally entitled to convey those rights to the full extent contemplated by the transaction. For example, another party might have a license to use those rights or, more importantly, a third party might be able contractually to restrict the transferor's ability to transfer the technology to the transferee.

When the right, title and interest in the technology are being purchased and, in some cases, even when the intellectual property is only licensed, an attempt should also be made to value those rights. The valuation of intellectual property rights, such as patents and copyrights, is exceedingly difficult. For example, the scope of a patent monopoly may be limited, and a competitor easily may be able to avoid the patent but still have a competing product. Copyrights are perhaps even more difficult to value than patent rights, both because the copyright in a work can be avoided by designing around the particular way in which an idea has been expressed and because of the possibility of independent creation. Another important valuation factor is that if, as is often the case, the rights had already been licensed to others, the overall value of the rights will be reduced. This might change the economics of the transaction and the transferee may wish to adjust the business terms accordingly.

The following steps also should form part of a due diligence exercise:

- Deciding what type of intellectual property rights are to be obtained and whether those are registered or unregistered rights.
- Determining whether the transferor is the owner or lawful licensee of the rights. If the rights are registered rights (such as patents, registered trademarks or registered designs) it is necessary to conduct a search in relation to those rights in the relevant national or supranational register. This search will reveal the legal owner of the rights. Determining the owner of unregistered rights is more difficult. For example, in many countries it would be impossible to state categorically that the transferor owns the copyright in a particular work unless copyright assignments have been obtained from all the people involved in producing the work. In the case of software, this may include assignments from all the participating programmers as well as any graphic designers employed to design the "look and feel" of the software and the artists responsible for any of the graphics or sound in the software.[219] If the owner does not own the rights, but is licensed to sublicense or otherwise use the rights as contemplated by agreement with the transferee, then the transferee needs to ascertain that the transferor indeed has the authority to enter into and fully implement the agreement with the

---

219. Even if all these assignments are obtained, because copyright is not a monopoly right, there remains the inescapable danger that another party might have independently written something substantially similar.

transferee. In certain cases, the transferee may wish to review a copy of the transferor's agreement with the party originally licensing the technology to the transferor; or, if this is not possible due to confidentiality and other reasons, the transferee may seek an express consent to the transaction from the original licensor.

- Seeking confirmation backed-up by a written representation and warranty from the transferor that it is the owner or lawful licensee of all relevant intellectual property rights. It is common for such a warranty to be accompanied by an indemnity protecting the transferee if the transferor violates this warranty.[220]

- Checking whether there is any flaw in the rights or any reason why the transferee may not obtain the rights for which it bargains. The transferee's ownership may be worth rather less if, for example, the transferor had already granted licenses in respect of any of the rights to other parties or there is ongoing litigation in relation to the rights which may ultimately prevent the transferee from using them. In the case of registered rights, the relevant register should be checked since important actions affecting the rights, such as licenses or security taken in the rights by a bank, may be registered.[221] The transferee should confirm whether the transferor knows, or has any reason to suspect, that a third party may have an interest in the rights or any litigation is expected, threatened or under way. Again, this should be backed-up by warranties and an indemnity.

IX. CONCLUSION

No technology business can afford to ignore its intellectual property rights. The identification and ongoing protection of intellectual property rights are key factors in assessing how best to maximize the value and use of technology. Failure to do so may have a significant adverse impact on a business' ability to exploit its rights effectively and, worse, may result in the loss or misappropriation of its intellectual property. As it is difficult to predict with certainty the directions in which technology may develop over time, a business should try to ensure that its rights are as broad as possible and that they are secured

---

220. *See* Chapter Three, Sections VII and VIII.
221. *See* Chapter Five, Part One.

for each aspect of its technology, even if some technologies appear of insignificant value at the time.

Any business whose plans include commercial relations with customers or strategic partners in other countries should be aware of the international dimensions of its intellectual property rights. Intellectual property protection should be obtained in all countries likely to be important both for the exploitation of the technology and due to its potential misappropriation by others. The institution and ongoing maintenance of a comprehensive international intellectual property program is costly and time-consuming. Technology businesses, therefore, should develop a well-thought-through intellectual property strategy based on prioritized cost-benefit considerations.

Table 1.1 Comparative Table of Intellectual Property Rights

Type of intellectual property right	What it protects	Scope of Protection	Term	Cost	Procedure	Registration of assignment	Registration of license
Patents	Invention	Monopoly right	17–20 years from filing	Drafting, filing and renewal fees	Apply to relevant Patent Office	Advisable, sometimes compulsory	Advisable, sometimes compulsory
Design Rights	Designs	Protection against copying but not independent creation	10–15 years from filing (where registration possible) or first exploitation	Drafting, filing and renewal fees where registered, otherwise none	Apply to relevant national office if registered, otherwise automatic	Advisable and sometimes compulsory, if registered design	Advisable and sometimes compulsory, if registered design
Copyright	Expression, original works	Protection against copying but not independent creation	Life of author plus 50 or 70 years	None	Automatic	No	No
Trade Secrets	Any information of a confidential nature	Absolute protection	No fixed term	Security measures	No formalities but confidentiality must be preserved	No	No

Table 1.2 Illustrative Comparative Table for Patents for Inventions by Country and Region

	China	France	United Kingdom	United States of America
Requirement of novelty	Yes	Yes	Yes	Yes
Requirement of inventiveness/ non-obviousness?	Yes	Yes	Yes	Yes
Requirement of industrial/ practical applicability?	Yes	Yes	Yes	Yes
Chemical/ medical patentable?	Yes except not methods for the diagnosis/ treatment of diseases, or animals or plant varieties.	Pharmaceuticals, processes or methods of preparation of them, and chemical components are patentable. Methods for treatment or of diagnosis are not patentable.	Yes, but not methods of performing mental acts, plant or animal varieties or any essentially biological process for the production of animals or plants.	Yes, except naturally occurring products and, possibly, methods of treatment.
Process may be patented?	Yes	Yes	Yes	Yes
Is there interim publication of the application before patent is granted?	Yes	Yes	Yes	No
Is there an opposition procedure?	Oppositions may be filed within three months of publication of specification.	Observations may be filed within 3 months after publication of novelty search report by Patent Office.	Observations may be filed between date of publication of patent and grant.	Only by attacking validity in infringement proceedings once a patent is granted.
Term	20 years for inventions; 10 years for utility models and designs.	20 years.	20 years.	17 years.
Can the patent's validity be challenged?	Yes	Yes	Yes	Yes
Licenses of right/ compulsory licenses available if invention not used?	Yes	Yes	Yes	No
PCT	Yes	Yes	Yes	Yes
EPC	No	Yes	Yes	No

Table 1.3 Illustrative Comparative Table for Registered Trademarks by Country

	People's Republic of China	France	United Kingdom	United States of America
What are the requirements for registration?	Mark must be distinctive of certain goods or services. Subject to certain absolute and relative prohibitions, any word, device or combination of the two can be registered.	Mark must be distinctive of certain goods or services.	Mark must be capable of being represented graphically and of distinguishing goods or services.	Mark must be distinctive of certain goods or services.
Term	10 years renewable for 10 year periods.	10 years renewable for 10 year periods.	10 years renewable for 10 year periods.	10 years renewable for 10 year periods.
What is the examination procedure?	Trademark applications are examined for conflict with trademark law (absolute prohibitions) and existing registrations and applications (relative prohibitions).	Trademarks are registered after their validity has been checked. The French trademark office does not check the existence of prior rights when conducting its examination.	Trademark applications are examined for conflict with trademark law (absolute prohibitions) and existing registrations (relative prohibitions).	The application is examined for whether it is *per se* unregistrable or is confusingly similar to a previously registered mark.
What is the opposition procedure?	Oppositions may be filed within 3 months of preliminary approval of an application.	The law is changing shortly and by 1995/96 the owner of a similar trademark registration or application or a notorious trademark may lodge an opposition within 2 months from the date of publication of the application.	Oppositions may be filed within 3 months of date of publication of application.	Within 30 days after publication of application.

INTELLECTUAL PROPERTY ASPECTS OF TECHNOLOGY TRANSFERS 57

What happens if mark is not used by owner?	Mark may be cancelled for non-use for 3 consecutive years.	Mark should be the subject of "serious and unequivocal" use in connection with the goods or services for which it is registered. If the trademark is unused for 5 consecutive years it may be cancelled at the request of any interested party.	Mark may be cancelled for non-use for 5 years.	Non-use for 2 consecutive years will be evidence that the mark has been abandoned but this may be rebutted by contrary evidence.
Definition of infringement	Use of mark or similar mark without permission on goods in respect of which mark has been registered, or knowingly selling infringing goods.	Use of the mark in respect of goods or services identical to those designated in the registration, suppression or modification of a regularly used mark, or use of the mark on similar goods to those designated in registration.	Use in the course of trade of a mark which is identical or similar in respect of goods or services which are identical or similar to the registration or when the use of the mark takes unfair advantage of the distinctive character of the registered trademark.	Use of a mark which so closely resembles another registered trademark as to cause a likelihood of confusion.
Can trademarks be licensed or assigned?	Yes	Yes	Yes	Yes
Do licenses/ assignments have to be registered?	Yes	No, but will not be effective as against third parties unless registered.	No, but assignment will not be effective as against third parties unless registered.	No, but assignment will not be effective as against third parties unless registered.

Table 1.4 Comparative Table of Adoption of Conventions

Country	Universal Copyright Convention Text of Geneva (1952)	Text of Paris (1971)	Rome Convention (1961)	Berne Convention	Madrid Arrangement concerning the International Registration of Marks	Hague Agreement on Designs	Patent Cooperation Treaty
Albania	N	N	N	Y 06.03.94	N	N	N
Algeria	Y 28.08.73	Y 10.07.74	N	N	Y 05.07.72	N	N
Andorra	Y 16.09.55	N	N	N	N	N	N
Argentina	Y 13.02.58	N	Y 02.03.92	Y 10.06.67	N	N	N
Armenia	N	N	N	N	Y 25.12.91	N	Y 25.12.91
Australia	Y 01.05.69	Y 28.02.78	Y 30.09.92	Y 14.04.28	N	N	Y 31.03.80
Austria	Y 02.07.57	Y 14.08.82	Y 09.06.73	Y 01.10.20	Y 01.01.09	N	Y 23.04.79
Bahamas	Y 27.12.76	Y 27.12.76	N	Y 10.07.73	N	N	N
Bangladesh	Y 05.08.75	Y 05.08.75	N	N	N	N	N
Barbados	Y 18.06.83	Y 18.06.83	Y 18.09.83	Y 30.07.83	N	N	Y 12.03.85
Belarus	Y 27.05.73	N	N	N	Y 25.12.91	N	Y 25.12.91
Belgium	Y 31.08.60	N	N	Y 05.12.1887	Y 15.07.1892	Y 01.04.79	Y 14.12.81
Belize	Y 01.12.82	N	N	N	N	N	N

INTELLECTUAL PROPERTY ASPECTS OF TECHNOLOGY TRANSFERS 59

Country	Universal Copyright Convention Text of Geneva (1952)	Text of Paris (1971)	Rome Convention (1961)	Berne Convention	Madrid Arrangement concerning the International Registration of Marks	Hague Agreement on Designs	Patent Cooperation Treaty
Benin	N	N	N	Y 03.01.61	N	Y 02.11.86	Y 26.02.87
Bolivia	Y 22.03.90	Y 22.03.90	Y 24.11.93	Y 04.11.93	N	N	N
Bosnia and Herzegovina	Y 11.05.66	Y 10.07.74	N	Y 06.03.92	Y 06.03.92	N	N
Brazil	Y 13.01.60	Y 11.12.75	Y 29.09.65	Y 09.02.22	N	N	Y 09.04.78
Bulgaria	Y 07.06.75	Y 07.06.75	N	Y 05.12.21	Y 01.08.85	N	Y 21.05.84
Burkina Faso	N	N	Y 14.01.88	Y 19.08.63	N	N	Y 21.03.89
Cambodia	Y 16.09.55	N	N	N	N	N	N
Cameroon	Y 01.05.73	Y 10.07.74	N	Y 21.09.64	N	N	Y 24.01.78
Canada	Y 10.08.62	N	N	Y 10.04.28	N	N	Y 02.01.90
Central African Republic	N	N	N	Y 03.09.77	N	N	Y 24.01.78
Chad	N	N	N	Y 25.11.71	N	N	Y 24.01.78
Chile	Y 16.09.55	N	Y 05.09.74	Y 05.06.70	N	N	N
China	Y 30.10.92	Y 30.10.92	N	Y 15.10.92	Y 04.10.89	N	Y 01.01.94

Country	Universal Copyright Convention Text of Geneva (1952)	Text of Paris (1971)	Rome Convention (1961)	Berne Convention	Madrid Arrangement concerning the International Registration of Marks	Hague Agreement on Designs	Patent Cooperation Treaty
Colombia	Y 18.06.76	Y 18.06.76	Y 17.09.76	N 07.03.88	N	N	N
Congo	N	N	Y 18.05.64	Y 08.05.62	N	N	Y 24.01.78
Costa Rica	Y 16.09.55	Y 07.03.80	Y 09.09.71	Y 10.06.78	N	N	N
Côte d'Ivoire	N	N	N	Y 01.01.62	N	Y 30.05.93	Y 30.04.91
Croatia	Y 11.05.66	Y 10.07.74	N	Y 08.10.91	Y 08.10.91	N	N
Cuba	Y 18.06.57	N	N	N	Y 06.12.89	N	N
Cyprus	Y 19.12.90	Y 19.12.90	N	Y 24.02.64	N	N	N
Czech Republic	Y 06.01.60	Y 17.04.80	Y 01.01.93	Y 01.01.93	Y 01.01.93	N	Y 01.01.93
Denmark	Y 09.02.62	Y 11.07.79	Y 23.09.65	Y 01.07.03	N	N	Y 01.12.78
Dominican Republic	Y 08.05.83	Y 08.05.83	Y 27.01.87	N	N	N	N
Ecuador	Y 05.06.57	Y 06.06.91	Y 18.05.64	Y 09.10.91	N	N	N
Egypt	N	N	N	Y 07.06.77	Y 01.07.52	Y 01.07.52	N
El Salvador	Y 29.03.79	Y 29.03.79	Y 29.06.79	Y 19.02.94	N	N	N
Estonia	N	N	N	Y 26.10.94	N	N	Y 24.08.94

INTELLECTUAL PROPERTY ASPECTS OF TECHNOLOGY TRANSFERS 61

Country	Universal Copyright Convention		Rome Convention (1961)	Berne Convention	Madrid Arrangement concerning the International Registration of Marks	Hague Agreement on Designs	Patent Cooperation Treaty
	Text of Geneva (1952)	Text of Paris (1971)					
Fiji	Y 10.10.70	N	Y 11.04.72	Y 01.12.71	N	N	N
Finland	Y 16.04.63	Y 01.11.86	Y 21.10.83	Y 01.04.28	N	N	Y 01.10.80
France	Y 11.01.56	Y 10.07.74	Y 03.07.87	Y 05.12.1887	Y 15.07.1892	Y 20.10.30	Y 25.02.78
Gabon	N	N	N	Y 26.03.62	N	N	Y 24.01.78
Gambia	N	N	N	Y 07.03.93	N	N	N
Georgia	N	N	N	N	N	N	Y 25.12.91
Germany	Y 16.09.55	Y 10.07.74	Y 21.10.66	Y 05.12.1887	Y 01.12.22	Y 01.06.28	Y 24.01.78
Ghana	Y 22.08.62	N	N	Y 11.10.91	N	N	N
Greece	Y 24.08.63	N	Y 06.01.93	Y 09.11.20	N	N	Y 09.10.90
Guatemala	Y 28.10.64	N	Y 14.01.77	N	N	N	N
Guinea	Y 13.11.81	Y 13.11.81	N	Y 20.11.80	N	N	Y 27.05.91
Guinea-Bissau	N	N	N	Y 22.07.91	N	N	N
Guyana	N	N	N	Y 25.10.94	N	N	N
Haiti	Y 16.09.55	N	N	N	N	N	N
Holy See	Y 05.10.55	Y 06.05.80	N	Y 12.09.35	N	Y 29.09.60	N

Country	Universal Copyright Convention Text of Geneva (1952)	Universal Copyright Convention Text of Paris (1971)	Rome Convention (1961)	Berne Convention	Madrid Arrangement concerning the International Registration of Marks	Hague Agreement on Designs	Patent Cooperation Treaty
Honduras	N	N	Y 16.02.90	Y 25.01.90	N	N	N
Hungary	Y 23.01.71	Y 10.07.74	Y 10.02.95	Y 14.02.22	Y 01.01.09	Y 07.04.84	Y 27.06.80
Iceland	Y 18.12.56	N	Y 15.06.94	Y 07.09.47	N	N	Y 23.03.95
India	Y 21.01.58	Y 07.01.88	N	Y 01.04.28	N	N	N
Indonesia	N	N	N	N	N	Y 24.12.50	N
Ireland	Y 20.01.59	N	Y 19.09.79	Y 05.10.27	N	N	Y 01.08.92
Israel	Y 16.09.55	N	N	Y 24.03.50	N	N	N
Italy	Y 24.01.57	Y 25.01.80	Y 08.04.75	Y 05.12.1887	Y 15.10.1894	Y 13.06.87	Y 28.03.85
Jamaica	N	N	Y 27.01.94	Y 01.01.94	N	N	N
Japan	Y 28.04.56	Y 21.10.77	Y 26.10.89	Y 15.07.1899	N	N	Y 01.10.78
Kazakhstan	Y 27.05.73	N	N	N	Y 25.12.91	N	Y 25.02.91
Kenya	Y 07.09.66	Y 10.07.74	N	Y 11.06.93	N	N	Y 08.06.94
Kyrgyzstan	N	N	N	N	Y 25.12.91	N	Y 25.12.91
Laos	Y 16.09.55	N	N	N	N	N	N

INTELLECTUAL PROPERTY ASPECTS OF TECHNOLOGY TRANSFERS 63

Country	Universal Copyright Convention Text of Geneva (1952)	Text of Paris (1971)	Rome Convention (1961)	Berne Convention	Madrid Arrangement concerning the International Registration of Marks	Hague Agreement on Designs	Patent Cooperation Treaty
Latvia	N	N	N	N	N	N	Y 07.09.93
Lebanon	Y 17.10.59	N	N	Y 30.09.47	N	N	N
Lesotho	N	N	Y 26.01.90	Y 28.09.89	N	N	N
Liberia	Y 27.07.56	N	N	Y 08.03.89	N	N	Y 27.08.94
Libya	N	N	N	Y 28.09.76	N	N	N
Liechtenstein	Y 22.01.59	N	N	Y 30.07.31	Y 14.07.33	Y 14.07.33	Y 19.03.80
Lithuania	N	N	N	Y 14.12.94	N	N	Y 05.07.94
Luxembourg	Y 15.10.55	N	Y 25.02.76	Y 20.06.1888	Y 01.09.24	Y 01.04.79	Y 30.04.78
Macedonia	N	N	N	N	Y 08.09.91	N	N
Madagascar	N	N	N	Y 01.01.66	N	N	Y 24.01.78
Malawi	Y 26.10.65	N	N	Y 12.10.91	N	N	Y 24.01.78
Malaysia	N	N	N	Y 01.10.90	N	N	N
Mali	N	N	N	Y 19.03.62	N	N	Y 19.10.84
Malta	Y 19.11.68	N	N	Y 21.09.64	N	N	N

Country	Universal Copyright Convention Text of Geneva (1952)	Universal Copyright Convention Text of Paris (1971)	Rome Convention (1961)	Berne Convention	Madrid Arrangement concerning the International Registration of Marks	Hague Agreement on Designs	Patent Cooperation Treaty
Mauritania	N	N	N	Y 06.02.73	N	N	Y 13.04.83
Mauritius	Y 12.03.68	N	N	Y 10.05.89	N	N	N
Mexico	Y 12.05.57	Y 31.10.75	Y 18.05.64	Y 11.06.67	N	N	Y 01.01.95
Monaco	Y 16.09.55	Y 13.12.74	Y 06.12.85	Y 30.05.1889	Y 29.04.56	Y 29.04.56	Y 22.06.79
Mongolia	N	N	N	N	Y 21.04.85	N	Y 27.05.91
Morocco	Y 08.05.72	Y 28.01.76	N	Y 16.06.17	Y 30.07.17	Y 20.10.30	N
Namibia	N	N	N	Y 21.03.90	N	N	N
Netherlands	Y 22.06.67	Y 30.11.85	Y 07.10.93	Y 01.11.12	Y 01.03.1893	Y 01.04.79	Y 10.07.79
New Zealand	Y 11.09.64	N	N	Y 24.04.28	N	N	Y 01.12.92
Nicaragua	Y 16.08.61	N	N	N	N	N	N
Niger	Y 15.05.89	Y 15.05.89	Y 18.05.64	Y 02.05.62	N	N	Y 21.03.93
Nigeria	Y 14.02.62	N	Y 29.10.93	Y 14.09.93	N	N	N
North Korea	N	N	N	N	Y 10.06.80	Y 27.05.92	Y 08.07.80
Norway	Y 23.01.63	Y 07.08.74	Y 10.07.78	Y 13.04.1896	N	N	Y 01.01.80

INTELLECTUAL PROPERTY ASPECTS OF TECHNOLOGY TRANSFERS 65

Country	Universal Copyright Convention Text of Geneva (1952)	Text of Paris (1971)	Rome Convention (1961)	Berne Convention	Madrid Arrangement concerning the International Registration of Marks	Hague Agreement on Designs	Patent Cooperation Treaty
Pakistan	Y 16.09.55	N	N	Y 05.07.48	N	N	N
Panama	Y 17.10.62	Y 03.09.80	Y 02.09.83	N	N	N	N
Paraguay	Y 11.03.62	N	Y 26.02.70	Y 02.01.92	N	N	N
Peru	Y 16.10.63	Y 22.07.85	Y 07.08.85	Y 20.08.88	N	N	N
Philippines	Y 19.11.55	N	Y 25.09.84	Y 01.08.51	N	N	N
Poland	Y 09.03.77	Y 09.03.77	N	Y 28.01.20	Y 18.03.91	N	Y 25.12.90
Portugal	Y 25.12.56	Y 20.07.71	N	Y 29.03.11	Y 31.10.1893	N	Y 24.11.92
Republic of Moldova	N	N	N	N	Y 25.12.91	Y 14.03.94	Y 25.12.91
Romania	N	N	N	Y 01.01.27	Y 06.10.20	Y 18.07.92	Y 23.07.79
Russian Federation	Y 27.05.73	Y 09.03.95	N	Y 13.03.95	Y 01.07.76	N	Y 29.03.78
Rwanda	Y 10.11.89	Y 10.11.89	N	Y 01.03.84	N	N	N
Saint Kitts and Nevis	N	N	N	Y 09.04.95	N	N	N
Saint Lucia	N	N	N	Y 24.08.93	N	N	N
Saint Vincent and the Grenadines	Y 22.04.85	Y 22.04.85	N	N	N	N	N

Country	Universal Copyright Convention		Rome Convention (1961)	Berne Convention	Madrid Arrangement concerning the International Registration of Marks	Hague Agreement on Designs	Patent Cooperation Treaty
	Text of Geneva (1952)	Text of Paris (1971)					
San Marino	N	N	N	N	Y 25.09.60	N	N
Saudi Arabia	Y 13.08.94	N	N	N	N	N	N
Senegal	Y 09.07.74	Y 10.07.74	N	Y 25.08.62	N	Y 30.06.84	Y 24.01.78
Singapore	N	N	N	N	N	N	Y 23.02.95
Slovakia	Y 06.01.60	Y 17.04.80	Y 01.01.93	Y 01.01.93	Y 01.01.93	N	Y 01.01.93
Slovenia	Y 11.05.66	Y 10.07.77	N	Y 25.06.91	Y 25.06.91	Y 13.01.95	Y 01.03.94
South Africa	N	N	N	Y 03.10.28	N	N	N
South Korea	Y 01.10.87	Y 01.10.87	N	N	N	N	Y 10.08.84
Spain	Y 16.09.55	Y 10.07.74	Y 14.11.91	Y 05.12.1887	Y 15.07.1892	Y 01.06.28	Y 16.11.89
Sri Lanka	Y 25.01.84	Y 25.01.84	N	Y 20.07.59	N	N	Y 26.02.82
Sudan	N	N	N	N	Y 16.05.84	N	Y 16.04.84
Suriname	N	N	N	Y 23.02.77	N	Y 25.11.75	N
Swaziland	N	N	N	N	N	N	Y 20.09.94
Sweden	Y 01.07.61	Y 10.07.74	Y 18.05.64	Y 01.08.04	N	N	Y 17.05.78
Switzerland	Y 30.03.56	Y 21.09.93	Y 24.09.93	Y 05.12.1887	Y 15.07.1892	Y 01.06.28	Y 24.01.78
Tajikistan	Y 27.05.73	N	N	N	Y 25.12.91	N	Y 25.12.91
Thailand	N	N	N	Y 17.07.31	N	N	N

INTELLECTUAL PROPERTY ASPECTS OF TECHNOLOGY TRANSFERS 67

Country	Universal Copyright Convention — Text of Geneva (1952)	Text of Paris (1971)	Rome Convention (1961)	Berne Convention	Madrid Arrangement concerning the International Registration of Marks	Hague Agreement on Designs	Patent Cooperation Treaty
Togo	N	N	N	Y 30.04.75	N	N	Y 24.01.78
Trinidad and Tobago	Y 19.08.88	Y 19.08.88	N	Y 16.08.88	N	N	Y 10.03.94
Tunisia	Y 19.06.69	Y 10.06.75	N	Y 05.12.1887	N	Y 20.10.30	N
Turkey	N	N	N	Y 01.01.52	N	N	N
Uganda	N	N	N	N	N	N	Y 09.02.95
Ukraine	Y 27.05.73	N	N	N	Y 25.12.91	N	Y 25.12.91
United Kingdom	Y 27.09.57	Y 10.07.74	Y 18.05.64	Y 05.12.1887	N	N	Y 24.01.78
United Republic of Tanzania	N	N	N	Y 25.07.94	N	N	N
United States of America	Y 16.09.55	Y 10.07.74	N	Y 01.03.89	N	N	Y 24.01.78
Uruguay	Y 12.04.93	Y 12.04.93	Y 04.07.77	Y 10.07.67	N	N	N
Uzbekistan	N	N	N	N	Y 25.12.91	N	Y 25.12.91
Venezuela	Y 30.09.66	N	N	Y 30.12.82	N	N	N
Vietnam	N	N	N	N	Y 08.03.49	N	Y 10.03.93
Yugoslavia (Serbia and Montenegro)	Y 11.05.66	Y 10.07.74	N	Y 17.06.30	Y 26.02.21	Y 30.12.93	N
Zaire	N	N	N	Y 08.10.63	N	N	N
Zambia	Y 01.06.65	N	N	Y 02.01.92	N	N	N
Zimbabwe	N	N	N	Y 18.04.80	N	N	N

Chapter Two

Structuring Alternatives for International Technology Transfers

Harry Rubin, Constantine J. Zepos and Thomas E. Crocker
Shaw, Pittman, Potts & Trowbridge, Washington, D.C.

A technology transferor should first secure the maximal protections for its technology under the applicable intellectual property regimes of its home country. The transferor should then identify clearly and specifically its long- and short-term business objectives for the exploitation of its technology. If those objectives include the transfer of the technology or its derivative products abroad, the transferor and prospective transferee should then select the appropriate legal structure in order to effect the technology transfer. The selected structure is of paramount importance to both transferor and transferee; for, as this Chapter will show, inherent in each structure are substantive characteristics which may either buttress or frustrate the parties' ability to achieve their business objectives. The selected structure should be the one that most easily enables the parties to achieve their business objectives throughout the life of their business relationship while simultaneously affording them enough flexibility to cope effectively with evolving business exigencies and unforeseen contingencies.

The parties should, therefore, resist the temptation to focus first on the operative terms of the technology transfer and only then agree on the structural framework of the transaction. They should, on the contrary, first resolve within their respective organizations and with one another which structure would be most suitable for their particular purposes. Accordingly, this Chapter will describe the available transfer vehicles and elucidate the salient business and legal implications that should figure most prominently in the parties' deliberations as they seek to identify the most appropriate technology transfer structure for their transaction.

I. FOUR BASIC FORMS OF TECHNOLOGY TRANSFERS

Technology, and its derivative products, can be transferred through a direct sale or license to end-users. Alternatively, it can be transferred by entering into one of two basic strategic alliance forms with a partner located in the target country. One form encompasses contractual alliances, which include distribution, agency, representative, and franchising arrangements; the other is the joint venture (JV) form, whereby two or more strategic allies establish a separate legal entity serving as the transfer vehicle. Finally, the transfer can – although rarely will – be accomplished through a merger or acquisition.

A. Direct Sale and Assignment

In an outright sale and assignment, products based upon the transferor's technology are sold without the transferor retaining any significant controls over their use and retransfer. This is the easiest form of technology dissemination. It is designed to produce revenues with a minimum of transaction costs and other impediments. This option, however, should only be considered if the transferor finds it impractical to impose restrictions on the products' uses, perhaps because they are high-volume or low-cost items, or because the transferor is persuaded that the technology used to create those products cannot be misappropriated in a viable commercial manner. A classic example in this category is consumer electronics. These products must be disseminated in large quantities, and it is unlikely that they could be marketed successfully if they were made available under license restrictions. Of course, marketing considerations, such as access to foreign markets and, particularly, the ability to distribute the product may actually require the transferor to link up with a strategic partner to market the product effectively.

The direct sale of products derived from the transferor's technology must be distinguished from a "sale" of the technology underlying the products. The latter would require the transferor irrevocably to assign all of its rights, title to and interest in the technology to the transferee. To that end, the transferor would have to identify the intellectual property elements embodied in the products – copyrights, trademarks, patents, trade secrets and know-how – and assign all those rights to the transferee.[1] This option would result in the complete divestiture of the transferor's rights in the technology. The transferor may decide to

---

1. *See* Chapter One and Chapter Five, Part One.

pursue such divestiture for many reasons, all of which would have to be predicated upon the transferor's fundamental decision no longer to market, develop, or otherwise exploit the technology. The transferor may have concluded, for example, that it has neither the capability nor the time or resources to exploit the technology. Or, the transferor may simply wish to generate immediate returns and forgo the potentially larger returns that the development and marketing of products based on the technology may generate over time.

B. Direct End-use Licensing

Technology and its derivative products can be licensed directly to end-users. While end-user licensing affords significant advantages by way of controls over the dissemination, use and protection of proprietary rights, it requires a suitable and elaborate marketing structure. Moreover, direct end-user licensing can subject the transferor to significant inefficiencies because there is no distributor, agent or representative offering warranty and maintenance services and absorbing the costs of establishing a marketing network in the target country.

Direct end-user licensing is appropriate mainly for products that are highly intellectual property intensive and when the need to control purpose, location of use and competition is substantial, provided that the transferor can reach consumers in foreign markets without the assistance of local parties. Technologies that primarily fit into this category are sophisticated or expensive technology packages directed at few easily accessible potential customers such as governmental authorities, utilities, well-known businesses or discrete market segments, or customized technology products, such as custom software packages, particularly if a close support and maintenance relationship is required with the end-user.

C. Strategic Alliance with Third Party

In transactions in this category, the transferor teams up with a strategic partner in order to market, support, customize, or further develop the technology in the target country. Strategic alliances include two types of structures: contractual alliances and JVs through a separate entity. In the strategic alliance context, it is particularly important for the parties to be aware of any political subdivisions in the target country, such as provinces or states, as those may impose separate requirements on the formation and operation of the JV entity.[2]

1. Contractual Alliances

The simplest and most popular form of international technology transfer is the contractual strategic alliance, whereby the technology or its derivative products are made available to end-users via a contractual partner, such as an agent, sales representative, franchisee, or distributor, acting as the immediate technology transferee who, in turn, is *licensed* to market the technology in the target country, whether separately or in the context of a value added reseller or other equipment manufacturer arrangement. Such contractual strategic alliances may result in the strategic ally in the target country ultimately becoming a manufacturing licensee or JV partner of the transferor.

The terms "agent," "distributor," and "representative" should be used interchangeably only at the user's own peril. Understanding the obvious and, frequently, subtle distinctions between those structures, as well as their variations, is critical because the rights and obligations of the parties in each case may vary substantially with the relevant jurisdiction.[3] Adding to the confusion is the cavalier usage of the term "licensee," which often is employed as a substitute for distributor, representative or agent. A licensee does not take title to the licensed technology or its derivative products, whereas a distributor – in its correct and purest usage as independent reseller – does. Moreover, all contractual strategic partners are licensees in the sense that they are licensed to use and retransfer all or parts of the technology, or its derivative products, and usually also the transferor's trademarks, goodwill and know-how *subject to specified conditions*. Conceptually, therefore, technology transferees in *all* strategic alliances forms are first and foremost licensees that are licensed in different ways and for distinct and well-defined purposes.

a. Agents

A typical sales agent, for practical and most legal purposes, is an employee of the technology transferor who carries out the transferor's instructions and represents and binds the transferor in the target country in all respects. Contrary to the distributor, the agent does not take title to the goods or purchase them for resale. The agent enjoys

---

2. *See* Chapter Six for a discussion on applicable law and choice of law.
3. INTERNATIONAL AGENCY AND DISTRIBUTION AGREEMENTS §§ 3.1-3.3 (Thomas F. Clasen ed., 1993).

limited freedom in carrying out its commission and its powers are finite and enumerated in the agency agreement.

Some jurisdictions recognize the concept of an "independent contractor agent." There are important differences between an employee agent and an independent contractor agent. Under most jurisdictions, if an agent is characterized as an employee, rather than an independent contractor, there are at least two possible disadvantages for the principal. First, the principal, much like an employer, may have to pay various social benefits (*e.g.,* unemployment compensation, health and social benefits, etc.) for its agent, which usually are not applicable to independent contractor agents. Second, the employee agent may be entitled to benefits under local labor law, which may include, among other provisions, mandatory vacations, premiums for overtime, special severance, and other benefits.[4]

An employee agent is in a dependent or subordinate relationship to the transferor and does not represent other principals or use its own capital.[5] To avoid the characterization of the agency relationship as one of employment and the consequent application of the relevant labor laws and regulations, the agent should be paid *commissions* rather than a salary. Engaging a corporation instead of an individual could further help prevent the characterization of an agent as an employee,[6] and may be particularly effective in countries where an individual is presumed to be an employee.[7] Generally, the more control the principal holds over the agent, the more likely it is that the agent will be characterized as an employee.

Probably the single most important characteristic of the agent is its ability to bind the transferor. Therefore, transferors concerned about the apparent or actual authority of their transferees to undertake commitments, assume liabilities or make decisions on their behalf should avoid using an agency structure altogether, whether independent or otherwise. It is critical, moreover, not to confer upon other types of transferees agency-like authority; for, even if the agreement does not refer to the transferee as agent, a court may read the agency status into the agreement based on its terms.

b. *Distributors*

In its purest form, a distributor, or "dealer," is an independent reseller of the transferor's product. The transferor sells the product embodying the technology to the dealer, who resells it in the target

---

4. *Id.* § 5.2.2.
5. Franklin C. Jesse, Jr., *Contracts with Foreign Representatives, in* INTERNATIONAL TRADE FOR THE NON-SPECIALIST § 7.02(d) (Paul H. Vishny ed., 1992).
6. Clasen, *supra* note 3, § 4.2.2.
7. *Id.* § 5.2.2.

country. The distributor's income is derived from its markup of the price of the goods resold to its customers. A distributor is permitted to set its own prices for the transferor's products so as to maximize its profit. Once the distributor has purchased the products from the transferor, it may resell them as it sees fit, subject to the restrictions in the distribution agreement. The distributor, by its resale activities, generally does not expose the transferor to the same liabilities as the agent or even the representative, and, consistent with that independence, the transferor should not be able to control the distributor to the same extent as the agent or representative.

It is not surprising, therefore, that the large majority of distribution arrangements in the high-technology area are not *pure* distribution arrangements. The transferor will not sell the technology or its derivative products to the distributor for resale. On the contrary, in order to safeguard its proprietary interests across the marketing chain all the way to the end-user and retain certain controls over the distributor's activities, the transferor will license a distributor to market the technology through what is loosely termed a distribution agreement, but what *de jure* and *de facto* is a well-defined and purpose-specific marketing license arrangement.

c. *Representatives*

Between the agent and the distributor is the representative, who usually is referred to either as a sales representative or a manufacturer representative. The representative differs from the sales agent in that he has less authority to bind the transferor than the agent, but also is more dependent on the transferor than the distributor. The representative's primary function is to promote and generate orders for the technology and constitute a liaison between the transferor and the customers in the target country. Significantly, however, the sales representative should not have the authority to bind the transferor, accept or reject orders, or independently offer representations or warranties on behalf of the transferor. These activities should be contractually reserved for the transferor.

d. *Franchising*

In a franchising arrangement, the transferor acts as the franchisor providing the transferee – the franchisee – with a franchise for the transferred technology. Franchising is a transfer from the franchisor to the franchisee of the complete package of technology and related know-how and trademarks that is necessary to establish a viable business rapidly. Trademarks, trade names, logos, know-how, and certain management assistance are provided to the franchisee in return for a down-payment, royalties and compliance with corporate and legal regulations, and elaborate quality and image control safeguards.[8] Through franchising, a transferor can expand its business and enter new markets using the same business name and a uniform corporate image, while retaining substantial controls over the transferred technology. Although franchising has been successfully employed in hotels, fastfood restaurants, convenience stores, and specialty services, it has not been a common means of high-technology transfer. This may be changing, however; ComputerLand Corp., a large international retailer of personal computers, recently originated the idea of the "full-service" franchise computer store, and several others have followed suit.

Transferors should be particularly careful when franchising in unfamiliar foreign markets. The success of international franchising often depends upon the franchisor's ability to adjust to a culture with different attitudes and preferences. Therefore, the transferor must ascertain the practicability of establishing its business in a foreign country and engage in thorough market research before attempting to expand internationally.

Three different commercial vehicles are available for international franchising. First, the transferor could franchise directly to franchisees located in the target country without the intervention of a third party. The transferor, under this method, would either franchise directly into the target country through its foreign subsidiary or branch office, or enter into a development agreement with a developer from the target country, under which the latter would develop and own all of the franchise operations in the target country. Alternatively, the transferor could enter into a JV arrangement in which the franchisor would operate the franchise, together with a local partner, through a JV company. The JV would then enter into either a development agreement or a master franchise agreement with the transferor. A JV is a particularly appropriate franchising vehicle if the transferor wishes to export its franchise system to target countries that:

(i) do not permit a foreign transferor to enter into a master franchise arrangement with a national of that country;
(ii) make it difficult for the foreign transferor to establish a branch or wholly owned subsidiary; or
(iii) place limitations on the ability of the foreign transferor to negotiate at arm's length with its franchisees.

The third option is for the transferor to enter into a master franchise agreement directly with a sub-franchisor, usually a foreign national, pursuant to which the sub-franchisor would develop and own franchise outlets. This type of arrangement is especially attractive when the

---

8. *See generally* GLICKMAN, FRANCHISING §§ 2.01.-2.02 (1993).

transferor does not have adequate financial and managerial resources to franchise directly into the target country.[9]

The defining terminology in an international franchise agreement is critical because the language and cultural barriers can easily result in different interpretations. Some of the particularly contentious issues in franchising are the degree of control the franchisor exercises over the franchisee and the franchisor's power to terminate the franchise.[10] Restrictive covenants with regard to territory and exclusivity must be carefully drafted to ensure enforceability under the target country's applicable law. Transferors are generally advised to agree to a longer franchise term for international franchises than they would for domestic franchises because often the foreign law governing post-term non-competition covenants and the protection of trade secrets is unclear, and the transferor may face uncertainty upon the expiration of a short-term agreement. Fees in franchise agreements usually include initial and continuing fees, and both are subject to negotiation between the parties. The parties also will have to decide whether the franchisee will have the right to grant sub-franchises. Transferors should note that in countries where sub-licensing of trademarks is not permissible, sub-franchising may not be feasible.[11] The parties also will have to negotiate provisions with regard to marketing and operations, training and support, project development schedule, payment of fees, and termination. Many of these provisions are similar to those in domestic franchise agreements. However, each provision should be examined in the context of the particular business and legal exigencies of the target country. While some countries do have discrete franchising legislation and regulations, in most countries, the legal environment for franchising depends not on the existence of discrete franchise legislation, which is usually unnecessary, but rather on the commercial laws and regulations that are applicable to the particular franchising arrangement.

---

9. *See* Alex S. Koningsberg, *Analyzing the International Franchise Opportunity, in* INTERNATIONAL FRANCHISING: AN IN-DEPTH TREATMENT OF BUSINESS AND LEGAL TECHNIQUES 12-28 (Gramatidis & Campbell eds., 1991) [hereinafter INTERNATIONAL FRANCHISING].
10. GLICKMAN, *supra* note 8, § 2.01.
11. Michael G. Brennan & David Mendelsohn, *Launching an International Franchise Program, in* INTERNATIONAL FRANCHISING, *supra* note 9, at 45. The rationale for such restriction is that sub-licensing of trademarks deprives the owners of the marks of direct control over their use which is necessary to protect the owners' rights in the marks. Nevertheless, a transferor may be able to "circumvent this problem by granting a direct trademark license to each sub-franchisee." *Id.*

ALTERNATIVES FOR INTERNATIONAL TECHNOLOGY TRANSFERS 77

The following diagram illustrates the relationship between three important criteria and the different contractual alliance forms from the perspective of the transferor.

Figure 2.1 The Relationship between Three Important Criteria and the Different Contractual Alliance Forms from the Perspective of the Transferor

Distributor	Franchisee	Manufacturer or Sales Representative	Independent Contractor Agent	Agent Employee

LOWEST   HIGHEST

< ....Transferee's dependence on transferor .... >

< .... Transferee's power to bind transferor .... >

< ... . Liability exposure of transferor .... >

Supranational Regimes

In October 1986, the European Council adopted Directive 86/653 in order to harmonize the laws of the EU member states relating to self-employed commercial agents.[12] The Directive defines a commercial agent as a self-employed intermediary who has continuing authority to negotiate the sale or purchase of goods on behalf of another person, *i.e.* the principal, or to negotiate and conclude such transactions on behalf of and in the name of that other person. The Directive does not apply to commercial agents whose activities are unpaid or to persons whose activities as commercial agents are considered secondary by the law of that member state. A commercial agent, as defined in the Directive, does *not* include, in particular:

12. Council Directive 86/653 of December 18, 1986 on the Coordination of the Laws of the Member States Relating to Self-employed Commercial Agents, 1986 O.J. (L 382).

(i) a person who, in his capacity as an officer, is empowered to enter into commitments binding on a company or association;
(ii) a partner who is lawfully authorized to enter into commitments binding on his partners; or
(iii) a receiver, manager, liquidator, or a trustee in bankruptcy.

The Directive sets forth the rights and obligations of commercial agents and principals, the remuneration of commercial agents (including the right to a commission and, in some cases, the right to be paid a commission before the principal has been paid by the customer), the conditions for concluding and terminating a contract (including the right to indemnity and compensation for damages), and the limits on agreements restricting the business activities of a commercial agent following termination of an agency contract. Under the Directive, commercial agents are allowed greater leeway in inspecting a principal's books than the principal's employees or even shareholders. Although by January 1, 1994, all EU member states had implemented the Directive, its importance has been significantly underestimated. Because the Directive protects commercial agents, particularly in the areas of payment and termination, it is imperative that transferors (*i.e.*, principals) carefully draft and negotiate agency agreements. Transferors of EU member states whose old agency laws gave agents "the thin end of the stick" (*e.g.*, the U.K.) should pay particular attention to the implications of the Directive. In certain instances (*e.g.*, where regular sales of relatively low-value items are involved), hiring the agent as an employee or distributor may be the better alternative. Finally, because EU member states may impose different obligations to compensate the agent when the agent is terminated by the principal, it is imperative that the parties decide which member state's laws will govern the agreement in case of a dispute. For example, under the Directive, a commercial agent is entitled to one month's average commission for each year of service to the principal, but only up to three-months' commission, if the agent sues in the U.K., and up to seven-months' commission, if the agent operates in Italy and takes action there.[13]

Country Focus

In the **United States**, a transferor can use a sales agent, sales representative, distributor, or franchisee to market its technology. The difference between a sales agent and a sales representative is that the former has the power to bind the transferor, whereas the latter usually does not. Thus, the transferor may be held liable for the sales agent's

---

13. *See* Ian Hamilton Fazey, *FT Exporter*, FIN. TIMES, Jan. 27, 1994. *See generally* Chapter Six.

actions, if made within the scope of the agent's engagement. The representative has less authority to bind the transferor than the agent, but is also less independent than the distributor.[14] The transferor's control of the distributor's activities may be subject to antitrust laws (see Section II.B.3). In addition, a foreign transferor is subject to several federal laws and regulations relating to imports in the United States, such as the Tariff Act of 1930,[15] the anti-dumping laws,[16] the Countervailing Duty Act, and Section 337 of the Tariff Act of 1930.[17] In the United States, franchises are regulated both on the state and federal levels. Several states have passed franchise disclosure acts, requiring franchisors to register with the state and provide prospective franchisees with a disclosure statement. State laws also regulate the established relationship between the franchisor and the franchisee, primarily with respect to the cancellation, termination, nonrenewal, or change of franchises. At the federal level, the Federal Trade Commission Rules require disclosures similar to those of the states, but without the registration requirement.[18]

In **Argentina**, because principals are jointly and severally liable for compliance with all labor and social welfare law obligations covering the subcontractor's employees, transferors may be able to limit the extent of their liability by including two provisions in their agreements. The first provision should give the transferor the right to inspect the books and records of the distributor to ensure that certain legal requirements are met. The second provision should give the transferor

---

14. *See* Clasen, *supra* note 3, § 1.1.
15. 19 U.S.C.S. § 1202 (1988); The Tariff Act imposes duties on imports according to their classification. 26 U.S.C.S. § 4218 (1988); *Agency and Distribution Agreements in the United States, in* Clasen, *supra* note 3, § 1.2.2.
16. 19 U.S.C.S. § 1673 (1983 and Supp. 1989); The Act provides that the Secretary of the Treasury is required to notify the U.S. International Trade Commission whenever the Secretary determines that foreign merchandise is being or is likely to be sold in the United States or elsewhere at less than its fair value and the Commission shall determine the injury to U.S. industry. If such imports are determined to be injurious to domestic sales of like products, such imports may be stopped. *Id.*
17. 19 U.S.C.S. § 1337 (a)(1)(A) (Supp. 1989). The section, as amended, prohibits "[u]nfair methods of competition and unfair acts in the importation of articles . . . into the United States, or in the sale of such articles by the owner, importer, or consignee, the threat or effect of which is . . . to destroy or substantially injure an industry in the United States[,] . . . to prevent the establishment of such an industry[,] or. . . to restrain or monopolize trade and commerce in the United States." *Id.*
18. *Franchises and Laws*, Bus. Franchise Guide (CCH) para. 105 (1-94).

the right to terminate the agreement, should the transferee fail to meet those requirements.[19]

In **Brazil**, it is important to distinguish between the *representante commercial*,[20] who is not an employee, but may solicit purchase orders in the name of the principal, and the *comissario mercantil*[21] – an individual merchant or commercial company that solicits purchase orders in its own name under its principal's instructions. Because agents in Brazil are well protected under applicable Brazilian labor laws, transferors desiring greater flexibility in certain aspects of their relationship (*e.g.*, termination or cancellation) with their contractual partner should consider transferring their technology through a distributor.[22] Although franchising is not governed by any special law in Brazil,[23] franchising contracts executed with a foreign transferor are regulated by Resolution 35/92, issued by the Brazilian Institute of Industrial Property (INPI).[24]

Transferors should engage an independent agent in **Mexico**, unless exercising complete control over the sales person is dispositive.[25] The General Commission Agent (*Commissionista*) is the most common type of independent agent used by transferors. When the transferor wishes to grant the agent limited authority, either in scope or time, and thus limit the former's liability, contracting with a Special Commission Agent might be a better choice.[26] Mexico's federal legislation regulating franchising generally requires presale disclosure of information to prospective franchise purchasers, filing of information about the franchisor, and registration of the transmission of trademark rights to the franchisee.[27] In **Canada**, only the Province of Alberta carries legislation expressly regulating franchising. The Alberta law provides for disclosure and registration requirements.[28]

Foreign technology transferors find it particularly challenging to penetrate the **Japanese** distribution network and find outlets for their products because distributors and retailers in Japan are loyal to a single or limited number of suppliers.[29] Therefore, foreign transferors should

---

19. *See Agency and Distribution Agreements in Argentina, in* Clasen, *supra* note 3, § 1.5.
20. Law No 48867, of Dec. 9, 1965, as amended.
21. Comm. Code, arts 165-190.
22. *See* Clasen (Analysis and Forms), *supra* note 3, § 5.3.1.
23. *See Agency and Distribution Agreements in Brazil, in* Clasen, *supra* note 3, § 1.1.
24. *See* W. Andrew Scott, *Technology Transfer Laws and International Franchising*, 22 INT'L BUS. LAW. 6, at 266 (1994).
25. *Agency and Distribution Agreements in Mexico, in* Clasen, *supra* note 3, § 1.1.6.
26. *Id.* § 2.1.
27. *Franchise Law*, Bus. Franchise Guide (CCH) para. 7200 (9-91).
28. *Franchise and Securities Laws*, Bus. Franchise Guide (CCH) para. 7000 (6-92).
29. William I. Schwartz & Takashi B. Yamamoto, *Doing Business in Japan: Strategies and Practical Insights*, 2 INT'L COMPUTER LAW. 1, 2-3 (Jan. 1994).

consider transferring their technology through a Japanese contractual ally that has an established distribution network. Although Japan has no special provisions applicable to agents and distributors, franchising is regulated by specific legislation.

Hong Kong has no specific legislation on franchising. The only relevant laws with respect to franchising are the laws concerning registration and licensing of trademarks and the law of contract. In addition, unlike many other countries, Hong Kong has no legislation setting out disclosure requirements and standards of conduct to be followed by franchisors. Thus, neither the franchisor nor the franchisee appear on public record, which makes the creditworthiness of the parties, especially of the franchisee, more difficult to ascertain.[30]

The **Korean** Commercial Code distinguishes between agency, brokerage, and consignment sales. Distributorship agreements are governed by the laws applicable to the sale of goods as a form of long-term sales contract. The main difference between an agent and a broker is that the broker cannot bind the principal. Consignment sales are prohibited in Korea.[31] Local agents must register with the Korean Trade Agents Association, and distributorships (for a duration of more than one year) must be reported to the Fair Trade Office of the Economic Planning Board.[32] Although the Korean Commercial Code distinguishes between a contracting agent and negotiating agent, this distinction is insignificant in international sales contracts. An agent in Korea is regarded as an independent contractor, rather than an employee of the transferor, and thus labor law will not apply to the principal/agent relationship.[33] Because the Korean language does not distinguish between an agent and a distributor, technology transferors are advised to deny explicitly any agency status in their distribution agreements.[34] In Korea, franchising, as any other investment or licensing arrangement involving a foreign party, is subject to prior government review and approval under the Foreign Capital Inducement Act. As of July 1994, there was no specific franchise legislation, even though the Korean government is considering passing such legislation. The most common method to secure government approval is to structure the franchise agreement as a license of the franchisor's trade or service mark and "technology," and to seek approval for the agreement from the relevant ministry as a technology inducement contract.[35]

---

30. *See* Ella Cheong, *Franchising in Hong Kong*, 20 INT'L BUS. LAW. 3, 136-137 (1992).
31. *Agency and Distribution Agreements in Korea*, *in* Clasen, *supra* note 3, § 1.2.
32. *Id.* § 1.3.3.
33. *Id.* § 2.1.
34. *Id.* § II.1 (Appendix A).
35. *See* Tae Hee Lee, *Korean Franchising Law and Practice*, 20 INT'L BUS. LAW. 3, at 142 (1992).

Franchise agreements are subject to review under the Korean Fair Trade Act and the unfair trade practice guidelines promulgated thereunder (the EPB Guidelines), which are designed to protect Korean licensees of manufacturing technology. Unless the franchisor convinces the appropriate authorities that the Unfair Trade Act and the EPB Guidelines should not be strictly applied to the underlying transaction, the franchisor may be unable to ensure the uniformity of its services and operations and to protect its service marks and goodwill effectively, because the EPB Guidelines prohibit certain controls placed upon the franchisees.[36]

In **France**, there are several types of commercial intermediaries. A *représentant de commerce* or *voyageur représentant placier* (VRP) is an employee who develops clients and obtains orders for the employer within a specified geographic area.[37] A VRP is not as independent as a representative, but at the same time, is not an employee. Significantly, despite the terms of the agency or distribution agreement, the French courts have sole authority to decide how to characterize the relationship.[38] Commercial agency agreements in France also are subject to the EU directive described above.

In **Germany**, the commercial agent (*Handelsvertreter*) is an independent contractor who either acts as a middleman in bringing about direct legal relations between the principal and the third party (*Vermittlungsvertreter*) or enters into binding agreements with the third party in the name of the principal (*Abschlußvertreter*). The *Vermittlungsvertreter* is similar to the U.S. sales representative and has no authority to bind the principal, but instead acts as a middleman and provides the principal with the opportunity to enter into a contract with a third party.[39] An agent with employee status is a commercial assistant or commercial employee (*Handlungsgehilfe*) and enjoys the same social protection as do other salaried employees.[40] Commercial agency agreements are subject to the EU directive described above. The distributor or dealer (*Vertragshändler* or *Vertriebsvertreter*) is an independent contractor, acts in its own name and on its own account,

---

36. *See* Scott, *supra* note 24, at 260.
37. Article L.751.1 of the Labor Code states that an agent will be considered a VRP if he: "(1) works for one or more employers; (2) performs his work in a selective or steadfast way; (3) does not carry out any commercial operation for himself; and (4) is bound to his employer by an agreement which settles the nature of the services or products offered for sale, the territory or kind of clients which he visits and the rate of remuneration." Jerome Depondt et al., *France*, *in* COMMERCIAL AGENCY AND DISTRIBUTION AGREEMENTS 268 (Guy-Martial Weijer ed.).
38. *Id.* at 288.
39. *Agency and Distribution Agreements in Germany*, *in* Clasen, *supra* note 3, § 1.
40. Rolf Beeker et al., *Federal Republic of Germany*, *in* WEIJER, *supra* note 37, at 172-173.

and generally shares the same characteristics as a distributor in other jurisdictions.

In **Italy**, like most other countries, several commercial intermediaries exist. An agent without the power to represent the principal (*agente senza rappresentanza*) generally promotes the conclusion of contracts on behalf of the principal within a specified territory.[41] An agent with the power to represent the principal (*agente con rappresentanza*) has the power to execute agreements in the name and on behalf of the latter, and thus, any contract prepared by the agent will be directly binding on the principal.[42] Another type of agent is the commission agent (*commissionario*), which always executes contracts on behalf of the principal but in its own name. Such contracts will be binding only between the commission agent and the third party, until the rights and duties of the contract are transferred from the commission agent to the principal.[43] Agents in Italy, who are characterized as employees, are entitled to the protection of collective bargaining agreements periodically negotiated among government, labor, and industry.[44] All agency agreements should be in writing and state the marketing area and any exclusive arrangements. Transferors should pay particular attention to the termination provisions of the agreement.[45] Commercial agency agreements in Italy also are subject to the EU directive described above. Italy has no specific rules for distribution agreements. These agreements are governed by the Italian Civil Code on the supply of goods.

In **Hungary**, there is no discrete franchise legislation. Although the approval of the Hungarian government is not required, a franchisee operating under a foreign franchise system is required to register with the Hungarian National Bank pursuant to the Foreign Trade Law.[46]

2. Joint Ventures via Separate Entity

The term "joint venture" is one of the most abused phrases in the business and legal vocabulary. The term is loosely used to describe many types of transactions ranging from a series of contractual obligations to the actual creation of a new entity that is jointly owned by two or more parties. For the purpose of this Chapter, a JV is a

---

41. Italian Civil Code, art. 1742.
42. *Id.* art. 1752.
43. *Id.* art. 1731.
44. *Agency and Distribution Agreements in Italy*, in Clasen, *supra* note 3, § 5.2.2.
45. U.S. DEP'T OF COMMERCE, *Marketing in Italy*, OVERSEAS BUSINESS REPORTS, Feb. 1993, at 14.
46. Philip F. Zeidman et al., *Franchising in Hungary*, 20 INT'L BUS. LAW. 9, at 474 (1992).

technology transfer mechanism whereby a foreign transferor and its strategic ally in the target country combine certain resources to establish a *new* legal entity designed to engage in particular activities in the target country. The overwhelming majority of jurisdictions provide no distinct legal definition for a JV as such. A JV entity can take two basic legal forms: a corporation or partnership. A variety of factors, including tax incentives, the business and operational objectives of the parties, and liability considerations ultimately should determine the most appropriate JV form for a particular transaction.

a. Joint Venture as a Corporation

In technology commercialization projects employing JVs as a transfer mechanism, the legal entity usually is a corporation. The transferor and its strategic ally form and invest in a corporation in the target country. The technology is then transferred from the transferor to that new corporation, which becomes the transferee. Each party forming the JV corporation may take a proportion of equity in that corporation. The respective equity shares of the parties will be determined through negotiations subject to the host government's regulations.

The most important advantage of the corporate JV form is that it provides limited liability up to the value of its stock. If the corporation is properly organized and capitalized, and all applicable formalities are observed, the corporate structure generally shields shareholders from liability. Other major benefits of the corporate JV include a possible public listing of its securities, thereby enabling capital expansion and absorption, perpetual succession, and legally a more internationally recognizable and credible structure. In addition, subject to local securities regulations, shares either can be made freely transferable, or reasonable restrictions can be instituted so as to prevent an undesirable transfer of stock to a third party. The corporate form's centralized management structure through the oversight by a board of directors also offers advantages for most business operations.

The primary disadvantage of a corporation is that its profits are taxed both at the corporate and the shareholder level. A corporation is also subject to greater governmental regulation, especially in countries with a two-tier regulatory framework, such as the state and federal levels in the United States.[47] A third disadvantage of the corporate form

---

47. Although, a benefit of such extensive regulation is that it provides the venturers with well-developed rules and standards of operation, thereby relieving the venturers from the need to interpret incomplete rules or enact their own.

is that a corporation must conduct its business with formalities (*e.g.,* comply with capitalization formalities, notice requirements, shareholder and board meetings and resolutions, etc.). Should some of these formalities be violated, a court may, based on that and other factors, "pierce the corporate veil" and impose liability beyond the corporation on the shareholders. Finally, a corporate JV has limited flexibility with respect to management and allocation and distribution of benefits and losses.[48]

Several corporate forms are available for structuring a JV, some of which are particularly well suited for smaller undertakings. They often provide greater flexibility in structuring the JV and impose greater restrictions on the transfer of the partners' interest to third parties, whether in the form of pre-emption or a right-of-first-refusal. Capital requirements for these corporate forms are significantly lower than those of standard corporations, and in many countries such corporations may not have more than a specified number of shareholders.

b. *Joint Venture as a Partnership*

The primary advantage of constituting the JV as a partnership is that partnership profits and losses pass directly to the partners, without being taxed at the partnership level. This tax transparency is advantageous to partners who can forecast their start-up expenses and losses, which are common in the incipient stages of a technology venture. Another advantage of the partnership is that it is not subject to intricate formalities (*e.g.,* minutes, notices, and meetings) and requirements (*e.g.,* minimum capitalization). The main drawback of the partnership is that, unlike the corporation, unless the partnership is properly structured as a limited partnership, the partnership's general partners can be found jointly and severally liable for the partnership's liabilities. Therefore, a partnership is more suitable for venturers having a close and trusting working relationship and transactions with limited liability exposure. That partnership interests may not be transferable without the unanimous consent of all partners is often considered an advantage for a party heavily relying on the contributions and commitments of its partner.

A JV can be constituted as a limited partnership (LP), which is similar to a general partnership, except that the general partner alone retains the right to manage the JV's business and the limited partners'

---

48. *See* James R. Bridges, *Structuring Joint Ventures, in* JOINT VENTURES AND OTHER COOPERATIVE ARRANGEMENTS (Michael A. Epstein et al. eds., 1989); *See also* JOINT VENTURES WITH INTERNATIONAL PARTNERS, 1-18 to 1-19 (Dobkin & Burt eds., 1989).

liability is limited to the extent of their investment. In certain countries[49] a limited partner is not allowed to participate in the "management" of the LP or to represent the LP with respect to third parties. The LP may be a good solution for a partner desiring to remain a passive investor in the JV and limit its liability.[50] On the other hand, such an arrangement may not be suitable for a partner wishing actively to participate in the management of the venture, while simultaneously limiting its liability.

Supranational Regimes

In the **European Union**, the European Economic Interest Grouping (EEIG) was created as a special form of JV.[51] The EEIG resembles the American general partnership, has a formal legal status, is subject to EU law and provides for a high level of cooperation among venturers. Specifically, it is an association of two or more persons or entities that does not change the independent existence of the participants. It may be established only by parties located in EU member states. Such parties may include the European subsidiary of a non-EU corporation, but not a branch of a non-EU corporation.[52] The participants can withdraw from the EEIG in accordance with the terms of the agreement establishing the EEIG. New participants may be included only with the consent of all existing members.[53] The participants are generally liable for the debts of the EEIG. There must be diversity between central administrations, or the places of principal activities, with respect to at least two of the EEIG founders.[54] EEIGs are limited to not more than 500 employees and may be limited by laws of the member states to not more than 20 members. Each member state is given the power to determine whether it will recognize an EEIG as having legal personality. The EEIG is not in itself a profit-seeking venture; an EEIG's activities are only ancillary to the economic activities of its members. Because of these limitations, the EEIG has not been a realistic alternative to the more prevalent JV forms.[55] The EEIG would, however, be an appropriate structure for pooling research and development projects.[56]

---

49. *E.g.*, Hungary, Company Act, § 6 (1988).
50. Some LP acts do permit granting the limited partners certain veto rights.
51. Council Regulation No. 2137/85 of July 1985 on the European Economic Interest Grouping (EEIG), 1985 O.J. (L 199) 1 [hereinafter EEIG Regulation].
52. *See* Jonathan S. Schwartz, *Economic Interest Groupings Appeal to EC Joint Ventures*, 3 J. INT'L TAX'N 1, at 12 (1992).
53. *See* EEIG Regulation, *supra* note 51, art. 26(1), at 7.
54. *Id.* art. 4, at 3.
55. *See* Schwartz, *supra* note 52, at 13.
56. *Id.*

Country Focus

In the **United States**, depending on the state of its formation, a JV may generally take the form of a corporation, closed corporation, limited liability company, or general or limited partnership. The corporate and partnership forms share the same general characteristics as those in other western countries. The close corporate form is available in several states[57] and is an attractive legal form for a U.S. JV because it allows greater management flexibility than the regular corporation, yet offers the same limited liability. The close corporation is usually limited to a small number of shareholders (*e.g.,* 30 in Delaware), the transfer of its shares is restricted, and the public offering of its shares is not allowed.[58] The purpose of close corporations is to reduce or eliminate the expense and inconvenience required to maintain the corporate characteristic of limited liability.

The general and limited partnerships in the United States share the basic characteristics of the equivalent partnerships in other Western countries. The general partnership has no separate legal entity and its partners are jointly and severally liable. In a limited partnership at least one general partner is liable to third parties and one or more limited partners are liable up to their contribution amount.[59] A foreign transferor wishing to establish a JV in the United States should note that it will subject itself to U.S. tax jurisdiction if it becomes a general or limited partner in an American partnership. The transferor, however, may be able to avoid this by becoming a shareholder in a U.S. corporation or in a foreign corporation doing business in the United States.[60]

As of September 1994, 45 states had enacted an additional form of business organization: the limited liability company (LLC),[61] which was designed to combine the most advantageous attributes of the partnership and corporation. It is treated like a corporation for limited liability

57. *See e.g.,* ARIZ. REV. STAT. ANN. §§ 10-201 to 10-218 (1993); CAL. CORP. CODE § 158 (WEST 1990); DEL. CODE ANN. tit. 8, §§ 341-56 (1991); FLA. STAT. § 607.017; ILL. REV. STAT. ch. 32, §§ 1201-1216; KAN. STAT. ANN. §§ 17-7201 to 17-7216 (1992); ME. REV. STAT. ANN. tit. 13-A, §§ 102(5) & 701 (1981); MD. CORPS. & ASS'NS CODE ANN. §§ 4-101 to 4-603 (1985), N.C. GEN. STAT. § 55-7-31 (1992); OHIO REV. CODE ANN. § 1701.59.1. (1992); 15 PA. C.S.A. §§ 2301-2309 (1993); R.I. GEN. LAWS § 7-1.1-51 (1992); TEX. BUS. CORP. ACT ANN. art. 12; WIS. STAT. § 180.1801 to 180.1837 (1992).
58. *See e.g.,* DEL. GEN. CORP. LAW, § 342(a).
59. DEL. CODE ANN. tit. 6, §§ 17-101 to 17-1109 (1993).
60. *See* 3 Dobkin & Burt, *supra* note 48, at 5-10 to 5-11.
61. *See* Edward A. Adams, *Firms Expected to Make Switch to New Format; Limited Liability Partnerships Seen Restricting Exposure,* N.Y.L.J., July 14, 1994, at 1; *See generally* RIBSTEIN AND KEATINGE ON LIMITED LIABILITY COMPANIES, §§ 1.02-1.04 (1992). The remaining five states are expected to enact LLC statutes by the end of 1995.

purposes but, if properly organized, as a partnership for federal tax purposes.[62] LLC members may participate in the management of the business without losing the protection of limited liability, and there is considerable flexibility in control, management, voting and sharing of economic benefits. The LLC is an attractive organizational form for JVs because its partners can share control with limited liability and avoid double taxation. Whether states without statutory authority for an LLC will honor the liability limitations of a foreign LLC remains unclear.[63] Since each state has its own laws, prospective JVs should bear in mind that the laws of each state may suggest a different type of organizational form for their JV.

In **Argentina**, JVs take the form of a corporation (*sociedad anonima* (SA)), a limited liability company (*sociedad de responsibilidad limitada* (SRL)), or one of the two types of JVs recognized in 1983 (a cooperative JV (*Union Transitoria de Empresas*) or a temporary JV (*Agrupacion de Colaboracion Empresaria*)). Of the two corporate forms, the SA is considered a better option for creating a JV because it is easily established and capitalized. In addition, a shareholder in the SA can be a corporation, whereas shareholders in an SRL must be real persons. If one of the JV partners plans to contribute only services or know-how to the JV, instead of capital goods or other assets, a corporate JV is not feasible under the Company Law.[64] "Temporary partnerships" may be organized for a renewable maximum term of ten years to provide or develop certain stages of their members' business or to improve or develop their mutual activities. Temporary unions of companies are permitted to develop or perform a specific and discrete job, service or supply, or an extension thereof, at home or abroad. Their duration is limited to the performance of that job or service, however. Unlike in cooperative JVs, partners in temporary JVs are not jointly and severally liable to third parties.[65]

The corporate form is the preferred vehicle for a JV in **Brazil**. Of the several types of corporate forms available under the Brazilian law, two are particularly common for JVs: the *sociedade por quotas de responsabilidade limitada* (the Limitada) and the *sociedade anonima* (SA). The SA resembles a corporation in the United States and most other countries, and it may be privately or publicly owned. Partners in an SA are given great flexibility in devising their equity or debt structures. Minority shareholders are granted special rights under the

---

62. *Id.*
63. *Id.*
64. *See* art. 39 of the Company Law, which requires that contributions be made in goods that can be attached by creditors. An exception is made for *sociedaded de capital e industria* (Articles 141 CL *et seq.*). Dobkin & Burt, *supra* note 48, at 2-8.
65. *Id.*

Brazilian Corporate Law. The Limitada is a private limited liability company which resembles a closely held company in the United States and a private company in the United Kingdom. The Limitada is an attractive form for a JV because it offers substantial flexibility in structuring the company's operations. Significantly, however, transferors planning to manage the JV from their home country, rather than Brazil, will have difficulty structuring their JV as an SA or Limitada because only physical persons residing in Brazil may manage those corporate forms.[66] A Brazilian JV may also take the form of a partnership or a consortium.

In **Canada**, as in most other countries, a JV has no legal standing, and thus, the JV will usually take the form of a corporation, general partnership, or limited partnership. The Canadian corporation bears many similarities to the equivalent U.S. and U.K. corporate forms. In Canada, however, once the JV partners decide to incorporate the JV, they must decide on whether to undertake a federal or provincial incorporation. Unlike a provincial corporation, a federal corporation can carry on business under its corporate name in each province and, therefore, does not have to qualify to do business in each province in which it operates. However, a federal corporation

(i) is required to publicly disclose its financial information and make such information available for public inspection, if certain requirements are met;[67] and
(ii) if the corporation potentially operates as an investment holding company, it may be subject to certain filing requirements under the Investment Companies Act.[68]

In addition to other relevant factors, if financial disclosure is of significant importance to the joint operation or if the entity is expected to operate primarily in one province, then the JV partners may decide on provincial incorporation. General and limited partnerships in Canada share the basic characteristics of those in other common law countries.[69]

Forms of business enterprise in both the **Czech Republic** and **Slovak Republic** are now governed by the Commercial Code and Act on Trades of January 1, 1992. Most JVs in the two countries take the form of a joint stock company or limited liability company. The joint stock company (*akciova spolecnost* - a.s.) shares the same basic attributes of a

---

66. Dobkin & Burt, *supra* note 48, at 17-11, 17-13.
67. The corporation must have gross revenues in excess of Canadian dollars 10,000,000 or assets in excess of Canadian dollars 5,000,000 (including all affiliates).
68. Canada Business Corporation Act, R.S.C. 1985, c. C-44, § 160.
69. *See* Barry R. Campbell & Candy L. Saga, *International Joint Ventures in Canada*, in Dobkin & Burt, *supra* note 48, at 14.6-14.9.

corporation in most other jurisdictions and is the preferred form of JV by the governments of the two countries.[70] A limited liability company (*spolecnost s rucenim omezenym* - spol. s r.o.) is often the preferred form when the JV partners are exclusively foreign investors.[71] The basic characteristics of the limited liability company are:

(i) it has a minimal capital requirement of Kc100,000 (compared to Kc1 million for the joint stock company);
(ii) the number of participants is limited to 50;
(iii) no shares are issued; and
(iv) participation can be transferred as specified in the establishment agreement.

Joint stock companies and limited liability companies are subject to the same corporate income tax. Other possible, but uncommon, legal forms of JV are the limited partnership (*komanditni spolecnost* - k.s.), the general partnership (*verjna obchodni spolecnost* - v.o.s.), and the silent partnership which is not a legal entity. The general and limited partnerships are similar to those equivalent partnerships of other jurisdictions. The silent partnership is an unregistered written agreement by which the transferor (silent partner) contributes funds or assets to a business but takes no part in its activity.[72]

Although **Russia** has no distinct legal entity for a JV, legislation concerning JVs was first introduced in 1987. A transferor may choose any of the existing forms of business enterprise allowed under applicable Russian law to create a JV. Among those forms, the joint stock company and the limited liability partnership are the most popular. The joint stock company may be "closed" – privately held – or "open," and its shares freely marketable. JV partners may find the closed joint stock corporation more suitable because its shares can only change hands with the consent of the majority of shareholders, unless otherwise provided in its charter. Aside from the foregoing and different capital requirements between the closed (100,000 Rubles) and the open (10,000 Rubles) corporations, there are no other significant differences between the two. The limited liability partnership is similar to the closed joint stock company, except for differences in the foundation documents and other regulatory issues. Significantly, unlike the Western partnerships, the limited liability partnership is a taxable legal entity and its partners enjoy limited liability.[73]

70. PRICE WATERHOUSE, DOING BUSINESS IN THE CZECH AND SLOVAK REPUBLICS 60 (1993) [hereinafter PW-CZECH & SLOVAK].
71. *See* Milan Ganik, *International Joint Ventures in Czechoslovakia*, *in* Dobkin & Burt, *supra* note 48, at 19-7.
72. *See* PW-CZECH & SLOVAK, *supra* note 70, at 57-68.
73. PRICE WATERHOUSE, DOING BUSINESS IN THE RUSSIAN FEDERATION 58-64 (1994) [hereinafter PW-RUSSIA].

ALTERNATIVES FOR INTERNATIONAL TECHNOLOGY TRANSFERS 91

In **Hungary**, most international JVs are registered as Hungarian companies with foreign equity participation under either the form of a limited company (Kft.) or a public limited company (Rt.). A Kft. is usually the preferred structure when the transaction involves a small number of investors who wish actively to participate in the management of the venture. The Kft. provides limited liability to its shareholders, is not overburdened by formalities, and its flexibility allows its investors to modify the venture. The structure of the Kft. resembles in many respects the structure of the German GmbH. A JV Agreement governing the aspects of the parties' cooperation as co-investors in the Kft. is not directly relevant to the creation of the Kft. The JV Agreement need only supplement the Contract of Association, which is the founding document of the Kft., and need not be reviewed by the Court of Registration. Few companies, if any, engaged in international technology transfer, will opt to create a public limited company (Rt.) in Hungary, because its cumbersome formalities were designed to protect a large number of investors, which is rare in a typical technology transfer JV.[74] The Rt. is similar to the German AG, and, unlike the Kft., the founders of an Rt. are given less flexibility to determine most aspects of the venture.[75] Although the Company Act contemplates that the Rt. be a public company, it is possible to create a closely held company as long as the founding partners are not all private persons.[76]

In **France**, there is no law that prescribes a specific legal form for JVs. JVs may be organized either as a corporation (*société anonyme* – SA), a limited liability company (*société à responsabilité limitée* – SARL), a silent partnership (*société en participation* – SEP), or as an economic interest group (*groupement d'intérêt économique* – GIE). The SA is similar in form to the American corporation. An SA must have at least seven shareholders and must be capitalized at a minimum of FF250,000. Shareholders are liable for the corporation's debt to the extent of their capital contributions. For most practical purposes, including regulatory and reporting standards and filing requirements, the SA and SARL are very similar. Nevertheless, certain key differences do exist between the two corporate forms. First, investors who desire to minimize their initial capital investment may opt for the SARL, as the minimum capital

---

74. *See* Theodore S. Boone, *International Joint Ventures in Hungary*, in Dobkin & Burt, *supra* note 48, at 16-6.
75. Act VI 1988 on Economic Associations (Company Act), § 233. *See also Laws Affecting Joint Ventures in Hungary*, Practising Law Institute (Apr. 15-16, 1991). Certain structural and operational aspects of the Rt., such as capitalization and voting rights, can be determined by the founders. *Id.*
76. Company Act, § 260(4).

requirement is only FF50,000, compared to FF250,000 for the SA.[77] Second, as many JVs involve a small number of partners, an SARL may be preferable to an SA, because it requires a minimum of two (and allows a maximum of 50) shareholders, compared to a minimum of seven shareholders required for the SA. Third, the SARL provides better managerial flexibility, because it can accommodate two managers, each having equal power, and, should the by-laws so provide, most shareholder decisions can be taken by written consent. On the other hand, a three-quarters majority vote of the SARL shareholders is required to adopt resolutions at extraordinary meetings, compared to a two-thirds majority for the SA. Fourth, the laws governing the SARL provide better protection against the transferability of shares than the SA. Specifically, SARL shares may not be transferred to third parties without the approval of shareholders representing three-quarters of the capital as well as a majority of the shares. It should be noted, however, that JV partners can restrict the transfer of shares in an SA by including a right-of-first-refusal provision in either the by-laws of the corporation or in a shareholder agreement. Fifth, managers holding a majority interest in an SARL receive less favorable tax treatment than the PDG, board members or the general manager of an SA. Thus, unless the SARL manager holds a minority interest, the SA may be the preferred JV form.[78] Finally, the transfer of the shares of an SA gives rise to no, or at most nominal, registration tax on the value of the shares transferred (compared to 4.8 per cent of the shares transferred for the SARL).[79]

A new corporate entity, the *Société par Actions Simplifiée* (SAS), was created in France on January 5, 1994.[80] The SAS, which can be described as a limited liability company organized on the basis of a contractual relationship, is particularly suitable for JVs. The SAS is a closely held corporation which can be formed with as few as two shareholders. The greatest asset of this new corporate entity is the structuring flexibility that it provides. Unlike the SA and SARL, the SAS' rules are contained in its by-laws and are subject only to minimum statutory limitations. In addition, the president of an SAS may be a legal entity and the transfer of shares in breach of by-law provisions is void. The SAS capital requirement is FF250,000; the same as that for an SA. To compensate for the structuring flexibility and minimum safeguards for shareholders,

---

77. Note, however, that the entire registered capital of an SARL must be paid in at the time of incorporation, while only 25 per cent of the SA's registered capital must be paid in immediately. *See* Jean-Luc Soulier & Carol Fox, *Creating and Structuring International Joint Ventures in France*, 19 INT'L BUS. LAW. 9, 427, at 428 (1991).
78. *Id.*
79. Joint Ventures, INT'L FIN. LAW REV. (Special Supp.), Feb. 1993, 11, at 12.
80. Law No. 94-1, of Jan. 5, 1994.

employees and third parties, shareholders of an SAS are subject to a minimum capital requirement of FF1,500,000.[81]

A different option for the JV vehicle in France is the silent partnership (SEP). Because the SEP is not a separate legal entity and is not recorded at the Registry of Commerce, its existence is not publicly known. That aspect of the SEP makes it an ideal structure for a JV involving a confidential project, which is not uncommon in international technology transfers. In addition, because there are no filing and publication requirements, SEPs are easy to form, which makes them an attractive JV structure for short-term projects.[82] Although the partners of the SEP are directly taxed for the JV's profits, the SEP is nevertheless required to file tax returns and, as such, is regarded as a legal entity for tax purposes. The three primary disadvantages of the SEP are that

(i) the SEP partners are jointly and severally liable for the SEP's obligations;
(ii) the SEP cannot acquire property or contract debts in its own name (only in the name of the partner(s)); and
(iii) third parties and government agencies often will not deal with an unregistered entity.[83]

Still another JV form in France is the Economic Interest Grouping (GIE). Although it was specifically created as a JV vehicle, it has not been as successful as anticipated, partly because it is still subject to many of the formalities that apply to French corporations. The activities of a GIE must be closely related to those of its members. GIEs are normally used for export activities and research and development pooling. Members of a GIE are taxed directly for the profits of the entity and are jointly and severally liable for its obligations. GIEs are particularly suitable for JVs engaged in research and development or some short-term activity with insignificant potential liability.[84]

Germany has no specific legislation to regulate JVs and, thus, JVs are subject to the same laws and regulations applicable to other forms of business enterprise. There are four basic forms of business enterprise in Germany: the limited liability company (GmbH), the stock corporation (AG), the general partnership (OHG), and the limited partnership (KG). Of those four, only the first two have full legal rights in their own names, offer limited liability to their shareholders, and are subject to

---

81. *The "Société par Action Simplifiee" or SAS – A New Corporate Entity*, 6 MCKENNA EUR. REV. 4-6 (Apr. 1994).
82. SIMEON-MOQUET BORDE & ASSOCIES, DOING BUSINESS IN FRANCE § 5.10[3], at 5-184.4 (1993).
83. *Joint Ventures*, INT'L FINANCIAL LAW REV. (Special Supp.), Feb. 1993, at 11.
84. Soulier & Fox, *supra* note 77, at 428.

taxation as separate entities. The GmbH is the most common form adopted by JVs. It has simple legal formalities and a flexible management structure. It is an attractive form for those seeking close control of the venture. In addition, a GmbH can be established with as few as one incorporator, compared to a minimum of five for the AG, and requires a lower minimum capitalization (DM50,000 compared to DM100,000 for the AG). Also, the 10 per cent minimum legal reserve restriction does not apply to the GmbH, as opposed to the AG, and thus, the GmbH may freely distribute and allocate its profits. However, as a stock corporation, an AG can issue stock which may be publicly traded, whereas shares in a GmbH must be registered, and equity investments in it may be transferred only by notarial deed. Both partnership forms are very similar to the general and limited partnership under U.S. law. Primarily for tax purposes, German law provides for a third partnership (the GmbH & Co. KG), which is a common form of JV. The GmbH & Co. KG is a limited partnership (KG) in which a GmbH is the only unlimited partner. The limited partners of the KG are the shareholders of the GmbH. Thus, none of the JV partners, as a limited partner of the KG, has to assume unlimited liability, yet can benefit from the advantages of a limited partnership. In certain cases, a GmbH & Co. KG may be preferable to a simple GmbH as a JV structure, particularly when tax considerations predominate, the local party desires to accrue profits and losses (as a limited partner in the KG), or when the foreign party seeks to limit the liability of the parent company (by participating through its German corporate subsidiary as an unlimited partner).[85]

In **Italy**, most JVs take the form of a corporation (SpA) and, less frequently, of a limited liability company (Srl). The advantages of a JV incorporated as an Srl, as opposed to an SpA, are that the former offers greater managerial flexibility, has a lower minimum capitalization requirement (20 million lire compared to 200 million lire for the SpA), is subject to fewer formalities, and allows for greater flexibility in imposing ownership transfer restrictions. In order to enhance the enforcement prospects of contractual provisions, parties incorporating a JV in Italy often are advised to restate most corporate provisions of the shareholder agreement in the JV company's by-laws.[86]

In **India**, the corporate form is usually the only form approved by the Indian government and financial institutions for JVs with foreign equity

---

85. *See* Gerhard Lang, *International Joint Ventures in the Federal Republic of Germany*, in Dobkin & Burt, *supra* note 48, at 5-3; *See Doing Business in Europe* (CCH) paras. 32-000 to 32-364.
86. *See* Vincenzo Sinisi (Dobson & Sinisi), *Joint Ventures – An Italian Perspective*, IBA Section on Business Law Seminar – "Joint Ventures: a Case Study," Mar. 14-16, 1993, Tel-Aviv, Israel, at 4.

participation. Partnership JVs are less common because, among other reasons, they:

(i) have unlimited liability (no concept of limited partnership exists in India);
(ii) can have a maximum number of 20 partners; and
(iii) are taxed at a higher rate (registered firm tax).

Indian law regards contractual arrangements between two or more parties as an "association of persons" (AOP) and such associations do not assume the form of a legal entity under Indian law. An AOP may not be the best form for the foreign partner because such association may (at the discretion of the Indian taxing officer) be taxed at the maximum marginal rate, or alternatively, each member of the AOP will be taxed at the maximum marginal rate of Indian tax, regardless of the normal rate of tax for such member.[87]

In **Japan**, most JVs take the form of a limited stock corporation (*Kabushiki Kaisha* (KK)) or a contractual agreement between the partners (*Kumiai*). The KK is similar to the American corporate form. The KK is generally preferred to other forms of corporate organization because it provides its shareholders limited liability, ease of operation, and a flexible structure to accommodate the small number of shareholders that is common in JVs. The second, and less frequently used JV form, the *Kumiai*, resembles the American partnership in some respects. Although the *Kumiai* takes the form of an agreement between the JV partners to carry on a common undertaking, it has no legal status by itself.[88] Theoretically, the *Yugen Kaisha* (YK) is an alternate and attractive corporate form for a JV in Japan, because it has greatly simplified requirements and limited liability. Practically, however, the YK is rarely used as a vehicle for a JV because it is used by small local companies and thus, perceived inferior to the KK form by the Japanese.[89]

China currently permits three forms of JV investment: equity JV, contractual or cooperative JV. An equity JV is governed primarily by the Chinese Joint Venture Law and Regulations. Liability is limited to the amount of capital contribution, and that capital may not be withdrawn or reduced during the life of the JV. The Joint Venture Law establishes a minimum capital contribution of the foreign participant of

---

87. Cyriil Shroff et al., *International Joint Ventures in India*, in Dobkin & Burt, *supra* note 48, at 21-80 to 21-90.
88. *See* ECKSTROM'S LICENSING IN FOREIGN AND DOMESTIC OPERATIONS § 3[2] [hereinafter ECKSTROM'S]; Dobkin & Burt, *supra* note 48, at 7-3.
89. Tsuneo Sato, *Joint Ventures in Japan*, INT'L FIN. LAW REV., Dec. 1989, at 35; *See also* Cynthia R. Perkinson & Janet L. Rich, *Foreign Business Entities*, *in* Vishny *supra* note 5, at 337, 343.

25 per cent and allows foreign participants to own 100 per cent of a JV. The Joint Venture Regulations, which were intended to supplement the Joint Venture Law, include several important provisions. Among those are the following:

(i) Chinese law must govern JV contract formation and settlement of disputes;
(ii) a JV can take the form of a limited liability company and the liability of its partners is limited to their capital contributions;
(iii) JVs may use, but may not own, the site of the venture in China; and,
(iv) most significantly from a technology transfer perspective, after the expiration of a technology transfer agreement or termination of a JV, the Chinese partner has the right to continue to use any technology obtained from the foreign partner.[90]

A JV is not recognized as a legal or taxable entity in **Korea**. A Korean JV, therefore, usually takes the form of a joint stock corporation (*Chusik Hosea*). Under the Korean Foreign Capital Inducement Law, the company's shareholders have limited liability for the obligations of the company. An alternative form of incorporation for the JV is the *Yuhan Hosea*. In a *Yuhan Hosea*, shareholder liability cannot exceed contributed capital and the number of shareholders cannot exceed 50. Besides other differences in interest transferability and the par value of share and capital stock minimum requirements, the two corporate forms bear many similarities.[91] In **Taiwan**, most JVs take the form of a corporation. Although a JV could theoretically take the form of an unincorporated partnership, no such JV has ever been approved by the Taiwanese government.[92]

D. Merger and Acquisition

A third, more infrequently used, basic structure for transferring technology is simply to merge with or acquire an entity that possesses the desired technology or has an attractive marketing network, R&D or manufacturing base in the target country. However, it is rare for parties to enter into a merger or acquisition for the sole purpose of effecting

---

90. *See International Joint Ventures in the People's Republic of China*, in Dobkin & Burt, *supra* note 48, at 5-6; The foreign participants may establish such ownership under the Law on Enterprises Operating Exclusively with Foreign Capital (FEL). *Id.*
91. PRICE WATERHOUSE, DOING BUSINESS IN KOREA 72 (1992) [hereinafter PW-KOREA]; 4B ECKSTROM'S, *supra* note 88, § 3[1].
92. *See* PRICE WATERHOUSE, DOING BUSINESS IN TAIWAN 64 (1991).

technology transfers. Indeed, the wisdom of such a move is questionable because an acquisition or merger invariably exposes a party to substantial costs and risks. The technology transfer rationale, when viewed in isolation, will usually, but not always, pale in comparison to the countervailing factors, such as the liabilities and the financial and managerial commitments associated with a merger or acquisition. Put differently, one does not acquire General Motors to have a better distribution network for one's cars. Therefore, and because mergers and acquisitions constitute a vast and discrete legal area, this book will not cover such transactions in any detail.

II. KEY CONSIDERATIONS AND RATIONALES DETERMINING THE SELECTION OF THE APPROPRIATE TECHNOLOGY TRANSFER STRUCTURE

A careful consideration of numerous complex and interdependent business and legal factors relevant to both transferor and transferee, as well as the particular characteristics inherent in the environment to which the technology will be transferred, should determine the selection of the appropriate vehicle for accomplishing the technology transfer.

A. Business Factors

1. Technology, Know-How, and R&D

The local partner's principal reason for entering into a business relationship with the transferor will be to gain access, for a variety of purposes, to the technology which the transferor seeks to market, develop or otherwise exploit. A strategic alliance provides access to new technology without the need to purchase assets and replicate laboratories or testing periods. JVs set up to exploit complementary technology and research activities usually involve parties from different industries or segments of the same industry cooperating in order to acquire knowledge they do not possess and could only develop or acquire independently at substantial expense or over a long period of time. Acquiring new technology and know-how is as important for a small aggressive company as it is for a large firm seeking to sustain its competitive advantage. IBM, for example, has numerous strategic alliances with key customers for developing specialized software.[93] If long-term development and exploitation of technology are the parties' key objectives, a JV usually would be the most appropriate transfer vehicle.

2. Capital

Either one or both parties may need capital to finance new or improve upon existing technologies or otherwise finance their respective enterprises. A JV allows one party to team up with others that can provide the necessary capital. Contractual strategic alliances, by contrast, will hardly ever involve capital infusion and, therefore, not satisfy capital needs.

3. Market Access

The transferor typically will seek a foreign strategic partner in order to penetrate the customer base in the target country and profit from that partner's connections, marketing assets and understanding of the local language, needs and business customs. Market penetration often is the single most important asset that a foreign party can bring to a strategic alliance. Contractual alliances are particularly suitable for transferors whose predominant purpose is to market their technology internationally. When the primary motivation underlying the transfer transaction is the transferor's desire to gain market access, JVs tend only to make sense in highly concentrated markets or those protected by trade and investment barriers. In the latter case, the transferor may associate itself with domestic firms to circumvent such barriers. Japanese companies frequently opt for JVs to overcome possible trade barriers. For example, Honda's JVs with British Leyland have provided the former with a degree of access to the European markets that it would otherwise be denied.[94] Indeed, in some Asian and Middle-Eastern countries effective market penetration can be accomplished only with the assistance and intervention of a local party.

4. Market Size

The present and projected size of the target country's market is an important variable in selecting the proper transfer method. Small

---

93. Peter Lorange et al., *Building Successful Strategic Alliances*, 25 LONG RANGE PLANNING 6, at 10 (1992).
94. COLIN GILLIGAN & MARTIN HIRD, INTERNATIONAL MARKETING: STRATEGY AND MANAGEMENT 113 (1986).

markets favor transfer methods with low break-even volumes, such as contractual alliances. Conversely, markets with significant demand potential may justify transfer structures with high break-even volumes, such as JVs or even the acquisition of, or merger with, an entity firmly entrenched in the target country.

5. Materials and Supplies

A JV, merger, or acquisition may enable the transferor to take advantage of cheap materials and supplies in the target country, particularly if the target country is a developing nation with both under-utilized resources and a need for technological development. Contractual alliances are rarely employed for that purpose.

6. Allocation of Risk

Parties to contractual alliances are able to shift the business and financial risks associated with the transaction to the party that is in the best position to assume those risks. The costs associated with a contractual alliance are small compared to JVs, or mergers and acquisitions, and contractual alliances shield the transferor from the overall business risk of entering into a new foreign market entirely on its own. Furthermore, a contractual strategic alliance may be used as a preliminary gauge of the target market to determine whether the market justifies a more substantial commitment. A technology transfer involving equity ownership, on the other hand, such as a JV, an acquisition or merger, is doubly risky because in such a structure, the transferor effectively also becomes the transferee through its partial ownership of the JV or the merged entity or its complete ownership of the acquired entity.[95]

7. Cost Differentials, Expenses and Financing

Through a JV with a foreign partner, the transferor may benefit from substantial cost differentials in production, salaries, raw materials, and R&D. In industries with significant economies of scale, a JV may produce substantial savings. In R&D intensive JVs, the pooling of research activities should enable the parties to pour more resources into large-scale projects. Cost differential considerations are relevant in contractual alliances only insofar as the transferor is able to realize cost

---

95. KATHRYN R. HARRIGAN, STRATEGIES FOR JOINT VENTURES 21 (1985).

savings by using a contractual ally in the target country as opposed to accessing the target country on its own; as such, the cost savings may or may not be significant, depending on the circumstances.

Contractual strategic alliances, however, do carry the lowest transaction costs, both to set up and on an ongoing basis, and require no equity investment in the transferee. The transaction costs of establishing and operating a JV are significantly higher than those of a contractual alliance. JVs, moreover, invariably also require equity investments. The transaction costs and equity investment associated with JVs, however, rarely reach those of mergers and acquisitions, which typically require expensive legal, accounting and expert services and significant investments.

8. Personnel

A common complaint voiced by technology transferors in many technology exporting countries is that they cannot find sufficient qualified scientists and technical experts at home to develop, maintain and diversify their products. When they do find the expertise, it comes at an exorbitant price. A common motivation for entering into a strategic alliance is to benefit from some of the most attractive high-technology labor markets in the world. The fall of communism and disassembly of the Soviet Union have exposed one of Russia's most precious jewels: its highly educated workforce. Many foreign companies have rushed to capitalize on such opportunities by establishing JVs in Russia.[96] India and Israel also are increasingly becoming a magnet for technology companies, as they offer an abundance of sophisticated technical personnel at exceedingly attractive comparative rates.

Transferors often erroneously believe, however, that a JV can solve recruitment problems. Since JVs tend to be regarded as inferior in status to the parent companies, the JV entity may find it difficult to attract committed management. When Digital Equipment Corporation established a JV with two local companies in Hungary in 1990, it easily found qualified professional computer engineers, but not the necessary management and consultancy skills.[97] A JV sometimes becomes a "dumping ground" for the strategic ally's less competent

---

96. *See* Paul Lawrence & Charalambos Vlachoutsikos, *Joint Ventures in Russia: Put the Locals in Charge*, HARV. BUS. REV., Jan.-Feb. 1993, at 45.
97. Ferenc Bati, *Technological Strategic Alliance: Digital Equipment Corporation in Hungary – As a case in Point*, 15 TECH. IN SOC'Y 159-163 (1993).

personnel.[98] Therefore, although qualified scientists and technical experts may be abundant in the target country, professionals with adequate managerial skills may be difficult to find, and the transferor may be required to add substantial managerial value to the transferee in a JV structure.

9. Business Cultures

Transferring technology through a contractual ally, such as a distributor or representative, is an excellent method to circumvent the plethora of complex management issues that must be resolved in order to form a successful JV. Resolving the ongoing conflicts stemming from differences in management styles or national business cultures between the transferor and the JV, merger partner, or the remaining personnel, if any, of an acquired entity, may prove a formidable task, which may altogether overwhelm small or medium-size companies.[99] Differences in both management styles and business cultures can be particularly acute in technology transfers between American and Asian entities. Contractual alliances are the best option from this perspective They require limited, well-defined and predictable interactions between the parties and, therefore, present only a narrow terrain for potential conflict.

10. Time Constraints

Although risky, early market entry can be a critical factor in technology transfers, especially when the technology is rapidly changing or the market is competitive.[100] Early entry also is appropriate when cost savings can be realized by early commitment to suppliers and distribution channels. Finally, early entry should give a party the considerable advantage of having more time to study the market and assimilate and adapt the technology.

A contractual alliance can be entered into and implemented much more rapidly than a JV. Indeed, if a JV can be concluded very quickly, it

---

98. *See* TIMOTHY M. COLLINS & THOMAS L. DOORLEY III, TEAMING UP FOR THE 90S: A GUIDE TO INTERNATIONAL JOINT VENTURES AND STRATEGIC ALLIANCES 299 (1991).
99. *Id.* at 111-12, 297.
100. *See* MICHAEL E. PORTER, COMPETITIVE STRATEGY: TECHNIQUES FOR ANALYZING INDUSTRIES AND COMPETITORS 232 (1980).

probably means that there either was no compelling need to constitute the transfer as a JV, or that the transaction had not been thought through carefully enough, and several potentially vexing issues may remain unresolved. A JV takes substantial time both properly to structure and manage. Mergers and acquisitions are even more time consuming as they require extensive due diligence and detailed documentation. Transferors primarily seeking rapid market entry should, therefore, take advantage of an established distributor or representative in the target country and forgo the JV option. Time can also be of the essence for the transferee, and obtaining technology through self- or joint development may take years. A contractual alliance enables the transferee to employ the technology developed by the transferor almost immediately.[101]

11. Term

In considering technology transfer structures, the parties should be mindful of the different lengths of the relationships that are associated with each structure. Contractual alliances are by far the most flexible in this respect. While the parties may agree on any length of term, most contractual alliances carry relatively short initial terms, from one to three years. If the relationship is successful, the parties may later extend or renew the term. As most JVs are designed not only to market technology, but also to adapt and frequently develop technologies, they inherently require much longer time commitments. JVs frequently contemplate an initial term of ten to 15 years before either party may implement any of the agreed upon exit mechanisms or seek to change the initial equity allocation between the parties. Mergers and acquisitions, of course, do not have a term as such. Once the transaction is consummated, it is irreversible because at least one of the parties entering into the merger and acquisition will cease to exist in its prior form. In this sense, mergers and acquisitions are of infinite duration. Therefore, parties seeking a strategic alliance with a party in the target country but wishing to avoid a long-term commitment are best advised to pursue contractual alliances with short initial terms.[102]

12. Proprietary Information – the Business Aspects

Every technology transfer inherently entails the transfer of proprietary information, such as patents, trademarks, trade secrets,

---

101. *See* SHARON M. OSTER, MODERN COMPETITIVE ANALYSIS 190 (1990).
102. *But see* Chapter Three, Section XII and Chapter Seven, Section IV.

and know-how. The disadvantage of a contractual alliance is that the transferor has little practical day-to-day control and supervision over the transferee. Notwithstanding the existence of contractual or legal safeguards, therefore, it may be difficult for the transferor to *police* the enforcement of its proprietary rights. This is particularly troubling since unauthorized disclosure of such information in a target country may result in even broader unauthorized international disclosure. A JV gives the transferor the opportunity to supervise and enforce the protection of its proprietary rights through its participation in the JV's day-to-day management. Levi Strauss Company, for example, after forming a production, distribution and retailing JV with four Hungarian firms, improved quality and proprietary rights' controls and became better positioned to counter the competitive threat of clandestine imports and counterfeit products in the Hungarian market.[103] On the other hand, the extent of proprietary information necessarily exchanged is considerably higher in a JV than in a contractual alliance, because the JV parties work together more closely on an ongoing basis, and because some prospective JV partners may prove more interested in discovering the transferor's proprietary information than in the JV's operations.

13. Strategy

Transferors are finding it increasingly necessary to share their technology as a way to secure business abroad,[104] and JVs are a popular means to that end. One drawback of JVs, however, is the loss of competitive advantage through the strategic inflexibility occasioned by the JV structure.[105] In order to create and maintain a successful JV, the transferor needs to accommodate the fundamental interests of the local partner. A JV, therefore, can frustrate the strategy of the transferor when the local partner's interests conflict with the transferor's. Transferring technology through a contractual alliance, by contrast, provides the transferor with greater flexibility. A merger or acquisition obviously provides optimal strategic freedom for the surviving party.

14. Goals

The longer the term of the alliance and the more complex, multidimensional and investment intensive the alliance form, the more

---

103. Neil Smith & Douglas Rebne, *Foreign Direct Investment in Poland, the Czech and Slovak Republics and Hungary: the Centrality of the Joint Venture Entry Mode*, 28 MID-ATLANTIC J. BUS. 3, at 189 (1982).
104. Richard W. Stevenson, *No Longer the Only Game in Town*, N.Y. TIMES, Dec. 4, 1988, § 3, at 1, 7.
105. HARRIGAN, *supra* note 95, at 36.

it is essential that the parties' objectives and interests be compatible and complementary. If one JV partner seeks to reinvest profits in product diversification and R&D, whereas the other partner's goal is to realize and repatriate its profits on a short-term basis in order to show quarterly revenues, the venture is likely to fall apart. Accordingly, the transferor should not enter into a JV, unless both parties share the same long- and short-term business objectives, and should instead focus on its barest needs and interests, such as enhancing market visibility and penetration in the target country by appointing a local distributor or sales representative. A thorough appreciation of one's partner's motivation is especially critical if the parties are potential competitors. For example, Japanese copier makers and automobile producers have often used an American distributor until they felt they had gained enough experience to start their own operation in the United States.[106] Contractual alliances require the least goal compatibility of all transfer structures involving a foreign partner. JVs cannot survive without it, and mergers and acquisitions represent the culmination of perfectly congruous interests.

15. Competitive Environment

The nature and magnitude of competition in the target country should be factored into the selection of the transfer structure. In highly competitive markets, the transferor may be better off choosing transfer methods, such as contractual alliances, that utilize few resources, because highly competitive markets are often associated with low returns on investment.[107] JVs, mergers and acquisitions, by contrast, require substantial resources, and may not, therefore, be the appropriate transfer vehicle for an intensely competitive market. Nevertheless, when the local JV partner, or the target-entity in a merger and acquisition, is well established in the competitive market, high-commitment transfer methods are justifiable if synergies from such transactions produce a significant competitive advantage or the target market is of particular strategic importance to the transferor.

16. Managerial Control

Transferring technology through contractual alliance forms provides the transferor with only limited operational control over the transfer,

---

106. Kenishi Ohmae, *The Global Logic of Strategic Alliances*, HARV. BUS. REV., Mar.-Apr. 1989, at 152.
107. *See* HARRIGAN, *supra* note 95, at 113-125; *See also* W. Chan Kim and Peter Hwang, *Global Strategy and Multinationals' Entry Mode Choice*, 23 J. INT'L BUS. STUD. 1, at 29 (1992).

and little, if any, control over the management, marketing strategies and operations of the contractual ally.[108] Some form of *joint* ownership is, by definition, an essential feature of any JV. Indeed, JVs can only succeed if each JV partner abdicates *some* measure of control in favor of the other JV partner. The parties' control over the JV will usually be proportional to their respective equity participation in the JV entity. But this is not always the case. The minority party may exert a dominant influence over the JV's operations, for example, if the JV is critically dependent on a continuing flow of technical assistance from the minority party.[109] The minority partner may also possess an influence that exceeds its equity stake, either because of the target country's minority protection rights or because it simply insisted on super-majority voting for a variety of issues. The joint ownership contemplated by the JV structure, unfortunately, is rife with potential conflict as the JV partners may disagree about investment, marketing, product development, strategy, and any number of other management matters. When the retention of complete managerial control is a key objective, therefore, an agent, manufacturer representative, merger, or acquisition may provide the only answer.[110]

17. Nature of Technology to be Transferred

Technology that requires considerable adaptation for its successful marketing in the target country favors transfer methods, such as a JV, merger or acquisition, that bring the transferor into close proximity with the foreign market. This is particularly true if adaptation requires new production facilities or when the adapted technology cannot viably be marketed in the transferor's own domestic market. In the 1980s, for example, Ford and General Motors manufactured vehicles in Europe that were fundamentally different from the vehicles they manufactured at home.[111] Moreover, transferors possessing technology that is difficult to duplicate, often may command substantial leverage, even in high investment risk countries, because the host government in those

---

108. Sanjeev Agarwal & Sridmar N. Ramaswani, *Choice of Foreign Market Entry Mode: Impact of Ownership, Location and Internalization Factors*, 23 J. INT'L BUS. STUD. 1, at 2-3 (1992).
109. FRANCIS R. ROOT, ENTRY STRATEGIES FOR INTERNATIONAL MARKETS 152-53 (1987).
110. *But see* J. Peter Killing, *How to make a Global Joint Venture Work*, HARV. BUS. REV., May-June 1982, at 120-27 (explaining different ways executives can tailor their management approach to the specific needs of the JV).
111. ROOT, *supra* note 109, at 13-14.

countries may be unable to find alternative sources of technology.[112] In such situations, the transferor may be able to extract favorable business and legal terms if it selects a technology transfer method that results in a direct market presence in the target country.

18. Political Environment

The political environment of the target country may dictate the mode of entry. In countries where the government plays a significant role in key business operations, a JV may permit better relationships with local authorities or labor unions, especially when the local partner can add political influence and government support to the undertaking.[113] Certifications or licenses also may prove easier to obtain because the authorities may not perceive the transferor as a foreign entity.

The diagram on the page opposite illustrates the relationships between the most important business variables and the different transfer forms from the perspective of the transferor.

B. Legal Factors

Each available technology transfer structure is inescapably interwoven with salient legal characteristics. Cumulatively, these legal characteristics together with the business factors discussed previously give significant substantive content to the choice of each transfer vehicle and, in some cases, impose important limitations on the parties' freedom to define the substantive dimensions of their transaction. The parties should, therefore, endeavor to understand the substantive ramifications of the contemplated transfer structure early in the negotiation process.

1. Ownership of Technology

The transferor's legal ability to retain ownership in the transferred technology may be enhanced or reduced depending upon the selected alliance form. A JV typically will involve at least the grant to the JV of some proprietary rights or a broad long-term license to the transferred technology and, most likely, to technology that is developed by the JV based upon the transferred technology. The licensing components of agency, representation and distribution transactions (other than in their purest sense as reseller arrangements), generally allow for the imposition of controls over how, where and for what purpose technology is used as well as over the reverse engineering, copying and dissemination of the transferred technology. By contrast, transfer methods which at the core

---

112. *See* Agarwal & Ramaswani, *supra* note 108, at 43.
113. *See* COLLINS & DOORLEY, *supra* note 98, at 207.

Figure 2.2 Relationships between the Most Important Business Variables and the Different Transfer Forms from the Perspective of the Transferor

	Direct End-User Sale/License	Contractual Alliance	Joint Venture via Separate Entity	Merger or Acquisition
	LOWEST			HIGHEST

BUSINESS FACTORS:

- Risk
- Potential return
- Control
- Requisite capital investment
- Transaction costs
- Requisite goal compatibility
- Typical term of relationship
- Market presence
- Implementation time
- Marginal savings/economies of scale
- Exploitation of competitive advantage
- Vulnerability to political change
- Ability to protect proprietary information

are outright *sales and assignments* of the technology or its derivative products – whether directly to end-users or through independent reseller distributors – are inherently antithetical to ownership controls by the transferors.

2. Control of Operations and Equity Ownership

Properly structured, agency and representation and, to a lesser extent, distribution arrangements, offer substantial controls over the strategic ally while requiring little or no compromise of the transferor's own freedom of action. While obtaining a majority equity position should secure control in a JV, an effective JV necessarily requires some form of joint governance and administration, thereby forcing the transferor to give up a measure of control over the JV in favor of its partner. For, even if the transferor is the majority owner of the JV, the minority equity holder will probably insist on, or be provided by local laws with, customary minority protections, such as super-majority voting for specified issues at the board and shareholder levels. Many countries, moreover, restrict equity participation by foreigners in local operations in order to reduce the control that foreign parties can exercise over local operations. As a basis for defining control, most countries have employed percentage levels of ownership.

In a two-partner JV, the minority equity holder should have at least 25 per cent of the equity in order to secure practical participation in the control and management of the JV. Many consider a minority partner owning less than 25 per cent of the equity merely to be a passive investor[114] and, thus, believe that such partner is not entitled to any meaningful management rights. A number of jurisdictions, moreover, accord statutory veto rights to minority owners with at least 25 per cent of the equity. In a JV involving more than three partners, a minority partner with an equity participation of as low as 10 per cent can still become a factor in the decision-making process, especially when neither one of the other two parties can control the venture by itself (*e.g.,* each having 45 per cent of the equity).[115]

Several nonequity devices are available to control a 50:50 JV. One is issuing two kinds of stock – voting and nonvoting – which will divide the profits evenly but give a majority of the voting stock to the transferor. The parties can also provide that the transferor will appoint the majority of directors. Alternatively, the parties could stipulate that the transferor's directors (even though equal in number to the other partner's directors) will appoint a management committee or agree that in the case of a tie vote, the position of one of the parties will prevail.

114. HARRIGAN, *supra* note 95, at 367-8.
115. *See* 4 ECKSTROM'S, *supra* note 88, § 1.02[1].

Finally, the parties may award a management contract to one party or execute a voting agreement favoring one party.[116]

Country Focus

Subject to compliance with antitrust and other regulatory requirements, there are generally no restrictions on foreign investment in the **United States**. Restrictions do exist, however, in certain industries of national interest, including communications, aviation and military sectors. Minority shareholder protections are complex matters that are typically reserved for statutory resolution under state statutes and case law construction. One form of minority shareholder protection is *cumulative voting*, which is a system of shareholder voting for a board of directors designed to ensure that minority shareholders obtain representation on the board. This is accomplished by allowing a shareholder to cast all its votes for a single position, unlike regular voting where each shareholder votes for all positions. In addition, minority shareholders may question the good faith of major transactions, thereby setting aside the sale of corporate assets, for example, if (i) the sales price was grossly inadequate, or (ii) fraud was committed. Although shareholders generally have no legal claim to the earnings of a corporation until a dividend has been declared by the directors, courts will set aside the directors' decisions if they are found to have acted in bad faith. Minority shareholders are also protected against *freeze-outs* by the majority. A freeze-out is a transaction in which the majority shareholders – most often of a close corporation – reduce or eliminate the proportional equity ownership or financial return of the minority shareholders in an effort to "persuade" the latter to liquidate their investment in the corporation on terms favorable to the majority. The most common form of a freeze-out is the *cash-out merger*, where the minority shareholder is required to accept cash for its shares while the majority shareholder receives shares in the continuing enterprise. Modern U.S. statutes generally authorize cash-out mergers, "though courts test such mergers on the basis of fairness and, in some states, business purpose."[117]

Except as otherwise specified by applicable state statutes, most corporate actions must be approved by a majority of a quorum of the shareholders. Certain actions, however, may require a larger vote under applicable state law and, as such, provide significant protection to the minority holders. For example, in New York, an amendment to the articles of incorporation requires the approval of a majority of all outstanding shares entitled to vote (*i.e.*, not just the quorum). In

116. ROOT, *supra* note 109, at 45.
117. *See generally* 1 Corp. Guide (P-H) paras. 1155, 2045, 2506, 2705.

addition, several states, including New York, require a super-majority vote (*e.g.*, a vote of two-thirds of all outstanding shares entitled to vote) for the sale of all or substantially all of the assets of the corporation. Most states, including Delaware, require the approval of a majority of the shares permitted to vote of the disappearing entity in the context of statutory mergers.

In **Argentina**, 100 per cent foreign ownership is generally permitted.[118] Joint venturers who choose to form the venture as a corporation (SA) should keep in mind that Argentine law places a number of restrictions on corporate decision making that are primarily intended to protect minority interests. Significantly, these restrictions cannot be waived in the articles of incorporation.[119] With the exception of certain sectors of national importance, there are generally no restrictions on foreign ownership in **Brazil**. However, some restrictions apply to the investment of foreign companies engaged in the manufacture and import of products that include electronic components.[120]

In **Mexico**, foreign-owned corporations are permitted without any authorization from the Foreign Investment Commission, so long as their activities are not specifically limited to foreign ownership and certain requirements are met. When acquiring an existing corporation, authorization is required only if foreign ownership exceeds 49 per cent. However, if foreign ownership was already greater than 49 per cent prior to the acquisition, no authorization is required.[121] Contrary to JV corporations, JV contracts (*asociacion* - A. en P.) are not subject to these ownership restrictions because they do not constitute separate entities. Nevertheless, if a JV agreement or contract involves the participation of a foreigner in more than 49 per cent of the total profits or control of the JV's activities, the parties are advised to submit the agreement to the Foreign Investment Commission for review.[122]

The foreign acquisition of a **Chinese** business is not permitted. However, with government approval, foreign investors can acquire an equity interest in a Chinese JV or a wholly foreign-owned enterprise. Mergers, as in many other East Asian countries, are not common.[123] All

---

118. PRICE WATERHOUSE, DOING BUSINESS IN ARGENTINA 3 (1992) [hereinafter PW-ARGENTINA]. Complete foreign ownership is still not permitted in some privatized industries, television and radio stations, and some financial enterprises.
119. Dobkin & Burt, *supra* note 48, at 2-4.
120. PRICE WATERHOUSE, DOING BUSINESS IN BRAZIL 39-40 (1991) [hereinafter PW-BRAZIL].
121. PRICE WATERHOUSE, DOING BUSINESS IN MEXICO 45 (1993) [hereinafter PW-MEXICO].
122. *Id.* at 47.
123. PRICE WATERHOUSE, DOING BUSINESS IN THE PEOPLE'S REPUBLIC OF CHINA 45 (1993) [hereinafter PW-CHINA].

foreign investment projects must be approved by the Ministry of Foreign Trade and Economic Development.[124] Foreign investors can establish foreign-owned enterprises in industries which are conducive to the development of the Chinese economy. Since the Chinese authorities are selective in granting approval to wholly owned enterprises, the enterprise must also satisfy one of the following requirements:[125] (i) it must use advanced technology and equipment, develop new products, be economical with respect to energy and raw materials, upgrade and replace existing products, or produce products that can be substituted for imports; or (ii) the value of the products it exports each year must account for more than 50 per cent of the total value of all the products produced during that year, and a balance between foreign exchange revenue and expenditure or a surplus of foreign exchange revenue must be achieved. Foreign investors are strongly advised to form a venture with Chinese partners, as opposed to creating a wholly foreign-owned enterprise, because the approval process will be simplified, and the Chinese partner can assist in areas where local know-how is essential. If the technology is transferred through an equity JV, the transferor must contribute a minimum of 25 per cent of the venture's registered capital, but no upper limit has been set.[126]

Although some restrictions on foreign ownership exist in certain industries of national interest, the participation of local parties is generally not required in **Japan**. Thus, up to 100 per cent foreign ownership of entities established in Japan is allowed. As a practical matter, however, the merger with, or acquisition of, a local Japanese company in order to penetrate the local market remains rare.[127] Equity holders in Japanese entities should note that ownership in excess of one-third gives the investor the right to veto changes in corporate by-laws and major assets.[128] In **Korea**, many investment opportunities are available to foreign investors willing to hold less than 50 per cent equity, and various tax and other incentives are available to approved foreign investments. In certain cases, investments of over 50 per cent are permitted if they are technology or export oriented.[129]

In **India**, the previous threshold limit of 40 per cent foreign equity interest has been changed to 51 per cent. Direct foreign investment of up to 51 per cent foreign equity participation in specified high-priority industries and export-oriented trading companies that meet certain

---

124. *Id.* at 25.
125. These requirements have recently been relaxed to some extent. *Id.*
126. *Id.* at 40-41.
127. *See, e.g.*, PRICE WATERHOUSE, DOING BUSINESS IN JAPAN 32 (1993) [hereinafter PW-JAPAN].
128. COLLINS & DOORLEY, *supra* note 98, at 280.
129. PW-KOREA, *supra* note 91, at 45.

prescribed criteria are granted automatic approval. In other areas, the earlier logic presumably continues and approvals are on a case-by-case basis. In high technology ventures, foreign equity participation beyond 51 per cent is allowed. For wholly export-oriented enterprises, even 100 per cent equity participation is permitted.[130]

In **Poland**, the 1991 Law on Foreign Investment (Joint Ventures Act) abolished the 1988 Foreign Investment Law requirement that a foreign JV partner invest a minimum of 20 per cent of the equity.[131] Thus, currently, foreign investors (*i.e.*, transferors) in Poland may hold any percentage (including 100 per cent) of equity in a JV.

In **France**, if the JV is incorporated as an SARL, the affirmative vote of three-quarters of the SARL's equity holders is generally required for extraordinary decisions. A provision in the articles providing for a higher majority is null and void. The sale of stock to a third party requires the affirmative vote of the majority of the shareholders. An action that would increase the financial liability of the shareholders requires unanimous shareholder consent.[132]

In **Germany**, minority shareholder interests are generally protected by various degrees of super-majority voting provisions. For example, if the JV is incorporated as a GmbH, share capital changes, amendments of the articles, or the dissolution of the company require the approval of three-quarters of the votes cast. In other situations, unanimity or the consent of the adversely affected shareholders may be required.[133] If the JV is organized as a stock corporation (AG), a minority shareholder holding at least 10 per cent of the stated capital has a right to veto any company waiver or settlement relating to the board members' or other persons' breach of duty or other improper action. Minority shareholders holding 10 per cent of the stated capital or stock with an aggregate value of DM 2 million may also petition the local court to replace the auditor or force a special audit of transactions relating to the formation of the AG or actions undertaken by the AG's management.[134]

In the **United Kingdom**, although no specific statutory minority protection exists, minority participants will generally protect their interests by providing in the shareholder agreement a list of important issues which, before implementation, require approval either by all of the directors appointed by each of the participants or

---

130. PRICE WATERHOUSE, DOING BUSINESS IN INDIA 23-49 (1993).
131. 4B ECKSTROM'S, *supra* note 88, at PO-24.
132. SIMEON - MOQUET BORDE & ASSOCIES, *supra* note 82, § 5.03[3][a][i][B].
133. DOING BUSINESS IN GERMANY (Dr. Bernd Ruster gen. ed., 1994) § 23.07[3][a].
134. *Id.* § 24.03[3][b][vii].

by a percentage of the directors.[135]

In **Italy**, both the purpose and the duration of a clause restricting each party from transferring its equity holdings must be reasonable. Restricting the transfer of shares for a period of five years is generally acceptable. If the JV, however, is incorporated as an Italian limited liability company (*i.e.,* an Srl), the parties are permitted to prohibit any sale of shares for an unlimited period of time. Parties to a JV are generally advised to include transfer restriction clauses not only in the shareholder agreement, but also in the by-laws of the company so that the non-breaching party may more effectively void a transfer in violation of the contractual provision. Certain transfer restrictions or rights, such as a call option on the shares of a JV partner, unless granted to all shareholders, cannot be included in the by-laws because "all shares must have the same rights under Italian law." With the exception of board of directors' and shareholder meetings, the protection of minority shareholders is often accomplished through super-majority provisions.[136]

3. Competition Law

Technology transfers may trigger competition (antitrust) laws because the parties invariably operate in the same industry and frequently are competitors. As such, the transaction could have anticompetitive effects. Moreover, transactions implemented in the target country may have more substantial competition ramifications for the transferor than would appear at first glance. For example, a separate subsidiary incorporated in the target country may subject the parent to the target country's competition law. Competition law analysis should be undertaken at the very incipient stages of the contemplated transaction. Particular care must be taken to ensure that the contemplated transaction does not violate the antitrust laws of the United States or the competition laws of the EU. If found to violate such laws, the transaction could be enjoined and the parties could face substantial civil and even criminal penalties.

Supranational Regimes

The primary sources of the **European Union's** competition laws are

---

135. 2 CLIFFORD CHANCE, DOING BUSINESS IN THE UNITED KINGDOM § 19.05[7] (1993).
136. *See* Sinisi, *supra* note 86, at 6-8.

Articles 85[137] and 86[138] of the Treaty of Rome. Article 85 prohibits practices, such as price fixing and market share arrangements between two or more enterprises, that could lead to a distortion of competition affecting trade between member states. Article 86 is aimed at the activities of monopolies and other powerful entities and prohibits them from abusing their dominant position in the market. Examples of this behavior include charging unfair prices and refusing to sell to a distributor for no objective reason.

Joint Ventures – EU competition rules are implicated when an undertaking creates, with another undertaking, a jointly owned subsidiary (or other entity) in the EU to produce or sell a product or perform research and development activities. The Commission assumes that an agreement to establish a JV between actual or potential competitors is inherently anticompetitive and, therefore, falls within the purview of Article 85(1). If a JV is formed by parties that are not actual or potential competitors, the provisions in the JV agreement which are necessary for the JV's proper operation are not covered by Article 85(1). Restrictions that are not essential to the operation of the JV, such as those concerning quantities, prices, and export bans, are not considered ancillary to a pro-competitive JV and will run afoul of Article 85(1).[139]

A JV agreement that triggers Article 85(1) might be exempt under the block exemption regulations for specialization or research and development agreements.[140] Alternatively, the Commission has generally shown a willingness to grant individual exemptions to JV agreements involving new and improved technologies. Several clauses often found in JV agreements, including the grant of exclusive rights to the JV, a

---

137. Article 85(1) prohibits "all agreements between undertakings, decisions by associations of undertakings and concerted practices which may affect trade between member states and which have as their object or effect the prevention, restriction, or distortion of competition within the common market." Examples of such agreements are set forth in Article 85(1)(a) to (e). Article 85(2) provides that any agreement or decision in breach of Article 85(1) "shall be automatically void." Under Article 85(3), Article 85(1) may, however, be declared "inapplicable" to agreements or decisions fulfilling a number of specified criteria.
138. Article 86 provides that: "Any abuse by one or more undertakings of a dominant position within the common market or in a substantial part of it shall be prohibited as incompatible with the common market in so far as it may affect trade between member states."
139. *See generally* COMPETITION LAW OF THE EUROPEAN ECONOMIC COMMUNITY § 7.03 (von Kalinowski gen. ed., 1988) [hereinafter EC COMPETITION LAW].
140. Commission Regulation No. 417/85 on the Application of Article 85(3) of the Treaty to Categories of Specialization Agreements, 1985 O.J. (L 53) 1; Commission Regulation No. 418/85 on the Application of Article 85(3) of the Treaty to Categories of Research and Development Agreements, 1985 O.J. (L 53) 5.

non-competition clause between the JV partners and the JV, and restrictions on sublicensing during the course of the JV agreement are sanctioned by the Commission under Article 85(3).[141]

The creation of a JV may in certain circumstances constitute a "concentration," as that expression is understood in the Merger Control Regulation,[142] which is limited to concentrations having a "Community dimension."[143] The Regulation defines a "concentration" as the merger of two or more previously independent undertakings, or the acquisition of direct or indirect "control" of all or part of one or more undertakings, by person(s) controlling such undertakings or by the undertakings themselves.[144] "Control" is defined as the actual or potential ability to exercise decisive influence over an undertaking. "Concentrative JVs," as distinguished from "cooperative JVs," are JVs "which [have] as [their] object or effect the coordination of the competitive behavior of undertakings which remain independent." Concentrations of a "Community dimension" are those where "(a) the aggregate worldwide turnover of all the undertakings concerned is more than ECU 5,000 million and (b) the aggregate EU-wide turnover of each of at least two of the undertakings concerned is more than ECU 250 million."[145] The Regulation prohibits a concentration if it "creates or strengthens a dominant position as a result of which effective competition would be significantly impeded in the common market or in a substantial part of it."[146] The Regulation also includes provisions for premerger notification of concentrations of a Community dimension.

Whether or not a JV is a concentration for the purposes of the Merger Control Regulation or whether it must pass muster under Articles 85 and 86 has been clarified by the 1990 Notice on Cooperative and Concentrative Operations under the Merger Control Regulation.[147] In order to be concentrative, the JV must (i) perform all the functions of an

---

141. EC COMPETITION LAW, *supra* note 139, § 7.3.
142. Council Regulation No. 4064/89 of December 21, 1989 on the Control of Concentrations Between Undertakings, 1989 O.J. (L 395) 1 [hereinafter Merger Regulation].
143. *Id.* art. 1(1).
144. *Id.* art. 3(1), 3(2).
145. *Id.* art. 1(2).
146. *Id.* art. 2(3).
147. Commission Notice Regarding the Concentrative and Cooperative Operations Under Council Regulation No. 4064/89 of December 21, 1989 on the Control of Concentrations Between Undertakings, 1990 O.J. (C 203) at 6; Common Mkt. Rep. (CCH) para. 2842 (1990).

autonomous economic entity on a lasting basis,[148] and (ii) not have as its object or effect the coordination of the competitive behavior between the parties to the venture or between the venture and themselves. Thus, a JV will be deemed to be concentrative where the parent companies are neither actual nor potential competitors in the JV's field prior to its establishment. Even if the parent companies remain active in the same product or service markets as the JV, the establishment of a JV may amount to a partial concentration if their activities are geographically separate. Conversely, where either one or both of the parent companies are actual or potential competitors of the venture, the JV will *not* be deemed concentrative and, thus, the JV will fall outside the scope of the Merger Control Regulation. Instead, it will have to pass muster under Articles 85 and 86, in which case, the JV will be subject to less favorable filing procedures, review standards and longer clearance procedures than if the JV were deemed to be concentrative.

Mergers and Acquisitions – Until the Merger Control Regulation was enacted in 1989, EU competition law with regard to mergers and acquisitions was based on the concept of abuse of a dominant position under Article 86. The Regulation gave the Commission the necessary powers to ensure that major corporate reorganizations did not impair competition within the EU. The Regulation applies only to concentrations having a Community dimension. As such, it replaces Articles 85 and 86 as the EU's legal instrument for the regulation of "concentrations." Furthermore, the Regulation also pre-empts national competition laws with respect to concentrations with a "Community dimension." The definitions of these terms were discussed in the previous paragraphs. Whether or not a concentration is compatible with the Common Market depends on the relevant product and geographic markets as well as the aggregate share of the parties in the affected market. The Commission will also take into account other factors, such as the existence of competitors and barriers to market entry, the extent of vertical or horizontal integration, and the stage of development of the markets concerned.[149]

Contractual Alliances – Certain categories of distribution agreements, such as those imposing blanket export bans on distributors, are systematically condemned by the Commission. Other agreements, such as selective distribution agreements, may fall outside Article 85(1) or, if they restrict competition, may benefit from individual exemption. In addition, the Commission has adopted exemption regulations for

---

148. That is, the JV must act as an independent supplier and buyer on the market and must be intended and able to conduct business in the long term.
149. *See* ANTITRUST LAW DEVELOPMENTS, *infra* note 170, at 957-961.

exclusive distribution agreements,[150] exclusive purchasing agreements,[151] franchise agreements,[152] and motor vehicles distribution and servicing agreements.[153]

The block exemption concerning exclusive distribution agreements applies to agreements pursuant to which a supplier agrees to supply certain goods only to a particular distributor for resale in all or part of the EU. Pursuant to this block exemption, the imposition of the following obligations on an exclusive distributor is permissible:

(i) a requirement that the distributor not manufacture or distribute goods which compete with the contract goods;
(ii) distributor's undertaking to obtain the contract goods only from the transferor; and
(iii) distributor's commitment to refrain from *seeking* customers, or establishing any branch or distribution depot, outside the contract territory.[154]

Significantly, an exclusive distributor may not be prohibited from selling outside its territory if those sales were not solicited or initiated by the distributor. The only restriction that may be imposed on the supplier (transferor) is that it should not supply the contract goods to users in the contract territory.[155]

The block exemption for exclusive purchasing agreements follows the structure of the block exemption for exclusive distribution agreements. The exemption applies only to transactions involving two parties, in which one party, the reseller, agrees with the other party, the supplier, to purchase goods for resale only from the supplier or from a connected undertaking or another source which the supplier has entrusted with the sale of its goods.[156] Significantly, agreements by a dealer who is not

---

150. Commission Regulation No. 1983/83 on the Application of Article 85(3) of the Treaty to Categories of Exclusive Distribution Agreements, 1983 O.J. (L 73) 1 [hereinafter Regulation 1983/83]; Common Mkt. Rep. (CCH) para. 2730 (1988).
151. Commission Regulation No. 1984/83 on the Application of Article 85(3) of the Treaty to Categories of Exclusive Purchasing Agreements, 1984 O.J. (L 173) 5 [hereinafter Regulation 1984/83]; Common Mkt. Rep. (CCH) para. 2733 (1988).
152. Commission Regulation No. 4087/88 on the Application of Article 85(3) of the Treaty to Categories of Franchise Agreements, 1988 O.J. (L 359) 46 [hereinafter Regulation 4087/88]. *See* ECKSTROM'S, *supra* note 88, § 18.29; Common Mkt. Rep. (CCH) para. 2061.079.184 (1992).
153. Commission Regulation No. 123/85 on the Application of Article 85(3) of the Treaty to Certain Categories of Motor Vehicle Distribution and Servicing Agreements, 1985 O.J. (L 15) 16; Common Mkt. Rep. (CCH) para. 2751 (1985).
154. Regulation 1983/83, *supra* note 150, art. 2(2); *See also* Chapter Three, Section II.
155. *Id.* art. 2(1).
156. Regulation 1984/83, *supra* note 151, art. 1.

given an exclusive territory are exempt, but agreements containing reciprocal exclusive purchasing obligations are not.

In 1989, the Commission adopted a block exemption regarding the application of Article 85(3) to certain categories of franchise agreements.[157] The block exemption will remain in force until December 31, 1999. The regulation applies to bilateral franchise agreements in which the franchisor grants the franchisee, in exchange for consideration, an exclusive territory in which to exploit a "franchise," which may consist of a

> package of industrial or intellectual property rights relating to trademarks, trade names, shop signs, utility models, designs, copyrights, know-how, and patents, to be exploited for the resale of goods or the provision of services to end-users.[158]

Only know-how which is "secret, substantial and identified" qualifies for protection.[159] The regulation exempts franchise agreements in which the franchisor grants an exclusive territory and agrees neither to grant another franchise nor exploit the franchise itself in that territory nor supply goods to third parties in the territory. The franchisor may require that the franchisee exploit the franchise only from specific premises and that it not solicit customers outside its territory. These provisions provide the transferor with tighter controls over retail outlets than the provisions in the block exemption on exclusive distribution. However, unlike the block exemption on exclusive distribution agreements, where the distributor may be obligated to purchase goods only from the transferor, franchisors cannot prevent their franchisees from obtaining their products from third parties, if such procurement would not harm the common reputation and identity of the franchise network. The benefit of the exemption will also be withdrawn where agreements include provisions that restrict the franchisee's right to challenge the relevant intellectual property rights, or the use of the know-how after the franchise term has ended and such know-how has entered into the public domain.[160]

By Official Notice, Article 85(1) of the Treaty does not apply to agency agreements.[161] Thus, contracts with commercial agents under which agents undertake to negotiate transactions in the name and on behalf of the principal do not fall within the prohibitions of Article 85.[162] However, this exemption is applicable only to commercial agents

157. Regulation 4087/88, *supra* note 152, art. 1.
158. *Id.* art. 1.3(a).
159. *Id.* art. 1.3(g), (h) & (i).
160. *Id.* art. 5(d) & (f).
161. Official Notice of December 24, 1962 on Contracts for Exclusive Representation Concluded with Commercial Agents, 1962 O.J. (139) 2921; Common Mkt. Rep. (CCH) para. 2697 (1971).
162. *Id.*

who are not independent traders. According to the Commission, the determining criterion for distinguishing a commercial agent from an independent trader is that the latter assumes financial risks connected with sales or carrying out of the contract. Whether the agent

(i) maintains at its own expense a substantial service to customers free of charge;
(ii) determines prices or terms of business; or
(iii) keeps or is required to keep on its own property a considerable stock of the products,

are all factors used by the Commission to determine that the agent is an independent trader.[163]

It is critical to understand that although the application of EU competition rules is confined to the geographic area of the EU, a non-EU transferor may be subject to EU competition rules without being physically present in the EU. Application of EU competition rules to a non-EU transferor depends on whether the agreement or practice has an *appreciable effect* on trade between EU member states, and whether its object or effect is to prevent, restrict or distort competition within the EU.[164] In addition, because the competition rules apply to any type of business, regardless of its form, the transferor cannot limit the application of such rules by selecting a specific technology transfer vehicle. Thus, whether the undertaking is a subsidiary, branch, partnership, distributorship, or JV has no effect on the application of EU competition rules.[165] However, as in the United States, JVs, mergers and acquisitions are subject to more complex and detailed controls and, therefore, subject the parties to greater competition law exposure than simple contractual alliances.

Country Focus

The principal sources of antitrust law in the **United States** are the Sherman Act,[166] passed in 1890, and the 1914 Clayton Act,[167] as amended in 1936 by the Robinson-Patman Act.[168] These laws were adopted to resolve the perceived problems caused by the monopolistic control of certain industries as well as anticompetitive agreements and certain prevailing business practices.

---

163. *Id.*
164. Common Mkt. Rep. (CCH) para. 2001.12 (1993); *See also* EC COMPETITION LAW, *supra* note 139, § 1.03.
165. Common Mkt. Rep. (CCH) para. 2001.12 (1993).
166. 15 U.S.C.A. §§ 1-7 (1988).
167. *Id.* §§ 12-27.
168. *Id.* §§ 13-13b, 21a. Only Section 1 of the Robinson-Patman Act is part of the Clayton Act.

The Sherman Act is the principal competition law statute in the United States. Section 1 prohibits price fixing, territorial or other customer allocations, tying arrangements, boycotts and other joint actions by two or more entities that unreasonably restrain competition. Section 2 prohibits monopolization of a market by a single entity in order to control prices or prevent competition, as well as conspiracy or other attempts to that effect.[169] The Clayton Act renders illegal specific trade practices restricting competition, such as certain tying arrangements, exclusive dealing agreements or requirement contracts. It also prohibits mergers or acquisitions of stock or assets where the effect "may be substantially to lessen competition, or tend to create a monopoly." The Robinson-Patman Act generally prohibits price discrimination, *i.e.,* charging competing customers different prices for like goods where the effect of such practice is to undermine competition. It also prohibits indirect favoritism of certain customers through disproportionate discounts, rebates, services or advertising allowances.[170] In addition, although not strictly an "antitrust" law, the Federal Trade Commission Act[171] passed in 1914, prohibits unfair methods of competition and unfair or deceptive acts in or affecting commerce. It is directed primarily against unfair merchandising and misleading or deceptive advertising. Most states in the United States have competition laws containing provisions similar to the federal antitrust laws. They may be asserted by state authorities, particularly if federal authorities do not act.

Certain practices and business arrangements presumptively violate antitrust law and are considered illegal *per se*; that is, they are deemed to harm competition and to be so lacking in potential benefit that they are illegal in and of themselves. Other practices are subject to a *rule of reason* analysis. Accordingly, the legality of restraints on trade is determined by weighing all the factors of the case such as the history of the restraint, the "evil" believed to exist, the reason for adopting the particular remedy, and the purpose or end sought to be attained. The rule of reason has been rejected for certain types of business conduct, such as price fixing agreements, which have been found to be illegal *per se.*[172]

---

169. These two Sections are analogous to Articles 85 (restrictive agreements) and 86 (abuse of dominant position) of the Treaty of Rome governing the EU.
170. *See* ABA ANTITRUST SECTION, ANTITRUST LAW DEVELOPMENTS 401 (3rd ed. 1992).
171. 15 U.S.C.A. §§ 41-58.
172. *National Collegiate Athletic Ass'n v. Board of Regents of the University of Oklahoma,* 468 U.S. 85 (1984); *See also* ANTITRUST LAW DEVELOPMENTS, *supra* note 170, at 41-48.

Joint Ventures – JVs are subject to challenge under Sections 1 and 2 of the Sherman Act, Section 7 of the Clayton Act, and Section 5 of the FTC Act.[173] JVs that are used as a vehicle to fix prices or divide markets have been held illegal *per se* under Section 1 of the Sherman Act.[174] In other situations, the legality of the venture is tested under the rule of reason.[175] The rule of reason requires a broad analysis of the purpose and effects of the JV. Generally, a threefold inquiry is undertaken to determine whether

(i) the creation of the JV unreasonably restrains any significant competition between the parties;
(ii) there are any unreasonable collateral or ancillary restraints associated with the transaction; and
(iii) the JV is an "essential facility" to which all should be entitled access on reasonable and non-discriminatory terms.[176]

Other considerations in determining the reasonableness of the JV are whether the entities are large in size or otherwise occupy a dominant market position, whether there are high barriers to entry into the relevant market or other market structure features inhibiting competition, and whether the entities are actual or potential competitors.[177]

Section 7 of the Clayton Act prohibits "acquisitions" of stock or assets where the effect of the acquisition may be to lessen competition substantially, or to create a monopoly, in any line of commerce. Accordingly, Section 7 applies to the formation of JVs when the JV partners acquire the JV entity's stock or the JV entity acquires assets from one or both of the JV partners. Section 7 focuses on the potential effects of the transaction on competition. Determining the relevant "product" and "geographic" markets constitutes the basic step in analyzing a transaction under Section 7. If the JV partners are actual or potential competitors with respect to the same product in overlapping

---

173. *See generally* ANTITRUST LAW DEVELOPMENTS, *supra* note 170, at 372–392.
174. For JVs involving American companies and domestic business operations, *see, e.g., United States v. Topco Associates*, 405 U.S. 596 (1972); *See also* ANTITRUST LAW DEVELOPMENTS, *supra* note 170, at 74-77.
175. *See National Collegiate Athletic Ass'n v. Board of Regents of the University of Oklahoma*, 468 U.S. 85 (1984) (Under the rule of reason test for determining whether alleged acts violated § 1 of the Sherman Act, fact finder must weigh all circumstances of the case to decide whether practice unreasonably restrains competition, and the test requires that plaintiff show anticompetitive effects, or actual harm to competition, and not whether the practices were unfair or tortious).
176. U.S. Department of Justice, *Antitrust Enforcement Guidelines for International Operations*, § 3.41 (Nov. 1988), *published in* 4 Trade Reg. Rep. (CCH) para. 13,109, at 20,000 [hereinafter International Guidelines].
177. *Id.; See also* Dobkin & Burt, *supra* note 48, at 10-7 to 10-9.

geographic markets, it is more likely that competition between the parties will be impaired, and Section 7 of the Act triggered. In that case, the market shares of the parties to the transaction and the overall concentration of the market will be the primary factors in determining whether Section 7 of the Clayton Act was violated.[178]

Section 5 of the Federal Trade Commission (FTC) Act, which proscribes unfair methods of competition "in or affecting commerce," may also be applied to JVs. However, unlike the Sherman Act, the FTC Act applies to potential as well as actual restraints. It applies to all "persons" and reaches activity affecting interstate or foreign commerce, including the import and export commerce of the United States. Thus, Section 5 can be used against acts or practices that are not specifically covered by the Sherman and Clayton Acts.[179]

There are certain special statutes relating to JVs that have been enacted at least in part to support U.S. enterprises in international competition. The Webb-Pomerene Act of 1918 exempts from antitrust all associations entered into for the sole purpose of engaging in export trade.[180] In addition, the National Cooperative Research and Production Act of 1984, as amended in 1993, was passed to govern JVs in research.[181] Pursuant to that Act, parties to a joint research and development venture may give notice to the U.S. government and thus be limited to single damages (rather than treble damages)[182] in any antitrust recovery resulting from a finding of illegality. The Act adopts the rule of reason standard for testing legality, taking into account all relevant factors affecting competition.[183]

The Hard-Scott-Rodino Act requires parties to mergers or acquisitions of stock or assets that meet certain criteria to file a premerger report with both the U.S. Department of Justice and the FTC and to wait a specified period of time before consummating the transaction. The purpose of the premerger report and the waiting period is to permit the U.S. government to review the transaction and challenge it, if it violates the Clayton Act. Notification must be filed with respect to ventures that are structured as corporations and meet the following three criteria:

178. *Id.* at 10-4 to 10-7.
179. *Id.* at 10-3; *See also* VON KALINOWSKI, ANTITRUST LAWS AND TRADE REGULATION § 2.05 (1993).
180. 15 U.S.C.A. §§ 61-65.
181. *Id.* §§ 4301-05.
182. Treble damages are damages mandated by statute in certain types of cases, consisting of the single damages found by the jury multiplied by three. *See, e.g.,* Section 4 of Clayton Act for treble damages for antitrust violations. 15 U.S.C.A. § 15.
183. 15 U.S.C.A. § 4302; *See also* International Guidelines, *supra* note 176, para. 13,109.

(i) the activities of any participant must be in, or must affect, interstate commerce, or the activities of the venture must reasonably be expected to be in or to affect interstate commerce;
(ii) either
   (a) one participant must have net sales or total assets of $100 million or more, the venture will have total assets of $10 million or more, and at least one other participant must have net sales or total assets of $10 million or more, or
   (b) one participant must have net sales or total assets of $10 million or more, the venture will have total assets of $100 million or more, and at least one other participant must have net sales or total assets of $10 million or more; and
(iii) a participant must hold 15 per cent or more of the voting securities or assets of the venture or an aggregate total amount of voting securities and the assets of the venture in excess of $15 million.[184]

Foreign transferors acquiring, or financing the acquisition of, an American company of national security significance may be subject to the Exon-Florio Amendment to an existing defense act.[185] The Amendment provides the President or its designee with the authority to review the effects on U.S. national security of mergers, takeovers and acquisitions by foreign persons, which could result in foreign control of U.S. firms. Thus, a transferor acquiring an interest in a U.S. company that appears to have a relation to national security should evaluate whether its transaction is an "acquisition" and would result in "control" under Exon-Florio. If the answer is affirmative, the transferor must examine whether the acquisition would impair "national security."[186]

An "acquisition" under Exon-Florio is defined collectively as an acquisition, merger or takeover. The term is interpreted rather broadly, however, also to include consolidations and JVs, if the U.S. entity contributes an existing business over which the foreign party would gain control through the JV.[187] "Control," also broadly defined in the regulations, means the power through the "ownership of majority or dominant minority" of the total voting securities or "by proxy voting, contractual arrangements or other means" to "determine, direct or decide matters affecting an entity."[188] JVs are subject to Exon-Florio

---

184. 16 C.F.R. § 801.40 (1988).
185. 50 U.S.C.A. App. 2170.
186. Schmidt, *Exon-Florio: A Primer for Foreign Investors and Foreign Lenders Doing Business in the United States*, 20 INT'L BUS. LAW. 9, 485-486 (1992).
187. *Id.*; 31 C.F.R. § 800.301(b)(5) (1933).
188. 31 C.F.R. § 800.204 (1993); *See also* Schmidt, *supra* note 186, at 487.

review only when an existing identifiable business in the United States is contributed to a venture, and then only if the foreign transferor controls the JV, *i.e.*, owns more than half of a JV. Conversely, a half interest in an existing U.S. business, or another form of business venture, might constitute foreign control.[189] Although "national security" is not defined in the regulations, the following factors are considered in evaluating a transaction's effect on national security: domestic production needed for projected national defense requirements; the capability and capacity of domestic industries to meet national defense requirements, including the availability of human resources, products, technology, materials and other supplies and services; and the control of domestic industries and commercial activities by foreign citizens as it affects the capability and capacity of the United States to meet the requirements of national security.[190]

To date, only one investigation has resulted in a Presidential Order mandating divesture. That divesture related to the acquisition of MAMCO Manufacturing Co. by the Chinese government's Aero-Technology Import and Export Corporation. The U.S. government committee that made the decision was concerned that the Chinese company might use its ownership of MAMCO to gain secret engine technology or access to the production facilities or technology of Boeing – MAMCO's largest customer. In other cases, the notifying parties withdrew their notice or restructured their transaction in order to alleviate the U.S. government's concerns.[191]

Mergers and Acquisitions – Mergers and acquisitions must pass muster under the same provisions of U.S. antitrust law that are applicable to JVs, such as Section 7 of the Clayton Act, Sections 1 and 2 of the Sherman Act, Section 5 of the FTC Act, and the other provisions discussed above.

Contractual Alliances – U.S. antitrust law distinguishes between horizontal agreements (*i.e.*, agreements among competitors at the same level of distribution to fix prices, divide foreign markets, or allocate customers) and vertical agreements (*i.e.*, agreements between entities operating at different levels of the manufacturing or distribution chain).[192]

Horizontal agreements can be found violative of U.S. antitrust law when those arrangements have the requisite "effect" on U.S. trade and

---

189. *Exon-Florio Back in Business*, INT'L FIN. LAW REV., Jan. 1992, at 9 [hereinafter *Back in Business*].
190. 31 C.F.R. § 800.204 (1993); *See also* Schmidt, *supra* note 186, at 487.
191. *Back in Business*, *supra* note 189, at 10.
192. *See generally* Theodore L. Banks et al., *Antitrust Aspects of International Business Operations*, *in* THE LAW OF TRANSNATIONAL BUSINESS TRANSACTIONS, § 9.03 (Nanda ed., 1993).

exports. Horizontal restraints are considered to be more serious and without justification, and constitute *per se* offences. Horizontal agreements are often used by a party to enter into, or increase sales or profits in, a foreign market.[193] Agreements among actual or potential competitors to fix prices, divide foreign markets, or allocate customers will violate Section 1 of the Sherman Act and are illegal *per se*.[194] In addition, agreements among distributors in a given market to limit imports or boycott certain suppliers in order to reduce prices or obtain other concessions also may violate U.S. antitrust laws.[195]

Vertical agreements are analyzed under the rule of reason rather than being *per se* illegal. If the justifications for the restraints are adjudged reasonable, no violation will occur. Vertical restraints include limitations on the territory or customers for resale and agreements prohibiting a customer (or supplier) from purchasing from, or selling to, competitors. Significantly, two vertical restraints – controlling resale prices and certain tying restrictions – are considered *per se* violations. "Suggesting" resale prices is, however, permissible.[196]

Under the seminal holding of *GTE Sylvania*, vertical non-price restraints, such as territorial and customer restrictions, are governed by the rule of reason.[197] An exclusive distributorship, in which a manufacturer agrees not to license any other party in a particular area or not to compete in that territory, is usually upheld.[198] Vertical price restrictions, however, such as resale price maintenance agreements, are *per se* illegal. Cases on resale price maintenance agreements have focused not on the reasonableness of the restraint as such, but on whether the restraint is unilateral or concerted, and the proper boundaries of the *per se* category, and whether the restraint should be characterized as falling within these boundaries. Some types of practices

---

193. See Clasen, *supra* note 3, § 6.2.2.
194. *See, e.g., Timkin Roller Bearing Co. v. United States,* 341 U.S. 593 (1951) (An "aggregation of trade restraints" that included, among other things, an allocation of trade territories and price fixing, was held illegal); *United States v. United States Alkali Export Ass'n,* 86 F.Supp. 59 (S.D.N.Y. 1949); *See also* Clasen, *supra* note 3, § 6.2.2.
195. See ANTITRUST LAW DEVELOPMENTS, *supra* note 170, at 77-80.
196. *Monsanto Co. v. Spray-Rite Service Corp.,* 465 U.S. 752, 761 (1984); *See also* ANTITRUST LAW DEVELOPMENTS, *supra* note 170, at 107-109.
197. *Continental T.V., Inc. v. GTE Sylvania, Inc.,* 433 U.S. 36, 54-57 (1977). *See also* International Guidelines, *supra* note 176, at § 3.5. Vertical non-price distribution restraints "can promote competition by allowing a manufacturer to achieve efficiencies in the distribution of its products and by permitting firms to compete through different methods of distribution." *Id.*
198. *See United States v. Arnold Schwinn & Co.,* 388 U.S. 365, 376 (1967); *See also* Clasen *supra* note 3, § 6.2.3.(b).

predominantly raise one or the other of these issues; other practices raise both.[199]

Conduct relating to U.S. import trade that harms consumers in the United States may be subject to the jurisdiction of the U.S. antitrust laws regardless of where such conduct occurs or the nationality of the parties involved. Restraints imposed outside of the United States, which have no impact on U.S. domestic, export or import commerce that is direct, substantial, and reasonably foreseeable, will avoid U.S. antitrust scrutiny. However, a restraint on "a U.S. distributor that prevents exports competing with an exclusive foreign distributor is actionable under the Sherman Act, since export commerce is restrained."[200] In antitrust, as in other areas of law, a U.S. court may obtain jurisdiction over a defendant if the latter has certain *minimum contacts* and the suit does not offend "traditional notions of fair play and substantial justice."[201] It seems that selecting one particular transfer vehicle over another, therefore, will not minimize antitrust liability. However, JVs, mergers and acquisitions – because the range of their contemplated activity is significantly broader than contractual alliances – subject the parties to potentially greater antitrust liability exposure than contractual alliance forms.

4. Competition Between the Parties

In addition to examining a technology transfer transaction's macroeconomic competitive effects and legal implications, a selected transfer structure's effect on competition as between both parties must also be considered. Strategic alliances frequently include the parties'

---

199. *See* ANTITRUST LAW DEVELOPMENTS, *supra* note 170, at 102.
200. Banks, *supra* note 192, § 9.03[1]. The RESTATEMENT (THIRD) OF THE FOREIGN RELATIONS OF THE UNITED STATES § 415 (1987) provides as follows: (1) Any agreement in restraint of U.S. trade that is made in the United States and any conduct or agreement in restraint of such trade that is carried out in significant measure in the United States are subject to the jurisdiction to prescribe of the United States, regardless of the nationality or place of business of the parties to the agreement or of the participants in the conduct; (2) Any agreement in restraint of the U.S. trade that is made outside of the United States and any conduct or agreement in restraint of such trade that is carried out predominantly outside of the United States are subject to the jurisdiction to prescribe of the United States, if a principal purpose of the conduct or agreement is to interfere with the commerce of the United States, and the agreement or conduct has some effect on that commerce; (3) Other agreements or conduct in restraint of U.S. trade are subject to the jurisdiction to prescribe of the United States if such agreements or conduct have substantial effect on the commerce of the United States and the exercise of jurisdiction is not unreasonable.
201. ANTITRUST LAW DEVELOPMENTS, *supra* note 170, at 871. *See also* Chapter Six, Section II.A.

undertaking not to compete with one another, thereby restricting their freedom to explore other markets or technologies. If this freedom is a key objective, a JV probably is not advisable. The transferor can usually altogether escape non-competition restrictions in contractual arrangements, whereas the strategic foreign partner in a JV will likely insist that the transferor not compete with it or the JV entity.

5. Payment, Repatriation and Convertibility

Contractual alliance forms typically make it easier for the transferor to realize payment for the transferred technology. Royalties or license fees are generally payable to foreign parties subject to withholding taxes. In situations where royalty fees cannot be repatriated, transferors may find that selling or assigning their technology may be a more viable option, especially when the technology is outmoded in the transferor's domestic market or is available to the transferee from other sources. Because JV arrangements often require equity investments in the target country, that country's profit repatriation and currency convertibility laws must be carefully examined. If the transferor's primary motivation for entering into a strategic alliance is to maximize revenues in the short term, the transferor should not make equity investments in a JV entity located in a country with extensive or unpredictable foreign currency and capital restrictions. The transferor may have difficulty repatriating those earnings or be prevented from converting earnings into a major currency. Even if the convertibility of the local currency is not feasible or repatriation of profits is problematic, a transferor may still opt for a JV, however, if it is able to commit itself for the long term. Although the Ruble is not convertible, for example, many foreign corporations have established JVs in Russia with a long-term perspective on those investments.

Country Focus

The **United States** and **Canada** do not have currency exchange control regimes. Income from royalty payments may be freely converted at the best prevailing rate of exchange at the time of conversion and repatriated. In the United States, a government insurance agency known as OPIC – Overseas Private Investment Corporation – finances and insures long-term U.S. investments in developing countries and emerging markets.[202] OPIC insures against inconvertibility of the target country's currency by guaranteeing that local currency in the target

---

202. OPIC programs are available to 138 countries and areas, including most Central and Eastern European countries, Greece, Ireland and Portugal from the EU, and most developing countries of Africa, South America, Middle East, and Asia. As of June 1994, OPIC programs were not available for investments in China and Korea.

country will continue to be convertible on the terms in effect at the time the insurance was issued.[203] OPIC inconvertibility insurance covers earnings, returns of capital, principal and interest payments, technical assistance fees, and other remittances related to investment projects. OPIC also insures against expropriation (*e.g.,* nationalization or, confiscation of an enterprise) and political violence (*e.g.,* loss of assets or income due to war, revolution, insurrection, or civil strife). OPIC programs are available only to U.S. citizens, U.S. companies more than 50 per cent owned by U.S. citizens, and foreign corporations that are at least 95 per cent U.S. owned.

In **Mexico**, there is no restriction on the remittance of profits or on the repatriation of initial or subsequent investments. In addition, no exchange control limitations exist for repayments of intercompany loans or for the remittance of dividends, intercompany interest or branch profits. No guarantees against inconvertibility are offered by the Mexican government, however, and all transactions in the exchange market depend on the availability of foreign currency funds.[204]

In **Argentina**, foreign investors may, without approvals or formalities, repatriate the full amount of the capital invested and transfer abroad their profits at any time. There are no waiting periods, and the same principles apply even if foreign ownership exceeds 49 per cent of an Argentine company. Access to foreign exchange markets is unrestricted.[205] Although there are generally no state guarantees against inconvertibility, on August 18, 1994, the Argentine government, in cooperation with the United States, enacted Law No. 24,356 on the Promotion and Protection of Investments in order to establish a system of guarantees for U.S. investors. This law provides protections against several risks, including exchange controls fluctuations and expropriation.

Repatriation of capital in **Brazil**, is limited to the amount registered in foreign currency with the Central Bank. Should the transferor wish to repatriate any amount in excess of the registered amount, the Central Bank's prior approval is necessary. In addition, any excess amount is subject to a withholding tax of 25 per cent. Profits may be distributed and remitted abroad only on the amount of the foreign registered capital and may be subject to a withholding tax. Remittances for technology transfers, including patents and trademarks, require the prior approval and registration with the appropriate authorities. There

---

203. Inconvertibility should be distinguished from currency devaluation, which is considered a commercial risk and is not insurable.
204. *See generally* PW-MEXICO, *supra* note 121, at 42.
205. *See generally* ARGENTINE MINISTRY OF ECONOMY AND PUBLIC WORKS AND SERVICES, A COMPENDIUM FOR FOREIGN INVESTORS (NOV. 1993) 23-24.

are no guarantees against inconvertibility.[206]

In **Hungary**, dividends and repatriation of capital are (subject to the payment of debts) automatically payable abroad in the currency of the original investment, provided that their payment is based on valid shareholder resolutions and that the association holds the equivalent sum in Forints. Remittance of profits abroad and repatriation of capital are guaranteed by law.[207] In **Poland**, foreign investors may freely withdraw capital in instances of liquidation, expropriation, or a decrease in share capital. The full repatriation of profits, dividends and capital gains is also allowed. The Polish Law on Foreign Investment (Joint Ventures Act) of June 14, 1991 and bilateral investment treaties guarantee the availability of hard currency in certain circumstances, including sums received from the liquidation of a JV and sums obtained from expropriations.[208] All foreign investment activity in **Russia** is regulated by the Law on Investment Activity of June 26, 1991 and the Law on Foreign Investment of July 4, 1991. The inconvertibility of the Ruble (it may not be imported or exported) presents a great challenge to the transferor. Only those profits from investments in Russia received in hard currency may be repatriated (subject to the availability of hard currency and the payment of relevant taxes). Since July 1, 1992, foreign investors also are required to sell 50 per cent of the hard currency earnings of all Russian legal entities (including those with foreign participation) on the domestic currency market for Rubles either at the market exchange rate quoted by authorized banks or the Central Bank rate.[209]

There are no restrictions on payments to foreign creditors of whatever nature or on repatriation of capital or earnings in the **European Union** and **Japan**. In **Korea** the repatriation of capital and earnings for properly registered investments under the Foreign Capital Inducement Law (FCIL) may be guaranteed at the prevailing rate of exchange at the time of the transfer, upon prior approval by the Ministry of Finance. The Korean government also guarantees the repatriation of proceeds from disposal of capital and the remittance of dividends and royalties if certain conditions are met under the FCIL.[210]

Taiwan has relaxed its foreign exchange controls, as it applies to royalties, interest and salaries, overseas loans, insurance payments, freight charges, capital investments abroad and dividends. Now, foreign investors may freely remit proceeds from investments that have been approved by the Investment Commission. Profits and dividends from

---

206. *See generally* PW-BRAZIL, *supra* note 120, at 36-38.
207. *See* PRICE WATERHOUSE, DOING BUSINESS IN HUNGARY 58-59 (1993).
208. *See* PRICE WATERHOUSE, DOING BUSINESS IN POLAND 49 (1992).
209. *See* PW-RUSSIA, *supra* note 73, at 38-39.
210. *See* PW-KOREA, *supra* note 91, at 42-44.

approved foreign investments, interest on approved foreign loans, as well as royalties and fees resulting from approved license agreements may be freely remitted.[211] Full repatriation of invested capital,[212] capital gains from authorized investments and principal from officially approved loans is also allowed.

In **Thailand**, license agreements calling for payment of fees overseas must be reviewed, approved by and registered with the Bank of Thailand, and if they are part of a larger-scale investment in Thailand, they must be approved by the Board of Investments.[213] In **China**, the repatriation of capital[214] depends on the type of the JV. In an equity JV, the transferor will be unable to recover and repatriate its invested capital until the end of the venture period. Conversely, in a contractual JV the transferor may recover and repatriate its invested capital during the term of the contract upon agreement of the authorities and the JV partners. Parties to a cooperative JV must state in the JV contract that the fixed assets of the venture will belong to the Chinese party after the expiration of the venture's operating period. Profits may be repatriated provided they are in foreign currency or foreign exchange certificates, all prior years' losses have been cleared, all relevant taxes have been paid, and contributions to certain funds have been made. China provides no guarantees against inconvertibility.[215]

6. Liability

This issue should be of paramount concern when the transferred technology may cause injury or damage. As a general rule, product liability is difficult to escape, but the magnitude of the potential exposure must be investigated, and, if the target country's laws permit, limited.[216] It is certainly possible to contain other liabilities, such as contractual liability *vis-à-vis* third parties, warranty claims, or damages

---

211. 3 ECKSTROM'S, *supra* note 88, § 48.05[2]-[8].
212. After one year has elapsed since from the commencement of business. *Id.*
213. 3 ECKSTROM'S, *supra* note 88, § 49.05[1].
214. Article 10 of the Chinese Joint Venture Law states:
  The net profit that a foreign participant receives as his share after executing its obligations under the pertinent laws and contracts, the funds it receives at the time when the joint venture terminates or winds up its operations, and his other funds may be remitted abroad through the Bank of China in accordance with the foreign exchange regulations and in the currency or currencies specified in the contracts concerning the joint venture.
  See International Joint Ventures in the People's Republic of China, in Dobkin & Burt, *supra* note 48, at 6.
215. *See generally* PW-CHINA, *supra* note 123, at 38-39.
216. *See also* Chapter Three, Section VIII.

for lost or anticipated profits. Contractual strategic alliance forms generally offer significantly greater liability protection to the transferor than the JV, as the JV entity invariably will be a business entity organized under the laws of the target country. Moreover, even within the contractual strategic alliance category, some structures offer better liability shields than others. Most notably, independent distribution is much preferable to agency, which offers little, if any, liability protection. By definition, an agent (or a representative with significant powers) has the express or apparent authority to bind, and assume certain obligations and liabilities on behalf of, the transferor.

Product liability claims are creatures of tort law and are brought under either a fault or no-fault (strict liability) theory. Under the former, the fault – willfulness, recklessness, gross negligence or negligence – of the manufacturer needs to be established, whereas under the latter theory the manufacturer will be held liable irrespective of fault. The underlying principle of the strict liability theory is that the cost of a product-related injury is more properly allocated to the manufacturer because the manufacturer is in the best position to ensure the safe and proper function of the product, obtain insurance and pass along any cost in a product's price.[217] Liability under warranty is a remedy of contract, rather than tort, law, and is covered in Chapter Three.

Supranational Regimes

In an effort to unite the market further in the **European Union**, the Council of Ministers passed a Directive[218] to harmonize product liability law throughout the EU member states.[219] The Directive sets forth an EU-wide strict liability standard for injuries caused by defective consumer goods and requires that member states bring their domestic law into compliance with the Directive. The Directive standardizes the definition of a defective product as one that "does not provide the safety which a person is entitled to expect" taking into account the presentation of the product, the use that could reasonably be expected

---

217. Hartwig Bungert, *Compensating Harm to the Defective Product Itself – A Comparative Analysis of American and German Products Liability Law*, 66 TUL. L. REV. 1192 (1992).
218. Council Directive of July 25, 1985 on the Approximation of the Laws, Regulations and Administrative Provisions of the Member-States Concerning Liability for Defective Products, 1985 O.J. (L 210) 29 [hereinafter Product Liability Directive]; Common Mkt. Rep. (CCH) para. 3330 (1985).
219. *See* Sandra N. Hurd & Frances E. Zollers, *Product Liability in the European Community: Implications for United States Business*, 31 AM. BUS. L.J. 245 (1993).

of the product, and the time the product was put into circulation.[220] The Directive defines the producer broadly to include the manufacturer of a finished product, the producer of any raw material, the manufacturer of a component part and any person who, by putting its name, trademark or other distinguishing feature on the product presents himself as its producer. The definition also includes importers of a defective product into the EU. Suppliers may be held liable as producers if the actual producer cannot be identified or, in the case of an imported product, if the product does not indicate the identity of the importer, even if the producer is known.[221] Thus, the EU will always have jurisdiction over someone who can be held liable for the defect. Although transferring technology through a JV, merger or acquisition in the EU will directly subject the transferor to potential product liability, a transferor will be held liable even if the technology is transferred through an agent or distributor; but, under certain circumstances, the JV structure actually may be more beneficial because it might enable the transferor to share the product liability risk with the transferee.

Country Focus

The **United States** was the first country to adopt strict product liability laws. Today, claims under product liability can be brought either under negligence or strict liability. For liability in negligence, the plaintiff has to show that a negligently made product created a foreseeable risk of injury, and that the use of the product by the purchaser or another person could have reasonably been foreseen by the manufacturer.[222] A manufacturer also may be held liable for negligence in mislabelling, failure to warn, negligent installation, or inspection, or for an unsafe or defective design. The strict liability doctrine imposes on the manufacturer, distributor, or vendor of a product, which has been placed in the stream of commerce and is dangerous because of a defect, strict liability to a user for injuries or damages proximately caused by the defect. Neither privity nor negligence need be shown. The plaintiff is required to prove only that:

(i)   the product was defective;
(ii) the defect existed at the time it left the hands of the defendant;
(iii) the defect made the product unreasonably dangerous; and
(iv) the defect was the proximate cause of the damage.

220. Product Liability Directive, *supra* note 218, art. 6.
221. *Id.* art. 3.
222. *MacPherson v. Buick Motor Co.*, 217 N.Y. 382, 111 N.E. 1050 (N.Y. 1916). (Held that a manufacturer or seller of a product would be liable for negligence in its manufacture or distribution even to parties not in any contractual relationship with it); *See* M. STUART MADDEN, PRODUCTS LIABILITY §§ 2.2-2.3 (2d ed., 1988).

The end-user can, under this theory, sue anyone in the distribution chain, from the manufacturer to the retailer, without regard to the relationship of the sellers to each other or to him.[223]

U.S. courts have general jurisdiction over foreign corporations if those corporations maintain "continuous and systematic" business contacts within the United States. When the foreign corporation does not retain sufficient contacts to support general jurisdiction, U.S. courts can still claim specific jurisdiction over foreign corporations that have minimum contacts with the United States. U.S. courts can exercise specific jurisdiction over foreign defendants for a particular claim if it was *reasonably foreseeable* that the activity giving rise to that claim might cause harm within the United States.[224] In *Oswalt v. Scripto, Inc.*, a Japanese cigarette lighter manufacturer who manufactured its products in Japan and sold them in the United States through American distributors was held liable for injuries caused by the defective function of one of the lighters in Texas because the manufacturer had the *knowledge* and *expectation* that the lighters would be sold in the forum state of Texas.[225]

Thus, choosing a particular type of transfer method will not necessarily limit a transferor's liability under tort liability theories. Paradoxically, however, while in a JV the foreign partner will have a significantly more substantial presence in the United States than with a contractual alliance, the foreign partner actually may be better off from a product liability perspective because the transferor will share the liability with the local U.S. partner.

American transferors should note that because product liability suits are common in the United States and their awards are substantial in comparison to those of other countries, American companies often are sued in the United States for products sold abroad, and in some

---

223. Peter E. Hergoz, *Recent Developments in Products Liability in the United States*, 38 AM. J. COMP. L. 539, at 541 (1990); *See also* RESTATEMENT OF TORTS § 402A.
224. *See International Shoe Co. v. Washington*, 326 U.S. 310 (1945); Jurisdiction of federal courts to adjudicate claims against foreign parties depends on the laws of the state where the court sits and on whether the foreign party (i) "regularly carries on business in the state;" (ii) "had carried on business in the state, but only in respect of such activity;" and (iii) "had carried on outside the state an activity having a substantial, direct, and foreseeable effect within the state, but only in respect of such activity." RESTATEMENT (THIRD) OF THE FOREIGN RELATIONS LAW OF THE UNITED STATES § 421(2)(h), (i) & (j) (1987); If a foreign holding company owns the transferred technology which is used by its wholly owned subsidiary in the United States, an American court may not have jurisdiction over the parent company if the parent did not exercise control over its subsidiary and was not in the same business as its subsidiary. *See* Prod. Liab. Rep. (CCH) para. 13,699, at 43,162.
225. 616 F.2d 191 (5th Cir. 1980); *See* MADDEN, *supra* note 222, § 19.16.

instances, even when manufactured and licensed there.[226] That the parent company in the United States and its foreign subsidiary are two distinct entities with different citizenships and that the subsidiary's contacts with the United States may not be sufficient to justify the jurisdiction of the American courts, may not prevent a U.S. court from extending its reach to activities that occur abroad based on the doctrines of corporate veil piercing, alter ego, or agency.[227]

Foreign transferors should be particularly concerned about the risks of potential liability in the United States. Product liability cases in the United States are tried by a jury, which often rules in favor of the injured plaintiff, and may award astronomical punitive damages to the plaintiff. The majority of American courts make no distinction between foreign and American manufacturers, regardless of whether their manufacturing facilities are located in the United States.[228] In addition to potentially huge damage awards – which frequently are in the millions – product liability suits in the United States are attractive to plaintiffs because in the American legal system, as opposed to others,

(i) plaintiffs may employ an attorney on a contingency fee, thus incurring minimal costs in the event of a loss;
(ii) extensive pretrial discovery is available, which allows easy access to defendant's records and deposition of its employees; and
(iii) the plaintiff is not required to pay the other party's expenses in the event of a loss.[229]

A product liability law came into force in **Australia** in July 1992, based on the EU system. In **Korea**, although no legislation exists to provide a statutory cause of action for product liability claims, manufacturers can be held liable in tort for injuries caused by a defective product.[230] Significantly, however, a foreign manufacturer or supplier "will not be held liable for an intermediary's violation of Korean law."[231] Therefore, a transferor may be able to limit its liability,

---

226. *See, e.g., Dowling v. Richards-Merrel Inc.*, 727 F.2d 608 (6th Cir. 1984), *aff'g*, 545 F. Supp. 1130 (S.D. Ohio 1982); *Whose Law Should Apply to Foreign Torts?*, NAT'L L. J., July 20, 1987, at 30.
227. *See e.g., In re Union Carbide Corp. Gas Plant Disaster*, 634 F. Supp. 842 (S.D.N.Y. 1986), *aff'd as modified*, 809 F.2d 195 (2d Cir. 1987); *See also* Davis, *The Bhopal Litigation*, 29 J. INDIAN L. INST. 321, 351-55 (1987); Westbrook, *Theories of Parent Company Liability and the Prospects for an International Settlement*, 20 TEX. INT'L L.J. 321, 327 (1985).
228. *See* MADDEN, *supra* note 222, § 19.16.
229. *See* Steven S. Bell et al., *US Product Liability Exposure for Asian Manufacturers*, ASIA LAW, July 1994, at 10.
230. *See* Tae Hee Lee, *Korean Franchising Law and Practice*, 20 INT'L BUS. LAW. 3, 142, 145 (1992).
231. *Agency and Distribution Agreements in Korea*, *in* Clasen, *supra* note 3, § 1.3.2.

by transferring its technology through a contractual alliance, rather than a JV, merger or acquisition.

In **Japan**, negligence provides the legal basis for finding product liability. Under Article 709 of the Japanese Civil Code, a claimant must prove that the product was defective; that the defect was the result of the defendant's conduct; the extent and type of injury; that the defective product caused the injury; and that the defendant breached its duty of care.[232] With the exception of certain mass tort actions, the plaintiff must prove negligence and causation beyond a reasonable doubt. In addition, the *res ipsa loquitur* doctrine is not generally accepted in Japan, and discovery of evidence is not allowed.[233] On April 12, 1994, however, after 20 years of debate, the Japanese government finally endorsed a strict product liability bill offering consumers improved protection against defective products. Under the bill, companies are only liable for ten years after the products are sold, and are exempt from liability if they can show that the defect could not have been foreseen in the light of technical standards at the time of sale. The bill, which is being introduced in the Diet, should be implemented by the middle of 1995.[234]

Neither **Canada**, nor **New Zealand**, nor **Turkey** has established a strict product liability system. In light of the Union Carbide accident in Bhopal, technology transferors should know that **India** implements a strict product liability doctrine. Significantly, furthermore, Indian interpretations of liability allow penalties to be based on ability to pay, not on damages. A transferor with substantial assets,[235] therefore, should consider structuring its JV through layers of corporate subsidiaries legally distinct from the parent entity.

7. Local Content

Many foreign countries require that products or services contain a specified percentage of local content (*i.e.*, value that is added to the product or service in that country) in order to qualify for benefits such as investment or export incentives, public procurement eligibility, or preferred tariffs. It is unlikely that local content rules be satisfied by any contractual alliance form, whereas, when properly structured, a JV entity may meet local content requirements. An acquisition of, or

---

232. Marcy Sheiwold, *International Products Liability Law*, 1 TOURO J. TRANSNAT'L L. 257, *citing* Mitsui, *Products Liability in Japan: A Review of Legal and Insurance Aspects*, 7 J. PROD. LIAB. 197 (1984).
233. Yukihiro Asami, *Product Liability Legislation in Japan: Turning Point Nears*, EAST ASIAN EXEC. REP., Aug. 1993, 16, at 21.
234. Michiyo Nakamoto, *Better Deal for Consumers*, FIN. TIMES, Apr. 13, 1994, at 5.
235. Barbara Crossette, *Corning Set to Pursue India Venture*, N.Y. TIMES, June 18, 1990, § D, at 6.

merger with, a local entity should satisfy local content requirements.

Supranational Regimes

The **European Union** does not require goods marketed within the EU to contain any specific minimum percentage of EU origin material or value added. However, the EU's public procurement policies generally have local content requirements. For example, Directive 90/531 on the Procurement Procedures of Entities Operating in Water, Transport, Energy, and Telecommunications Sectors (the Utilities Directive) allows EU authorities to reject foreign bids even if they are up to three per cent cheaper than the local tender.[236] The Directive also allows the EU to exclude foreign firms from the tender process if the local content of their equipment is less than 50 per cent. These two EU preferential provisions appear in Article 29 of the Directive, which has ignited considerable controversy between the United States and EU.[237] The Directive became effective January 1, 1993, for all EU member states, except for Greece, Spain and Portugal, for which the Directive will enter into force at a later date. Non-EU transferors also should note that the rules under the Directive do not apply to offers of non-EU origin where the benefit of the provisions of the Directive had been extended to that country pursuant to a bilateral agreement concluded between the EU and that country.

Under **NAFTA**, Mexico has agreed to drop its local-content requirements (currently 36 per cent on cars, 40 per cent on light and heavy trucks) to 34 per cent effective on January 1, 1994, and decrease them to 29 per cent by 2003.[238] In addition, to provide further regional integration of the auto industry, the definition of a North-American-made auto will be expanded from one containing 50 per cent U.S. or Canadian local content (parts or labor added in North America) to one containing 62.5 per cent U.S., Mexican, or Canadian local content. The purpose of this rule is to ensure that non-NAFTA goods do not gain duty-free treatment.[239]

---

236. Council Directive 90/531 of September 17, 1990, on Procurement Procedures for Entities Operating in Water, Energy, Transport, and Telecommunications Sectors, 1990 O.J. (L 297) 1.
237. *See* Andrew Hill, *Indignant EC Springs to Defence of its Directive – Community Officials See Utilities Ruling as an Important Market-Opening Initiative*, FIN. TIMES, Feb. 3, 1993, at 7.
238. North American Free Trade Agreement, App. 300-A.2.
239. *Id.* ch. 4, art. 403, para. 5(a). The 62.5 per cent rule will be phased in over four years. A 60 per cent rule will apply to auto parts.

Country Focus
China requires a JV to give "first priority" to utilize Chinese resources for its operation.[240] Local content requirements are particularly popular in motor vehicle manufacturing. The following countries have motor vehicle local content requirements: **Argentina, Australia, Brazil, Chile, China, Egypt, Indonesia, Malaysia, Mexico, New Zealand, Nigeria, Pakistan, Philippines, Portugal, South Africa, Spain,** and **Taiwan.**[241]

Public procurement contracts for foreign companies are difficult to obtain in the **United States**. The Buy American Act establishes a general preference for the acquisition of domestic "articles, materials, and supplies" acquired for public use in the United States.[242] The Act provides that

> unless the head of the [U.S. government] department... concerned shall determine it to be inconsistent with the public interest, or the cost to be unreasonable, only... materials... produced in the United States shall be acquired for public use.[243]

The Act also provides that domestic firms should win government orders even if their prices are six per cent higher than those of foreign competitors.

8. Regional Blocks

Regional trading blocks have recently been proliferating. As the number and sophistication of trading blocks increase, so does the impact and significance of the legal and regulatory regimes governing those blocks. The selection of the technology transfer vehicle will affect the extent to which the transferor may benefit from the general advantages conferred by regional or supranational regimes or suffer from the consequences of being deemed a foreign entity.

Supranational Regimes
By establishing a JV entity in a **European Union** member state, the JV entity will be treated as an EU enterprise, thereby enabling the transferor to take advantage indirectly of most EU benefits. The removal of physical, technical and fiscal barriers within the EU has created a single market with the free movement of goods, persons, services, and capital within the EU. The EU has been removing internal physical barriers (customs and immigration controls), fiscal barriers

---

240. Joint Venture Law, art. 9; *See International Joint Ventures in the People's Republic of China, in* Dobkin & Burt, *supra* note 48, at 6.
241. U.S. Dep't of Commerce, Office of Automotive Affairs, Motor Vehicle Division.
242. 41 U.S.C.A. § 10a (1988).
243. *Id.*

(taxation and financial inconsistencies between member states), and technical barriers in the form of regulations and standards in most industries. The effect of eliminating such barriers and harmonizing technical standards is that compliance with the appropriate regulations in one member state obviates the need to adapt the technology in order to transfer it to another member state and substantially reduces the transaction costs of doing business in Europe.

Although non-EU based transferors also benefit from the EU system (for example, they need obtain certification from only one EU authority for the technology to be considered duly acceptable throughout the EU) the benefits for companies operating from within the EU are greater. By transferring technology through an EU-based vehicle, such as a JV, merger with an EU entity or simply establishment of a subsidiary in the EU, a non-EU transferor becomes an "insider" and, thus, may benefit from all the legal and business advantages of the unified European market. Such transfer methods provide a more permanent presence in the EU which can also increase the transferor's marketing ability. Another advantage of transferring technology through a JV, merger or acquisition in the EU is that the transferor will be eligible to qualify for public procurement programs otherwise inaccessible to non-EU transferors. Conversely, transferring technology through a contractual alliance would offer the transferor significantly fewer opportunities as the transferor's operations would primarily remain outside the EU. The question of whether to establish a permanent presence in Europe has been endlessly debated, and its resolution ultimately should rest primarily on business considerations. In many cases, the benefits from having a presence in Europe are the same as those that would lead to the establishment of a local presence in any other market. The industries that tend to benefit most from establishing an EU entity are those that are subject to heavy and preferential EU regulation.

The implementation of **NAFTA** is in an embryonic stage. While it is, therefore, difficult to predict its impact, several key features emerge. Trade barriers between the United States, Mexico, and Canada will either be eliminated or significantly reduced, which ultimately will provide transferors access to a market of 360 million consumers. The three countries will eliminate tariffs in various stages on goods meeting North American rules of origin, ranging from immediate elimination to a 15-year phaseout.

NAFTA contains several provisions which are potentially germane to consideration of alternative forms of technology transfer between the NAFTA countries. Subject to any applicable reservations by the parties, NAFTA requires national treatment and market access for goods (Chapter 3), limits standards-related and other technical barriers to trade (Chapter 9); establishes national treatment and non-discrimination in government procurement (Chapter 10); mandates national treatment and most-favored-nation treatment for investment, services and related matters (Chapter 11); guarantees intellectual property protection (Chapter 17); and provides for numerous other measures designed to facilitate free trade between the United States, Mexico and Canada.

The rules under NAFTA governing country-of-origin for purposes of eligibility for NAFTA protections are complex and can vary from sector to sector. Consequently, any party contemplating an in-bound investment or technology transfer to the United States, Mexico or Canada for purposes of taking advantage of the market access provisions of NAFTA should carefully review the applicable country-of-origin rules prior to making such a transfer or investment.

Mexico's local content requirements in manufacturing will be eliminated, thus increasing demand for U.S.- and Canadian-made products. NAFTA will eliminate many border restrictions, such as quotas and import licenses, and will end duty drawback, customs user fees, and performance-based duty waivers. NAFTA will favor firms established in Mexico, compared with other firms from non-NAFTA countries, by granting Mexican firms privileged access to the U.S. market through the elimination of trade and non-trade barriers between the United States and Mexico and the enactment of several NAFTA preferential trade provisions, such as local content rules (*see* Section II.B.7.). NAFTA is designed to remove investment barriers, provide for fair treatment of investors, and eliminate government requirements that distort business decisions. NAFTA-based transferors will benefit from the reduced cost of input materials and economies of scale. The comprehensive intellectual property provisions negotiated by the United States will protect the competitive advantage of high-technology companies. Finally, NAFTA provides for guaranteed access to lucrative government contracts in several sectors, including heavy electrical equipment, communications and computer systems, and electronic products in all three countries.[244] In order to take advantage of NAFTA, transferors should select the proper transfer vehicle based on the same principles as outlined for the EU.

9. Export Controls

Export controls, in one form or another, apply to most technology transfers. Any party contemplating a technology transfer into or with another country should review the export controls (and in certain cases

---

244. *See* Anne M. Driscoll, *Embracing Change, Enhancing Competitiveness: NAFTA's Key Provisions*, BUS. AM., Oct. 18, 1993, 14-27.

import controls) of the countries involved. Although export licensing requirements may apply, they are likely to have only a limited impact on the particular form of technology transfer used. Export controls thus tend to be transparent or neutral in that, with certain minor exceptions discussed below, they should not materially affect a decision on whether directly to sell and assign, license, or enter into a particular strategic alliance form for effecting the technology transfer.

The export control regimes over dual-use,[245] munitions and nuclear-related goods and technology of the **United States, Western Europe** and **Japan** have developed in close coordination with one another under the auspices of the Coordinating Committee on Multilateral Export Controls (COCOM). Established in 1949, COCOM maintained lists of controlled dual-use, munitions and nuclear-related goods and technology which were implemented by the individual member countries of COCOM. At its height, COCOM consisted of all NATO countries (except **Iceland**), **Japan** and **Australia**. It also included such non-member "cooperating countries" as **Austria, Finland, Ireland, Singapore, Sweden, South Korea** and **Switzerland**. Although COCOM ceased to exist on March 31, 1994, because of the end of the Cold War, its former members have agreed in principle to replace it with a successor regime to counter proliferation of weapons of mass destruction. Negotiations for the successor regime were still under way at press time and it possibly might include **Russia** and other former members of the Soviet Bloc. In the meantime, many of the COCOM-based controls continue to be administered by its former member countries on a unilateral basis.

In addition to the COCOM-based controls, most major Western countries currently administer certain export controls pursuant to multilateral nonproliferation regimes, including in particular the Australia Group (dealing with chemical and biological weapons), the Nuclear Suppliers Group (NSG) and the Missile Technology Control Regime (MTCR).

As a result of the multilateral base of the above export control regimes, the types of controls, as well as their impact on the various forms of technology transfer, tend to be similar from country to country.

Supranational Regimes

The **European Union** has undertaken to eliminate controls on intra-EU trade on dual-use goods and technologies and to harmonize dual-use export controls through common standards. The EU harmonization

---

245. Dual-use goods and technical data are goods and technical data that have both commercial and military applications, *e.g.*, computers.

effort is driven by the perception that export controls pose a problem for the completion of the EU internal market in which goods and technology should move as freely between member states as they do within each member state.

The harmonization regulation under consideration would mandate a special authorization for the export or re-export to third countries of any dual-use item. The EU member state in which the exporter is located would issue the authorization for export, which then would be valid throughout the EU. In order to combat "license shopping," EU member countries are considering a requirement that would prevent exporters from routeing their licensable exports through subsidiaries based in countries with relatively lax licensing standards. The likely effect of the EU harmonization effort should be to diminish further the implications raised by export controls for the different forms of technology transfer within the EU. **NAFTA** does not contain export controls.

Country Focus

United States export controls on dual-use goods and technical data are administered through the Department of Commerce's Export Administration Regulations (EARs) under authority of the Export Administration Act of 1979, as amended.[246] The Export Administration Act formally expired as of August 20, 1994. Pending efforts by the U.S. Congress to rewrite the Act in a substantial manner, at press time the President continues to administer the controls set forth in the Act under the authority of a separate statute, the International Emergency Economic Powers Act, 50 U.S.C. 1701. It is possible that Congress will in the near future enact legislation which significantly changes the requirements of the Export Administration Act.

The general principle is that any "export" from the United States requires a license. There are two broad types of license under the EARs: general licenses, which do not require the express prior written approval of the Department of Commerce for the export, and individual validated licenses (IVLs) which require such approval. The EARs contain a number of different categories of general license, including, most prominently, General License G-DEST, as well as general licenses applicable to shipments by and among certain favored groups of countries, such as COCOM. If any of these general licenses applies to the technology transfer in question, the effect of U.S. export controls on the form of the technology transfer is minimized even further.

Section 16(5) of the EAA defines "export" broadly to mean:

(i) an actual shipment, transfer, or transmission of goods or technology out of the United States;

---

246. 50 U.S.C. App. 2401-2420.

(ii) a transfer of goods or technology in the United States to an embassy or affiliate of a controlled country; or
(iii) a transfer to any person of goods or technology either within the United States or outside the United States with the knowledge or intent that the goods or technology will be shipped, transferred, or transmitted to an unauthorized recipient.

The EARs provide a further definition of "export" in the context of technical data (but not as to goods). Section 779.1(b)(1) of the EARs[247] defines "export of technical data" to mean:

(i) an actual shipment or transmission of technical data out of the United States;
(ii) any release of technical data in the United States with the knowledge or intent that the data will be shipped or transmitted from the United States to a foreign country; or
(iii) any release of technical data of U.S.-origin in a foreign country.

Thus, no matter which form of technology transfer is used, the event of the "export" itself triggers the licensing requirement under the EAA.[248] In that the actual "shipment," "transfer" or "transmission" of goods or technology out of the United States is the "export" that triggers the licensing requirement, it makes little practical difference which form of technology transfer is involved.

However, the form of transfer could affect how to complete the appropriate application for an IVL (Department of Commerce Form BXA-622P – "Application for Export License"). Thus, in a direct sale, the end-user stated on the IVL application likely would be the party to whom the sale is made. In contrast, use of an agent, sales representative or distributor might result in the need to list that party as an "intermediate consignee" on the license application, with the ultimate end-user to be listed as the "ultimate consignee." However, this consideration is essentially one of procedure rather than substance, and it should not affect the basic decision about which form of technology transfer to use.

Moreover, the significant liberalization of control levels by the United States in the last several years has resulted in a sharp decline in the universe of goods and technologies subject to IVL requirements and a concomitant increase in the number of goods and technologies which now may be exported under general license, which does not require the prior express approval of the Department of Commerce. Consequently, dual-use export controls are likely to be of concern only as to the finite

247. 15 C.F.R. 779.1(b)(1).
248. Import controls do not apply under the EARs. However, U.S. Customs Service entry procedures and duties would apply.

ALTERNATIVES FOR INTERNATIONAL TECHNOLOGY TRANSFERS 143

and shrinking list of high-technology items which are controlled by virtue of their inclusion on the Commerce Control List (CCL) under the EARs.

Assuming that the good or technology that is to be exported from the United States is controlled on the CCL, Section 773.3 of the EARs establishes the Distribution License (DL) as a special licensing procedure. The DL authorizes exports of certain commodities under an international marketing program, generally to three or more consignees that have been approved in advance as foreign distributors or users. The DL procedure is a special privilege reserved for firms with a thorough knowledge of and experience with the EARs and an internal control mechanism to assure strict compliance with the requirements of the license. The DL procedure may authorize exports and re-exports to most countries in what used to be called the "Free World," *i.e.*, countries other than the former Soviet Bloc, the People's Republic of China and certain countries in the Middle East. Although the DL can be useful in facilitating exports of commodities controlled on the CCL to a distributor, the qualification and documentation requirements to establish a DL are extensive and onerous. Therefore many otherwise eligible U.S. exporters have elected not to pursue the DL. Other special licenses, such as the Project License and Service Supply License, are available under the EARs to cover exports for a defined period for use in specified activities or to provide servicing for previously exported goods, respectively. Both licenses are subject to significant restrictions and qualification requirements under the EARs.[249]

A unique feature of U.S. dual-use export controls is their *extraterritorial application*. Thus, under Section 774.1 of the EARs,[250] unless the re-export of a commodity previously exported from the United States has been specifically authorized by the Department of Commerce or is authorized under the limited permissive re-export provisions of the EARs,[251] no person in a foreign country may re-export that commodity to another destination without the Department of Commerce's prior approval. Similar provisions apply under Section 779.8 of the EARs[252] as to re-exports of technical data and of any product manufactured abroad by use of U.S.-origin technical data. The United States thus asserts jurisdiction under the EAA on the goods or technical data themselves, and U.S. jurisdiction travels with the goods or technical data once they leave the United States.

The practical effect of this extraterritorial jurisdiction is that the selection of transfer vehicles involving intermediary third parties in the

249. *See* 15 C.F.R. 773.2 and 773.7.
250. *Id.* 774.1.
251. *Id.* 774.2.
252. *Id.* 779.8.

form of strategic alliance partners located in one country – who would then market the technology in another country – does not constitute a viable strategy for escaping U.S. export controls. In other words, the choice of one form of technology transfer over another is irrelevant to the application of U.S. export controls because of their extraterritorial reach. No matter which form is used, the U.S.-origin goods or technical data will continue to be subject to U.S. jurisdiction. Even in the most attenuated example, *e.g.*, if a JV results in the transfer of U.S.-origin data to a foreign country and that technical data is either improved or merged with foreign-origin technical data to create new technical data, the resulting technical data would be subject to U.S. jurisdiction, and depending on the destination and whether it is eligible for the permissive re-export provisions of the EARs, its re-export could be subject to prior licensing by the Department of Commerce.

In the context of the U.S. dual-use export control regime, it should be noted that in late 1991 the Department of Commerce began to implement the Enhanced Proliferation Control Initiative (EPCI). EPCI was promulgated to control the spread of nuclear, chemical and biological weapons and missile technology. It imposes new and expanded export controls on commodities and technical data, including software. EPCI requires an IVL for the export, re-export or transfer of any commodity or technical data which the exporter "knows," "has reason to know," or "is informed" is destined for any end use which may involve development of nuclear, chemical or biological weapons or missiles. EPCI thus effectively imposes on all U.S. exporters a "know your customer" rule. EPCI's prohibitions originally extended not only to sensitive weapons-related technology, but also to commodities not otherwise controlled, when the exporter "knows" or "has reason to know" that they might be involved in a prohibited end use. Thus, the controls covered seemingly innocuous items like paper-clips and rubber bands. However, the Department of Commerce subsequently issued an "advisory notice" to clarify that the controls apply only to items that can be "directly employed" in illicit end uses, thereby narrowing the reach of the regulation.[253] Nevertheless, EPCI imposes a new, stringent requirement that exporters and their employees know what and to whom they are selling, as well as where the exported item is going and how it will be used.

The U.S. Department of State administers separate controls on munitions exports through the International Traffic in Arms Regulations (ITAR)[254] issued under authority of the Arms Export Control Act.[255] If a particular "defense article" or "defense service" (including technical data) is listed on the U.S. Munitions List, it is subject to this separate regulatory regime. Prior licensing requirements similar to those under the EARs apply. However, the ITAR is generally a more rigid and controlling

253. Reg. 68029 (1993).
254. 22 C.F.R. Part 120.
255. 22 U.S.C. 2751.

regulatory regime than the EARs, and it does not make provision for general licenses. Thus, if an item is controlled, it must be specifically licensed by the Department of State's Office of Defense Trade Controls (ODTC).[256] The ramifications (or lack thereof) of this requirement for the alternative forms of technology transfer are essentially the same as under the EARs, with three major exceptions. The three exceptions are the specific licensing requirements that the ITAR imposes on (i) manufacturing licensing agreements, (ii) technical assistance agreements and (iii) distribution agreements. Each of these agreements is defined below.

A manufacturing licensing agreement under Section 120.21 of the ITAR is an agreement whereby a U.S. person grants a foreign person an authorization to manufacture defense articles abroad and which involves or contemplates, *inter alia*, the export of technical data or defense articles or the performance of a defense service.

A technical assistance agreement under Section 120.22 of the ITAR is an "agreement for the performance of a defense service(s) or the disclosure of technical data, as opposed to an agreement granting a right or license to manufacture defense articles." Assembly of defense articles is included under technical assistance agreements, unless production rights or manufacturing know-how are conveyed, in which case the arrangement is deemed to be a manufacturing license agreement.

A distribution agreement under section 120.23 of the ITAR is an

> agreement . . . to establish a warehouse or distribution point abroad for defense articles exported from the United States for subsequent distribution to entities in an approved sales territory.

In any of the above cases, the approval of ODTC must be obtained *before* the agreement goes into effect. This requirement applies whether or not technical data is disclosed or used in the performance of defense services pursuant to such an agreement. Part 124 of the ITAR[257] also contains numerous and significant provisions which must be inserted in manufacturing license agreements, technical assistance agreements and distribution agreements, as well as other requirements, before such an agreement can enter into force. The practical effect of these requirements under the ITAR is that if covered munitions or related technical data are involved and the vehicle for the technology transfer is either a manufacturing licensing agreement, technical assistance agreement or distribution agreement, ODTC must approve the agreement in advance and the agreement must contain certain

---

256. Import controls also apply to items on the U.S. Munitions List. Depending on the item, and on whether its importation is temporary or permanent, licensing authority could be exercised either by ODTC or by the Department of the Treasury's Bureau of Alcohol, Tobacco and Firearms.
257. 22 C.F.R. Part 124.

mandatory provisions. These requirements are in lieu of separate requirements in the ITAR, analogous to those in the EARs, requiring individual licensing for specific exports of goods or technical data in contexts other than those involving manufacturing license, technical assistance or distribution agreements. Re-export controls apply extraterritorially under the ITAR, as under the EARs.

Separate controls on the export and import of nuclear-related goods and technical data are administered by the Nuclear Regulatory Commission (NRC) and Department of Energy (DOE), both operating under authority of the Atomic Energy Act of 1954, as amended. The NRC's jurisdiction extends over the export and import of any listed "nuclear equipment or material" and requires a specific license under 10 C.F.R. Part 110, unless the export is otherwise eligible for a general license under the NRC's regulations. The NRC's controls are thus broadly analogous to those administered by the Departments of Commerce and State above and should not necessarily affect the choice of form used for technology transfer.

In contrast, the DOE regulates persons subject to U.S. jurisdiction who engage directly or indirectly in the production of "special nuclear material" outside the United States (10 C.F.R. § 810.2). The DOE's regulations do not apply to exports licensed by the NRC. The DOE licensing covers technical assistance or services provided by U.S. persons to foreign nuclear programs, unless otherwise subject to general license under the DOE's regulations. The DOE's licensing requirements thus extend primarily to transfers of technical data or services and potentially could apply to any of the forms of technology transfer considered above, including in particular transfers pursuant to JVs.

Finally, the United States currently prohibits transactions (including financial arrangements relating to technology transfers) with embargoed countries, *i.e.*, **North Korea, Cuba, Iran, Libya, Iraq**, the UNITA faction in **Angola** and the Federal Republic of Yugoslavia (**Serbia** and **Montenegro**) (S&M). While certain of these embargoes (*e.g.*, Iraq and S&M are pursuant to United Nations resolutions, others are unilateral (*e.g.*, Cuba). Whether multilateral or unilateral, these controls, which generally take the form of absolute prohibitions backed up by significant civil and criminal penalties, are administered through regulations[258] issued by the Department of the Treasury's Office of Foreign Assets Control (OFAC) pursuant to either the Trading with the Enemy Act[259] or the International Emergency Economic Powers Act.[260] The practical effect of these requirements is to prohibit all technology transfers between persons subject to U.S. jurisdiction (a term which can

---

258. 31 C.F.R. Parts 500 through 585.
259. 50 U.S.C. App. 5(b).
260. *Id.* 1701.

include non-U.S. branches or subsidiaries of U.S. persons, depending on the regulation in question) and the above countries. The list of embargoed countries can be amended at any time.

The **United Kingdom** maintains export controls similar to those of the United States on the export of goods or technology to various proscribed destinations. As in the United States, these controls are largely based on the former COCOM controls and include dual-use, munitions and nuclear items. However, in addition, its dual-use control list is based on a list agreed among the EU member states. The U.K. is a full participant in the MTCR, NSG and Australia Group, and its control list also incorporates the MTCR, NSG and Australia Group control lists.

As under U.S. law, an "export" is the triggering event which requires a license, and, as in the United States, there is little impact on the choice between the basic forms of technology transfer. Although the primary regulatory basis for U.K. export controls, the Export of Goods (Control) Order 1994 (Statutory Instrument 1994 No. 1191) and Amendments, extends only to exports of "goods," "technology" and "software," there is some question as to whether it expressly covers intangible technologies. The U.K. has analogues to the U.S. DL through various bulk licensing procedures, including in particular the Open Individual Export License (OIEL), and to U.S. General License G-DEST through the Open General Export License (OGEL). The U.K. also has "end use" or "catch all" controls intended to prevent the proliferation of weapons of mass destruction and missiles which are comparable to the EPCI provisions under U.S. law.

In addition, the U.K. maintains controls on a similar (but slightly different) list of embargoed countries comparable to those implemented in the United States by OFAC. The U.K. also participates in UN-sanctioned embargoes, such as those against Iraq and S&M. However, the U.K. does *not* have the extraterritorial re-export control provisions of U.S. law. Thus, the particular problems posed by those provisions for the various modes of technology transfer should not be a factor under U.K. law.

The export control regimes of **Germany, France, Italy, Japan** and the other former COCOM member states, with minor variations, follow the same general pattern established by the U.S. and U.K. export control regimes. An example of one variation is that the German Foreign Trade Act stipulates that all trade between **Germany** and other nations is in principle unrestricted. However, this presumption in favor of trade can be limited by the Act itself, other laws and, most importantly, by international agreements to which Germany is a party. Similarly, Germany has limited extraterritorial licensing provisions in that participation in chemical or biological weapons or missile development outside Germany is subject to German government permission.

Japan also has a law establishing the principle of free export trade, subject to restrictions which are regarded as "exceptional measures." Japan in particular has restrictions on the export of defense-related equipment.

Because most producers of defense equipment in **France** are state-owned or supervised, the prospect of an international contract or JV to transfer munitions would be an issue for intergovernmental oversight from the start, with the Ministry of Defense playing a particularly prominent role.

10. Exit Mechanisms

The ease with which a party can extricate itself from the relationship with the other party should be a critical consideration in selecting the transfer structure. With the exception of direct end-use sale or licensing and subject to potential termination liabilities which may befall transferors acting as principals in contractual alliances in certain jurisdictions,[261] both parties will find that a contractual alliance offers the easiest and lowest risk exit procedures as well as the typically shortest term of all transfer structures.

Most JVs incorporate exit devices of varying degrees of complexity and sophistication. In addition to typical termination provisions, such as termination for uncured breaches and insolvency, JVs usually contemplate exit based on a party's divestiture of its equity holdings in the JV entity. A JV partner's ability to sell out and transfer its assets to a third party should be one of the most sensitive and heavily negotiated aspects of a JV. The complexity and idiosyncratic nature of the JV account for the restrictions each JV partner will seek to impose on the other's ability to transfer its shares to a third party. Invariably, therefore, a JV agreement will include any combination of equity transfer restrictions.

A party may be able to transfer its shares only upon obtaining the prior consent of the other party. Such approval may be granted in the other party's sole discretion with some (more or less) meaningful modifications. But, in any event, the approving party basically will retain a veto right over the other party's share transfer, thereby locking the other party into the JV relationship. JV agreements also frequently include buy-out provisions of different forms. For example, a *put* provision would require one JV partner to purchase the "putting" partner's interest in the JV. Conversely, a *call* provision would require

---

261. *See* Chapter Three, Section XII.

one partner to sell its interest in the JV to the "calling" partner. Puts and calls are used to break deadlocks or are tied to the occurrence or non-occurrence of particular events specified in the agreement, such as failure to achieve sales or development goals. The purchase price (for a put) and sale price (for a call) can either be predetermined by the parties based on a specified formula or determined by independent appraisal. Unlike the independent appraisal, the use of a predetermined formula often increases the likelihood that a call or put will be exercised, because the predetermined formula may undervalue or overvalue the future profitability or worth of the JV, thus creating speculative incentives for the holder of the put or call. To discourage the use of either measure, parties to a JV are advised to discount the purchase price of a put or include a premium for the purchase price of a call. Depending on the financial resources of the parties (especially for a put), their motives and valuation method used, both forms of buy-out provisions may lead to instability and encourage a "first strike."

The most common and least strategically destabilizing buy-out provision is the *right-of-first-refusal*, which gives one party the opportunity to match the terms of the proposed sale of the other party's interest in the JV before the sale is executed. The holder of such a right will have the option to purchase the seller's interest in the JV on the same terms and conditions of a good faith offer made by a third party to purchase such interest, provided it is an offer that the seller is otherwise willing to accept. A right-of-first-refusal should be distinguished from a *pre-emptive right*, which grants to existing shareholders the first opportunity to buy a new issue of stock. The purpose of pre-emptive rights is to protect the shareholders from the dilution of their ownership interest in the corporation. Because new shares are usually priced below the market, a financial incentive exists to exercise such rights. Pre-emptive rights are usually included in the articles of incorporation and are most commonly used in close corporations, as opposed to publicly held corporations.

The parties should consider the following termination and post-termination factors when deciding what exit provisions should be included in the JV agreement:

(i) the relative financial resources of the parties;
(ii) the events and timing at which the exit mechanisms may be triggered;
(iii) the likely value of the parties' interest in the JV;
(iv) the ability to protect confidential information after termination;
(v) the ability to repatriate capital;
(vi) the division of assets and liabilities;
(vii) successor liability problems;
(viii) indemnification obligations;

(ix) tax consequences; and
(x)   the effect of termination on the JV partners and third parties.

The common denominator of JV exit mechanisms that are not related to a party's breach or insolvency is that they involve the transfer of equity stakes. As such, they are significantly riskier and costlier than contractual alliances.

The following diagram summarizes the relationship between several legal factors and the respective transfer vehicles from the perspective of the transferor.

ALTERNATIVES FOR INTERNATIONAL TECHNOLOGY TRANSFERS   151

Figure 2.3   Relationship between Legal Factors and Transfer Vehicles from the Perspective of the Transferor

	Direct End-User Sale/License	Contractual Alliance	Joint Venture via Separate Entity	Merger or Acquisition
	LOWEST			HIGHEST ⟶

LEGAL FACTORS:

- Retention of ownership in technology
- Competition law sensitivity
- Potential difficulty in repatriating and converting payment and profits
- General liability exposure
- Local content/public procurement eligibility
- Ability to benefit from regional regimes
- Complexity of exit mechanisms/exit difficulty

III. CONCLUSION

A host of complex business and legal considerations should be factored into the selection of the most appropriate technology transfer vehicle. Inevitably, one form will offer advantages that other forms do not. Rarely will – and should – one factor be dispositive. Rather, the parties should weigh all factors, assign the proper relative weight to each factor in the transaction, understand the trade-offs presented by each structure, and base their deliberations on well-defined priorities dictated by their overall business objectives.

The business objectives and the parties' circumstances will vary greatly from case to case. Therefore, while the authors did state which structure would be most suitable in reference to certain factors *in isolation*, it would be an imprudent over-simplification to proffer a *cumulative* formula for when each structure should be used.

However, notwithstanding the authors' reluctance to prejudice the outcome of the parties' search for the proper transfer structure, experience does teach one important lesson time and again. It is that a JV is a task-specific merger, not an upgraded marketing arrangement. In a JV partner, each party should look not only for objective characteristics such as capabilities, resources, experience, and local contacts, but also for compatibility on a more subjective level, including objectives, business philosophies, attitudes and styles. More than anything, the JV partners must be able to trust and communicate well with one another. A JV is too complex and intimate a relationship to be driven solely by objective business reasons. While it is essential that the parties expend adequate time and resources to select the appropriate partner for all strategic alliance structures, the selection of the right JV partner is the single most important prerequisite for a successful JV. Indeed, the parties would be well advised to enter into a JV arrangement on somewhat less favorable terms with an experienced and reliable partner with similar objectives, rather than entering into a JV on superficially better terms with a more questionable partner. JVs may offer great rewards, but most JVs fail precisely because of the "soft" or subjective factors. Consequently, and since in most cases the transferor's primary goal in considering a strategic alliance will be to penetrate a foreign market and the transferee's main purpose will be to gain access to the transferor's technology, the presumption should be *against* a JV and in favor of entering into a contractual strategic alliance, at least as the first step in the relationship.

Chapter Three

Contractual Allocation of Rights and Obligations in Technology Transfers

Harry Rubin and Daniela Feldhausen
Shaw, Pittman, Potts & Trowbridge, Washington, D.C.

A technology transferor's primary concern should be to obtain the maximum legal protection possible for its proprietary rights before embarking on technology transfer transactions. Chapter One describes the protections afforded to different types of intellectual property under international regimes and domestic legal systems. The transferor's next step should be to determine the most advantageous legal and business transfer structure. The competing considerations and characteristics of the alternative transfer structures are discussed in Chapter Two. After having secured the maximum protection available under intellectual property regimes and selected the appropriate transfer structure, the transferor must carefully examine what rights in the technology it will grant to the transferee, how the liabilities associated with the technology will be allocated and how best to safeguard the transferor's residual proprietary interest in the technology. This Chapter, therefore, focuses on the contractual allocation of rights and obligations between the transferor and transferee and discusses the principal issues that arise during the negotiation and drafting of a technology transfer transaction, from both the transferor's and the transferee's perspectives.

A standard outright sale and assignment of technology is conceptually inconsistent with the imposition of restrictions on the use of that technology or its derivative products by the transferee. Therefore, the technology should be *licensed*, either directly or in the context of one of the structural alternatives discussed in Chapter Two. Since in the overwhelming majority of technology transfers the technology is, in fact, licensed to the transferee, this Chapter will usually refer to the technology transferor and transferee as licensor and either licensee or distributor, respectively, regardless of the actual structure – end-user license, contractual alliance or joint venture (JV) – that is selected to effect the transfer.[1]

I. GOVERNMENT APPROVALS AND REGULATORY SCHEMES

In many countries, government approval is required before a license agreement can become effective. Unless the licensor is familiar with local law and is confident that all legal requirements have been met, it should require the licensee to warrant that all necessary approvals have been obtained from the licensee's government or will be obtained before the agreement becomes effective. The licensee should be made responsible for obtaining such approvals and undertaking all required registrations at its own expense. If the licensor has not had much experience transferring technology to a particular country, it should require the licensee to defend and indemnify the licensor from any claims, liabilities and expenses suffered by the licensor as a result of the licensee's failure to obtain such approvals. Finally, the license should provide that obtaining the requisite approvals and registrations is a precondition for the effectiveness of the agreement and that if such approvals or registrations are not obtained by a certain date, the licensor will have the option to terminate the relationship without any further liabilities. Significantly, the parties' proprietary rights and confidentiality obligations should be binding as of the execution of the agreement – not as of its registration or approval date.

Supranational Regimes

If an agreement *prima facie* triggers the application of the competition (antitrust) laws of the **European Union**, formerly the European Community, it should be notified to the European Commission (the "Commission") unless it falls squarely within one of the "block exemptions." Registered agreements are considered valid unless challenged, and, if the challenge is effective, the Commission will generally reform the agreement rather than subject the parties to fines. Unregistered licenses, on the other hand, can be declared void from their inception and are subject to penalties of up to ten per cent of the licensor's total turnover.[2] If a licensor enters into the identical

---

1. *See* general discussion on different technology transfer structures in Chapter Two.
2. Joel Davidow, *International Licensing and Foreign Antitrust Rules, in* DRAFTING LICENSE AGREEMENTS 225 (Michael A. Epstein & Frank L. Politano eds., 1993 Supplement).

agreement with different licensees in the EU, approval by the Commission of one of these agreements may be considered approval of all such agreements.[3]

All agreements that are entered into with a party in the EU or that have effects in the EU are subject to the EU's competition laws. Certain patent and know-how licenses that are not entered into in the context of a JV, as well as certain distribution agreements, exclusive purchasing agreements and franchise agreements, have been granted block exemptions from these laws. Commentators generally categorize these block exemptions into "white," "grey" and "black" lists. If the agreement itself falls within the scope of the block exemption, contractual obligations that are on the white list need not be notified to the Commission or justified. Black list practices, on the other hand, must be notified, but are unlikely to be approved. Grey list provisions are not required to be notified to the Commission, but are automatically allowed if the Commission is notified of them and does not object within six months. Notifications of grey list practices should include an explanation as to why they are necessary for competition and not significantly harmful from a practical point of view.[4] Many parties file proposed agreements with the Commission in order to predetermine their validity.[5] Since fines are rare for grey list practices, however, many license agreements with those practices are never notified to the EU.[6] The white, grey and black lists are discussed further in this Chapter's subsequent sections on competition law and particular licensing practices.

The Commission currently is considering a draft regulation on technology transfers (the Draft).[7] The Draft proposes a block exemption for technology transfer agreements and is designed to replace both the block exemption for patent agreements and the block exemption for know-how license agreements (see Section II) by June 30, 1995 and December 31, 1999, respectively. It applies to "pure" patent license agreements and "pure" know-how license agreements as well as combined patent and know-how license agreements, whenever the patents are "essential for the achievement of the objects of the licensed

---

3. 3 STEVEN Z. SZCZEPANSKI, ECKSTROM'S LICENSING IN FOREIGN AND DOMESTIC OPERATIONS § 19.02[2][b][iii] [hereinafter ECKSTROM'S].
4. Davidow, *supra* note 2, at 226.
5. W.A. Hoyng & M.B.W. Biesheuvel, *The Know-How Group Exemption*, 26 COMMON MKT. L.REV. 219, 220 (1989).
6. Davidow, *supra* note 2, at 228.
7. Preliminary Draft Commission Regulation of 30 September, 1994 on the application of Article 85(3) of the Treaty to certain categories of technology transfer agreements.

technology" and the know-how is "secret, substantial and identified in any appropriate form." This new block exemption applies only to situations in which the licensee itself manufactures the licensed products or has them manufactured on its behalf. It does not apply to agreements between members of a patent or know-how pool or certain agreements entered into in the context of a JV. Agreements concerning only the sale of licensed products continue to be governed by the block exemption for exclusive distrubution agreements (see Section II).

In what is probably the most controversial aspect of the Draft, many of the license restrictions that were on the white list and thus exempted from scrutiny under the old patent and know-how block exemptions would now be subject to additional, market-based tests. For example, under the Draft, a licensor will only be permitted to grant an exclusive license to a potential licensee if the licensee has a market share before entering into the proposed license agreement of no more than 40 per cent and the licensee will not be operating in an oligopolistic market. Other contractual restrictions formerly presumed permissible are only exempt under the Draft if the party protected by those restrictions has a market share of 20 per cent or less.

Country Focus

In general, technology licenses are not subject to registration requirements or approval in the **United States**. However, the U.S. Federal Trade Commission (the U.S. FTC) will apply the Hart-Scott-Rodino Act to exclusive intellectual property licenses. If no exemptions apply, the exclusive license has a value of at least $15 million and the parties meet certain asset and sales thresholds (*i.e.*, one of the parties has total assets or annual sales of at least $100 million and the other party has total assets or annual net sales of at least $10 million), the parties must notify the U.S. FTC of the proposed license and wait at least 30 days before implementing its provisions.[8] The U.S. FTC may seek to undo the consummated transaction and/or impose a penalty of up to $10,000 per day for noncompliance with these reporting and waiting requirements.

The **Argentine** Technology Transfer Law governs the transfer of technology for consideration, whether between unrelated parties or affiliated companies, and requires that all international technology transfers be registered with the Argentine National Institute of Industrial Technology (INTI).[9] Although failure to register will not

---

8. 15 U.S.C. § 18(a); 16 C.F.R. 801.40.

9. Elmer J. Stone & Kenneth H. Slade, *Special Considerations in International Licensing Agreements*, 1 TRANSNAT'L LAW. 161, 174 (1988).

affect the validity of the contract, royalty payments will not be deductible for tax purposes if the agreement is not registered.[10] Even agreements between foreign companies and their Argentine subsidiaries are subject to review to determine whether they are in line with commercially reasonable business arrangements between unrelated parties. During such a review, consideration in the amount of up to five per cent of net sales will be assumed to be appropriate. The parties to any international technology transfer must pay a stamp tax within five business days of the date the agreement is signed or takes effect, and before the agreement is submitted to INTI.[11] The parties can request that INTI issue an opinion on the arrangement before they execute the agreement.

All contracts concerning a trademark or patent filed in **Brazil**, as well as all technology transfers to Brazilian parties or that require the performance of contractual obligations in Brazil, must be filed with the Brazilian National Institute of Industrial Property (INPI). According to the recently enacted Normative Act No. 120, the contracting parties may now negotiate the terms of such agreements without interference by the INPI. The parties must still comply with the Industrial Property Code and the rules of the Ministry of Finance, however, which limit the tax deductibility of royalty payments to between one per cent and five per cent, and prohibit restrictions on manufacturing or "commercialization."[12]

Although **Mexico** does not formally require the registration or approval of technology transfer agreements, assignments of patents and trademarks must be recorded in the Patent and Trademark Office in order to be effective against third parties.[13] In addition, there may be adverse tax consequences for a licensee who makes payments on unregistered transfers.[14]

Foreigners seeking to license technology into the **People's Republic of China** will generally negotiate the agreement not with the intended licensee, but with the relevant Chinese Foreign Trade Corporation (the "Chinese FTC"). The intended licensee, in turn, may be asked to

---

10. Marval & O'Farrell, *Argentina*, in INTERNATIONAL AGENCY AND DISTRIBUTION AGREEMENTS § 5.5 (Thomas F. Clasen, ed., Butterworths 1993) [hereinafter INTERNATIONAL AGREEMENTS].
11. *Id.* § 30.05.
12. Adriana Casella, *Brazil: Technology Transfer*, INT'L FIN. LAW REV. 42 (Feb. 1994).
13. John B. McKnight & Carlos Müggenburg R.V., *Mexico's New Intellectual Property Regime: Improvements in the Protection of Industrial Property, Copyright, License, and Franchise Rights in Mexico*, 27 INT'L LAW. 27, 40-41 (1993).
14. ECKSTROM'S, *supra* note 3, at § 26.03[1].

provide the Chinese FTC with the technical information required to conclude the agreement. Historically, the Chinese FTC has been the only Chinese party to sign license agreements as licensee. More recently, however, an increasing number of intended licensees are being permitted by the Chinese authorities to co-sign such agreements. Foreign licensors may discover that potential licensees are reluctant to diverge from standardized license agreements developed by the China National Technical Import Corporation. Significantly, although the words "agreement" and "contract" are used interchangeably throughout this Chapter, in China, a "contract" is binding and enforceable, whereas an "agreement" is not.[15]

According to China's Foreign Economic Contract Law, all economic contracts between Chinese and foreign entities, and all modifications to such contracts, must be approved by the Chinese government in order to become effective. In addition, contracts relating to the assignment or licensing into China of patent or other industrial property rights, know-how, proprietary technology and technical services are also subject to the Regulations on Administration of Technology Import Contracts of the People's Republic of China and the Detailed Rules for the Implementation of the Administrative Regulations of the People's Republic of China on Technology Import Contracts. Software licensors should also consult the Computer Software Protection Regulations (1991) and the related 1992 Procedures, which may require them to register the licensed software with the Center for Software Registration.[16]

This Chapter deals only with those laws relevant to the transfer of technology to Chinese entities generally. Licensors must keep in mind that different laws apply for transfers of equity contributions to joint ventures formed in China and for transfers into China's special economic development zones.

Under **Japan's** Foreign Exchange Law, many international commercial agreements, including technology licenses, must be filed with and approved by Japan's Ministry of Finance before being implemented. Without this approval, the Japanese party may not make payments to the foreign party. International transfers of patent licenses must also be registered in and validated by the Japanese Patent Office (JPO). In addition, many international licensing and distribution agreements must be filed with Japan's Fair Trade Commission (Japan's FTC).[17]

15. *Id.* § 27.04[8].
16. Henry Hong Lui, *Legislative Update – Legal Aspects of Software Protection in China: The Computer Software Protection Regulations*, 9 COMPUTER & HIGH TECH. L.J. 469 (1993).
17. Davidow, *supra* note 2, at 230.

Although notice need not be provided to Japan's FTC until after the agreement has been executed, parties often seek unofficial assurances before finalizing negotiations.[18] In the alternative, the agreement should provide that the approval of Japan's FTC is a condition precedent to effectiveness of the agreement.

All technology transfer arrangements involving the **Philippines**, including the transfer of all forms of industrial property rights, must be registered with and approved by the Philippine Technology Transfer Registry (TTR). The speed with which the TTR renders its decision on license agreements and the outcome of that decision largely depend upon whether the proposed royalty rate is higher than the rate set by the government for that type of transaction and whether the local licensee will earn sufficient foreign exchange to cover the remittances for royalties.[19] Even after obtaining approval, the parties will be required to provide the TTR certain information regarding the licensee's progress in mastering the technology on an annual basis.[20]

Currently, all technology transfer agreements involving at least one **Korean** party must be registered in order to be enforceable. In general, those agreements with a term exceeding three years (including renewal periods) whose

(i) total royalty payments exceed U.S. $100,000,
(ii) initial royalty payment exceeds U.S. $50,000, or
(iii) running royalty rate exceeds two per cent of the "total net sales,"

must be approved by the relevant ministry in accordance with Korea's Foreign Capital Inducement Act (FCIA).

Other agreements require approval by a Class A Korean foreign exchange bank, which is generally considered a mere formality.[21] Separate maintenance service agreements require governmental approval, as do renewals of the original license agreement. However, Korea's Fair Trade Commission (Korea's FTC) has announced plans to abolish these registration requirements.[22]

Whether or not license agreements are notified to the Commission, those entered into with a **French** party must be registered with the French fiscal authorities, the French Commission on Technical

18. William I. Schwartz & Takashi B. Yamamoto, *Doing Business in Japan: Strategies and Practical Insights*, 2 INT'L COMPUTER LAW. 2, 10 (1994).
19. ECKSTROM'S, *supra* note 3, § 34.07[8].
20. *Id.* § 34.04.
21. Duck Soon Chang, *Technology Licensing in Korea: Validation Procedures, Effects of Trade Secret Protection Act*, E. ASIAN EXEC. REP., Sept. 15, 1992.
22. C. Leon Kim, *Approval Process for Technology Transfer Agreements to be Abolished*, 8 WORLD INTELL. PROP. REP. 233 (1994).

International Transfers and, in many cases, the French Patent Office (whether or not a patent is being transferred). Although failure to complete the fiscal registration does not invalidate the agreement, it will prevent an aggrieved party from enforcing the license in court.[23] The French Patent Office will not register a patent license whose underlying patent has been applied for, but not yet granted.

Unless transfers of patent rights are registered with the **Russian Federation**'s Patent Department, they will be null and void.[24] Patent registrants should be careful to mark the application "secret," as all applications not so marked will be published within 18 months.[25] Licensors of patents will be required to employ a Russian patent agent in order to enforce their rights in Russia.[26] Trademark licenses must also be registered with the Russian Patent Department and must contain minimum standards for quality control.[27] Agreements on the protection of intellectual property rights have been reached with various former Soviet republics, including **Armenia**, the **Ukraine**, **Belorussia**, **Moldova** and **Kazakhstan**.[28]

All license agreements entered into with **Indian** parties must be registered with the Indian government, the Reserve Bank of India and appropriate agencies, and the parties must receive an approval letter from these organizations before royalty payments can be remitted to the foreign licensor. Government approval, however, may be difficult to obtain. In addition to extensive rules about permissible and non-permissible license arrangements, the Indian government has set a ceiling on various types of imports.[29] Parties wishing to do business in India should be especially careful to deal only with trustworthy, reputable counterparts and attempt to obtain governmental pre-approvals wherever possible.

Licenses of technology rights entered into with a **Nigerian** party must be registered with and approved by the Nigerian National Office of Industrial Property, which will analyze the agreement from a technical, legal and economic point of view, and various other Nigerian government agencies. Contracts that provide for the payment of royalties to a party outside Nigeria are invalid without this approval.[30]

---

23. ECKSTROM'S, *supra* note 3, § 19.02[4]; § 19.03[4].
24. Ksenia Orlova, *A Summary of Intellectual Property Rights in Russia* 3 (Denton Hall, 1993) (on file with Shaw, Pittman, Potts & Trowbridge).
25. *Id.,* at 5.
26. *Id.*
27. *Id.,* at 10.
28. *Id.,* at 13.
29. ECKSTROM'S, *supra* note 3, § 40.14[1][a].
30. *Id.* § 39.02.

II. COMPETITION LAW

In many countries, technology licenses, especially exclusive licenses, must pass muster under applicable competition law. In fact, the TRIPs[31] Agreement, which is part of the Final Act of GATT's Uruguay round, specifically provides that member countries may prohibit certain licensing terms and practices that have an adverse impact on competition. According to TRIPs, such terms and practices may include, for example, exclusive grant-back provisions and no-challenge clauses that prevent the licensee from challenging the validity of the intellectual property rights underlying the license.[32] Other provisions that are generally prohibited include resale price maintenance schemes and tying arrangements, whereby the licensor in effect forces the licensee to buy certain additional products or services from the licensor as a condition for receiving a license for the desired technology. Significantly, because competition regulation is of major public policy importance to the country in which the license agreement is performed or has an effect, competition legislation invariably will override the choice of a foreign law in the agreement. Thus, the parties cannot "contract out" of competition law restrictions.

Supranational Regimes
Articles 85 and 86 of the Treaty of Rome form the core of the EU's competition laws. Technology transfers may violate Article 85 if the agreement has as its object or effect the prevention, restriction or distortion of competition within the Common Market. Article 86 may be violated if a party to such an agreement abuses its dominant position within the Common Market, or a substantial part thereof, and that abuse has an effect on trade between member states. Examples of such prohibited abuse include:

(i) directly or indirectly imposing unfair purchase or selling prices or unfair trading conditions;
(ii) limiting production, markets or technical development to the prejudice of customers;
(iii) applying dissimilar conditions to equivalent transactions with other parties;
(iv) making the conclusion of contracts subject to acceptance by the other party of unrelated supplementary obligations; and

---

31. Agreement on Trade-Related Aspects of Intellectual Property Rights, Including Trade in Counterfeit Goods [hereinafter, TRIPs].
32. *Id.* art. 40.2.

(v) granting rebates to purchasers who agree to buy all or most of their requirements of a particular product from a supplier who has a dominant position in the relevant market.[33]

There is a *de minimis* exception to Article 85 which exempts transactions if the goods or services which are the subject of the agreement, together with licensor's and licensee's essentially equivalent goods or services, represent no more than five per cent of the total market for such goods or services and the licensor's and licensee's aggregate annual turnover does not exceed 200 million ECU.[34]

In addition, patent[35] and know-how[36] licenses that are not entered into in the context of a JV, as well as exclusive distribution agreements,[37] exclusive purchasing agreements and franchise agreements, have been granted "block exemptions" from the provisions of Article 85. These block exemptions only apply to those agreements that meet the specified criteria, and generally include white, grey and black lists that set out permissible, potentially allowed and presumptively impermissible practices.

Under the patent block exemption, for example, the grey list includes minimum royalties; field of use restrictions; obligations not to sublicense or assign the patent; restrictions on divulging know-how after expiration of the agreement; minimum quality specifications; non-exclusive grant-back provisions; and most favored nations clauses. Black list restrictions include control of licensee pricing; mandatory assignment back of improvements; bars on research and development; no-challenge clauses; patent tying; and maximum quantity limits.[38]

The guidelines for know-how licenses are substantially similar to those for patent licenses, but are somewhat more favorable to the licensor. For example, they allow the licensor to terminate the licensee's exclusivity if the latter engages in competitive activities and permit the

33. Art. 86; ECKSTROM'S, *supra* note 3, § 18.08.
34. Commission Notice of September 3, 1986, Concerning Agreements of Minor Importance Which Do Not Fall under Art. 85(1) of the Treaty Establishing the European Economic Community.
35. Commission Regulation 2349/84 of 23 July, 1984 on The Application of Article 5(3) of the Treaty to Categories of Patent Licence agreements, 1984 O.J. (L 219/ 15), corrected by O.J. (L 113/34) [hereinafter Regulation 2394/84].
36. Commission Regulation No. 556/89 of November 30, 1988 on the Application of Article 85(3) of the Treaty to Categories of Know-how Licence Agreement, 1989 O.J. (L 61) [hereinafter Regulation 556/89].
37. Commission Regulation 1983/83 of 22 June, 1983 on the Application of Article 85(3) of the Treaty to Categories of Exclusive Distribution Agreements, 1983 O.J. (L 173) [hereinafter Regulation 1983/83].
38. Davidow, *supra* note 2, at 227-229, 230.1-232.

licensor to require the licensee to adhere to quality standards in a wider range of circumstances.[39]

The block exemption for exclusive distribution agreements explicitly permits restrictions prohibiting the licensor/supplier from supplying the contract goods directly to users in the licensed territory, and prohibiting the exclusive licensee/distributor from:

(i) manufacturing or distributing goods which compete with the licensed goods;
(ii) obtaining the contract goods from third parties; and
(iii) seeking customers, establishing branches and maintaining any distribution depot outside the contract territory in relation to the contract goods.[40]

The block exemption does not apply to distribution agreements between competitors, and may not apply if either party attempts to prevent end-users from obtaining the contract goods from other sources inside or outside the EU.[41]

Country Focus

Antitrust enforcement in the **United States**, which was somewhat lax during Republican administrations, is on the upswing under the present Democratic administration. Under President Clinton, the Antitrust Division of the U.S. Department of Justice has set up a task force to focus on the Division's policies on intellectual property and antitrust. The task force is generally expected to concentrate on tying arrangements and grant-back provisions.

U.S. antitrust law generally views anticompetitive behavior in terms of horizontal agreements (between competitors) or vertical agreements (between entities in different positions on the distribution chain, *e.g.*, between a manufacturer and a distributor of the manufacturer's products).[42] Agreements between a licensor and a licensee primarily implicate the body of law on vertical restraints. Most vertical restraints, including exclusivity and noncompetition clauses, as well as territorial and customer restraints, will be analyzed under the "rule of reason," in which a court analyzes the anticompetitive effects of the restraint in light of the surrounding circumstances, such as the potential

---

39. James S. Venit, *Technology Licensing in the EC*, 59 ANTITRUST L.J. 485, 490 (1991).
40. Regulation 1983/83, *supra* note 37, art. 2.1 - 2.2.
41. *Id.* art. 3.
42. *See also* Chapter Two, Section II.B.3.

procompetitive effects of the restraint.[43] Other restraints, most notably resale price maintenance and certain tying arrangements, are considered *per se* illegal under U.S. antitrust laws. U.S. antitrust analysis of international agreements will also depend upon whether the technology is being imported into or exported from the United States. Because parties found violating the U.S. antitrust laws may be subject to treble (triple) damages and, in some cases, criminal penalties, parties should carefully monitor the evolution of U.S. antitrust laws and take antitrust concerns very seriously.

According to guidelines to **Japan's** Antimonopoly Law, Japan's FTC can require parties to delete or modify provisions it considers unfair trade practices or unreasonable restraints of trade.[44] The licensor's acquisition of a market share of 25 per cent may be considered an unfair business practice, as may territorial restrictions, restrictions on a licensee's use of improvements to the licensed technology, restrictions on the resale prices of the technology, restrictions on dealing in competing goods or technology after the termination of the agreement, obligations to purchase other products from the licensor, and unduly hindering parallel importation of the technology.[45]

Agreements that fall within the scope of the FCIA will be examined for unfair trade practices by **Korea's** FTC. Unfair trade practices may include unreasonable tie-ins, sales or export territorial restrictions, resale price restrictions, tie-outs[46] during the contract term of a non-exclusive license, tie-outs after termination of the agreement, restrictions on the licensee's continuing use of the technology after expiration of the underlying patent or copyright protection, and, in general, the imposition of unreasonable conditions on the licensee.[47] Whether or not a practice is unfair may in some cases be determined in light of international practices and customs,[48] but Korea will closely scrutinize agreements which restrict exports from Korea or grant exclusive sales

---

43. Lynn D. Krauss, *Antitrust Issues and Pitfalls in Distribution Relationships*, 72 MICH. BUS. L. J. 538 (1993); *Legal Issues, in* Marval & O'Farrell, *supra* note 10.
44. Steven C. Nelson, *Selling from the United States to Japan: Representation Sales and Distribution Agreements with Japanese Business*, 2 INT'L Q. 31, 45 (1990). For a translation and explanation of the white, grey and black lists of Japan's patent and know-how licensing guidelines, *see* Davidow, *supra* note 2.
45. Nelson, *supra* note 44, at 44. *See* the 1972 Antimonopoly Guidelines for Sole Import Distributorship Etc. Agreements.
46. Arrangements whereby the licensee is prohibited from dealing in competitive or similar products or technology.
47. Chang, *supra* note 21.
48. Fred M. Greguras & Moon Sung Lee, *Computer Software License Agreements*, E. ASIAN EXEC. REP., June 15, 1992.

rights.[49] As in Japan, discussing the proposed agreement with the relevant government authorities prior to its formal submission is highly advisable.

In **Israel**,[50] the Restrictive Trade Practices Law of 1988 regulates restrictions on "the price that is demanded, offered or paid" and "the division of the market, in its entirety or in part, in accordance with the location of business or in accordance with the persons or class of persons with whom business is to be carried on." There is an exception, however, for restraints pertaining to patents, trademarks, and copyrights, so long as either:

(i) "the arrangement is between the owner of such intellectual property and the recipient of the right of use in it *and* the intellectual property has been registered, if such registration is required by law," or

(ii) it is "[a]n arrangement the parties to which are a company and its subsidiary."[51]

III. DEFINITION OF TECHNOLOGY TO BE PROVIDED

The license agreement should list in excruciating detail all aspects of the technology that will be provided. The agreement should discuss whether replacements, enhancements, corrections, improvements, additions or new technologies that are later developed by the licensor will also be provided to the licensee under the agreement, and if so, when, under what conditions and at what additional cost, if any. The licensor may wish to retain the unilateral right to revise this list. A licensee/distributor will invariably resist granting the licensor the right to revise the product list, however. If forced to grant the licensor that right, the licensee may require the licensor to reduce any applicable minimum sales quota in the event a product or any subsequent version of that product is deleted from the scope of the agreement.

---

49. ECKSTROM'S, *supra* note 3, § 32.06[1]. *Note* that Korea's FTC has announced a plan to issue lists of permissible and non-permissible licensing practices, similar to the EU's block exemptions.
50. Barry Levenfeld, Business Opportunities In Israel – Intellectual Property 10-11 (June 1994) (Yigal Arnon & Co.) (on file with Shaw, Pittman, Potts & Trowbridge).
51. *Id.*

It is in both the licensor's and the licensee's interest that the licensee be granted the right to use the licensor's trademarks in the licensee's territory, but solely in connection with the marketing and distribution of the goods or technology.[52] The licensor may seek to retain the right to refuse to accept a licensee/distributor's orders, in case demand exceeds availability. In this case, the distributor should demand a fair allocation of the product among all distributors.

IV. OWNERSHIP

The allocation of rights in the transferred technology is the single most important issue in the license arrangement. The agreement must clearly specify which aspects or portions of the technology will be owned by the licensor and which by the licensee. As a general rule, the licensor will want to retain and secure its rights in all of the base technology being licensed as well as in any ancillary proprietary rights such as trademarks, copyrights, patents and trade secrets. In addition, the agreement should carefully define the ownership and exploitation rights in technology developed either singly by the licensee or jointly by the licensor and licensee that is derived from or based upon the technology transferred to the licensee.

Preliminarily, licensors should examine their licensee countries' overall reputation for protecting intellectual property. On April 30 and June 30, 1994, the U.S. Trade Representative's office declared **China** a "priority foreign country." China was cited for poor enforcement of its intellectual property laws: ". . . China's enforcement of its [intellectual property rights] laws and regulations is sporadic at best and virtually non-existent for copyrighted works."[53] **Argentina**, the **EU, India, Japan, Korea, Saudi Arabia, Thailand** and **Turkey** were all placed on the USTR's priority watch list, while **Australia, Chile, Colombia, Cyprus, Ecuador, Egypt, El Salvador, Greece, Guatemala, Indonesia, Italy, Pakistan, Peru,** the **Philippines, Poland, Spain, Taiwan,** the **United Arab Emirates** and **Venezuela** were placed on the watch list.[54]

According to the report, **Argentina** lacks full and effective patent protection. **Japan** was included on the priority watch list for problems in

---

52. Nagel & Anderson, *Software Distribution Agreements, in* II DRAFTING COMMERCIAL DOCUMENTS SERIES 821.
53. *USTR Announces Special 301 Decision,* OFFICE OF THE U.S. TRADE REPRESENTATIVE, June 30, 1994.
54. *USTR Announces Three Decisions: Title VII, Japan Supercomputer Review, Special 301,* OFFICE OF THE U.S. TRADE REPRESENTATIVE, April 30, 1994.

the patent area, extensive software piracy, lack of adequate enforcement mechanisms for trade secrets, and a proposed amendment to its copyright law that would permit decompilation of computer software. **Korea** was cited for the inadequacy of its intellectual property laws generally as well as inadequate enforcement of those laws, inadequate customs regulations to prevent the export of infringing goods, and inadequate trade secrets laws. The **EU** was retained on the priority watch list mainly for problems affecting the audiovisual and telecommunications industries. **India** was once again cited for the inadequate protection provided by its intellectual property laws generally, although it was commended for enacting important amendments to its copyright law and for introducing new trademark legislation. Although the lack of intellectual property protection is theoretically most egregious in priority foreign countries, followed by the priority watch list countries, and then countries on the watch list, in practice, the decision to place a country on one list rather than another is highly political. Thus, licensors should be concerned if their target country is placed on any one of these lists for reasons relating to the proposed transfer of technology.

Irrespective of the overall intellectual property climate in the licensee's country, the parties should make the most of the contractual devices at their disposal. The license agreement should specify either that the licensor is the exclusive owner of the technology, including all trademark, patents, copyrights and other intellectual property rights in the technology, or that such technology is licensed subject to a valid license or other authorization duly obtained by the licensor. At a minimum, the licensee should require a warranty to the effect that the licensor has the full right and authority to enter into the agreement and provide the technology to the licensor. The licensee should also require the licensor to indemnify it for any breach of this warranty. In addition, the agreement should identify who owns any derivative technology, which is developed by the licensee based on the licensed technology, and define exactly what is meant by such derivative technology. In simple strategic alliances, the licensee may own such technology. In more complex arrangements, such as JVs, joint ownership of derivative technology is a popular option.

The parties should resolve which of them will own and file the applications for the trademarks associated with the technology. This is particularly important in international technology transfers because in the overwhelming majority of jurisdictions outside the United States, the first person to file an application for a trademark will own the rights in that mark.[55]

---

55. *See* Chapter One for a more detailed discussion of this issue.

Licensors should understand the target country's laws on ownership of intellectual property in order to provide adequately in the agreement for the ownership of various by-products of the technology, from translations of documentation to patentable improvements. For example, many countries require that marketing materials and documentation be translated into the local language, and the licensor, for obvious marketing reasons, may want such documents to be translated into the local language even if that is not required. If such translations cannot be performed in the licensor's home country, the licensor should ensure that the rights in all translations prepared by the foreign licensee be assigned to the licensor, and that the licensee waive any moral rights to such translations or consent in advance to their infringement by the licensor. In order to judge the effectiveness of the proposed assignment provision, the licensor must know whether the licensee or the licensee's employee (who actually performs the translation or makes the invention) will own the rights in those translations and inventions under local law. If the employee owns those rights, the licensor or licensee will have to enter into a separate agreement with that employee in order to obtain an assignment of the employee's rights.

Country Focus

Under **U.S.** copyright law, works made for hire – works created by employees in the scope of their employment – belong to the employer. If, however, the works are created by an independent contractor, rather than an employee, title remains with the independent contractor. In that case, the licensee should sign a separate agreement with the independent contractor assigning the rights in the work to either the licensor or the licensee. A licensor in a particularly strong bargaining position may insist on owning derivative works that are developed by or for the licensee as works made for hire or, if applicable law does not deem such works to be works made for hire, insist on an irrevocable assignment to the licensor of all of the licensee's rights in such derivative works. In the latter case, the licensee should also be required to execute all necessary documents to effect the transfer of rights to the licensor.

In **Mexico**, the licensee's reason for hiring the employee will determine whether the licensee or the employee owns inventions created by the employee during the course of employment. If the employee was hired for research and development, the employee's inventions belong to the licensee, and the employee is entitled to special compensation for the invention. If, on the other hand, the employee was hired for other purposes, the invention belongs to the employee, although the employer may be entitled to be reimbursed for time and expenses.[56] Mexico grants authors moral rights, which are not assignable.[57]

Under **Japanese** law, the first to file a trademark application will own the rights to the registration. Consequently, the foreign licensor should file the trademark application itself. If for some reason the Japanese licensee must file the trademark application, the agreement should require the Japanese party to effect the registration in the licensor's name. The agreement should also carefully restrict the licensee's use of the trademark to the licensor's products and prohibit the licensee from using the trademark upon termination of the agreement.[58]

Under Japanese copyright law, authors of derivative works, such as those made as adaptations or translations of software for use in the Japanese market, may have pre-emptive ownership rights over the author of the original software. Therefore, foreign licensors should have all adaptations and modifications made in their home country.[59] If this proves impractical or if there is any possibility that Japanese law will govern the agreement, the parties should expressly agree that, for purposes of the Japanese Copyright Act, any modification will be considered a "secondary work." Because a copyright owner has the exclusive right to prepare secondary works, the original owner – the licensor – will thus have a colorable claim to ownership of all proprietary rights in such modifications.[60] If the agreement is governed by non-Japanese law which would provide better protection to the licensor, the agreement should contain an acknowledgment by the licensee that all translations of the technology and related documentation and any of the technology's enhancements, corrections, modifications or additions are governed by the copyright laws of the other jurisdiction. If any adaptations will be made by the Japanese licensee, the agreement should further require that they be made by the Japanese party's employees, rather than by independent contractors (to prevent a third party from acquiring moral rights in the adaptations), and grant the licensor a non-exclusive, royalty-free license to exercise any moral rights to the modification owned by the Japanese party.[61]

---

56. ECKSTROM'S, *supra* note 3, § 26.06[3].
57. *Id.* § 26.01[7].
58. Nelson, *supra* n. 44, at 36.
59. *Id.*, at note 39.
60. Fred M. Greguras, *Legal Issues Related to Entering the Japanese Software Market* 14-15 (September 4, 1991) (on file with Shaw, Pittman, Potts & Trowbridge).
61. *Id.*

Other than in exceptional circumstances, the **Philippine** TTR will not approve clauses in technology transfer agreements which restrict the technology recipient from access to continued improvements in techniques and processes related to the transferred technology, as long as the licensee is willing to make additional payments therefor.[62]

Korea grants patent protection to the first person to file the application rather than the first to invent the technology being patented.[63] Similarly, trademark protection is granted to the first person to register the mark; thus, the licensor should register all trademarks itself, or at least provide contractually that the licensee will do so on the licensor's behalf.[64] Licensors must also take into account the moral rights of Korean licensees who adapt the technology to the local market. The Korean party's moral rights to localized software include, for example, the right to make its work public, state its name on the program and preserve the integrity of the program.[65] Although the Korean licensee cannot assign its moral rights, it may be able to waive those rights or give advance consent to their infringement by the licensor.[66]

Taiwan's 1992 Copyright Law presumes that the employee – not the employer – is the author of a work. Given the scope of protection provided to authors, including non-assignable moral rights, licensors who contemplate continuing work on the technology in Taiwan should insist on side agreements with all potential authors. Licensors of software should note that Taiwan's new copyright law specifically protects software authors against alterations that go beyond correcting obvious program errors.[67]

Some countries, including **France**, will not permit a licensor to license a trademark with respect to goods not specifically covered by the trademark's registration, even though the trademark will otherwise be held to protect goods that are merely similar to those for which the trademark was registered.[68]

---

62. Rules and Regulations to Implement the Intent and Provisions of Sec. 5 PD No. 1520 Creating the Technology Transfer Board Within the Ministry of Industry, Rule V., Sec.1(c) [hereinafter Philippine Rules and Regulations].
63. Greguras & Lee, *supra* note 48.
64. *Id.*
65. *Id.*
66. *Id.*
67. Francis S.L. Wang and Laura W. Young, *Taiwan's New Copyright Regime: Improved Protection for American Authors and Copyright Holders*, 27 INT'L LAW. 1111, 1113 (1993).
68. ECKSTROM'S, *supra* note 3, § 19.04[6].

Under the copyright laws of the former Czechoslovakia, which were broadly adopted by both the **Czech Republic** and **Slovakia**, the author of a work is the owner of its copyright, even if the work was created during the course of the author's employment. The rights granted to the author include moral rights and *droit de suite*, according to which the author is entitled to a fair share of the profit made by someone who later sells a copy of the work for a "socially unjustifiable profit."[69] Licensors must thus provide for the transfer of copyright from the employee to the licensor and the employee's waiver of moral rights in the work. In contrast, patent rights are presumed to belong to the inventor's employer if:

(i) made in the course of employment, unless otherwise agreed upon by the employer and employee or
(ii) the employer does not make a claim upon the patent within three months of having received notice from the employee of the invention.[70]

Finally, licensors should inquire into any agreements the licensee has entered into with its employees regarding the ownership of inventions, and insist on notice to the licensor of new inventions before the rights thereto revert to the employee.

Patent rights are presumed to belong to the employer in the **Russian Federation**, unless employer and employee have provided otherwise. However, the employee has the right to remuneration from the employer/patentee.[71] Inventions made in the Russian Federation may not be patented abroad until three months after a patent has been applied for in Russia, unless the inventor receives special permission to do so from the Patent Department.[72] Computer programs created in the course of employment belong to the employer, unless the parties have otherwise agreed.[73] Although an employee in the same situation would be considered the author of a work for copyright purposes, the employer has the exclusive right to use that work, unless otherwise provided.[74] Licensors are advised to inform themselves about any agreements between the licensee and its employees that allocate intellectual property rights.

---

69. LEGAL ASPECTS OF INVESTMENT IN THE CZECH AND SLOVAK FEDERAL REPUBLIC Chapter 11, § 1.5 (Allen & Overy et al. eds.) [hereinafter LEGAL ASPECTS OF INVESTMENT].
70. *Id.* § 2.4.
71. Orlova, *supra* note 24, at 3.
72. Christopher Osakwe, *Introductory Note*, 32 I.L.M. 1614 (1993).
73. Orlova, *supra* note 24, at 15.
74. *Id.*, at 23.

Under **Egyptian** patent law, the patent on an invention made by an employee during the course of employment belongs to the employer, although the inventor may be entitled to additional compensation for such an invention.[75]

V. LICENSE GRANT AND RESTRICTIONS

Once the allocation of ownership in the transferred technology is well defined, the parties should consider several provisions detailing the scope and purpose of the license granted to the licensee. These provisions will help the licensor safeguard its proprietary interest in the technology and promote the parties' overall business objectives. At a minimum, the agreement should cover the following issues.

A. Purpose

The agreement should specify the purpose, whether commercial, internal or for particular products or uses, for which the licensed technology may be used by the licensee. The agreement should then state that the technology may not be used by the licensee for any other purpose. The agreement should also specify whether the licensee may use or modify the technology to produce its own technology or incorporate it into other technology in an Original Equipment Manufacturer (OEM) or Value-Added Reseller (VAR) arrangement, and whether the licensee may then re-license that new technology. These provisions not only force the parties to agree on how and under what conditions the licensee may use the technology, but also help clarify what will be considered a breach of the contract in this particularly opaque and contentious area.

B. Territorial Restrictions

The agreement should state the geographic area in which the technology can be used, sold or sublicensed. The licensor should consider retaining the right to delete part of the licensee's territory for a variety of business reasons or to terminate the entire agreement in the

---

75. Steven D. Jamar, *The Protection of Intellectual Property Under Islamic Law*, 21 CAP. U. L. REV. 1079 (1992).

event either party's government imposes restrictions on delivery of the technology to, or transfer of the royalty payments from, the territory.

One reason the licensor may wish to exercise control over the licensee's exports is to assure compliance with the export control regime of the licensor's country.[76] Another reason may be either party's desire to prevent parallel imports. Parallel imports, also known as grey-market goods, are products that are manufactured outside the target country with a valid trademark and then marketed in the target country, usually at a lower price than the identical products bearing the same trademark which are brought into the target country through authorized distribution channels. By contractually preventing parallel imports through territorial restrictions on the licensee, the licensor can protect itself against competition from the licensee in the licensor's home country and protect its other licensees from parallel imports into their territories. Thus, the prevention of parallel imports is in the interest of both the licensor and licensee, especially if the latter is granted exclusive rights.

Many export-oriented countries restrict a licensor's ability to prevent the licensee from exporting the products to other countries. Depending on the underlying purpose of the license arrangement, a licensor licensing technology into such countries may choose to control the territory in which the end products are distributed by requiring the licensee to sell all of its output exclusively to the licensor. Such an arrangement in effect transforms the underlying deal from a marketing arrangement to one in which the licensee acts as the licensor's overseas manufacturer.

Supranational Regimes

Although licensors may grant their licensees certain exclusivity rights in the EU, the parties may be in breach of EU competition laws if they agree to prevent parallel imports from distributors located in other EU member states. In other words, a French licensee may require the licensor not to sell in France or appoint any additional distributors in France. Neither the foreign licensor nor the French licensee, however, may prevent goods sold in Germany with the licensor's consent from being resold into France.

The EU's patent block exemption permits prohibiting the licensor from licensing others to "exploit" (which includes any means of exploitation afforded by patent law and in particular the ability to manufacture, use or market) the licensed invention in the licensed territory and exploiting the licensed invention in the territory itself, as

76. *See also* Chapter Two, Section II.B.9.

long as one of the licensed patents remain in force. That exemption also permits prohibiting the licensee from:

(i) exploiting the licensed invention in territories the licensor has reserved for itself (*i.e.*, in which it has not granted any licenses);
(ii) manufacturing or using the licensed technology in territories which the licensor has granted to other licensees;
(iii) actively marketing the licensed technology in territories within the EU which are licensed to others, including advertising and establishing any branch or distribution network in such territories; and
(iv) passively marketing the licensed technology, *i.e.*, responding to unsolicited requests for the technology from territories within the EU licensed to other licensees,[77] for a period of up to five years.

Significantly, the patented technology must always be protected by a parallel patent in the forbidden territories and the licensee must manufacture the licensed product itself or have it manufactured in order for the above restrictions to be permissible.[78]

Thus, the patent block exemption permits a licensee to demand and receive protection from active sales in its territory by another licensee for the duration of the license and from passive sales into its territory for five years. The know-how block exemption permits similar exclusivity provisions, although the exemption period will only last as long as the know-how remains secret and substantial, and at most for five or ten years, depending on the type of restriction.[79] According to the block exemption for exclusive distribution agreements, by contrast, the licensor can prohibit the licensee/distributor from actively seeking customers, establishing branches and maintaining any distribution depot outside the territory with respect to the licensed technology, but cannot prohibit passive sales by the licensee.[80] Again, any attempt by the parties to prevent parallel importation of the goods by third parties is prohibited.

---

77. Regulation 2349/84, *supra* note 35, art. 1. *See also* BERNARD VAN DE WALLE DE GHELCKE & GERWIN VAN GERVEN, COMPETITION LAW OF THE EUROPEAN ECONOMIC COMMUNITY § 9.05[4] (von Kalinowski ed., Matthew Bender, 1992) [hereinafter COMPETITION LAW].
78. COMPETITION LAW, *supra* note 77, § 9.05[4]; Regulation 2349/84, *supra* note 35, art. 1.1 - 1.2.
79. Regulation 556/89, *supra* note 36, art. 1.
80. *See supra* note 40, and accompanying text.

Country Focus

Under U.S. antitrust laws, territorial restrictions in an exclusive distribution agreement are *per se* illegal if they constitute "an integral part of an agreement to maintain resale prices."[81] If the territorial restrictions are not part of a scheme to fix prices, they will generally be subject to the rule of reason, in which the court analyzes the purpose for the restriction, its effect on competition, the licensor's market share, and any procompetitive benefits of the restrictions.[82] Although such restrictions are often upheld if imposed unilaterally by the licensor, they are more likely to be declared illegal if the restriction is imposed at the licensee's request.[83]

In the United States, both Section 526 of the Tariff Act of 1930 (which prohibits importing foreign goods into the United States that bear a registered trademark owned by a U.S. entity without the trademark owner's written permission) and Section 42 of the Lanham Act (which prohibits importing merchandise that copies or simulates a registered trademark) have been used in the fight against parallel imports.[84] Despite the apparently strong protection afforded by the Tariff Act, there has been a great deal of controversy regarding the implementation of Section 526 by the U.S. Customs Service (Customs). Customs regulations currently permit imports of foreign goods that bear trademarks identical to those registered in the United States if (i) the U.S. and foreign trademark are owned by the same business entity or (ii) the domestic and foreign trademark owners are affiliated with each other as parent and subsidiary or are under common ownership and control (the "Affiliation Exception"). Another exception to Section 526 created by the Customs regulations, one that permitted parallel imports if the U.S. owner authorized the foreign manufacturer to use the mark, was struck down by the U.S. Supreme Court.[85] The Supreme Court did not, however, decide whether the parallel import had to be identical to the domestic product in order for the Affiliation Exception to apply. Other legal tools used in the fight against parallel imports into the United States include copyright infringement and trademark dilution theories; Section 337 of the Tariff Act, which prohibits unfair methods of competition and unfair acts in the

---

81. ABA Antitrust Section, I ANTITRUST LAW DEVELOPMENTS 119 (3d ed. 1992).
82. *Id.*, at 123-6.
83. *Id.*, at 126-7.
84. Harry Rubin, *Destined to Remain Grey: The Eternal Recurrence of Parallel Imports* 26 INT'L LAW. 597.
85. *K Mart Corp. v. Cartier, Inc.*, 486 U.S. 281 (1988).

importation of products into the United States; and fraud and misrepresentation theories.[86]

China's Regulations require special government approval for "unreasonable" export restrictions.[87]

Export restrictions on **Japanese** licensees may run afoul of Japan's competition laws. Japan restricts a licensor's ability to control the geographical distribution of its technology. Unless the licensor already has patent rights or does business in a country, or has granted another party an exclusive license to do business in that area, the licensor may not be able to prevent the Japanese licensee from distributing to that country.[88]

Other than in exceptional cases, the **Philippine** TTR will not approve clauses in a technology transfer agreement that directly or indirectly restrict the export of products manufactured by the technology recipient under the agreement.[89]

Agreements requiring the licensee to sell all of its contract goods exclusively to the licensor are permitted and practised in **Taiwan**.[90]

Poland's 1990 Law on Counteracting Monopolies prohibits certain practices, including the division of markets along territorial lines, unless the practice is economically necessary, involves the minimum restriction on competition possible, and does not cause an overall significant reduction in competition.[91] Breaches of this law are subject to more severe penalties than breaches of similar laws of the EU or other Eastern European countries.[92]

In order to gain approval from the **Indian** government, agreements must generally permit the Indian licensee to export to all countries except those in which the foreign licensor has already concluded a licensing agreement.[93]

The **Nigerian** government similarly disapproves of provisions that restrict the licensee's ability to export the resulting products, or that require the licensee to sell the products to the licensor or an entity designated by the licensor, although the National Office of Industrial

---

86. Rubin, *supra* note 84.
87. Regulations on Administration of Technology Import Contracts of the People's Republic of China, art. 9 [hereinafter Technology Import Regulations].
88. ECKSTROM'S, *supra* note 3, § 31.02[3].
89. Philippine Rules and Regulations, Rule V, Sec. 1(c).
90. Dr. C.Y. Huang, *Technology Transfer to Taiwan Through Foreign Direct Investment and Licensing*, ANNUAL CONFERENCE ON INTELLECTUAL PROPERTY 2-1 (1990).
91. ECKSTROM'S, *supra* note 3, § 51.01[3][d][i].
92. *Id.*
93. *Id.* § 40.16.

Property appears to make exceptions for countries in which the licensor has previously granted another party exclusive rights.[94]

Israeli law[95] does not protect exclusive distributors from competition by another business that has lawfully acquired the products from another source. In *Leibovitch v. Eliyahu Ltd.*, the Israeli Supreme Court held that the exclusive distributor had no proprietary right in the goodwill of the products. The Court also held that because the competing importer did not act "without legal cause," the exclusive distributor did not have a cause of action for unjust enrichment. The Court held that the public's interests in free competition and the individual's freedom to choose an area of business endeavor outweighed the exclusive distributor's right to continue a commercial relationship with its customers, uninterrupted by the activities of the competing importer. Thus, parallel imports are sanctioned in Israel.

C. Exclusivity

If the technology is licensed directly to end-users, exclusivity is not an issue, although even in that case, the agreement should clarify that the end-user licensees may not resell or sublicense the technology. However, if the technology is provided to end-users through a contractual alliance partner, such as a distributor or sales representative, the license should specify whether the partner is granted an exclusive or non-exclusive license to market the technology in the target country. The agreement should also specify whether the licensee has the right to appoint sub-distributors or representatives. Licensors contemplating sub-distributorships should inquire whether the relevant jurisdiction restricts the licensor's right to *approve* sub-distributors. A non-exclusive license should specify whether the licensee is required to provide warranty service for, and otherwise maintain, products marketed by a competing licensee.

Whether or not a potential licensee should be granted exclusive rights to a particular territory is often a hotly contested issue, both between the licensor and its licensee and internally, within the licensor's organization. On the one hand, the licensor can minimize its transaction costs by using as few licensees as possible; or, the market may simply be too small to support multiple licensees. The licensor, moreover, will be able to extract substantially more significant contractual undertakings from the licensee in an exclusive arrangement. On the other hand, licensors often prefer

---

94. *Id.* § 39.05.
95. Levenfeld, *supra* note 50, at 12, citing Civ. App. Motion 371/89, 44(ii) 309.

non-exclusive arrangements out of fear that they will be locked into an exclusive arrangement with an ineffective licensee, thereby forgoing potential revenues and a larger market share. Presumably, if the licensor has several licensees working in the same territory, at least one will be diligent, knowledgeable about the industry and possess the right contacts. Generally, the licensor should only confer an exclusive license if it is convinced that appointing an exclusive licensee will result in better market penetration than having several non-exclusive licensees competing with one another in the same territory. The licensor should also be aware that granting a licensee non-exclusive rights now may preclude the licensor from subsequently granting another distributor exclusive rights in even a small fraction of that territory.

The licensee, of course, will generally prefer exclusive rights, and will likely argue that it will have the requisite incentive to dedicate its full resources and otherwise exert its best efforts to market the technology only if it can be assured that it will actually derive the optimum benefit from its marketing efforts. If the licensor is not certain that the licensee will be able to meet its expectations, the licensor should condition the licensee's exclusivity on the licensee's meeting certain performance quotas.[96] In addition, licensors should require all exclusive licensees (and many non-exclusive ones) to expend a specified amount of funds on technology promotion, including, for example, participation in trade shows and trade fairs, and to engage qualified personnel to promote and support the technology adequately.

Usually there is room for compromise between a licensee insisting on exclusivity and a licensor fearing an ineffective exclusive licensee. The agreement can be structured so as to be exclusive as to some, but not all, of the licensor's technology or as to some, but not all, applications or industries. The agreement could be exclusive in only a limited geographical area or for only a specified period of time. Alternatively, an exclusive license could be structured to convert into a non-exclusive license at any time the licensee fails to meet specified performance quotas.

Supranational Regimes

Licensors planning to enter into exclusive distribution agreements that have an effect in the EU should review both the *de minimis* exception to Article 85 and the block exemption for exclusive distribution agreements.[97] That block exemption permits restrictions prohibiting the licensor/supplier from supplying the contract goods directly to users in the licensed territory, and prohibiting the exclusive licensee/distributor from:

96. *See* Section IX.B of this Chapter.
97. *See supra* note 34, and accompanying text.

(i) manufacturing or distributing goods which compete with the licensed goods;
(ii) obtaining the contract goods from third parties; and
(iii) seeking customers, establishing branches and maintaining any distribution depot outside the contract territory in relation to the contract goods.[98]

Significantly, distribution agreements covered by the block exemption must permit a distributor in any EU member state to make a sale to any customer located in the EU but outside of that distributor's exclusive territory, provided that the distributor did not actively solicit the sale. This is in keeping with the general principle that passive competition should not be restricted.[99]

Country Focus
A licensee dealing with a **French** patent owner must bear in mind that, unless carefully spelled out to the contrary, an exclusive license only prevents the licensor from licensing to other parties; the patent owner may continue to use the patent itself unless it specifically abandons that right in the agreement.[100]

D. Use Restrictions

The agreement should detail how the licensee may use the technology and accompanying rights and clarify whether the licensee may reproduce or copy the licensed technology and, if so, under what conditions. Although the licensor may feel adequately protected by local patent law, for example, license agreements should always include use restrictions in order to permit the licensor to sue based on breach of contract instead of, or in addition to, relying on straight intellectual property protection. Use restrictions are obviously especially important when the licensor is not confident that its rights will be protected under local law.

Licensors should take the special nature of the licensed technology into account when imposing restrictions on its use by the licensee. Very specific use restrictions are extremely important for software, which is easily duplicated, and trade secrets, which may not be protected by local intellectual property laws. Software licensors often specify that the software may be used on only one particular machine, or at least on only one machine at a time. In the alternative, a license may be for a

---

98. Regulation 1983/83, *supra* note 37, art. 2.1 - 2.2.
99. COMPETITION LAW, *supra* note 77, § 6.10[7].
100. ECKSTROM'S, *supra* note 3, § 19.03[5].

particular number of users, for a particular number of central processing units (CPUs) or for a particular site. Frequently, additional royalties will be due the licensor if the licensee uses the software on a larger CPU or for more transactions or users than originally foreseen.

A software license must specify whether it is an end-user license for the use and internal reproduction of the software only, or a license and distribution agreement. In both cases, the licensee usually should only be granted rights to the object code version[101] of the software and should be prohibited from reverse engineering or decompiling the software.[102] If the licensee is allowed to modify the software or incorporate it into its own software, the licensee will also need a license to modify the software's source code. Whether or not the licensee receives access to the source code, a software license should always explicitly set out the purpose for which the licensee is being granted the license and prohibit the licensee from using the software for any other purpose.

Software manufacturers and their licensee/distributors around the world have attempted to restrict in-store or mail-order purchasers' use of the software by including a license agreement in the form of a "shrink-wrap" contract in the product's packaging. Shrink-wraps arose for marketing reasons, because it is generally not feasible for licensors to execute separate agreements with each end-user of mass-marketed software. The purported "agreement" is typically printed on a form included in the box that also contains the diskette, and the diskette in turn is wrapped in a plastic casing that states that by tearing the plastic, the user has read and agreed to the terms printed on that form. In more recent adaptations of the shrink-wrap concept, the license appears on the computer screen, and users are asked to read the terms and continue to use the program on the diskette only if they agree to those terms. Although the extent of enforceability of a shrink-wrap agreement is often unclear, using one is preferable to having no agreement at all.

Supranational Regimes

When the licensee is manufacturing products under license, both the patent and the know-how block exemptions to the EU's competition

---

101. Object code is the machine-readable set of instructions for the computer. Programs called "assemblers" convert the language software programmers actually write – source code – into object code.
102. A licensee distributor will often require the licensor to place a copy of the software's source code in escrow and to grant the licensee a right to use the source code to maintain and support the software for its end-user sublicensees if the licensor materially breaches the agreement.

CONTRACTUAL ALLOCATION OF RIGHTS AND OBLIGATIONS   181

laws allow the licensor to require the licensee to use the licensor's trademark or trade dress to distinguish the licensed technology. However, when a licensee manufactures under license, it must be permitted to identify itself as the manufacturer of the technology. The licensor of a patent may also require the licensee to mark the licensed technology with an indication of the patentee's name, the licensed patent or the patent licensing agreement.[103] The patent and know-how block exemptions both specifically permit field of use restrictions by placing them on the white list.

Any software license with a licensee located in the EU must comply with the EU Software Directive, according to which the licensee must be permitted to reverse engineer a software program to the extent necessary in order to make the software interoperable with other software and hardware. This right to decompile the software may only be exercised

(i) to the extent necessary to achieve the interoperability of an independently created computer program with the program that is being decompiled;
(ii) by a person having the right to use the program (*e.g.*, a licensee); and
(iii) if the licensor of the program that is to be decompiled has not made its source code "readily available" to such a person.[104]

Country Focus
Distribution arrangements that operate in the **United States** should be carefully structured to avoid being considered franchises, since franchises are heavily regulated by the U.S. FTC and state franchise laws. These laws typically require franchisers to provide potential franchisees with detailed disclosure documents (which must be filed with the state) with respect to the franchisee's costs, risks and obligations.[105] Franchise laws also generally protect franchisees from termination without cause. Software distributors, in particular, have unwittingly run afoul of U.S. federal and state franchise laws.

Licensors may be able to protect themselves by

(i) strictly limiting the licensee's use of the licensor's trademarks to the actual goods to be distributed by the licensee;

---

103. Regulation 2349/84, *supra* note 35, art. 2(1)(7).
104. Council Directive 91/250 of 14 May 1991 on the Legal Protection of Computer Programs, 1991 O.J. (L 122) 42.
105. *See* Chapter Two, Section I.C.1.d.

(ii) prohibiting the licensee from using the licensor's trademarks to identify the licensee's business itself or any of the licensee's other products; and

(iii) avoiding charges that could be characterized as franchise fees.[106]

This is an area of law that is still evolving; thus, licensors should be sure to check with local counsel before entering into distribution agreements with U.S. parties.

Although relatively few U.S. courts have been asked to review shrink-wrap contracts, the prognosis for their enforceability is not good.[107] The few cases that have been decided have tended to be very fact-specific, with courts analyzing the transactions in terms of traditional contract law principles in order to determine whether the end-user assented to the terms of the license or whether the licensor conditioned the transaction on the licensee's acceptance of the terms of the license. In *Step-Saver Data Systems, Inc. v. Wyse Technology*,[108] for example, the Third Circuit examined the enforceability of a shrink-wrap contract against a licensee who was a distributor, not an end-user of the software, and determined that the contract between the licensor and the distributor was formed based on the distributor's phone order of the software from the licensor, and that the provisions of the shrink-wrap contract constituted additional terms that did not become part of the licensor's contract with the distributor.

Prohibitions on reverse engineering may be considered unfair trade practices under the **Japanese** Anti-Monopoly Act.[109] In fact, the Japanese government is considering amending its copyright law to permit decompilation of computer software. If a licensor licensing technology into Japan or **Korea** intends to restrict the use of the technology to the licensee, the agreement should carefully define the term "licensee," as the licensor may be precluded from separately licensing its technology to two separate but related entities if "licensee" is defined too broadly.[110]

---

106. Training fees and required initial and minimum inventory orders have been construed as franchise fees. Philip D. Porter, *High Tech Distribution Agreements: Domestic*, in GEORGE WASHINGTON UNIVERSITY CONTINUING LEGAL EDUCATION PROGRAM (March 9, 1994).

107. David L. Hayes, *Shrinkwrap License Agreements: New Light on a Vexing Problem*, 15 HASTINGS COMM. & ENT. L.J. 653 (1993).

108. 939 F.2d 91 (3d Cir. 1991). See also, *Vault Corp. v. Quaid Software Ltd.*, 655 F. Supp. 750 (E.D. La. 1987), aff'd, 847 F.2d 255 (5th Cir. 1988); *Arizona Retail Sys., Inc. v. Software Link, Inc.*, 831 F. Supp. 759 (D. Ariz. 1993).

109. Jeffrey P. Cunard, *How to Protect Technology That's Transferred to Japan*, E. ASIAN EXEC. REP., February 15, 1990, at 12.

110. Greguras, *supra* note 60.

There is no clear statutory or case law authority in **Israel** regarding the enforceability of shrink-wrap contracts. Besides taking all possible steps to ensure that the terms of the shrink-wrap will be deemed part of the contract between the parties, such as ensuring that the agreement is clearly visible to a prospective licensee, licensors should consider obtaining an "advance ruling" from a Standard Contracts Tribunal that the contract does not contain any "unduly disadvantageous" terms, which are prohibited by the Standard Contracts Law.[111] Obtaining such a ruling generally takes two to four months.

E. Subsequent Transfer of Technology

The agreement should define the conditions for the subsequent transfer of the licensed technology by the licensee to third party sub-licensees or end-users. The licensor may wish to prescribe the entire sublicense agreement to be used by the licensee or require the licensee to use certain key provisions in its agreement with end-users in order to ensure that the licensor's intellectual property is sufficiently protected and that its liability to end-users is limited as foreseen in the original license agreement.[112] The parties should also note that in most countries, assignments of technology rights must be registered in order to be enforceable (*see*, Chapters One and Six).

Supranational Regimes

As signatories of **NAFTA**, Mexico, Canada and the United States must grant the owner of a registered trademark the right to assign its trademark with or without the transfer of the underlying business.[113]

The **EU's** competition regulations on patents and know-how licenses expressly allow the licensor to prohibit sublicenses of the technology.[114]

Country Focus

India may require licensors to permit an Indian licensee to sublicense the technical know-how, technology or engineering design to another Indian party "should it become necessary."[115] Such a sublicense would also be subject to Indian government approval.

---

111. Levenfeld, *supra* note 50, at 19-20.
112. Nagel & Anderson, *supra* note 52, at 835.
113. North American Free Trade Agreement, art. 1708(11).
114. Regulation 2349/84, *supra* note 35, art. 2(1)(5); Regulation 556/89, *supra* note 36, art. 2(1)(2).
115. ECKSTROM'S, *supra* note 3, § 40.16.

F. Resale Price Maintenance

The licensor often seeks to control the price at which a licensee resells or sublicenses the licensed technology, in order to prevent the licensee from harming the licensor's image in the marketplace by discounting the technology or in order to secure minimum revenues. The licensee, by contrast, will seek free rein to set its own prices to maximize its profit. Competition laws around the world favor the licensee and invariably have outlawed resale price maintenance schemes.

Several options are available to a licensor seeking to ensure a minimum revenue stream, however. First, the licensor can require the licensee to pay a royalty equal to the higher of (i) a particular percentage of revenues actually realized by the licensee or (ii) a specified amount or a particular percentage of the price set forth in a licensor's price list. Alternatively, the licensee can be required to pay a flat minimum royalty. The foregoing, of course, can be varied or combined. The underlying idea is that these alternatives only impose a minimum royalty payout requirement, and not a floor or a ceiling on the prices that the licensee may actually charge for marketing the technology in its territory. Indeed, it is good practice to specify that nothing in the agreement shall be construed to infringe upon the licensee's right to charge any price it deems appropriate for the technology.

Supranational Regimes

The **EU's** block exemptions for patent and know-how licenses will not apply if the licensee is restricted in the free determination of prices, components of prices or discounts for the licensed products.[116]

Country Focus

Agreements in which a licensor sets a minimum price at which a licensee may resell the technology constitute resale price maintenance, which is *per se* illegal under Section 1 of the U.S. Sherman Act.[117] A manufacturer may suggest that the licensee resell or sublicense at a certain price, generally known as the "Manufacturer's Suggested Retail Price" (or MSRP). The licensor may not, however, coerce the distributor into selling at that price. Whether particular actions taken by the licensor constitute coercion is a question of fact to be decided at

---

116. Regulation 2349/84, *supra* note 35, art. 3(6); Regulation 556/89, *supra* note 36, art. 3(8).
117. Lynn D. Krauss, *Antitrust Issues and Pitfalls in Distribution Relationships*, 72 MICH. B.J. 538; ABA ANTITRUST SECTION, I ANTITRUST LAW DEVELOPMENTS 100-15 (3d ed. 1992).

trial, but several recent cases have permitted manufacturers to pressure dealers to adhere to the MSRP by, for example, telling the distributor that failure to adhere to the MSRP will result in termination of the distribution agreement.[118] This approach, nevertheless, should be avoided.

According to **Japan's** Guidelines on Unfair Trade Practices with respect to Patent and Know-How Licensing Agreements, agreements setting the price at which the licensed technology will be sold in Japan most likely will be regarded as unfair by Japan's FTC, while agreements setting prices for exports from Japan are permissible as long as the licensor has patented the technology in the export market, is marketing the technology itself in that market or already has an exclusive distributor in that market.[119]

Russian competition law also prohibits resale price maintenance agreements, by prohibiting any activity aimed at fixing prices.[120] Likewise, **Polish** law, which was heavily influenced by the recommendations of various United Nations groups on competition legislation, forbids price-fixing provisions in technology transfer agreements.[121]

G. Tying and Quality Control

A licensor, especially one licensing trademarks associated with the technology, should require the licensee to maintain quality controls for the technology associated with these trademarks. The licensor should retain the ability to cancel the license, if the licensee does not maintain the licensor's quality standards, or to obtain injunctive relief and specific performance of such provisions.

The licensor may try to increase its sales and profits by requiring the licensee to buy related products and services from the licensor or a related entity. If the licensor is able, due to its market power in one technology, to require its licensee to purchase or license other products from the licensor, the licensor has "tied" the second technology to the first. Formal tie-in arrangements are prohibited by the competition laws of many countries. Therefore, some licensors attempt to achieve the same goal by setting quality standards the licensee can only achieve by using the "recommended" products, which happen to be the licensor's. Licensors must consult local laws to see whether such arrangements will

---

118. *Id.* at 108-9.
119. ECKSTROM'S, *supra* note 3, § 31.02[1].
120. Orlova, *supra* note 24, at 24.
121. ECKSTROM'S, *supra* note 3, § 41.10[6][c].

trigger competition concerns. Tie-ins generally have a better chance of surviving local legal scrutiny if they can be justified as a necessary quality control device or as appropriate to ensure the proper servicing of the licensed technology.

Supranational Regimes

The **EU's** patent block exemption allows the licensor to require the licensee to buy products and services from the licensor or someone chosen by the licensor in so far as such products or services are necessary for a technically satisfactory exploitation of the licensed invention.[122] The EU know-how exemptions are somewhat more liberal, and also allow tie-ins that ensure that the licensee conform to standards observed by other licensees.[123]

Country Focus

China's Regulations on the Administration of Technology Import Contracts require special government approval for "unnecessary" tie-ins.[124] **Japanese** competition laws permit tie-ins if the licensor can demonstrate that they are necessary to guarantee the effectiveness of the licensed patent or know-how, to maintain the goodwill of the licensed trademark, or to maintain the secrecy of the licensed know-how.[125] **Korea's** FTC will not permit "unreasonable" tie-ins, but will consider whether the tie-in is necessary in order to uphold quality standards in determining if the tie-in is reasonable.[126] **India** generally does not permit restrictions on the Indian party's choice of raw materials or components.[127] Tie-ins are also on **Nigeria's** list of inappropriate restrictive provisions, but may be permitted. Quality controls that attempt to achieve the same purpose may be rejected by the Nigerian government if they impose "unnecessary and onerous" obligations on the licensee.[128]

---

122. Regulation 2349/84, *supra* note 35, art. 2(1)(1).
123. Regulation 556/89, *supra* note 36, art. 3(3).
124. Technology Import Regulations, *supra* note 87, art. 9.
125. Japanese Guidelines for the Regulation of Unfair Business Practices with Respect to Patent and Know-how Licensing Agreements (Executive Bureau FTC, February 15, 1989), *translated* and *reprinted in* ECKSTROM'S, *supra* note 3, App. 31C.
126. Note that Korea's FTC has announced a plan to issue lists of permissible and non-permissible licensing practices, similar to the EU's block exemptions.
127. ECKSTROM'S, *supra* note 3, § 40.16.
128. *Id.* § 39.03[1].

H. Assignment of Agreement

Most licensors, especially of exclusive licenses, do not simply rely on a "best efforts" clause to provide them with the highest possible income stream; instead, they carefully choose the licensee they believe will most aggressively distribute their technology. Likewise, licensees will choose to work with licensors they trust to continue to provide any necessary support. As a result, many license agreements prohibit both parties from assigning the agreement to third parties. As an alternative to strict denial of assignment rights, the agreement might provide that neither party may assign the agreement without the written consent of the other party, which consent may not be unreasonably withheld.

Freedom of assignment generally tends to be more important for the licensor than the licensee. The license arrangement is a source of market share and income for the licensor and, as such, may be a valuable asset in other transactions, particularly in the context of a merger with, or acquisition of the licensor by, a third party. The licensor should insist on being able to assign its rights under the agreement and offer to obtain for the licensee a writing whereby the licensor's assignee assumes the licensor's obligations under the agreement. Licensors should not allow their licensees to assign the agreement unless the proposed assignee has certain minimum net assets and agrees, in writing, to assume all of the licensee's obligations.

Country Focus

License agreements governed by **Mexican** law are freely assignable by both parties, unless they have specifically provided otherwise.[129]

Agreements concluded with a **Chinese** FTC alone or with both a Chinese FTC and the intended Chinese licensee should clearly address the consequences of a dissolution of the legal entity or a change in the relationship between the Chinese FTC and the intended licensee.[130]

Unless the parties specifically provide otherwise, a licensee in a license governed by the Commercial Code of the **Czech Republic** or **Slovakia** may not sublicense or assign its rights.[131]

---

129. ECKSTROM'S, *supra* note 3, § 26.02[6].
130. Richard L. Thurston, *Country Risk Management: China and Intellectual Property Protection*, 27 INT'L LAW. 51, 58.
131. LEGAL ASPECTS OF INVESTMENT, *supra* note 69, at Chapter 11, § 7.

I. Grant-Back and Cross License

The licensor may seek to require the licensee to register all patentable improvements in the transferred technology in the licensor's name. At minimum, the licensor may want to secure an exclusive or non-exclusive (preferably, perpetual and royalty-free) license to use and, perhaps market, any technology that is developed by the licensee based on the licensor's technology. Particularly when complex technology is provided to a licensee in order to produce some other technology, the licensor will seek a grant-back or cross license for the technology so developed by the licensee.

Supranational Regimes

The **EU** permits grant-back provisions as long as they are reciprocal and non-exclusive. The licensor may not, however, require the licensee to assign rights to the licensor in whole or in part.[132]

Country Focus

According to **China's** Detailed Rules, proprietary rights to improvements in the technology, including patent applications, belong to the party making the improvement. Any grant-backs to the licensor should be reciprocal; *i.e.*, they should be made on the same terms on which improvements to the technology made by the licensor are supplied to the licensee.[133] Non-reciprocal grant-backs require special government approval.

Agreements which require an assignment or exclusive grant-back to the licensor most likely will be considered unfair by **Japan's** FTC. Instead, such technology transfers should be structured as non-exclusive grant-backs or, preferably, impose obligations on both parties to grant licenses to each other for new developments.[134] Grant-back and cross license provisions of high technology goods may require a prior license from Japan's MITI or its Ministry of Finance.[135]

The **Philippine** TTR prohibits clauses which provide that patentable improvements made by the licensee be:

---

132. Regulation 2349/84, *supra* note 35, art. 3(8); *see also* Regulation 556/89, *supra* note 36, art. 3(2).
133. Detailed Rules for the Implementation of the Administrative Regulation of the People's Republic of China on Technology Import Contracts, art. 12 [hereinafter, Detailed Rules].
134. ECKSTROM'S, *supra* note 3, § 31.02[9].
135. *Id.* § 31.01[2].

(i) patented in the name of the licensor;
(ii) exclusively assigned to the licensor; or
(iii) provided to the licensor free of charge.[136]

Although prior **Korean** guidelines prohibiting unilateral and unbalanced bilateral grant-backs were omitted from their more recent counterparts, it is unlikely that such practices will be permitted, as Korean law tends to track Japanese law on intellectual property issues.[137]

Because a general assignment of future works is void for indefiniteness under the Islamic principle of *"gharar"* (indefiniteness), licensors licensing technology into **Muslim** countries may have to forgo crosslicense and grant-back provisions altogether.[138]

Nigeria's National Office of Industrial Property disapproves of "onerous or gratuitous obligation[s]" on the licensee to assign to the licensor innovations made by the licensee without the licensor's help.[139] Such clauses are on Nigeria's list of restrictive provisions which must be eliminated, but may be granted special approval by the Nigerian Commissioner. Reciprocal arrangements will be permitted, however, as will provisions granting the licensor a preferential license to the improvements, as long as that license is not onerous.

J. No Challenge Clauses

The licensor frequently wishes to prohibit the licensee from challenging the validity of the underlying patent or other intellectual property rights. Many countries do not allow such clauses.

Supranational Regimes

Licenses taking advantage of the patent and know-how exemptions to the **EU's** competition laws may not require the licensee to acknowledge the validity of the underlying intellectual property protection or prohibit the licensee from challenging it.[140] However, a

---

136. Philippine Rules and Regulations, Rule V., § 1(c).
137. ECKSTROM'S, *supra* note 3, § 32.06[4]. Note that Korea's FTC has announced a plan to issue lists of permissible and non-permissible licensing practices, similar to the EU's block exemptions.
138. Jamar, *supra* note 75.
139. ECKSTROM'S, *supra* note 3, § 39.03[1].
140. Regulation 2349/84, *supra* note 35, art. 3(1); Regulation 556/89, *supra* note 36, art. 3(4).

know-how licensee can be prevented from challenging the secrecy of any know-how it has directly or indirectly disclosed.

Country Focus

The **Philippine** TTR generally prohibits clauses which require the technology recipient not to contest the validity of any of the patents of the technology supplier.[141]

VI. CONFIDENTIALITY

Confidentiality is of the essence in technology transfers. Due to the proprietary nature of technology, licensors should require their licensees to take specified steps to safeguard the confidentiality of proprietary information learned in the course of the transaction. In complex transfer transactions such as JVs, moreover, the licensee is likely to provide the licensor with confidential information as well. Confidentiality provisions are important even if the party providing such information believes it may be protected by patent, copyright, trade secret or other intellectual property laws in its home country, because the same information may not qualify for protection abroad. In addition, careful drafting will permit the injured party to sue for breach of contract, collect liquidated damages and seek injunctive relief. Different countries have different levels of tolerance for confidentiality provisions, however. Therefore, the laws of the target country must be consulted to ensure their enforceability.

Confidentiality provisions should cover at least the following three points.

A. Scope

The agreement should outline which materials, items and information are confidential, and specify whether they must be marked or otherwise identified as confidential in order to be treated as such. Licensors providing their licensees with a great deal of confidential information over a long period of time will resist being required to mark all of that information as confidential and will insist that all information provided to the licensee be considered confidential. Another consideration in deciding whether to require marking is how frequently *oral* confidential information will be provided to the other party. If the parties agree to

---

141. Philippine Rules and Regulations, Rule V, Sec. 1(c).

identify all confidential information, they will need to remember to summarize the contents of every confidential conversation in a writing stating that such information was given confidentially, and promptly send these summaries to the other party.

In addition, the agreement should state how long after termination or expiration of the agreement the information must be kept confidential. Providing for the survival of confidentiality provisions after the termination or expiration of the agreement is especially important in order to prevent the licensee from using trade secrets to re-create similar technology.

B. Procedures

The agreement should describe the procedures that the licensee must institute in order to protect the confidential information. Under the laws of most countries, only those who actually sign an agreement will be bound by its non-disclosure provisions. Thus, the licensee's employees will not be bound under a typical license agreement. As a result, the licensor should require the licensee to execute separate agreements with each person who has access to the technology. If this proves impossible, a second-best alternative is to hold the licensee liable for any breach of the non-disclosure provisions by its employees.[142] Additionally, the licensor may require the licensee to lock up the confidential information. Many agreements will require that the confidential information only be accessible to individuals with a need to know, even within the licensee's organization.

C. Exceptions and Reciprocity

Licensees should require the inclusion of several standard exceptions to the definition of confidential information. These exceptions should, at a minimum, consist of

(i) information generally available to the public other than as a result of the breach of the agreement;
(ii) information already in the possession of the receiving party prior to any disclosure thereof under the agreement;

---

142. Sue Holloway, *Black Box Agreements: The Marketing of U.S. Technical Know-How in the Pacific Rim*, 23 CAL. W. INT'L L.J. 199.

(iii) information that has been disclosed to the receiving party without conditions of confidentiality by an unaffiliated third party;
(iv) information independently developed by the receiving party without using the information disclosed to that party under the agreement; and
(v) information which is revealed as a result of a judicial proceeding or other legal requirement.

The disclosing party generally should bear the burden of proving these exceptions. It is typical, moreover, to require the licensor to abide by the same confidentiality restrictions concerning the licensee's confidential information that the licensee must abide by with respect to the licensor's confidential information.

Country Focus

Because the concept of confidentiality may not be well understood or appreciated in **China**, confidentiality provisions should be carefully spelled out, and the licensor should make it clear to the Chinese licensee that it will not hesitate to enforce the rights spelled out in the contract for breach of confidentiality provisions. When the agreement is signed not by the intended licensee, but only by one of the Chinese FTCs, its confidentiality provisions literally do not apply to the party receiving the technology. This is one of the reasons why many parties now insist that the intended Chinese licensee also sign the license agreement.

The Chinese are extremely reluctant to sign long-term secrecy clauses.[143] In fact, confidentiality provisions generally may not exceed the term of the agreement without special approval by governmental authorities.[144] If, however, the licensor provides the licensee with improvements to the technology during the term of the agreement, the confidentiality provision with respect to the improvements may extend beyond the termination of the agreement, but at most for the term provided for the original technology.[145] Another problem when transferring patented information to China is that confidentiality provisions only extend to information which has not been made public, and registering for patent protection requires publication of the information.

When exporting technology to **Japan**, it is essential to specify precisely the steps that the licensee must take in order to protect the

---

143. ECKSTROM'S, *supra* note 3, § 27.04[12].
144. Detailed Rules, *supra* note 133, art. 13.
145. *Id.*

licensor's confidential information. A typical statement that the licensee will protect the licensor's confidential information to the same extent that it protects its own would be insufficient because Japanese licensees generally do not protect confidential information. Thus, the licensor must impose obligations on the Japanese licensee which survive the expiration of the agreement in order to protect its trade secrets. Licensors should note that although there are criminal penalties and civil remedies in Japan for trade secret theft, trade secrets that are exposed in the course of a lawsuit to protect such rights are considered public information. Japan is currently considering adopting protective orders in cases alleging trade secret theft.[146]

Japanese employees should be compensated for signing a confidentiality agreement; otherwise, the agreement may be found to interfere with the employees' "freedom to choose [their] occupation."[147] An agreement with a Japanese licensee should specifically state that the licensor is entitled to injunctive relief for breach or threatened breach of the confidentiality provisions of the agreement, and liquidated damages for actual breach. However, as previously noted, in order to enforce the confidentiality provisions, the information would have to be revealed in a judicial enforcement action, as Japanese law does not recognize protective orders for such circumstances. As a result, the licensor's only recourse may be a claim for damages.

Licensors licensing into Japan should also be aware of special dangers involving patented technology. The Japanese Patent Office (JPO) discloses the contents of a patent application to the public during its review. Others can then use this public information to design around the patent. In addition, if the JPO considers the changes valuable improvements, it may require the inventor to grant the improver a license to use the patent.[148]

Agreements with licensees in **Korea** should specifically provide for injunctive relief for breach of confidentiality provisions. The agreements should also provide for liquidated damages for such breach, because it may be difficult to enforce injunctions.

---

146. James A. Forstner, *Japan Considers Adoption of Protective Orders*, 8 WORLD INTELL. PROP. REP. 99 (1994).
147. Todd F. Volyn, *Agreement Consummation in International Technology Transfers*, 33 IDEA: J.L. & TECH. 241 (1993).
148. Holloway, *supra* note 142; *See also* Chapter One, Section III.

VII. WARRANTIES AND DISCLAIMERS

Warranties are an exceptionally contentious topic. Most licensors prefer to give few or no warranties. However, it is difficult to market technology with inadequate warranties. Moreover, some jurisdictions will not permit the exclusion of implied warranties. The parties should also decide whether the licensor's original warranty to the licensee should be passed through to the end-user, or whether the licensee's distributor or sales representative will provide a different set of warranties to the end-user. The licensor should not permit the licensee to pass the licensor's warranty on to the end-user unless the licensee agrees to indemnify the licensor if the scope of the latter warranty exceeds the scope of the original warranty from the licensor to the licensee. In the case of software, the licensor should limit the warranty to the most current version of the software.

A. Non-Infringement

The most prevalent warranty is an intellectual property non-infringement warranty, whereby the licensor warrants that its technology does not infringe upon the proprietary rights (copyright, trademark, patents, and trade secrets) of third parties. The licensor should seek to exclude from this warranty any liability for infringement caused by the licensee's or end users' modification of the technology or any combination of the technology with the licensee's other technology that is not expressly permitted by the licensor.

The licensor should resist giving an unqualified warranty to the effect that the technology does not infringe a third party's patent rights, because third party patents rights are always difficult to ascertain. This is partly because patent offices often have a backlog of up to several years to process patent applications, and because patents can be invalidated even after they have been granted, if, for example, a challenger can demonstrate a prior publication that was overlooked by the patent examiner. Consequently, the licensor of a patent may want to include a clause in the agreement that states that the licensee has examined the patent and believes it to be valid, or one that specifies the extent of the novelty search that was undertaken and that the licensee is satisfied with that search. Another acceptable compromise may be for the licensor to warrant that to the best of its knowledge the transferred technology does not infringe upon any third party's patent rights.

Parties to a technology transfer also frequently debate who should assume the potential infringement risk in the target country. The licensor will argue that it is not able to search for potential infringement in the target country; the licensee will assert that since it is the licensor's technology, it is the licensor's responsibility to ensure that the technology is non-infringing. These arguments are invariably resolved in favor of the party that has the stronger bargaining power or better negotiating skills.

B. Performance – Use, Operation and Results

The licensor must decide which warranties, if any, to give for the use, operation and results of the technology. Licensors should condition such warranties on the licensee's exact compliance with the licensor's technical specifications, use conditions, service requirements, and minimum quality of raw materials and other components, and except from such warranties any uses of the technology in extreme weather or other aberrant conditions. If the licensor is required to provide a performance warranty for technology developed specifically for the licensee, it will often insist on a clause stating that the licensee's only recourse in case the technology does not perform as warranted is to require the licensor to use commercially reasonable efforts to make it perform as warranted. If the licensed technology is standard, the licensor will often limit the licensee's sole remedy in the event of a breach of a performance-type warranty to the correction or replacement, at the licensor's option, of the defective technology.

C. Conformity to Laws and Regulations

The successful marketing of sophisticated technologies with significant environmental impact, or that are governed by national or international standards, may require a warranty that the technology conforms to all applicable domestic and international laws, regulations and standards.

Country Focus

In the **United States**, under contracts governed by, or interpreted by analogy to, the Uniform Commercial Code (the UCC), a licensee may receive damages equal to the difference between the value of the goods accepted and the value of the goods had they conformed to the warranty,[149] plus incidental and consequential damages (unless these

---

149. UCC § 2-714(2). *See also* Chapter Five of this book for UCC provisions on protecting rights in licensed technology after its transfer.

are effectively limited or excluded by the parties). Courts will imply a warranty of merchantability (that goods are "fit for their ordinary purpose") and may also imply a warranty of fitness for a particular purpose (if the licensor knows the purpose for which the licensee will use the goods, and the licensee relies on the licensor's judgment in selecting the goods). Although these and other warranties can be disclaimed under the UCC, any such disclaimer must strictly follow the procedures set forth in the UCC in order to be effective. UCC Section 2-316(2) requires that any exclusion of the implied warranties of merchantability and fitness for a particular purpose must be in writing, specifically mention the word "merchantability," and be conspicuous (capitalized or in bold, for example). The exclusion of implied warranties is standard practice in the United States.[150]

Under **Mexican** law, registered licensees of patent and trademark rights (but not copyrights) may sue infringers, unless the licensor and licensee have specifically provided to the contrary.[151] In addition, "the licensee may have a valid action for unjust enrichment...if the technology is inadequate or inapplicable."[152]

A foreign licensor must guarantee the **Chinese** licensee that the licensor is the lawful owner of the transferred technology or that it is authorized to assign or license the technology. In addition, the licensor will be required to defend and indemnify the Chinese licensee from any third party infringement action.[153] Significantly, these requirements will override any attempted limitation of liability. In addition, foreign licensors must guarantee Chinese parties that the technology provided is capable of accomplishing the technical functions prescribed in the contract.[154]

In **Japan**, the Commercial Code governs the provision and disclaimer of warranties between merchants, while the Civil Code's warranties for purchased goods will likely apply to license arrangements with end-users.[155] Warranties can generally be disclaimed, although the law restricts disclaimers for liability arising from intentional or grossly negligent acts.[156]

---

150. *Id.*
151. ECKSTROM'S, *supra* note 3, § 26.01[8].
152. *Id.* § 26.04[6].
153. Detailed Rules, *supra* note 133, art. 11.
154. *Id.* art. 9.
155. William I. Schwartz & Takashi B. Yamamoto, *Doing Business in Japan: Strategies and Practical Insights,* 2 INT'L COMPUTER LAW 2, 8 (1994).
156. *Id.*

Likewise, the government of **Korea** requires licensors to warrant that the technology does not infringe upon third parties' patent rights, and to defend infringement suits bought by third parties.[157] Although general disclaimers with respect to the licensed technology's quality and fitness for its intended use may not be permitted in Korea, "disclaimers specifically related to the licensee's application of the licensed technology have been acceptable."[158] At least in a commercial context (as opposed to a consumer context), U.S.-style disclaimers of warranty are generally enforceable in Korea.[159]

As a matter of **French** law, the licensor is presumed to warrant to a patent licensee that use of the patent will not infringe another party's prior patent rights; if the warranty fails, the licensor will be required to reimburse the licensee for all of the latter's expenses, including all royalties paid to the licensor. The licensor can negate this warranty, however, by requiring the licensee to stipulate in the agreement that the licensee accepts the license at his own risk.[160] Under French law, an exclusive patent licensee may sue to enforce a patent if the licensor/patentee refuses to sue the infringer, or intervene and claim damages from the infringer.[161] A trademark licensee, on the other hand, is not permitted to sue for infringement by a third party, or join the trademark owner and claim damages.[162] A licensor entering into an agreement with a French licensee should specify that the licensee accepts the license at his own risk. Otherwise, the licensor may be required to reimburse all royalties earned for any patent that is later found to contain hidden faults, and, in addition, may be required to pay damages if it knew of those faults.[163]

The Commercial Codes of the **Czech Republic** and **Slovakia** provide that, unless the parties specify to the contrary, the licensee must notify the licensor of any infringement of the licensed rights. Those codes also provide that the licensor must do everything necessary to protect the exercise of the rights by the licensee.[164]

Unless the contract between the parties specifies otherwise, a **Nigerian** licensee may sue the infringer of a trademark if the trademark's owner refuses to commence proceedings against the infringer within two months after the licensee has brought the infringement to the trademark owner's attention. In addition, the Nigerian government analyzes the agreement's

---

157. Chun Wook Hyun, *Legal Aspects of Technology Licensing in the Republic of Korea*, 27 COLUM. J. TRANSNAT'L L. 53, 80 (1988).
158. ECKSTROM'S, *supra* note 3, § 32.06[4].
159. Greguras & Lee, *supra* note 48, at 103.
160. ECKSTROM'S, *supra* note 3, § 19.03[6].
161. *Id.* § 19.03[10].
162. *Id.* § 19.04[5].
163. *Id.* § 19.03[6].
164. LEGAL ASPECTS OF INVESTMENT, *supra* note 69, at Chapter 11, § 7.

warranties for production and quality levels as a part of its technical evaluation in deciding whether to approve a license agreement.[165]

VIII. REMEDIES; INDEMNIFICATION; LIMITATION ON LIABILITY

In order to provide greater certainty as to damages and other remedies in countries whose legal systems are unfamiliar, the agreement should clearly spell out contractual remedies. Generally, remedies will fall into three categories:

(i) replace, repair or pay,
(ii) indemnity, and
(iii) damages.

When licensing technology into countries whose legal systems do not provide for, or whose laws restrict, the application of injunctive relief, the parties may demand injunctive relief in appropriate third countries in case of breach by a party. If specific performance is not available, the parties should specify the remedies available to the injured parties for various types of breaches of the agreement. The number of countries in which injunctive relief and specific performance are unavailable should shrink, however, as the signatories to NAFTA and GATT (in particular, the TRIPs segment of the Uruguay Round's Final Act) implement the enforcement provisions of those agreements.[166]

The license should specify how damages are to be calculated and provide for liquidated damages in the case of breach of provisions that do not allow for the calculation of damages. Any liquidated damages clause should state why actual damages would be difficult to calculate, explain why the amount decided upon is reasonable, be backed by a bank guarantee (if feasible), and state that the liquidated damages are not intended as a penalty.

Licensees will invariably insist that the licensor indemnify the licensee from any successful claims brought against the licensee for infringement of a third party's intellectual property rights. In the alternative, the licensor may either obtain for the licensee the right to use the technology, modify the technology so that it becomes non-infringing, or permit the licensee to return it to the licensor with an appropriate

---

165. ECKSTROM'S, *supra* note 3, § 39.03[1].
166. NAFTA, art. 1714 - 1718; TRIPs, *supra* note 31, at Part III.

adjustment to the payment stream. The licensor should only agree to defend and indemnify the licensee against such claims if

(i) the licensee promptly notifies the licensor of any such claim;
(ii) the licensor has sole control over the defense and settlement of the claim; and
(iii) the licensee agrees to provide the licensor with all reasonably necessary assistance in defending and settling the claim.

The licensor should not indemnify the licensee against infringement claims arising out of modifications to the technology made by the licensee or use of the technology (*e.g.*, software) with materials (*e.g.*, the licensee's software) not supplied by the licensor. The licensee should insist that the licensor's duty to indemnify the licensee be exempt from the licensor's limitations on liability.

The extent of the licensor's indemnity obligations will vary greatly with the parties' relative size, resources, experience, expertise and other relevant factors. For example, a relatively large and sophisticated software licensor will likely be more willing to defend and indemnify the licensee from potential infringement actions than an unsophisticated patent inventor/licensor.

Both parties will attempt to limit their potential liability to each other under the contract. Often, the licensor will attempt to relate its liability under the contract to the particular breached provision. For example, the parties may negotiate specific remedies for breach of various warranties.[167] Both parties will seek to disclaim liability for lost profits, indirect, incidental, consequential, punitive or other special damages suffered by the other arising out of or related to the agreement. The parties may also set a maximum aggregate liability, such as the total amount to be paid by the licensee under the agreement. However, the parties frequently decide that certain types of claims, particularly tort liability and indemnification for intellectual property right infringement, will be excepted from that cap on liability.

If legal remedies are limited, the license agreement should provide that upon termination of the agreement, the licensee must immediately cease using the technology and pay the licensor a certain sum for each day it continues to use those rights. Particularly in patent licenses, termination of the agreement will be only a last resort, because the sunk costs of typically long development phases tend to be very high. In countries in which legal remedies are difficult to enforce, a licensor may wish to take technical precautions to minimize or prevent unauthorized practices. For example, licensors of customized software should license

---

167. *See also* Sections VI and VII of this Chapter.

object – not source – code, protect the software from unauthorized copying, limit the software's operation to a CPU with a specific serial number, and include a timing or "time out" mechanism that renders the software inoperable after a specific term.[168]

Supranational Regimes

Prior to **NAFTA**, Mexican law did not permit specific performance. Therefore, it was extremely important to provide alternate remedies such as liquidated damages for breaches of specific provisions. NAFTA requires its signatories to ensure that enforcement procedures be available under domestic law so as to permit effective action against infringement of intellectual property rights, including expeditious remedies to prevent infringement.[169] Mexico's customs administration has three years from the date of execution of NAFTA to comply with the requirements for enforcement of intellectual property rights at the border, including, for example, preventing the importation of counterfeit trademark goods.[170]

Country Focus

In the **United States**, the UCC permits the limitation or exclusion of remedies, but the licensor may not exclude all forms of remedy for breach of contract. As a result, many licensors grant the licensee a limited repair remedy. If, however, the licensee's only remedy is repair, the licensor must actually be able to repair the goods and do so in a timely manner.[171] If the licensor fails to perform the only remedy available to the licensee under the contract, the courts of some states will deem any limitation of remedies to have failed as well, and permit the licensee to pursue the general remedies provided by the UCC.[172]

Chinese law provides that damages for breach of contract must equal the loss suffered by the other party as a consequence of the breach. However, those damages must have been foreseeable at the time the contract was signed.[173] Liquidated damages are also permitted, although if they substantially exceed or fall short of the actual loss, the parties may request an arbitration board or court to adjust that

---

168. Greguras, *supra* note 60; Greguras & Lee, *supra* note 48.
169. NAFTA, art. 1714.
170. *Id.*, at Annex 1718.14.
171. Thomas L. Lockhart & Richard J. McKenna, *Software License Agreements in Light of the UCC and the Convention on the International Sale of Goods*, 70 MICH. B.J. 646 (1991).
172. *Id.*
173. Foreign Economic Contract Law of the People's Republic of China, art. 19 [hereinafter FECL].

figure appropriately.[174] Chinese courts also may find that limitations of liability infringe upon the principle of equality and mutual benefit required by Article 3 of the Foreign Economic Contract Law of the People's Republic of China.

The **Japanese** legal system does not provide for the recovery of lost profits, but may grant the plaintiff damages for loss of reputation.[175] In general, Japanese courts are willing to award specific performance.[176] If it finds that intellectual property rights have been abused, a Japanese court may even impose fines and prison terms, and/or cause patent rights to be forfeited.[177]

In the **United Kingdom**, remedies for breach of contract are designed to put the plaintiff in the position it would have been in had the contract not been breached. Exemplary (punitive) damages are not available for breach of contract. Liquidated damages are permitted, but they may not be so great as to be, in effect, a penalty.[178]

In **Israel**, warranties pertaining to personal and property damage arising from a defective product are non-excludable. Israel's Defective Products (Liability) Law 1988, imposes a non-waivable strict liability standard on the manufacturer, importer and seller of a defective product that causes death or personal injury. While injured individuals have recourse against the licensor regardless of any contractual provision to the contrary, the licensor, in turn, can seek indemnification from the Israeli distributor if their contract so provides.[179]

IX. REVENUES

Any license arrangement should be particularly specific as to the payment mechanism whereby the licensee remunerates the licensor. Such mechanisms must pass muster under the applicable laws and regulations of the country from which revenues are remitted to the licensor.

---

174. *Id.* art. 20.
175. Holloway, *supra* note 142, at n.123.
176. Volyn, *supra* note 147.
177. *Id.*
178. CLIFFORD CHANCE, DOING BUSINESS IN THE UNITED KINGDOM § 7.09 (Matthew Bender) (1993).
179. Levenfeld, *supra* note 50, at 12. *See also* Chapter Two, Section II.B.6.

A. Forms of Payment

Several payment methods are available to the licensor in order to realize revenues from the transfer transaction. Technology can be licensed on a perpetual basis in return for one or more lump sum payments. Alternatively, the technology can be licensed for a definite period of time in exchange for an ongoing license fee from the licensee. If the technology is transferred into a JV entity, the JV entity may provide the licensor with dividend-generating equity in return. If the technology is transferred to a strategic ally whose principal function it is to market the technology, the licensor can secure an ongoing income stream requiring the licensee to pay a royalty on the marketed technology and awarding the licensee a percentage of the revenues it derives from marketing the technology, thereby giving the licensee an incentive to maximize technology dissemination. If the licensor is interested in stretching out the payment for its technology over a long period of time for any number of reasons, it can license the technology in return for periodic (quarterly, monthly, yearly) royalty payments. The licensor may be able to link license payments to the various uses to which the technology is put and require higher royalty payments for one type of use than another. Of course, the parties can also agree on any combination of the foregoing.

Country Focus

Although in the past the **Mexican** government limited royalties to specified percentages, the parties are now free to set royalty rates without government interference.[180] A foreign licensor who does not wish to accept payments in pesos should demand that royalty payments be made outside of Mexico in the agreed-upon foreign currency. If the agreement merely states that the payments are to be in that foreign currency, Mexican law permits the licensee to make payment in pesos at the official exchange rate.[181] It is currently unclear what effect the abolition of an official exchange rate for the peso will have on this practise.

According to **China's** Detailed Rules, the price and form of payment for the imported technology must be "appropriate." In order to assist the approving authorities in making this determination, the agreement must break out the prices of individual items.

Royalty and license fees may not be paid by letter of credit in **Korea**. Thus, licensors should demand a large up-front payment followed by

---

180. *Mexico Updates Regulations on Transfer of Technology*, 4 WORLD INTELL. PROP. REP. 31, 32 (1990) [hereinafter *Mexico Updates Regulations*].
181. ECKSTROM'S, *supra* note 3, § 26.02[5].

instalments through an open account. Whenever possible, such instalments should be tied to other deliveries or services for practical leverage.[182] In addition, government policy in Korea sets maximum running royalty rates. Depending on the uniqueness and value of the technology, as well as the licensor's bargaining power, a royalty rate of up to ten per cent may be permissible, although limits in low priority industries may be set much lower.[183]

Entities licensing technology into **Poland** should be aware of the 1990 Law on Counteracting Monopolistic Practices, which prohibits "unjustified profits."

The royalty rate for license agreements with Indian licensees must be approved by the **Indian** government. That royalty rate, however, will only apply up to a maximum "capacity" level, which is likewise set out in the government's approval letter. New government approvals will be required for any units distributed beyond that level. The royalty base will be calculated according to a predetermined formula, and the royalty rate may generally not exceed five per cent and will be subject to Indian taxes. The Indian government will generally not allow either minimum guaranteed royalties or interest on overdue royalty payments.[184]

Royalty rates from Indian parties must also take into account that the Indian government considers whatever royalty is agreed upon to constitute full compensation for use of a patent for the life of the patent, even if the term of the license is shorter.[185] If the parties cannot convince the government to permit sufficiently high royalty rates to take all of these factors into account, the parties may wish to structure the deal to include separate fees for technical services, for example.[186]

One of the factors the **Nigerian** National Office of Industrial Property (NOIP) will take into account in its technical evaluation of the proposed agreement is whether the overall price for the technology is in line with its value to the country. The NOIP will refuse to register agreements "where the price or other valuable consideration therefor is not commensurate with the technology acquired or to be acquired."[187] Royalties from Nigerian parties are generally based on net sales, which is defined to exclude taxes and duties and the landed cost of imported components or raw materials. The latter are excluded in order to

---

182. Greguras & Lee, *supra* note 48.
183. ECKSTROM'S, *supra* note 3, § 32.06[2][a].
184. ECKSTROM'S, *supra* note 3, § 40.16.
185. *Id.*
186. *Id.*
187. *Id.* § 39.04.

encourage the use of local materials and increase the local value added of the final technology.[188]

B. Minimum Performance Requirements

The licensor should require exclusive licensees whose primary function it is to market the technology in their territory, to purchase (or license) or sell (or sublicense) a minimum quota or target number of items. The licensor may reserve the right to terminate the agreement if those targets are not met.[189] In lieu of termination, a failure to meet the quota could result in the licensor reducing the licensee's territory and/or technology range, or changing the license from an exclusive to a non-exclusive one. In the case of patent licenses, the minimum quotas will often not kick in until the second or third year of exploitation, and increase every year thereafter until the annual sales are expected to reach their peak. By contrast, in small markets for a particular technology or in markets in which there are many substantially similar technologies that compete with the transferred technology on the basis of price or functionality, minimum quotas may remain the same or even decline from one year to the next. Experience shows that quotas must be realistic and congruent with market conditions and exigencies. Unreasonably low or unrealistically ambitious quotas are detrimental to both licensor and licensee.

Minimum sales and purchase requirements are likely to generate different results. The minimum *purchase* requirement guarantees the licensor minimum revenues, but does not ensure that a market is developed for the technology in the territory. In the extreme case, the licensee could simply pay the minimum amount without marketing the technology. Thus, the licensor could be "bought out" of the market. A minimum *sales* or *sublicense* requirement, by contrast, does not guarantee specified minimum revenues (because resale prices cannot be controlled) but does ensure market development efforts.

Supranational Regimes

In general, minimum performance provisions in patent and know-how licenses are exempt from the purview of the EU's competition laws. If, however, the parties were competitors prior to entering into the license agreement, and the minimums are so high that they effectively

---

188. *Id.*
189. The failure to meet the quota is often the safest basis on which to terminate a distributor in countries that have agency protection laws. *See* Section XII.

prevent the parties from competing with each other, the Commission may withdraw that protection of the know-how block exemption.[190]

C. Royalty Structure

Licensors will often need to structure the royalty arrangements so as to comply with local laws. For example, in most countries, the licensor may not continue to collect royalties after expiration of the underlying patent. If royalties are to be calculated as a percentage of sales price, the parties should exclude value added and other taxes from that calculation. If royalties are calculated as a fixed sum per unit distributed, the agreement should stipulate how that sum will change if the distributor raises or lowers its price to end-users.

Licensors of patent rights should check individual countries' laws on charging royalties beyond the life of the patent. If necessary, a licensor should restructure the agreement to provide for separate royalty streams on patents and on any accompanying know-how, with the patent royalties terminating at the expiration of the relevant patent, and the royalties on the know-how terminating at the expiration of the agreement. Licensors should also check whether they may continue to change royalties for know-how after it has become publicly known.

Supranational Regimes

The EU's block patent exemption[191] permits royalty payments to be spread out over a period longer than the life of the patent or past the entry of know-how into the public domain in order to facilitate payment by the licensee or if the licensee has the right to terminate the agreement upon reasonable notice. In addition, if the license transfers both patents and know-how, royalties may continue beyond the expiration of the patents for as long as the licensee uses the related know-how. However, the greater the value of the patent in relation to the know-how, the more the royalties should be reduced upon expiration of the patent. The patent group exemption prohibit royalties

(i) on goods which are not entirely or partially produced by means of the licensed technology and
(ii) for the use of know-how which has entered the public domain other than by fault of the licensee.

The EU's know-how block exemption, on the other hand, permits clauses in a license agreement that require the licensee to continue to pay royalties on know-how that has become publicly known other than

---

190. Regulation 556/89, *supra* note 36, art. 7(8).
191. Regulation 2349/84, *supra* note 35.

through the fault of the licensor, and, in addition, provide for damages if the know-how becomes publicly known through the fault of the licensee.[192] Like its patent counterpart, the know-how exemption prohibits royalties

(i) on goods which are not entirely or partially produced by means of the licensed technology, and
(ii) for the use of know-how which has entered the public domain by the action of the licensor.

Country Focus

Japan's competition laws will not permit the licensor to charge royalties on expired patents. On the other hand, royalties on know-how may continue for at least a short time after the know-how is disclosed.[193]

The **Philippine** TTR prohibits clauses which require payments for patents and other industrial property rights after their expiration, termination or invalidation.[194]

D. Records and Audit Right

Royalty-based agreements should require the licensee to keep accurate and complete records of all transactions involving the licensed technology (including, where applicable, the provision of any support and maintenance services to end-users) and permit the licensor to inspect, upon reasonable notice and during normal business hours, the licensee's books and records to verify the calculation and payment of royalties. The licensee may refuse to permit the licensor to conduct the audits, and may instead suggest that the audits be carried out by a mutually agreeable third party, often an accounting firm. In any event, the licensee should be required to provide reasonable assistance to the person conducting the audit. If the audit reveals that the licensee has underpaid royalties, that unpaid amount, plus interest (set at a fixed per cent not exceeding the highest interest rate permitted by law) should become immediately due and payable. In addition, if the underpaid amount exceeds a certain percentage (often five per cent) of the licensee's total royalty payments, the licensee should be required to reimburse the licensor for the audit's costs.

---

192. Regulation 556/89, *supra* note 36, art. 2(1)(7).
193. ECKSTROM'S, *supra* note 3, § 31.02[8].
194. Philippine Rules and Regulations, Rule V., Sec.1(c).

Significantly, the licensee should be required to maintain and make available for inspection all records for several years *after* termination or expiration of the agreement.

X. MAINTENANCE AND TRAINING

Maintenance and training arrangements are frequently complex enough to warrant a separate maintenance and support agreement. Those agreements allocate the maintenance and training obligations for the technology between licensor and licensee and provide for corresponding payment. Licensors should not hesitate to require separate royalties or payments for the technical assistance furnished by the licensor; for, the know-how transferred to the licensee allows the licensee to begin using the technology sooner and more efficiently.

Since licensees in different countries will have different expectations as to how much support and maintenance the licensor will provide, it is important to clarify these obligations in the agreement. In particular, licensees should make sure that they will always have access to maintenance and support services throughout the term of the agreement and provide for contingencies allowing them the requisite access to the technology to take over maintenance and support in the event the licensor goes out of business or otherwise fails to perform its maintenance and support obligations. A software licensee will often require the licensor to place a copy of the software's source code into escrow and grant the licensee a right to access that source code to maintain and support the software upon the occurrence of certain triggering events.

Country Focus

Licensors concerned with their continuing maintenance and support obligations should set out extremely detailed acceptance and verification procedures in all agreements with **Chinese** licensees, because Chinese licensees generally maintain that the foreign licensor has continuing duties to assist the licensee unless limitations on that duty are spelled out in the contract.[195]

---

195. ECKSTROM'S, *supra* note 3, § 27.04[8].

XI. NON-COMPETITION

Whether the technology is licensed to a contractual strategic partner or a JV, the licensor should prevent the licensee from simultaneously marketing or manufacturing competitive technology. This is important not only for business reasons, but also in order to protect the proprietary rights of the licensor. The licensor may also want to prevent the licensee from competing with the licensor after termination of the agreement. However, different jurisdictions limit the scope and enforceability of non-competition provisions. A good non-compete provision should define the activities which are deemed competitive, the products which cannot be marketed and, particularly, the duration and territory to which non-competition applies.

Supranational Regimes

The **EU's** patent and know-how block exemptions prohibit clauses that prevent the licensee from competing with the licensor in research and development, manufacture, use or sales, although the know-how exemption allows the licensor to require the licensee to use its best efforts to exploit the licensed technology and to terminate the exclusivity of a licensee who engages in such competing activities.[196]

In addition, the EU's Council Directive on Self-Employed Commercial Agents[197] permits restraints for a period of up to two years on a commercial agent's business activities following termination of the distribution agreement – but only to the extent that such restraints relate to the geographic area or the group of customers entrusted to the distributor and to the kind of goods covered by the agreement. A commercial agent is defined as a self-employed intermediary who has the continuing authority to negotiate the sale or purchase of goods on behalf of another person (the principal) or to negotiate and conclude the sale or purchase of goods on behalf of and in the name of that principal. This directive does not apply to part-time commercial agents and may not apply to non-exclusive commercial agents in general.

Country Focus

In the **United States**, non-compete agreements are generally subject to a reasonableness test. In order to be considered "reasonable," and thus

---

196. Regulation 2349/84, *supra* note 35, art. 3(3); Regulation 556/89, *supra* note 36, art. 3(9).
197. Council Directive 86/653 of 18 December, 1986 on the Coordination of the Laws of the Member States Relating to Self-employed Commercial Agents, 1986 O.J. (L 382).

enforceable, they must be reasonably limited in time and scope, protect a legitimate interest of the principal, be supported by valid consideration and not contravene public policy. In many states, covenants not to compete entered into in the context of a sale of a business are more liberally enforced than those entered into in an employment context, because courts generally feel that the seller of a business is in a better position to negotiate the terms of such a covenant than an employee.[198] In states that draw this distinction, courts must decide whether covenants entered into in the course of a franchise or distributorship relationship should be analyzed under the standard applicable to the sale of a business or under the traditional standard applied to the employer/employee context. In some states, non-compete covenants in a distribution or franchise agreement will be treated as if they were entered into in the context of the sale of a business, and, therefore, be more liberally enforced than if they were treated as employment covenants.[199] However, good arguments can be made that the bargaining power of a distributor entering into a distribution agreement is more comparable to that of an employee entering into an employment agreement than that of the owner of a business selling that business and its goodwill in an agreement not to compete with the new owner's business. Some states have prohibited non-compete agreements altogether, or at least severely restricted their use.[200] Covenants ancillary to patent licenses, however, are likely to be enforced.[201]

Canada's courts will also review the reasonableness of covenants not to compete, focusing, like their U.S. counterparts, on the duration and geographic scope of the particular covenant.[202]

Under **Japanese** law, an agreement may generally prohibit the distributor from dealing in competing products. However, the contract should explicitly state which products compete with the licensor's.[203] Patent licensing agreements governed by Japanese law should refrain from restricting the licensee's ability to deal in competing goods or use competing technologies upon termination of the agreement, as such restrictions are likely to be regarded as unfair by Japan's FTC.[204]

---

198. KURT H. DECKER, I COVENANTS NOT TO COMPETE § 3.9 (1993).
199. DONALD J. ASPELUND & CLARENCE E. ERIKSEN, EMPLOYEE NONCOMPETITION LAW § 3.06.
200. *Id.* § 3.8.
201. *Id.* § 3.13.
202. Cameron D. Stewart, *Agency and Distribution Agreements in Canada* § 6.2, *in* INTERNATIONAL AGREEMENTS, *supra* note 10.
203. Nelson, *supra* note 44, at 34.
204. ECKSTROM'S, *supra* note 3, § 31.02[4].

Israeli law[205] permits the licensor to impose a reasonable restraint on the distributor's ability to compete with the licensor, provided that the two parties are not both in the business of manufacturing the goods. The latter could be considered a cartel under Israel's Restrictive Trade Practices Law. The reasonableness of the restraint depends on various criteria, including the subject matter of the restraint and the time period and territory for which it is imposed. Similar criteria are used to evaluate restraints that take effect after termination of the agreement.

XII. TERM AND TERMINATION

Although deciding upon the term of the agreement may initially appear uncomplicated, it may prove to be quite vexing. The remaining term of licensed patents; the possibility that licensed know-how will enter the public domain; the impact of local labor laws; the overall evolution of the parties' business relations and performance, as well as the impact of independent dynamics on each party, are only a few of the significant variables that should determine the nature of the termination provisions.

A. Duration and Renewal

Certain patent laws prohibit the licensor from licensing patents beyond the expiration of the patent. Licensors, therefore, must carefully structure such transfers as mixed patent/know-how transfers whose know-how-related royalty, confidentiality and other provisions extend beyond the expiration of their patent-related counterparts.

In jurisdictions where agency protection laws extend or are applied by analogy to licensees (whether as distributors or representatives), the agreement should be limited to a specific short term and avoid automatic or vague renewal language in order to limit the impact of such laws. Cautious licensors will provide that neither party has any hope or expectation that the agreement will be renewed or extended at termination. Upon expiration of the agreement, the parties may simply execute another agreement.

Many developing countries, moreover, have instituted policies designed to promote the rapid absorption of technology and have set maximum terms for technology licenses at five or ten years. Most countries that require the initial registration of a license agreement will

---

205. Levenfeld, *supra* note 50, at 11. *See also* Chapter Two, Section I.1.a.

also require its extension or renewal to be registered. Countries that set time limits on the duration of an agreement will generally not permit renewals.

Supranational Regimes

Many **European** countries have enacted strong labor laws to protect the domestic workforce. In addition, all members of the EU have been required to implement the Council Directive on Self-Employed Commercial Agents.[206] Under this Directive, agreements that continue to be performed after their expiration will be deemed to be converted into agency contracts for an indefinite period, which in turn means that the commercial agent will be due certain minimum notice requirements based on the entire duration of the parties' relationship. The Directive also requires member countries to pass legislation granting commercial agents the right to compensation or an indemnity upon termination of the agency contract, unless the licensor terminates the arrangement for a default by the commercial agent which would justify immediate termination of the agency contract under national law. The commercial agent has one year following termination of the contract to pursue these claims for compensation or indemnity.

In addition, the EU's competition laws require Commission approval of a clause that calls for the automatic extension of a patent license agreement beyond the term of the original patent to cover new, related patents obtained by the licensor. The approval mechanism can be avoided, *i.e.,* there will be an exemption from this application of the competition laws, if each party has the right to terminate the agreement at least annually after the expiration of the original patent. The EU's know-how group exemption prohibits automatic renewals of an agreement for improvements, unless the licensee can refuse to accept the improvements, or either party has the right to terminate the agreement at the end of the initial term and at least every three years thereafter.[207]

Country Focus

Distribution agreements that do not have a definite duration may not be terminated "arbitrarily or abusively" in **Argentina**.[208]

The **Mexican** government no longer strictly limits the duration of license agreements to ten years, and permits licensors to extend

---

206. Council Directive 86/653, *supra* note 197. *See also* Chapter Two, Section I.1.a.
207. Regulation 556/89, *supra* note 36, art. 3(10).
208. Marval & O'Farrell, *supra* note 10, at § 4.3.

agreements beyond ten years if they have made improvements to the technology.[209]

Under **Chinese** law, "the duration of the contract shall conform to the time needed by the recipient to assimilate the technology provided and, unless specially approved by the approving authority, shall not exceed ten years."[210]

In countries in which licensees have a royalty-free right to use any technology which is not subject to registration rights (*e.g.*, patents and trademarks) after the expiration of the agreement, such as **Korea**, it may be in the licensor's interest to provide for a long license term. However, the government of Korea is particularly reluctant to approve license terms of more than ten years.[211] In this situation, the best a foreign licensor can do with respect to trade secrets and know-how is to impose strict confidentiality terms which extend beyond the expiration of the agreement.[212]

Most license agreements in **Taiwan** and the **Philippines** are valid for five years, and any extension of this term is subject to further government approval.[213]

Licensors should also inquire as to any obligations local labor laws may impose. In **Belgium**, for example, even if the parties have agreed on a fixed term for a distribution agreement, the licensor must serve the distributor notice of termination of the agreement more than three but less than six months before its expiration in order for the agreement actually to terminate.[214] If the licensor fails to do so, unless the parties have provided for a specific renewal period, the agreement will be subject to the more onerous laws applicable to agreements of indefinite duration.[215] In **Italy**, on the other hand, labor laws concerning notice provisions for termination apply only to agency agreements, and not to distributorship relationships.[216]

209. *Mexico Updates Regulations*, *supra* note 180, at 32.
210. Technology Import Regulations, *supra* note 87, art. 8.
211. ECKSTROM'S, *supra* note 3, § 32.06[2][b]. Note that Korea's FTC has announced a plan to issue lists of permissible and non-permissible licensing practices, similar to the EU's block exemptions.
212. *Id.* § 32.06[4].
213. Dr. C. Y. Huang, *Technology Transfer to Taiwan Through Foreign Direct Investment and Licensing*, Ann. Conf. on Intell. Prop. 2-20 (Georgetown 1990); ECKSTROM'S, *supra* note 3, § 34.04.
214. J. Leo Goovaerts, *Agency and Distribution Agreements in Belgium*, in INTERNATIONAL AGREEMENTS, *supra* note 10.
215. *Id.*
216. Dr. Carlo Croff & Edoardo Andreoli, *Agency and Distribution Agreements in Italy*, in INTERNATIONAL AGREEMENTS, *supra* note 10. *See also* Chapter Two, Section I.C.1.

The Commercial Code which has been adopted by both the **Czech Republic** and **Slovakia** provides that, unless otherwise agreed by the parties, a license is terminable by either party on one year's notice.[217]

License agreements in **India** may generally extend for only ten years,[218] while the **Nigerian** government will not permit "unreasonable" terms or terms exceeding ten years, whichever is less.[219]

Distribution agreements with **Israeli** distributors should be entered into for a fixed period of time, since courts will require that notice of termination of an agreement with an unlimited term be given a "reasonable" time in advance. A "reasonable" time period is one that enables the distributor "to cover its costs, to arrange for the end of the contract by searching for another business, and to enjoy the fruits of its investment." If the parties enter into an agreement for a fixed period and the licensor terminates the agreement within that period without good cause, the licensor will likely be liable for damages for breach of contract. Distribution agreements should also require the distributor to acknowledge and agree that the term of the agreement (including the period for advance notice of termination) is sufficiently long to permit the distributor to recoup its investment of time, labor and money in developing the market for the distributed products. In addition, the contract should explicitly state that the licensor will not be liable "for any compensation or reimbursement in connection with the establishment, development or maintenance of any market or goodwill created," and that any and all goodwill developed by the distributor in connection with the products will belong exclusively to the licensor.[220]

B. Termination Reasons

Even if the parties intend for the license to be in force for a specified period of time, they often agree on causes for termination before the expiration of the agreement's original term. Most agreements will permit a party to terminate the agreement if the other party breaches a material provision, or materially breaches any provision, in the agreement and fails to cure such breach within a given number of days after receiving notice from the non-breaching party. The inability to achieve performance targets or quotas is a typical criterion for termination, as is the licensee's failure to observe the licensor's

---

217. LEGAL ASPECTS OF INVESTMENT, *supra* note 69, at Chapter 11, § 7.
218. ECKSTROM'S, *supra* note 3, § 40.16.
219. *Id.* § 39.03[1].
220. *See generally* Levenfeld, *supra* note 50, at 9, for a particularly good discussion on this subject.

confidentiality, proprietary rights or license restrictions. Some agreements will be terminated if the licensed technology infringes upon third party intellectual property rights and the licensor cannot obtain the right to continue to use the technology, modify the technology so that it becomes non-infringing or replace the technology with a non-infringing technology. Agreements also typically terminate if either party becomes bankrupt or ceases to operate as a going concern. In addition, licenses of multiple products may terminate with respect to a particular technology if the licensor's rights in that technology are conveyed to another party, for example.

Significantly, a licensor should insist on the right to terminate the agreement in the event it acquires, is acquired by or merges with a third party – even if some form of compensation is required to induce the licensee's consent to such a provision – because the existence of effective non-terminable agreements with licensees in major markets could be a significant obstacle for a potential acquiror or merger partner.

Discretionary termination, or termination at will, may be important to the licensor if the licensee has exclusive rights in a particular territory. In that context, the licensor's commercial success in that territory depends entirely upon the performance and overall business relationship with the one exclusive licensee. The exclusive licensee, by contrast, will resist termination at will by the licensor because, in most cases, an exclusive licensee will be required to devote most or all of its time, efforts and resources to marketing the licensee's technology, thereby leaving the licensee vulnerable in the event of termination. In non-exclusive arrangements, by contrast, termination at will by either party is a sensible option.

Country Focus

Chinese courts may not enforce onerous or unreasonable termination provisions. For example, a provision that permits the licensor to terminate the agreement based on third party infringement over which the licensee had no control may be held to be unreasonable.[221]

Unilateral termination of a **Japanese** distributor requires "just cause," which, even if explicitly defined in the agreement, is subject to review by Japanese courts. The licensor is advised to provide in the agreement for a specific amount of compensation due the distributor regardless of the reason for termination, or to have the distributor waive

---

221. Letter from Robert W.H. Wang & Co. (Dec. 24, 1993) (on file with Shaw, Pittman, Potts & Trowbridge).

its right to damages in case of unilateral termination for the reasons stated in the agreement.[222]

C. Post-Termination Rights and Obligations

The agreement should expressly state that upon termination or expiration of the agreement, the licensor will not owe the licensee any amounts for loss of profit, goodwill, creation of clientele or other like or unlike items, nor for advertising costs, costs of samples or supplies, termination of employees, employees' salaries and other like or unlike items.[223] The agreement should also require the licensee to

(i) return or, at the licensor's option, destroy all copies of all marketing and publicity materials and all confidential information provided to the licensee and
(ii) immediately cease all use of the licensor's trademarks and names.

The licensor should insist that the provisions regarding payment, audit rights, confidentiality, proprietary rights, indemnification, limitations on liability and any other similar provisions survive expiration or termination of the agreement for any reason.

The licensee, in turn, should insist that the indemnity provisions survive termination or expiration of the agreement and that any sublicense agreement in effect at the time of termination of the license agreement will continue in full force and effect until it is terminated in accordance with the terms of that sublicense. Licensee and licensor must decide who will provide maintenance and support for all products that have been distributed by the licensee. If the responsibility for these obligations is shifted to the licensor, the licensor must receive a list of all then-existing sublicensees from the licensee.

Supranational Regimes

The EU's patent block exemption expressly permits clauses that prohibit the licensee from exploiting an unexpired patent after termination of the agreement.[224] A licensor may also prevent the licensee from using licensed know-how after the expiration of the agreement, as long as the know-how is still secret at that time. A post-termination use ban combined with an otherwise permissible grant-back

---

222. Nelson, *supra* note 44, at 35.
223. Nagel & Anderson, *supra* note 52, at 825.
224. Regulation 2349/84, *supra* note 35, art. 2(4).

clause (*i.e.,* one that is non-exclusive and reciprocal) will be blacklisted for the licensee's protection, however, if the licensor's right to use improvements lasts longer than the licensee right to use the licensor's know-how.

Country Focus

Licensors licensing into **Mexico** should be especially careful when spelling out the licensee's rights upon termination of the license agreement, as Mexican law presumes that the licensee acquires the licensed technology at the expiration of the agreement and may then transfer it freely.[225] The parties may, of course, provide otherwise.

China's Regulations require special government approval for prohibitions on the Chinese party's continued use of the technology after expiration of the agreement.[226]

Licensors licensing technology into **Korea** may not prevent the licensee from using any technology that is not the subject of a registered right (such as a patent) after the termination of the license agreement. As a result, the licensor of a trade secret, for example, could enforce confidentiality provisions in the agreement, but could not prevent the licensee from continuing to use the trade secret after those obligations expire.[227] Similarly, other than in exceptional cases, the **Philippine** TTR will not approve clauses which restrict the use of the technology after expiration of the agreement.[228]

XIII. CERTAIN MISCELLANEOUS PROVISIONS

There are various miscellaneous contractual provisions that are particularly relevant to an international transfer of technology. The agreement should, of course, also include other provisions customarily found in international contracts.

---

225. ECKSTROM'S, *supra* note 3, § 26.06[4].
226. Technology Import Regulations, *supra* note 87, art. 9.
227. Chang, *supra* note 21. Note that Korea's FTC has announced a plan to issue lists of permissible and non-permissible licensing practices, similar to the EU's block exemptions.
228. Philippine Rules and Regulations, Rule V., Sec. 1(c).

A. Payment of Fees

Often the licensee's country will require annual fees for upkeep of the patent, trademark or other registrations. The licensor may make the payments itself, or require the licensee to do so and send the licensor proof of such payment at least one month before the deadline for payment expires. The parties should provide for a similar mechanism to register and pay for future registration fees and fulfil all other recurring obligations.

Country Focus

The Commercial Code of the **Czech Republic** and **Slovakia** provides that, unless the parties agree otherwise, the licensor must pay the requisite fees and otherwise maintain the intellectual property rights throughout the term of the license.[229]

B. Relationship of the Parties – Independent Contractor; Labor Laws

For tax, competition, warranty and tort liability reasons, among others, the relationship of the parties in any form of strategic alliance should be that of independent contractors. The agreement should expressly state that neither party is the other's employee, agent or partner or will hold itself out as such. The agreement should also state that neither party has the right to bind the other except as otherwise provided in the agreement and that neither is liable for the debts, torts or contracts of the other.

In countries with strong labor laws, licensors should attempt to avoid the application of such laws by using corporate, rather than individual persons, as licensees.

Country Focus

In **Argentina**, most distributorship contracts are subject to labor laws that make principals or manufacturers jointly and severally liable for their distributor's compliance with labor and social welfare laws. Licensors should demand the right to inspect their Argentine distributor's books and records for compliance with such laws and terminate the agreement in case of the distributor's non-compliance with such laws.[230]

---

229. LEGAL ASPECTS OF INVESTMENT, *supra* note 69, at Chapter 11, § 7.
230. Marval & O'Farrell, *supra* note 10, § 1.5.

C. Export Controls

The agreement should contain an export controls provision according to which the licensee agrees not to export any of the products or technology without first obtaining all requisite licenses.[231] Moreover, in sensitive cases, the licensor may wish to require the foreign licensee to keep records and permit the licensor to inspect those records, so that the licensor can verify compliance with re-export restrictions. When the agreement actually contemplates re-exports by the licensee, the parties may wish to provide that any failure to export the technology resulting from the inability to obtain the necessary government approvals will not constitute a breach of the agreement.

D. Most Favored Nations Clause

Some licensees are able to require the licensor to grant the licensee any and all more favorable terms that the licensor subsequently grants to another licensee. The EU's patent and know-how block exemptions expressly permit such clauses.[232]

---

231. *See* Chapter Two, Section II.B.9.
232. Regulation 2349/84, *supra* note 35, art. 2(1)(10); Regulation 556/89, *supra* note 36, art. 2(1)(10).

Chapter Four

International Tax Aspects of Technology Transfers

D. Kevin Dolan
Weil, Gotshal & Manges, Washington, D.C.

Kevin McMahon
Weil, Gotshal & Manges, New York, N.Y.

Michael F. Walsh
Weil, Gotshal & Manges, Washington, D.C.

Technology transfers have important tax implications. Even companies with large accumulated net operating loss (NOL) deductions must be sensitive to tax issues, since poor tax planning can result in unnecessary tax liabilities in future years. This Chapter summarizes the salient tax implications of international technology transfer transactions. The Chapter focuses on general principles of tax law that are applicable and most relevant in most of the world's major tax jurisdictions, with special emphasis on the United States. While the discussion of proposed structures emanates from a U.S. tax law perspective, the concepts are also applicable, in many instances, to non-U.S. tax jurisdictions.

Much of technology planning centers on deciding which affiliate within a multinational group should derive technology income, that is income arising from the use of technology. In many countries, the affiliate deemed to own the technology for tax purposes is the affiliate that incurs the financial risk related to the development or acquisition of the technology. That affiliate is also entitled to the income derived from that technology. Financial risk can take the form of either bearing the costs of development or making available without adequate compensation property or services related to the development of the technology.[1] The owner, therefore, is not necessarily the affiliate that performs the R&D

---

1. Treas. Reg. § 1.482-1(d)(3)(iii).

that developed the technology but, if different, is the affiliate that incurs the costs of development and, thereby, assumes the financial risk with respect to the development of the technology.

I. TAX DIMENSIONS OF DIFFERENT TRANSFER STRUCTURES

If the technology transferor is a resident of country X, a high tax jurisdiction, and the transferor licenses or transfers technology to a foreign affiliate or gives the foreign affiliate the right to use the technology, the transferee generally must compensate the owner, depending upon the nature of the transfer.

A transfer of technology can take many forms. Using the term "transfer" loosely to encompass all forms of a license, sale, or exchange of an intellectual property right, a transfer of technology can be effected by various types of transactions:[2]

- a license for a lump sum and/or a periodic royalty;
- a sale for lump sum and/or contingent consideration other than stock;
- a cross license for the use of the transferee's technology;
- a transfer for no consideration by way of a capital contribution to a subsidiary or a distribution to a parent corporation; or
- a transfer to a corporation in exchange for stock in the transferee.

The country X tax consequences of those transfer forms may differ dramatically in terms of whether the transferor recognizes no income as a result of the transfer, full gain on the transferred technology at the time of transfer, or periodic royalty amounts over the life of the technology. Many countries restrict certain types of transfers. Some have particular rules, for example, restricting transfers to foreign subsidiary corporations. In many cases, however, transfers can be achieved by a number of alternative means (including a drop down of assets into a subsidiary) that achieve the appropriate end with respect to a desired technology transfer. The remainder of this Section discusses the potential tax consequences of the different technology transfer structures.

---

2. *See generally* Chapter Two.

A. Sale vs. License

The characterization of a transfer of technology under country X tax law may not necessarily follow the treatment of a transfer under that country's commercial law. For example, a license in exchange for a periodic royalty may be considered for country X tax purposes to be either a license (in exchange for royalty payments) or a sale of the technology (in exchange for contingent sale proceeds) depending upon the facts. In addition, in certain circumstances, an assignment for lump sum consideration may be characterized as a license and not a sale.

The difference between a license and a sale is one of the most pervasive distinctions affecting the tax consequences of technology transfers. Although the law that articulates this distinction is quite extensive in certain jurisdictions (including the United States), a license of technology rights in perpetuity or for a period of time at least equal to the useful life of the technology often will be considered a sale, whereas a license for less than the useful life of the technology is more likely to be deemed a license. The distinction does not depend upon whether the consideration received from the transfer is in the form of periodic payments or a lump sum payment.

In the United States, Congress has provided certain statutory safe harbors that characterize particular types of transactions as either licenses or sales. These safe harbors contain extensive definitions and rules for characterizing various transactions. In general, however, a transfer of "all substantial rights" to a patent or an undivided interest in a patent is considered, under the safe harbor, to be a sale or exchange. This treatment results whether or not the payments are to be received in instalments or are contingent on the productivity, use, or disposition of the property transferred.[3] Moreover, certain transfers of trademarks, trade names, and franchise rights will not be treated as a sale or exchange under a safe harbor if the transferor retains any significant

---

3. I.R.C. § 1235(a). For a discussion of the legislative history and purposes of § 1235, see J. Olson, FEDERAL TAXATION OF INTELLECTUAL PROPERTY TRANSFERS, at App. B (1986); and James O. Liles, "*All Substantial Rights" under IRC 1235 and its Application to Patent Transfers Containing "Field of Use" and Geographical Restrictions,* 58 J. PAT. [& TRADEMARK] OFF. SOC'Y 288 (1976). *See also* Stephen P. Jarchow, *Recent Hooker Chemicals Case Examines Patent Sale/License Dichotomy,* 57 TAXES 623 (1979); and M. Susan Stiner, *The Tax Consequences of Transferring Patent Rights in an Invention,* 31 PRAC. LAW. 81 (1985).

power, right or continuing interest in the subject matter of the trademark or trade name.[4]

As in many other countries, the U.S. tax treatment of a license and a sale for either periodic or lump sum consideration differs in certain respects, although various provisions added to the U.S. Internal Revenue Code of 1986, as amended (the "Code") in recent years have reduced the importance of these differences.

- *Ordinary vs. Capital* – Payments received from a license agreement constitute royalty income, which is ordinary income. Payments received from a sale result in capital gain or loss, absent certain provisions of the Code that treat gain or loss from the sale or transfer of technology as ordinary income or loss.[5]
- *Instalment Sale Treatment* – Sales involving deferred consideration (including periodic payments) fall under the instalment sales rules. Unless an election to accelerate tax is made, tax on amounts received subsequent to the year of the sale will be subject to an interest charge.
- *Source Rules*[6] – Royalty income generally is sourced according to the place where the technology is used, whereas income from the sale of the technology generally is sourced according to the residence of the seller. The source rules applicable to royalties generally apply, however, to income from sales if the consideration is contingent upon productivity, use or disposition of the technology.

---

4. I.R.C. § 1253(a). *See generally* Olson, *supra* note 3, at Chapter 8A and Appendix E (containing legislative history of § 1253).
5. *See* I.R.C. §§ 1239, 1245, 1249, and 1253, which provide that certain transfers will result in ordinary income or loss. *Cf.* § 1235, which provides that certain transfers will result in capital gain or loss.
6. Those are rules that determine, for tax purposes, which country is considered to be the source (*i.e.* from which country income arises) of the income in question. Source issues frequently determine, among other matters, which jurisdiction may tax certain income.

- *PHC,[7] FPHC[8] or Sub S Status[9]* – The transferor's status as a personal holding company, foreign personal holding company, or S Corporation, which depends on the amount of royalty income received, may be affected.[10]
- *Subpart F[11]* – Royalties received from related parties on a license of technology are includable in subpart F income (as foreign personal holding company income), unless the royalties are paid and received within the same country. Royalties received from unrelated parties are includable in subpart F income, unless they qualify under a certain exception for royalties paid in connection with an active trade or business. Gain from the sale of technology is included in subpart F income unless:
    (i) it is considered to be inventory property;
    (ii) it is sold in connection with the sale of a trade or business;
    (iii) the technology had previously been licensed for royalties, and the royalties qualified under the active trade or business exception; or
    (iv) it is depreciable or amortizable property (under § 167 or 168) used in a controlled foreign corporation's[12] (CFC) trade or business.

7. For U.S. tax purposes, a "personal holding company" is a corporation that meets both an income and a stock ownership test. The income test requires that at least 60 per cent of the adjusted ordinary gross income be certain types of passive income. The stock ownership test requires that five or fewer individuals own, directly or indirectly, over 50 per cent of the stock by value.
8. For U.S. tax purposes, a "foreign personal holding company" is a foreign corporation that meets both an income and a stock ownership test and that is not excluded from the definition of "foreign personal holding company." Certain tax-exempt organizations and certain foreign branches are excluded from this definition. A foreign corporation meets the income test if at least 60 per cent of its gross income consists of certain types of income including certain dividends, interest and rents.
9. An S Corporation is generally treated as a partnership for U.S. tax purposes, while also maintaining limited liability.
10. I.R.C. §§ 542, 552 and 1361; *Tomerlin Trust v. Commissioner*, 87 T.C. 876 (1986).
11. Subpart F income is the most common form of income that the Code treats as passing through from the foreign corporation that owns it to its U.S. shareholders. Subpart F income generally consists of (1) insurance income, (2) foreign base company income, (3) certain income to the extent that the controlled foreign corporation has an "international boycott factor," (4) certain illegal payments to government officials and (5) certain income from blacklisted countries.
12. A controlled foreign corporation is a foreign corporation which is at least 50 per cent owned (by vote or value) by "United States Shareholders." For these purposes, a "United States Shareholder" is a U.S. person who owns at least ten per cent of the voting power of the foreign corporation.

- *PFIC Status*[13] – Whether a foreign corporation is a passive foreign investment corporation (PFIC) depends on the percentage of its income and assets that are passive. "Passive" income is defined by reference to the subpart F definition of foreign personal holding company income, except that royalties and certain other income received from a related person is not passive income to the extent allocable to income of a related person that is not passive income. Because the characterization of income from the transfer of technology as passive income under subpart F may depend upon whether the transfer is a sale or license, the characterization of a transfer as a sale or license may have PFIC ramifications.
- *Foreign Tax Credit* – The foreign tax credit is subject to separate limitations for foreign taxes relating to specified categories of income including "passive" income. For purposes of the foreign tax credit, passive income is defined generally by reference to the subpart F definition of foreign personal holding company income, subject to various exceptions. Because the characterization of income from the transfer of technology as passive income under subpart F may depend upon whether the transfer is a sale or license, the characterization of a transfer as a sale or license may have foreign tax credit ramifications.
- *The Amount and Timing of Income Recognized* – If the transfer is a sale, income equals receipts in excess of basis; if the transfer is a license, income equals the amount received less any amortization allowed.[14]
- *The Applicability of the Imputed Interest Rules* – Parties to a deferred sale or exchange must usually provide minimum stated interest to avoid imputed interest.

---

13. A foreign corporation is generally a "passive foreign investment corporation" if it meets the requirements of either an income test or an asset test. First, a foreign corporation is considered to be a PFIC if 75 per cent or more of its gross income for a taxable year is "passive income" (generally investment-type income such as dividends and interest, as opposed to "active income" that arises from a company's non-investment activities). Second, a foreign corporation is a PFIC if the average percentage of assets held during the taxable year that produce passive income, or that are held for the production of passive income, is at least 50 per cent.
14. David G. Harris and Karl B. Putnam, *Minimizing the Tax Costs of Foreign Transfers of Patents and Trademarks*, 14 INT'L. TAX J. 231 (1988).

B. Cross Licenses

International cross licenses are fairly common and are generally assumed in most jurisdictions not to have tax consequences, including either withholding tax consequences, recognition of gain or royalty income. In the United States, a grant by a company of a royalty-free license to an affiliate in exchange for a royalty-free license to use technology owned by the affiliate may be characterized in a number of different ways that trigger various tax consequences, and there are indications that the tax regimes of other countries may assume similar characteristics.

In the United States, the transfer may be considered a sale if, for example, the transfer is for the use of technology rights in a specific geographic market in perpetuity or otherwise for the useful life of the technology. On the other hand, it may be considered a license, if it is a non-exclusive license or the cross licenses can be terminated at will by either party.

If the cross license is a sale, then such a transfer would result in recognition of gain subject to the exception discussed below for "like-kind" exchanges. In the case of cross licenses with related parties, the amount of gain recognized may be subject to certain periodic adjustments to reflect the actual value of the technology as demonstrated by the income actually derived from the use of the technology. If it is a license, the U.S. Internal Revenue Service (the IRS) may impute royalty income equal to the value of the license right received. However, it would also be required to grant concurrent deductions for imputed royalties paid to the affiliate with which the company entered into the cross license.

Under certain circumstances, a cross license that otherwise would be treated as a taxable sale may be treated as an exchange of "like-kind" property. Under the Code, gain or loss is generally not recognized on the exchange of like-kind property, unless the exchanged property rights are *not equal in value*. In general, this treatment applies to a transfer of technology that is held for productive use in a trade or business or for investment in exchange for property of "like-kind" that is also held for productive use in a trade or business.[15] Although no gain or loss would be recognized on an exchange of like-kind property if the exchanged properties are equal in value, a cross license may have withholding tax implications as a result of imputed royalties, if withholding tax would be required when actual payments of royalties are made.

---

15. I.R.C. § 1031(a)(1).

The term "like-kind" refers to the nature or character of the rights in the technology exchanged and to the nature of the underlying property to which the technology relates. Thus, the exchange of copyright on software for a copyright on different software is a good "like-kind" exchange, as the technologies are the same and the underlying properties are the same. But, an exchange of a copyright on software for a copyright on a software manual is not a good "like-kind" exchange, as the underlying properties are different.[16] In addition, goodwill or going concern value of a business is not of "like-kind" to the goodwill or going concern value of another business.[17]

C. Contributions to Capital and Transfers for Stock

In many countries, certain transfers of technology as a contribution to capital of a corporation or partnership, certain transfers of technology in exchange for an interest in a corporation or partnership, and certain transfers pursuant to a reorganization potentially qualify as tax-free exchange or "rollover treatment." In the United States, qualification for treatment as a transfer exchange requires that a transfer of technology in exchange for an interest in a partnership or corporation qualify as a "transfer of property" under special rules in the Code.[18] If the transferor that receives stock in a corporation does not

---

16. Treas. Reg. §§ 1.1031(a)-2(c)(3).
17. Treas. Reg. § 1.1031(a)-2(c)(2). Under the proposed regulations, goodwill was treated as "like-kind" in rare and unusual circumstances. However, in issuing the final regulations, it was concluded that the nature and character of goodwill and going concern value are so inherently unique to, and inseparable from, the business that they can never be of like-kind with another business. T.D. 8343 at 167. As one commentator noted, it is not clear if it is the nature and character of goodwill which cannot be of "like-kind" or the nature and character of two businesses which cannot be of "like-kind." Howard J. Levine and Allen J. Littman, *The Final Regulations on Exchanges of Personal Property, Multiple-Asset Exchanges and Deferred Exchanges Under Section 1031*, 19 J. REAL ESTATE TAX'N 91, 94 (1992).
18. *See* § 721 in the case of a transfer to a foreign partnership and § 351 in the case of a transfer to a foreign corporation. Under § 367(c)(2), a contribution to capital to a controlled foreign corporation generally is considered to be in exchange for stock in the transferee foreign corporation. It is not clear, however, that the transferor would be considered to receive stock equal in value to the intangible rights contributed to the foreign corporation if the transfer were not considered to be a "transfer of property" for § 351 purposes. If so, then the transferor would have an imputed advance royalty equal to the value of the right received and not merely an annual royalty imputation under § 482.

qualify for tax-free treatment, then the value of the stock received will be considered to be an advance royalty to the extent not attributable to other property or services transferred or rendered to the corporation. Certain rules, however, essentially preclude the tax-free transfer of technology by a U.S. corporation to a foreign corporation. In such case, an annual "royalty" is imputed in the transferor's U.S. income in perpetuity, and the imputed amount may be periodically adjusted in subsequent years to reflect the actual value of the technology as demonstrated by the income actually derived from the use of the technology.[19]

D. Distributions

A country X subsidiary, in many cases, may also transfer technology across borders by making a distribution of the technology rights (*i.e.* a transfer of property from subsidiary to parent based on stock ownership) to its foreign parent. Gain on the distributed technology generally would be recognized, possibly subject, in the case of a U.S. distributing subsidiary, to potential periodic adjustments to reflect the technology's actual value over time. In the case of a U.S. subsidiary, this would be the result even if the distribution occurs pursuant to a complete liquidation of the U.S. subsidiary, since the non-recognition treatment normally accorded in the context of subsidiary liquidations is not permitted in the liquidation of a U.S. subsidiary into a foreign parent corporation.

---

19. Section 367(d) requires that the intangible be treated as having been sold in exchange for payments that are contingent upon the productivity, use, or disposition of the intangible. In addition, the imputation is treated as U.S. source income for foreign tax credit purposes – an essentially penal result. The regulations contain exceptions for goodwill and going concern value relating to the active conduct of a trade or business to be conducted outside the United States. Treas. Reg. § 1.367(d)-1T(b). In addition, in *lieu* of including an annual imputation, the § 367(d) regulations permit the U.S. transferor to recognize gain in the case of: (1) the transfer of certain operating intangibles relating to the active conduct of a trade or business outside the United States (presumably subject to periodic adjustments under the commensurate-with-income standard); intangible transfers that are mandated by certain foreign law requirements; and transfers of intangibles to certain foreign corporations that are joint ventures with unrelated parties. Treas. Reg. §§ 1.367(d)-1T(g)(2)(i), (ii) and (iii), respectively.

II. TAX IMPLICATIONS FOR DIFFERENT TECHNOLOGY OWNERSHIP AND DEVELOPMENT STRUCTURES

The above discussion illustrates that technology owned by a country X corporation may not be transferable to a foreign affiliate without the country X corporation being taxed on gain or a royalty-equivalent amount of income from the technology. The only way to avoid country X tax on technology income, therefore, may be to avoid country X ownership of the technology in the first instance – *i.e.* by relying on alternative arrangements for the development and acquisition of technology whereby foreign affiliates incur the cost and risk of development or acquisition.

Four basic arrangements are available for structuring the development, ownership, and exploitation of technology from a tax perspective:

(1) *ad hoc* arrangements;
(2) a centralized contract research arrangement;
(3) a cost sharing arrangement; and
(4) a joint venture (JV).

Ad hoc arrangements are agreements whereby multiple affiliates develop and own their technology and then permit the use of developed technology by other members of the group pursuant to a license or otherwise. Such arrangements should generally be avoided as they involve uncertainties and may result in a deemed sale, contribution, or distribution of technology, all of which would result in the recognition of gain, subject to possible exceptions if there is a *bona fide* cross license of technology of equivalent value that may not rise to the level of an exchange (*e.g.,* either party can terminate the cross license at will) or may qualify as a tax deferred, "like-kind" exchange. In any event, the *ad hoc* approach may be undesirable from a managerial perspective in the context of a multinational group that wishes to centralize the management of technology research and development. Moreover, U.S. tax advisers frequently review foreign-based structures and uncover that no provision has been made for the U.S. tax consequences of *ad hoc* arrangements. Foreign tax authorities frequently ignore the tax implications of cross licenses; consequently, so do many foreign tax advisers.

"Contract research and licensing" arrangements refer to a fairly common arrangement in which one affiliate funds the cost of all R&D performed by other affiliates and owns all interests in the resulting technology. If the developed technology is to be used by other affiliates, they are licensed for fair market royalties or sold for fair market consideration. Assume, for example, that a foreign affiliate reimburses a country X affiliate for all of the expenses incurred by the country X affiliate in developing technology (plus a service fee). Because the foreign affiliate incurs all of the risk of development of that technology, it will own 100 per cent of the rights to the technology and will charge a royalty or other consideration to any user. Thus, there is no sharing of costs or risks.

Cost sharing is a contractual arrangement in which each participant bears a specified percentage of the costs of developing technology and, in return, receives an ownership interest in the technology that results from the development efforts financed under the arrangement. The cost sharing contract specifies the scope of the research, the contributions and percentage of costs to be borne by each participant, and the ownership rights to be received by each participant. Foreign tax authorities frequently sanction cost sharing arrangements, although they rarely have formal requirements for them. The **Netherlands, Norway, Switzerland, Germany** and the **United Kingdom**, for example, all sanction cost sharing arrangements.

A cost sharing arrangement is obviously very different from research and license arrangements in which one party owns all of the rights in the technology and licenses (or sells) rights in the technology to other parties in exchange for a royalty (or purchase price consideration). In contrast, by incurring up-front development costs and sharing the risk of development, each participant in a cost sharing arrangement owns an identified interest in the technology and can exploit that interest without paying royalties once the technology is developed. Because no royalties are paid, cost sharing avoids transfer pricing issues as to whether royalty rates are adequate. On the other hand, the participants to a cost sharing agreement buy into a host of issues regarding the validity of the arrangement and the amount of costs required to be incurred by each participant. Significantly, however, notwithstanding the view of some that cost sharing is a panacea for avoiding transfer pricing issues, the reality is that cost sharing arrangements merely produce a trade-off of one set of transfer pricing issues for another.[20]

---

20. There are various kinds of license or sale arrangements that involve a limited sharing of development costs but are not cost sharing arrangements. Assume, for example, that a party A pays to a party B a fixed amount, or series of fixed amounts at various stages of development of an intangible ("benchmark payments"), which gives party A the right to use the intangible, if and when development is successful, in exchange for periodic royalties equal to a specified

Because a cost sharing arrangement avoids the need to pay royalties, it avoids withholding taxes that may be imposed on royalties paid under a research and license arrangement. The avoidance of withholding tax, however, does not necessarily mean that a cost sharing arrangement is more beneficial than a research and licensing arrangement. As pointed out above, a research and licensing arrangement may be preferable, for example, if the 30 per cent statutory withholding rate has been reduced by treaty or if technology income can be captured through product sales.

JV arrangements involve joint development, ownership, and *exploitation* by two or more parties. The JV entity generally owns the technology developed under such an arrangement. In the United States, JV arrangements are generally governed by the partnership provisions in the Code.[21] The partners in the JV can claim tax deductions for R&D and other costs (and R&D tax credits if available) generally to the extent those costs are borne by the partners subject to any applicable limitations.

The primary difference between a JV and a cost sharing arrangement is that the JV partners share the costs and profits of production and perhaps marketing – *i.e.*, of income producing activities – whereas the participants in a cost sharing arrangement share only the costs of development and do not share the costs and profits of production or marketing. Furthermore, a JV may be initiated either before or after the development of the technology. Thus, while the costs of development are shared in a cost sharing arrangement, the costs of development may or may not be shared in a JV.

Within the context of a multinational group, partnerships generally are inefficient vehicles for developing and exploiting technology in

cont.
>percentage of net sales. The arrangement is not a cost sharing arrangement but, instead, is either a license or sale arrangement that gives party A the right to use the intangible developed by party B in exchange for payments required under the agreement. The fixed payments during development are in the nature of "option" payments that involve a limited sharing of risk and give the payer the right to use or acquire the resulting intangible at an advantageous royalty rate or contingent purchase price. In determining the amount of the royalty or contingent purchase price that must later be paid by party A to party B where they are related parties, the IRS should take into account that party A made the "option" payments and, thereby, assumed a limited amount of risk, such that the royalty or contingent purchase price can be legitimately reduced to reflect the financial risk undertaken by party A.

21. Among other things, contributions of pre-existing intangibles to the partnership are governed by § 721 and other applicable partnership provisions, including § 1491 in the case of a transfer by a U.S. person to a foreign partnership, and not by whatever "buy-in" rules ultimately will apply to cost sharing arrangements.

multiple jurisdictions. It usually is not efficient, for example, for a U.S. and foreign affiliate to share the profits of exploiting technology in the United States and in foreign markets. In that event, the foreign affiliate would have U.S. trade or business income taxable in the United States or U.S. source dividends subject to U.S. tax, and the U.S. affiliate would have business profits in foreign jurisdictions potentially subject to tax in those jurisdictions or foreign source dividends subject to foreign tax. By contrast, it is generally more efficient for the U.S. affiliate to exploit the U.S. rights to the technology and for foreign affiliates to exploit foreign rights to the technology, regardless of whether the technology rights are owned by the party exploiting the technology or by another party to whom a royalty or other consideration must be paid.

The remainder of this Section describes in detail centralized research and cost sharing contracts and discusses the relative merits of each. Appendices A-1 and A-2 compare research and cost sharing contracts in the context of U.S. or foreign multinational groups.

A. Arrangements Within Foreign Multinational Groups

As noted above, *ad hoc* arrangements should be avoided except in limited circumstances and, in any event, are often not effective from a managerial perspective. In addition, JVs are generally unattractive for multinational groups. Consequently, a multinational group's alternatives in many, if not most, circumstances will be limited to research and licensing contracts or cost sharing arrangements.

1. Research and Licensing Contracts Within a Foreign Multinational Group

In general, a research and licensing arrangement makes more sense than a cost sharing arrangement for most foreign multinational groups. This generalization may not be true, however, in particular circumstances in which, for example, a foreign affiliate holding technology rights is subject to high foreign tax rates.

Consider the example of a publicly traded non-U.S. parent corporation (non-U.S. parent) that is resident in a low tax third country or, alternatively, owns a subsidiary (third country subsidiary) that is resident in a low tax country.[22] The non-U.S. parent (or the third country subsidiary) forms U.S. and foreign operating subsidiaries to conduct manufacturing and sales operations in relevant markets. The non-U.S. parent (or the third country subsidiary) finances R&D performed by a U.S. affiliate.

Because the non-U.S. parent or the third country subsidiary has financed all R&D performed by the U.S. operating subsidiaries, that entity would own the resulting technology. The U.S. operating subsidiaries do not receive R&D deductions because the cost of the R&D is borne by the non-U.S. parent or third country subsidiary. The benefit of forgoing the R&D deductions in the United States, however, is that future technology income will not be taxed in the United States, because the technology income will be paid to the non-U.S. parent or the third country subsidiary in the form of deductible royalties or sale price for the product.

In general, royalties paid for the use in the United States of technology are subject to 30 per cent U.S. withholding tax absent relief under a U.S. income tax treaty.[23] Any U.S. withholding tax would partially negate the deduction for royalties paid by U.S. affiliates and result in U.S. taxation of at least U.S. source technology income.

Most U.S. income tax treaties, however, contain specific royalty articles under which royalties are either exempt or are subject to reduced U.S. withholding tax. The non-U.S. parent or third country subsidiary may not qualify for a reduction or exemption from U.S. withholding tax under a U.S. income tax treaty, however, either because there is no income tax treaty between the United States and its country of residence or because the non-U.S. parent or third country subsidiary may not be considered a qualified resident under the "Limitations on Benefits"[24] article contained in the more recent U.S. tax treaties. The "Limitations on Benefits" article is intended to preclude the use of U.S. tax treaties by treaty country corporations that are predominantly owned by non-treaty country residents.

---

22. It will be assumed that, if the non-U.S. parent is resident in a high tax country, it can operate in low tax country through a third country subsidiary without all income of the third country subsidiary being currently taxed to the non-U.S. parent under non-U.S. anti-deferral rules (*e.g.,* U.S. Subpart F, **Canadian** FAPI, or **U.K.** CFC-type rules) in the country of residence of the non-U.S. parent.
23. I.R.C. § 1442(a).
24. The "Limitations on Benefits" articles contained in recent tax treaties are generally designed to prevent treaty shopping. These articles typically restrict certain entities that are owned by non-treaty country residents from qualifying for treaty benefits.

INTERNATIONAL TAX ASPECTS 233

Figure 4.1A

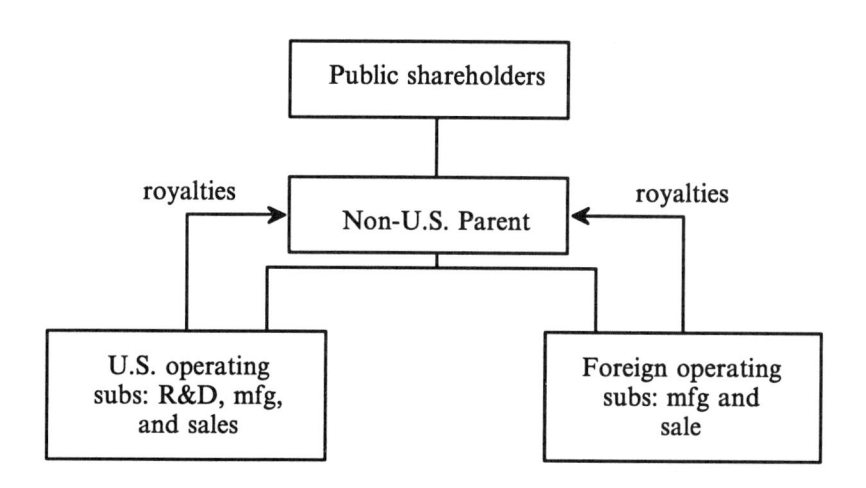

```
              ┌─────────────────────┐
              │ Public shareholders │
              └──────────┬──────────┘
                         │
   royalties   ┌─────────┴─────────┐   royalties
   ────────►   │  Non-U.S. Parent  │   ◄────────
              └─────────┬─────────┘
                  ┌─────┴─────┐
    ┌─────────────┴───┐   ┌───┴──────────────┐
    │ U.S. operating  │   │ Foreign operating│
    │ subs: R&D, mfg, │   │  subs: mfg and   │
    │   and sales     │   │      sale        │
    └─────────────────┘   └──────────────────┘
```

Figure 4.1B

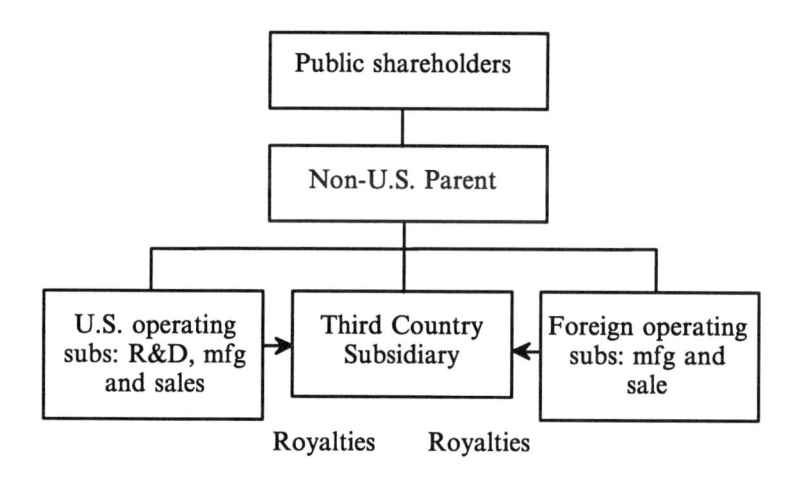

```
              ┌─────────────────────┐
              │ Public shareholders │
              └──────────┬──────────┘
              ┌──────────┴──────────┐
              │   Non-U.S. Parent   │
              └──────────┬──────────┘
     ┌───────────────────┼───────────────────┐
┌────┴─────────┐  ┌──────┴──────┐  ┌─────────┴────────┐
│U.S. operating│  │Third Country│  │Foreign operating │
│subs: R&D, mfg│─►│ Subsidiary  │◄─│  subs: mfg and   │
│  and sales   │  │             │  │      sale        │
└──────────────┘  └─────────────┘  └──────────────────┘
                Royalties    Royalties
```

If the non-U.S. parent or the third country subsidiary does not directly qualify for a treaty exemption from U.S. withholding tax on royalties, it is difficult to avoid the U.S. withholding tax without incurring substantial foreign tax cost by structuring royalty payments through a treaty country corporation – *e.g.,* by licensing technology through a **Netherlands** or **Swiss** licensing company that claims exemption from U.S. withholding tax under the United States-**Netherlands** or **Swiss** income tax treaty for the royalties received by the licensing company.

In certain circumstances, the only viable alternative for avoiding U.S. withholding tax, which may present a host of operational problems, may be to have the products for U.S. markets manufactured outside the United States by the non-U.S. parent or other foreign affiliate. In that event, the income derived from the use of technology is incorporated into the price received on the sale of the manufactured product to the U.S. operating subsidiaries. Assuming that the manufacturing affiliate has been careful, it will not have a U.S. trade or business, and the sale proceeds received by it on the sale of products to U.S. affiliates will not be subject to U.S. tax regardless of whether a U.S. tax treaty is applicable.

2. Cost Sharing Arrangements Within a Non-U.S. Multinational Group

Although the generalization made above that research and licensing arrangements are usually preferable in structuring the use of technology in non-U.S. multinational groups, in some circumstances it may be preferable to rely on cost sharing arrangements for the ownership and use of technology. Such would be the case, for example, if the non-U.S. affiliate that would own technology rights is subject to high rates of tax. In such circumstances it would not make sense, in the long run, to pay large amounts of royalties out of the United States into the non-U.S. affiliate's home country under a license arrangement.

The arrangement could be structured as follows:

Figure 4.2

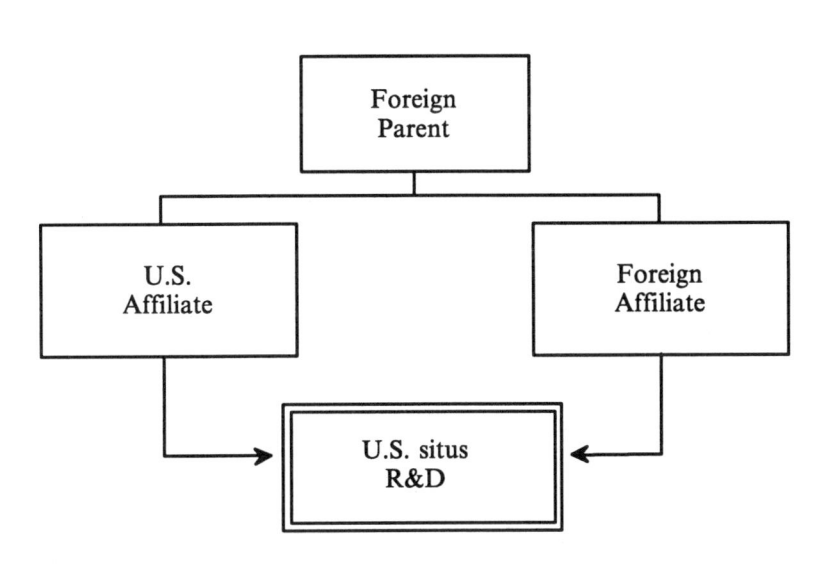

```
                    ┌──────────────┐
                    │   Foreign    │
                    │   Parent     │
                    └──────┬───────┘
            ┌──────────────┴──────────────┐
    ┌───────┴────────┐            ┌───────┴────────┐
    │     U.S.       │            │    Foreign     │
    │   Affiliate    │            │   Affiliate    │
    └───────┬────────┘            └───────┬────────┘
            │         ┌──────────────┐    │
            └────────▶│  U.S. situs  │◀───┘
                      │     R&D      │
                      └──────────────┘
```

A U.S. affiliate and a non-U.S. affiliate (*e.g.*, the non-U.S. parent) enter into a cost sharing arrangement. Under the arrangement, the non-U.S. affiliate will incur only a portion of the development costs and own only a portion of the resulting technology (*e.g.*, the non-U.S. rights), and the U.S. affiliate also will incur a portion of the development costs and own a portion of the resulting technology (*e.g.*, the U.S. rights).

Because the U.S. and the non-U.S. affiliate each owns the technology rights that it will exploit, neither will pay royalties to the other or to any other affiliate. Consequently, technology income relating to products sold in U.S. markets will be subject to U.S. tax, and technology income relating to products sold in non-U.S. markets will not be subject to U.S. tax.

Short-term considerations – particularly cash flow needs – may also dictate the use of a cost sharing arrangement, even though long-run considerations might favor the use of a research and licensing arrangement. For example, if a U.S. affiliate does not have net operating losses or loss carryforwards, the non-U.S. multinational may opt for having the U.S. affiliate claim a current deduction for a cost sharing payment in order to avoid having to provide additional funding to pay the additional U.S. tax that would occur if the U.S. affiliate were to forgo the current deductions for R&D expenses that are available under a cost sharing arrangement but are not available under a contract research and licensing arrangement.

B. Arrangements Within a U.S. Multinational Group

As in the case of a non-U.S. multinational group, the alternatives for structuring the ownership, development, or use of technology in U.S. multinational groups are generally limited to research and licensing contracts and cost sharing arrangements.

1. Contract Research Arrangements Within a U.S. Multinational Group

A U.S. multinational group has two options for structuring a research and licensing contract:

(1) *U.S. Ownership* – A U.S. affiliate can finance all of the R&D costs and own all of the resulting technology.
(2) *Foreign Ownership* – A foreign affiliate can finance all of the R&D costs and own all of the resulting technology.

Assuming that the foreign manufacturing affiliate is subject to a low foreign effective tax rate, such that it potentially would be beneficial for the foreign affiliate to earn income, the issue then becomes whether U.S. or foreign ownership is more beneficial.

a. Foreign Ownership

Under the foreign ownership alternative, a foreign affiliate would own the technology rights. If, in such circumstances, the foreign affiliate does not itself exploit the technology rights by manufacturing products, then it would generally exploit the technology rights that it owns by licensing the rights to other (U.S. or foreign) affiliates or to unrelated parties and derive technology income in the form of royalties.

Given that, under the subpart F rules, royalty income received by a foreign affiliate from a related party generally will be taxed to the U.S. parent of the foreign affiliate, the U.S. affiliate would receive no benefit for forgoing deductions for the development costs that are borne by the foreign affiliate, because the U.S. group would be required to include in income the net royalty income derived by the foreign affiliate. The arrangement would have a current cost in the form of lost deductions without an offsetting U.S. tax benefit.

INTERNATIONAL TAX ASPECTS 237

Figure 4.3A

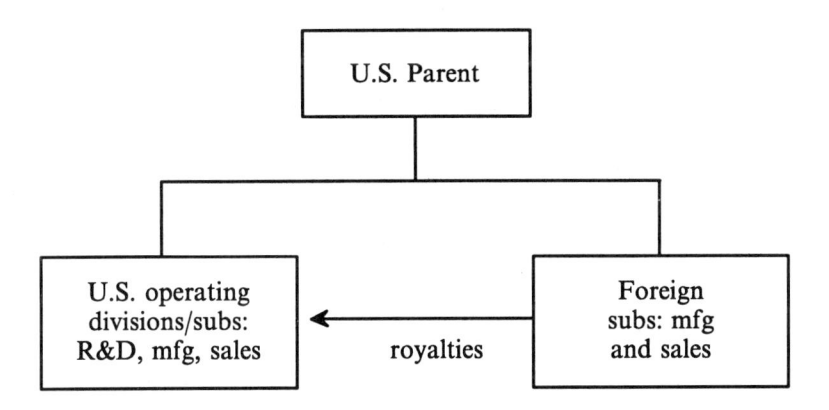

```
                    ┌─────────────┐
                    │ U.S. Parent │
                    └──────┬──────┘
                  ┌────────┴────────┐
    ┌─────────────────┐        ┌─────────────┐
    │ U.S. operating  │◄───────│  Foreign    │
    │ divisions/subs: │royalties│ subs: mfg  │
    │ R&D, mfg, sales │        │  and sales  │
    └─────────────────┘        └─────────────┘
```

Figure 4.3B

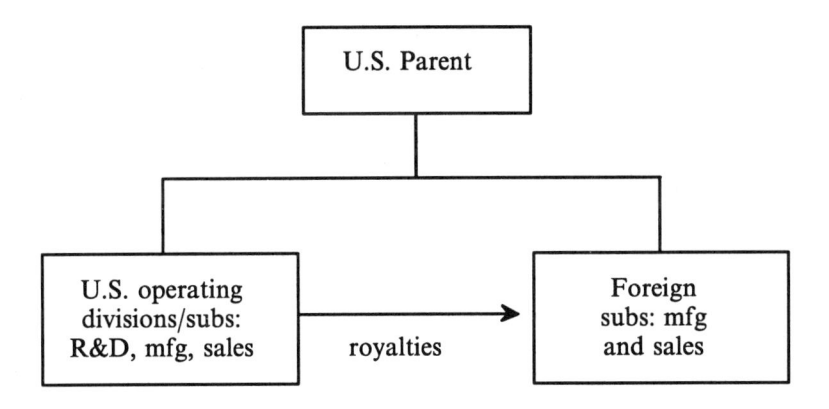

```
                    ┌─────────────┐
                    │ U.S. Parent │
                    └──────┬──────┘
                  ┌────────┴────────┐
    ┌─────────────────┐        ┌─────────────┐
    │ U.S. operating  │───────►│  Foreign    │
    │ divisions/subs: │royalties│ subs: mfg  │
    │ R&D, mfg, sales │        │  and sales  │
    └─────────────────┘        └─────────────┘
```

In general, the deferral benefit of foreign ownership is not available unless the foreign affiliate uses technology in the manufacture of products – including, in the context of foreign ownership of worldwide rights, products for the U.S. market as well as for foreign markets. In these circumstances, the foreign affiliate will capture technology income related to the technology that it owns in the form of sales income derived by a manufacturer, which will not be included in subpart F income. If a foreign affiliate manufactures products offshore for both domestic and foreign markets, then the foreign ownership alternative will permit the deferral of technology income from products sold in both U.S. and foreign markets (at a cost of the U.S. affiliates forgoing a U.S. tax deduction for all R&D costs).

b. U.S. Ownership

If the foreign manufacturing affiliates are located in moderate tax or high tax jurisdictions, it is unlikely that the U.S. multinational group would consider the foreign ownership alternative to be attractive. In the long run, a U.S. multinational group generally is better off reducing its foreign effective tax rate because of the limitations placed on its use of foreign tax credits. The U.S. ownership alternative, under which a U.S. affiliate incurs all R&D costs and owns all technology rights, should reduce the U.S. multinational group's foreign effective tax rate more than other alternatives over the long run, because the royalties received by the U.S. group in licensing those rights to foreign affiliates should be greater (even on a present value basis) than the R&D deductions to which the foreign affiliate would be entitled under foreign law under other alternatives.[25] A moderate or high foreign effective rate would weigh in favor of foreign ownership of technology (or a cost sharing arrangement) only if short-term considerations (*i.e.* obtaining current deductions for R&D in the foreign country) are paramount.

25. In addition, the royalty income received by the U.S. group under a licensing arrangement generally would be foreign source income, whereas the increased income to the U.S. group resulting from reduced R&D deductions under a cost sharing arrangement may only be partially foreign source income. This is because the R&D deductions lost under a cost sharing arrangement would be only partially apportioned by the U.S. affiliate to foreign source income, notwithstanding special rules under which a portion of the expenses for R&D performed in the United States may be apportioned exclusively against U.S. source income. Treas. Reg. § 1.861-8(e)(3)(ii); but *see* Rev. Proc. 92-56, 1992-2 C.B. 409 (July 13, 1992), which provides a temporary alternative method to the regulations pending the Service's conduct of a review of its regulations. In contrast, if the U.S. affiliate incurs all development costs and later licenses the resulting intangible to the foreign affiliate, the U.S. affiliate's future royalty income will be foreign source income in its entirety.

2. Cost Sharing Arrangements Within a U.S. Multinational Group

A U.S. affiliate may enter into a cost sharing arrangement with one or more foreign affiliates whereby each affiliate bears a portion of the development costs and the U.S. affiliate owns the U.S. rights to the resulting technology and the foreign affiliates own the foreign rights.

Figure 4.4

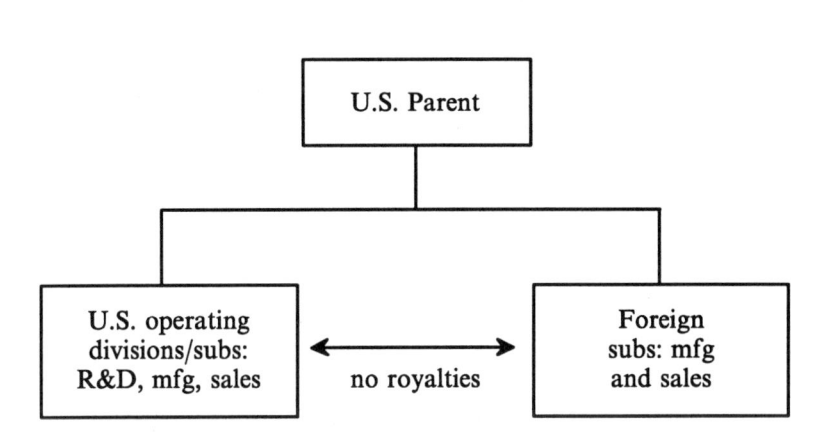

```
                    ┌─────────────┐
                    │ U.S. Parent │
                    └──────┬──────┘
              ┌────────────┴────────────┐
    ┌─────────┴─────────┐      ┌────────┴────────┐
    │ U.S. operating    │      │ Foreign         │
    │ divisions/subs:   │◄────►│ subs: mfg       │
    │ R&D, mfg, sales   │      │ and sales       │
    └───────────────────┘ no royalties └─────────┘
```

If the foreign affiliate does not itself exploit the technology rights by manufacturing products, then it generally would exploit the technology rights it owns by licensing the technology rights to other (U.S. or foreign) affiliates or to unrelated parties and derive technology income in the form of royalties. Because related party royalties and possibly unrelated party royalties may be includable in the U.S. group's income under subpart F, the arrangement would involve a current cost in the form of lost deductions (smaller R&D deductions for the U.S. group) without necessarily an offsetting U.S. tax benefit (royalty income currently taxable under subpart F).

The deferral benefit of cost sharing thus generally is not available unless the foreign affiliate uses technology in the manufacture of products for foreign markets. In such a case, the foreign affiliate will capture technology income related to the technology in the form of sales income derived by a manufacturer, which will not be included in subpart F income.

If, therefore, a foreign affiliate manufactures products offshore for foreign markets, then a cost sharing arrangement under which the foreign affiliate incurs a portion of R&D costs and owns the foreign rights to the resulting technology will permit the deferral of technology income from products sold in foreign markets (at the cost of the U.S. affiliate forgoing a U.S. tax deduction for the portion of the R&D costs incurred by the foreign affiliate). If the foreign manufacturing affiliate is located in a moderate tax or high tax jurisdiction, it is unlikely that a U.S. multinational group would consider a cost sharing alternative to be beneficial. Alternatively, if the foreign manufacturing affiliate is located in a low tax jurisdiction, then cost sharing may be beneficial. Whether foreign ownership of foreign rights through a cost sharing arrangement or foreign ownership of worldwide rights through a contract research arrangement is preferable is, however, a complex issue that requires careful consideration.

III. SPECIAL ISSUES IN JOINT VENTURES WITH A UNITED STATES PARTY

Outside the context of multinational groups, JVs are often useful for structuring the ownership, development, and use of technology among unrelated parties. Among the issues that arise are whether the JV entity should be a partnership or a corporation and whether it should be a home country or foreign entity. Those issues turn, in large part, on the need to structure the contribution of technology by one or both parties to the JV in a tax-efficient manner. In most cases, such technology is licensed for no royalties as the technology owner's contribution to the JV.

Special considerations that generally are peculiar to U.S. law arise in the context of technology transfers to a JV. These issues often have to be understood by the non-U.S. partner to the JV, because they frequently will cause the U.S. party to require that the JV be structured in ways that affect the legal structure or the economics of the JV. For tax purposes, the license of technology to the JV may be structured as either a contribution to the capital of the JV or as a sale or license to the JV. These options are explored below on the alternative assumptions that the JV either is (1) a foreign corporation or (2) a domestic or foreign partnership.

A. Contribution of Technology

Perhaps the most obvious way to structure a JV results in considerable disadvantageous tax consequences. Consider the case in which the JV is structured as a foreign corporation (FC) to which the U.S. partner (USP) contributes technology in exchange for stock of the foreign corporation and the foreign partner (FP) contributes cash and other property.

Figure 4.5

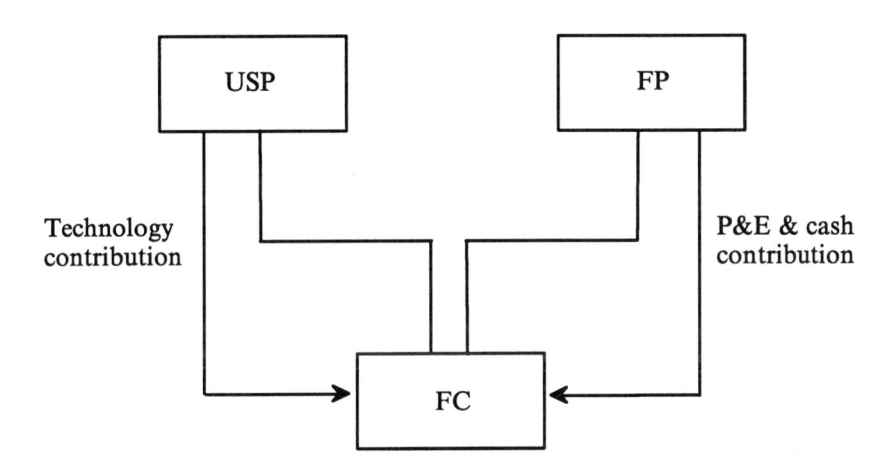

In such a case, except in certain circumstances, the U.S. partner must include annually in income an imputed royalty amount for the use by the foreign corporation of the technology.[26] Moreover, the imputed royalty amount is treated as U.S. source income, which precludes USP from offsetting the U.S. tax on the imputed royalty amount with foreign tax credits – including those incurred by the JV. Some of the alternatives to this basic structure that seek to avoid the consequences of a U.S. source imputed royalty amount while preserving the 50:50 business deal (and avoiding up-front recognition of income) are discussed below. Foreign tax authorities rarely impose exit taxes, such as imputed

---

26. I.R.C. § 367(d).

royalties, on these transactions. **Canada** is an exception. Rollover (*i.e.*, nonrecognition) treatment is more common.

B. Sale or License of Technology

One way to avoid a contribution of technology that would be subject to an imputed royalty is for the USP to sell or license the technology rights to the FC for a fair market value royalty or sale price:

Figure 4.6

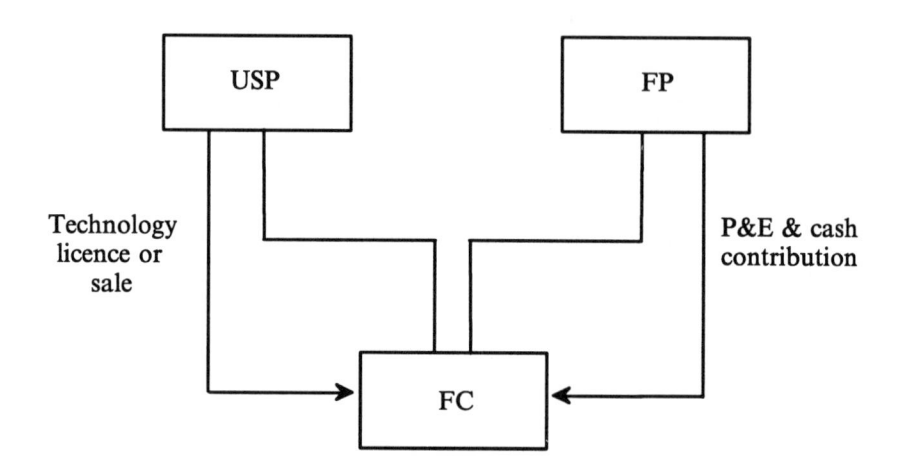

```
        USP                         FP
         |                           |
Technology                      P&E & cash
licence or                      contribution
  sale    |                      |
         └──────→  FC  ←─────────┘
```

Because a royalty "off the top" changes the commercial arrangement of a 50:50 profit split, the parties would attempt to make the FP whole as a result of any royalty or sale price paid to the USP. One such alternative could involve the FC issuing debt or preferred stock to the FP. The payments on that debt would approximate the value of the royalties paid from the FC to the USP. Attempts such as this to make the FP whole, however, may not achieve the desired commercial results of equalizing the returns to the two partners or, if they do so, may create tax risks that are better avoided.

C. Domestic or Foreign Partnership

Consider the case in which the JV entity is, alternatively, a domestic partnership (DPS) or a foreign partnership (FPS) and that USP contributes technology to the JV entity:

Figure 4.7

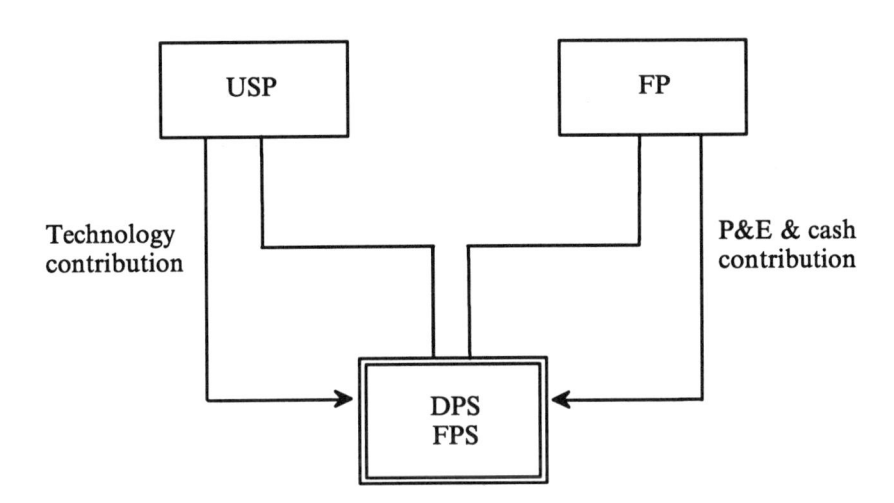

If the JV entity is a domestic partnership, then no income is recognized on the receipt by the USP of its interest in a DPS provided that the contribution satisfies certain requirements.[27]

If, on the other hand, the JV entity is a foreign partnership then contributions by the USP to an FPS are subject to either an excise tax[28] or an income tax on the gain on all contributed property. The excise tax can be avoided if the USP licenses technology to an FPS for a royalty instead of contributing the technology in exchange for stock. Such a structure would, however, raise the difficult issues discussed above associated with attempting to compensate the FPS to balance out the royalties paid to the USP.

In general, partnerships are potentially more beneficial than corporations because they permit more flexibility in structuring special

---

27. *See* I.R.C. § 721.
28. I.R.C. § 1491.

allocations. In addition, use of a partnership instead of a corporation probably reduces the risk that a portion of the JV interest received in the formation of the JV would be taxable compensation received for services.[29] The primary disadvantage of a partnership is that U.S. tax on JV income – even income in excess of technology income – cannot be deferred but, instead, is imposed currently. The following alternatives suggest structures that potentially result in some deferral of income.

1. Use of a U.S. Partner's Foreign Subsidiary

Consider the case in which the USP, a U.S. corporation, licenses or sells technology rights to a wholly owned foreign subsidiary, FS, for a fair market royalty or contingent sale proceeds. The FS in turn contributes for no consideration its right to use the technology under the license to a JV foreign corporation (JVFC) in exchange for one-half of the stock in a JVFC.[30]

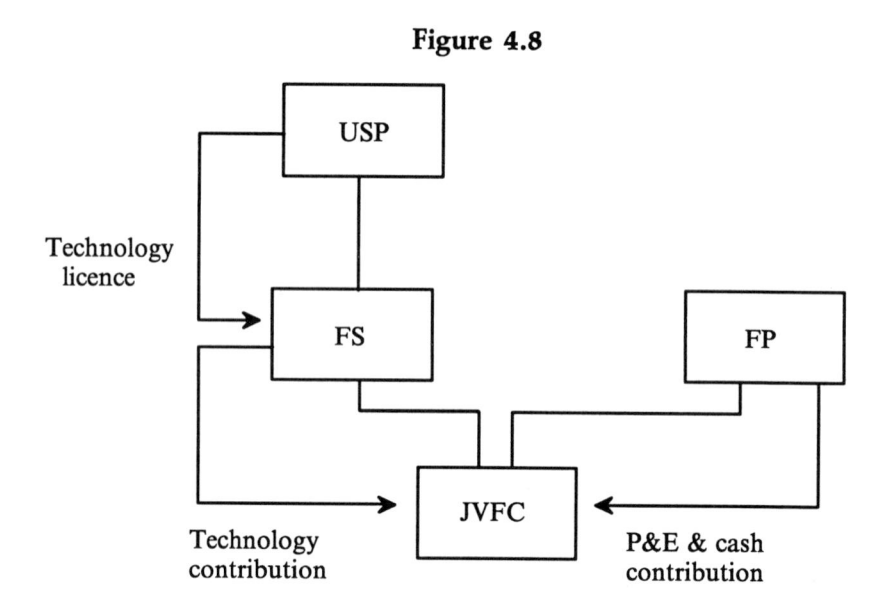

Figure 4.8

```
                    ┌─────────┐
                    │   USP   │
                    └────┬────┘
Technology               │
licence                  │
                    ┌────┴────┐        ┌─────────┐
                    │   FS    │        │   FP    │
                    └────┬────┘        └────┬────┘
                         │                  │
                         └──┐  ┌────────────┘
                            ▼  ▼
                         ┌─────────┐
                         │  JVFC   │
                         └─────────┘
         Technology                     P&E & cash
         contribution                   contribution
```

---

29. *Cf. Campbell v. Commissioner*, 943 F.2d 815 (8th Cir. 1991).
30. For foreign tax credit purposes, some approach should be considered to assure that JVFC is a CFC notwithstanding the 50:50 ownership split.

Because the USP has licensed its technology to its foreign subsidiary, FS, for a fair market royalty or contingent sales proceeds, there will be no tax on the transfer of the technology to the FS. The FS is then free to contribute to JVFC as a contribution to capital the rights to the technology.[31] The benefit of this arrangement is that, although the USP will suffer an inclusion of technology income (in the form of the royalty received from the FS), the profits of the JV over and above the technology income generally would not be currently taxed to the USP under the subpart F rules.[32] This structure, therefore, permits the deferral of manufacturing and marketing profits in excess of the technology income.

2. Use of U.S. Partnership with Foreign Subsidiary

Lastly, consider the case in which the USP, a U.S. corporation, contributes technology rights, and the FP, a foreign corporation, contributes plant and equipment and cash, to a U.S. partnership, a DPS, each for a one-half interest in the DPS.[33] The DPS then licenses the technology rights for no consideration to a wholly owned foreign subsidiary, FS, of the partnership and contributes the cash and other property to the FS as a contribution to capital.[34]

---

31. Since the FS is contributing to JVFC whatever rights it has to the intangibles, § 351 logically should apply to the contribution, notwithstanding that the contributed right is merely a right of use. This issue would have to be carefully considered, however.
32. The intangible income received by the USP from the FS should be foreign source income (assuming foreign use of the intangible) whether the license of intangibles from the USP to the FS constitutes a license or a contingent sale for U.S. tax purposes. I.R.C. §§ 862(a)(4) and 865(d)(1)(B).
33. Assuming that the intangibles contributed by the USP to the DPS will revert to the USP on dissolution of the partnership, it is not clear whether the USP is considered to transfer merely the right to use the intangible for the life of the partnership and whether § 721 applies to such a right.
34. The FS is a CFC because it is owned by a U.S. partnership – notwithstanding that the U.S. partnership is only 50 per cent owned by U.S. shareholders. The status of the FS as a CFC is important for purposes of avoiding a separate foreign tax credit limitation for the USP's share of dividends received by the DPS from the FS and characterizing USP's share of royalties received by the DPS from the FS under the look-through rules of § 904(d).

Figure 4.9

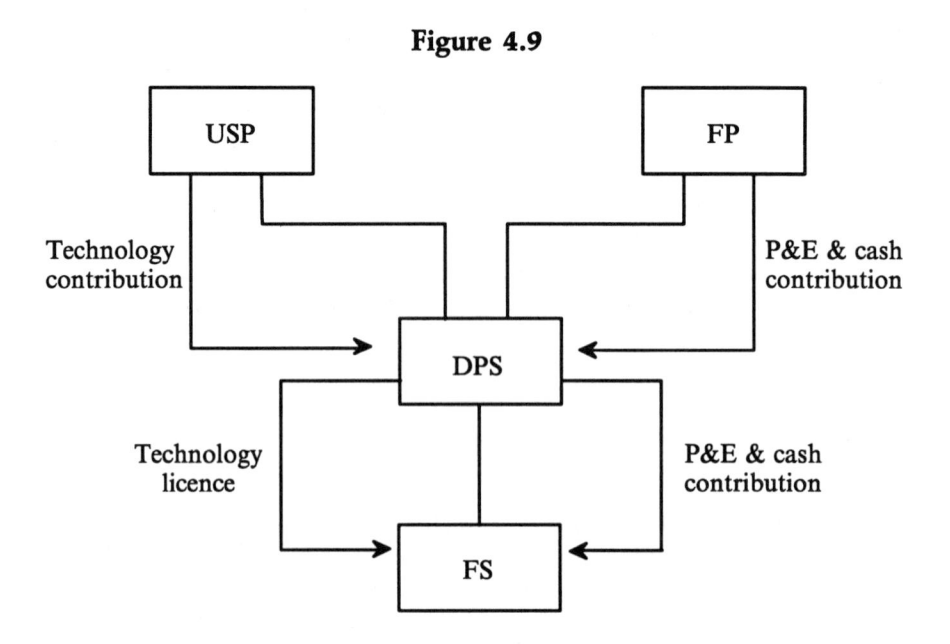

```
    ┌─────┐                    ┌─────┐
    │ USP │                    │ FP  │
    └──┬──┘                    └──┬──┘
       │                          │
Technology                    P&E & cash
contribution                  contribution
       │      ┌─────┐            │
       └─────▶│ DPS │◀───────────┘
              └──┬──┘
       ┌─────────┴─────────┐
Technology              P&E & cash
licence                 contribution
       │      ┌─────┐       │
       └─────▶│ FS  │◀──────┘
              └─────┘
```

Because the technology is contributed by the USP to a domestic partnership, there is no excise tax or other tax on the transfer of technology. Because the technology is exploited by a foreign corporation (FS) through the license arrangement, however, this alternative potentially achieves deferral of JV profits in excess of the technology income (which is paid by the FS to the DPS in the form of royalties).[35]

This alternative is potentially beneficial even with respect to technology income, because it splits the technology income between the USP and the FP, so that only half (USP's half) is currently subject to U.S. tax. The fact that only one-half of the technology income is taxed to the USP should not be problematic since that result is a natural consequence of any partnership arrangement.

---

35. This alternative may be tax efficient even if foreign withholding tax is imposed on royalty payments made by the FS to the DPS. A withholding tax imposed on royalties paid by the FS to the DPS would have the effect of merely recapturing the deduction for royalties paid by the FS to the DPS. The USP may be no worse off paying a withholding tax than if the USP did not have to contend with § 367(d) and had simply contributed intangibles to the FS. If the intangibles were contributed, there would have been no royalty deduction.

Unfortunately, the natural aversion of the foreign partner to the utilization of a U.S. partnership may preclude the use of this alternative – notwithstanding the absence of substantive U.S. tax ramifications.

Based on an examination of some of the major alternatives for structuring JVs, it appears there is no perfect solution for structuring the use by an international JV of technology owned by a U.S. party to the JV. Most, if not all, of the possible alternatives involve some tax risks. The JV parties should consider all of the possible alternatives, choose an approach that reasonably accommodates their commercial and tax objectives, and structure the details of the selected approach in a manner that reduces the tax risks given the competing commercial considerations. Most importantly, the selection of the appropriate structure should involve tax analysis and planning *early* in the process so that the tax implications of the contemplated structures figure prominently in each party's overall decision making as well as the negotiations between the parties. Finally, while tax considerations certainly are critical to the selection and implementation of technology transfer vehicles, they rarely are and never should be the sole determinants; tax considerations should be weighed together with the other significant factors described throughout this book.

Table 4.1 Non-U.S. Multinational Group

Non-U.S. Parent Finances R&D performed by U.S. Affiliate

Non-U.S. Parent Jurisdiction	Contract Research Arrangements		Cost Sharing
	Products Manufactured in U.S.	*Products Manufactured Outside U.S.*	
High Tax	Contract research arrangement probably not beneficial	Contract research arrangement probably not beneficial	No royalties, therefore, no withholding tax
	Royalty income subject to high tax	Royalty income subject to high tax	Technology income from products sold in U.S. subject to U.S. tax but not foreign tax
			Technology income from products sold in non-U.S. market not subject to U.S. tax
Low Tax	U.S. subs get no R&D deductions	No U.S. withholding tax	Contract research agreement generally preferable
	Technology income not taxed in U.S. (paid in the form of deductible royalties) except to extent subject to withholding	Manufacturing affiliate potentially has no U.S. trade or business	Maybe beneficial if cash flow concerns are important
		Sales to U.S. affiliates therefore not subject to U.S. tax	
		But operational and other problems	

Table 4.2 U.S. Multinational Group

Foreign Affiliate Jurisdiction	Contract Research Agreement			Cost Sharing	
	U.S. Ownership of Technology	Foreign Ownership of Technology			
	Use of Technology by Foreign Affiliate in Manufacturing	Use of Technology by Foreign Affiliate in Manufacturing	Use of Technology by U.S. Affiliate in Manufacturing	Foreign affiliate licenses technology rights to other affiliates, (not participants in the cost sharing arrangement) or to unrelated parties	Foreign affiliate uses technology in manufacturing of products
High Tax	Reduction of foreign effective tax rate through deductible royalties to U.S. U.S. ownership is, therefore, more beneficial unless short-term cash considerations are paramount	Foreign ownership is generally not beneficial	Foreign ownership is generally not beneficial arrangement	Foreign ownership is generally not beneficial arrangement	Because sales income not subject to subpart F deferral of income from products sold in foreign markets (at the cost of the U.S. parent forgoing a U.S. R&D tax deduction for all the group's R&D) Foreign ownership is generally not beneficial arrangement
Low Tax	Reduction of foreign effective tax rate through deductible royalties to U.S., but this is less important in a low-tax jurisdiction	Sales income not subject to subpart F Therefore, deferral on manufacturing sales income	Royalty income to foreign affiliate may be taxed to U.S. parent under subpart F Lose R&D deductions in U.S. without offsetting U.S. tax benefit Overall, not beneficial arrangement	Royalty income to foreign affiliate may be includible under subpart F Contract research agreement preferable	Whether cost sharing on contract research agreement is preferable requires closer analyses

Chapter Five

Assignment and Protection of Rights in Technology: Security Interests and Insolvency

Dr. Klaus Günther
Oppenhoff & Rädler, Cologne

Lynn A. Soukup
Shaw, Pittman, Potts & Trowbridge, Washington, D.C.

Increasingly in technology transfers, the transferor assists the transferee in financing the licensing, leasing or acquisition of the technology from the transferor. When a transferor participates in the financing effort, it should seek to retain an interest in the transferred technology, both to protect against the default of the transferee and to secure its rights *vis-à-vis* third parties. The possibilities and limits of securing the transferor's right in financed technology, as well as the formal requirements for effecting an assignment of rights in technology,[1] are the focus of Part One of this Chapter. Part Two discusses the effects of insolvency proceedings on technology transfers and highlights the risks assumed by, and protection available to, parties to technology transfer transactions in the event of the insolvency of one of the parties.

---

1. *See also* the "Country Focus" sections of Chapter One in order to determine whether, in certain countries, assignments must be registered in order to be effective.

PART ONE – SECURED TRANSACTIONS

A technology transferee frequently will borrow the funds necessary to obtain the technology, either by paying the purchase price or license fees to the transferor in instalment or royalty payments, or by borrowing funds from a bank or other third party lender. The transferor or lender may seek to retain an interest in the financed technology, as well as in the rights to payment arising from the sale or licensing of the technology by the transferee to third parties, in order to secure rights that are superior to those of the transferee's other creditors. Similarly, a lender financing a technology company's operations or a licensor expecting license fee payments or royalties from its licensee may wish to obtain an interest in the revenue stream generated by the technology in order to obtain rights superior to those of the owner's or licensee's other creditors.

I. UNITED STATES

The discussion of U.S. laws applicable to secured transactions refers to the transferee, licensee or distributor of the technology that obtains financing or will make a series of payments as the "debtor" and to the party providing the financing or receiving the payments as the "secured party." Under U.S. law, the interest taken by a secured party in property of a debtor in order to provide the secured party with superior rights to the debtor's assets is referred to as a "security interest" or a "lien," and the property in which the interest is retained is referred to as "collateral."

A security interest provides the secured party with significant protections against the rights of third parties to the collateral. For example, the holder of a security interest that has been properly documented and registered with the applicable U.S. federal or state offices generally will have the right to have its claims against the debtor satisfied from the collateral before any part of the collateral is used to satisfy the claims of the debtor's other creditors. If the security interest has not been properly documented and registered, the secured party will be treated as a general creditor of the debtor and will share *pro rata* with all other general creditors of the debtor in the value of the debtor's assets if the debtor becomes insolvent (including in a bankruptcy of the debtor). Therefore, the secured party can significantly enhance the likelihood of recovering the amounts due to it from the debtor if it takes a security interest in the debtor's assets and if its security interest is properly documented and registered. In addition, upon a default by the debtor the secured party may pursue remedies with respect to its collateral without the need for judicial process.[2]

A. Applicable Legal Framework

In the United States, two bodies of law must be consulted in order to ascertain the requirements for the documentation and registration of a security interest in technology and related rights to payment. The laws of individual states[3] within the United States, primarily the Uniform Commercial Code (UCC),[4] govern many aspects of security interests in such property. U.S. federal laws, including the Copyright Act, the Patent Act and the Lanham Act (which govern trademarks), also contain a number of relevant provisions.

Security interests in personal property (including technology and related payment rights) are generally governed by Article 9 of the UCC ("Article 9").[5] Article 9 establishes the requirements for an enforceable

2. See UCC §§ 9-501–9-507. See generally note 4, infra, for background on the Uniform Commercial Code, which provides for the rights of a secured party after the debtor's default.
3. References in this section to states within the United States include the 50 states, the District of Columbia and the U.S. Virgin Islands.
4. The UCC is a model law that was first proposed for adoption by the states in the 1950s in an effort to make commercial law (which in the United States is largely a matter of state rather than U.S. federal law) more uniform throughout the United States. The UCC has been adopted in each of the states of the United States (although Louisiana has adopted only certain portions of the UCC, including Article 9 of the UCC). In enacting the UCC, each state may adopt variations to the UCC's Official Text, and many have done so. Also, there have been several versions of the UCC Official Text, as revisions have been made to reflect changing commercial practices, developments in technology and judicial interpretations of the UCC. Most states now have adopted the 1978 Official Text, with variations as enacted in a particular state. In addition to the Official Text, the UCC contains Official Comments to aid in the interpretation and construction of the statute. Although the Official Comments generally have not been enacted into law, they are given significant weight in interpreting the Official Text. Unless otherwise noted, references in this section to the UCC will be to the 1978 Official Text of the UCC.
5. Article 9 of the UCC is not applicable to sales, other absolute transfers or licenses of technology. Article 9 is applicable to any transaction (regardless of its form) that is intended to create a security interest in personal property, and therefore covers pledges, collateral assignments, chattel mortgages, chattel trusts, trust deeds, factors' liens, equipment trusts, conditional sales, trust receipts, other lien or title retention contracts and leases or consignments intended as security. See UCC § 9-102.

agreement between the debtor and the secured party to create a security interest in personal property. This is referred to as the "creation" or "attachment" of the security interest. Article 9 also sets out the requirements that must be met in order for the secured party's rights in that personal property to be superior to the rights of third parties (including other parties claiming a security interest in that same property) and for the secured party to be protected in a bankruptcy or other insolvency proceeding of the debtor. This is referred to as the "perfection" of the security interest.[6]

State law (including the UCC) can, however, be pre-empted by U.S. federal law. In addition, Article 9 provides that it does not apply "to a security interest subject to any statute of the United States, *to the extent* that such statute governs the rights of parties to and third parties affected by transactions in particular types of property" [emphasis added].[7] Article 9 also provides that the system for filing notices of security interests in personal property may be pre-empted by U.S. federal statutes and treaties.[8] A secured party must, therefore, consider both U.S. federal laws and treaties and state laws in evaluating the documentation and registration of a security interest in intellectual property and other technology under U.S. law.

Four types of intellectual property rights are subject to U.S. federal law: copyrights and applications for registration of copyrights; patents and applications for patents; federally registered trademarks[9] and applications for federal registration of trademarks; and "mask works" (the equivalent of blueprints for computer chips) and applications for federal registration of mask works.[10] Other types of intellectual

---

6. Other state laws may also be relevant to the creation and perfection of security interests in personal property, including general contract laws and, in the case of trademarks that are registered under state but not federal law, state trademark law.
7. *See* UCC § 9-104(a). Official Comment 1 to UCC § 9-104 highlights that if the federal statute contains no relevant provisions, Article 9 could be looked to for the applicable law. The comment cites the Patent Act as a federal statute that "would not seem to contain sufficient provisions regulating the rights of the parties and third parties" so as to exclude security interests in patents from the provisions of Article 9.
8. *See* UCC § 9-302.
9. For purposes of this discussion, the term "trademarks" also includes service marks.
10. In addition, the federal Assignment of Claims Act (41 U.S.C. § 15; 31 U.S.C. § 3727) prohibits assignment of contracts with the U.S. government and provides that the U.S. government is not obligated to recognize a secured party's security

property (such as customer lists, other trade secrets and unregistered trademarks) are not subject to federal law.

Article 9 and the Official Comments do not state whether, or to what extent, Article 9 is pre-empted by federal laws applicable to intellectual property, and the relevant federal laws do not contain specific provisions pre-empting state law. A secured party must therefore look to case law to determine to what extent federal laws applicable to intellectual property pre-empt Article 9. Unfortunately, the case law on this issue is sparse, and most commentators and practitioners recommend compliance *both* with Article 9 and with the federal laws applicable to copyrights, trademarks, patents and mask works, in order to create and perfect security interests in such intellectual property and related payment rights.

The following paragraphs describe the authority available in evaluating whether, and to what extent, federal law applicable to intellectual property pre-empts Article 9.

1. Copyrights

Cases have held that filing under the Copyright Act[11] is the sole effective means of perfecting a security interest in a copyright and in related accounts receivable (and possibly in related contract and distribution rights) and that the federal copyright law determines the priority of the security interest.[12] One bankruptcy court has held that security interests in U.S. copyrights in works of foreign origin can only

cont.
    interest in payments due from the U.S. government to the debtor, and may continue to make such payments to the debtor, unless the requirements for assignment of payments due under a contract with or claim against the U.S. government to the secured party under the Assignment of Claims Act and the regulations promulgated thereunder have been complied with. A secured party should be aware that the Assignment of Claims Act permits assignments of such payments only under limited circumstances; for example, the assignment must be made to a financing institution (*i.e*, a person engaged in lending money as a regular part of its business operations) and must be made for the purpose of financing the debtor's performance of the government contract.

11. The Copyright Act of 1976, as amended, 17 U.S.C. § 101 *et seq.* (the "Copyright Act").
12. *See In re Peregrine Entertainment, Ltd.*, 116 B.R. 194, 198-204 (C.D. Cal. 1990); *In re AEG Acquisition Corp.*, 127 B.R. 34, 40 (Bankr. C.D. Cal. 1991). *But cf. In re C Tek Software, Inc.*, 117 B.R. 762, 763, 767 (Bankr. D.N.H. 1990) (court noted that security interest in copyrights "was properly perfected in New York;" case refers only to filing under Article 9). Although the *Peregrine* and *AEG Acquisition* cases do not expressly address applications to register copyrights, the reasoning in the cases would be applicable to such applications.

be perfected by registering the U.S. copyright and filing under the Copyright Act.[13]

2. Patents

Cases have held that the perfection of a security interest in a patent or application for patent under Article 9 is valid against another security interest perfected under Article 9, a lien creditor and a trustee or debtor in possession in bankruptcy.[14] The Patent Act[15] provides that a "subsequent purchaser or mortgagee for a valuable consideration, without notice" takes free of any assignment, grant or conveyance of a patent or application for patent that is not recorded with the Patent and Trademark Office.[16] One case has indicated that such a purchaser or mortgagee that properly records under the Patent Act, or a secured party that perfected by filing under the Patent Act rather than under Article 9, would have priority over a security interest perfected under Article 9.[17]

3. Trademarks

All reported cases to date apply Article 9, rather than federal trademark law, to security interests in federally registered trademarks and applications for federal registration of trademarks.[18] The Lanham

---

13. *AEG Acquisition*, 127 B.R. at 42.
14. *See Chesapeake Fiber Packaging Corp. v. Seabro Packaging Corp.*, 143 B.R. 360 (Bankr. D. Md. 1992); *City Bank & Trust Co. v. Otto Fabric, Inc.*, 83 B.R. 780, 782 (D. Kan. 1988); *In re Transportation Design & Technology, Inc.*, 48 B.R. 635, 638-40 (Bankr. S.D. Cal. 1985); *but see Peregrine*, 116 B.R. at 203-04 (stating that the *City Bank* and *Transportation Design* cases misconstrue Article 9).
15. The Patent Act, as amended, 35 U.S.C. § 1 *et seq.* (the "Patent Act").
16. 35 U.S.C. § 261.
17. *See Transportation Design*, 48 B.R. at 639-40 (filing under the Patent Act would be necessary to protect the secured party's position against such a *bona fide* purchaser, mortgagee or secured party).
18. *See, e.g., In re 1992, Inc.*, 137 B.R. 778, 781-82 (Bankr. C.D. Cal. 1992); *In re C.C. & Co., Inc.*, 86 B.R. 485, 486-87 (Bankr. E.D. Va. 1988); *In re Chattanooga Choo-Choo Co.*, 98 B.R. 792, 797-98 (Bankr. E.D. Tenn. 1989); *In re Roman Cleanser Co.*, 43 B.R. 940, 943 (Bankr. E.D. Mich. 1984), *aff'd*, 802 F.2d 207 (6th Cir. 1986); *In re TR-3 Industries*, 41 B.R. 128, 131-32 (Bankr. C.D. Cal. 1984); *see also Peregrine*, 116 B.R. at 204 n.14.

Act[19] provides that "[a]n assignment [of a trademark or application] shall be void as against any subsequent purchaser for a valuable consideration without notice, unless it is recorded in the Patent and Trademark Office."[20] To date there are no reported decisions on whether such a purchaser would have priority over a holder of a security interest perfected under Article 9, although cases have held that a security interest is not, prior to default, an assignment within the meaning of the Lanham Act.[21]

4. Mask Works

The Semiconductor Chip Protection Act[22] provides for federal recording of interests in mask works. There have been no reported cases to date evaluating whether the Semiconductor Chip Protection Act pre-empts Article 9; however, the Act is very similar to the Copyright Act, which has been held to pre-empt Article 9 as discussed above.

B. Creation and Perfection of Security Interests

Federal laws generally do not speak to the content of the agreement between the secured party and the debtor that creates a security interest in technology, but only to the filing to be made with the Patent and Trademark Office or the Copyright Office so that the security interest in copyrights and applications for federal registration of copyrights and related property, patents and applications for patents, federally registered trademarks and applications for federal registration of trademarks and mask works and applications for federal registration of mask works will be enforceable against third parties. Accordingly, state law (*i.e.*, Article 9 as adopted by the applicable state and general principles of contract law)[23] generally governs the creation of the

---

19. The Lanham Act, 15 U.S.C. §§ 1051-1127 (the "Lanham Act").
20. 15 U.S.C. § 1060.
21. *See, e.g., Roman Cleanser*, 43 B.R. at 944.
22. The Semiconductor Chip Protection Act, 17 U.S.C. § 901 *et seq.* (the "Semiconductor Chip Protection Act").
23. Generally, the choice of law provision in the parties' agreement will determine the state law applicable to creation or attachment of a security interest and, as discussed below under "Technology Not Subject to Federal Law – Uniform Commercial Code Article 9," if Article 9 is applicable to the collateral UCC § 9-103 will determine the state law applicable to issues of perfection (and the effect of perfection or nonperfection) of a security interest.

security interest in intellectual property, whereas the perfection of that security interest and its priority over other claims to the property are governed by Article 9 or, in the case of the types of intellectual property described above, federal law.

UCC Section 9-203 provides that a security interest is created between the debtor and the secured party when the following requirements are met

> (i) the collateral is in the possession of the secured party pursuant to agreement, or the debtor has signed a written security agreement[24] that contains language granting a security interest and a description of the collateral that "reasonably identifies" the collateral,[25]
> (ii) the debtor has rights in the collateral,[26] and
> (iii) the secured party has given value.[27]

As noted above, further actions are needed in order for the security interest, once created between the debtor and the secured party, to be "perfected" (*i.e.*, enforceable against third parties and effective in a bankruptcy or other insolvency proceeding of the debtor). The following paragraphs describe the law applicable to the perfection of a security interest in various types of intellectual property.

1. Copyrights

Section 101 of the Copyright Act defines the term "transfer of copyright ownership" as an

> assignment, mortgage, exclusive license, or any other conveyance, alienation, or hypothecation of a copyright or of any of the exclusive rights comprised in a copyright, whether or not it is limited in time or place of effect, but not including a nonexclusive license.[28]

---

24. *See* notes 28 and 36, *infra*, regarding provisions in the federal laws relating to the form and execution of the security agreement.
25. Issues related to the description of the collateral are discussed below under "Documentation Issues."
26. Due diligence procedures to verify that the debtor has rights in the collateral, and whether those rights are already subject to encumbrances, are discussed below under "Due Diligence – Debtor's Rights in the Collateral."
27. Value is defined in UCC § 1-201.
28. § 204 of the Copyright Act states that a "transfer of copyright ownership, other than by operation of law, is not valid unless an instrument of conveyance, or a note or memorandum of the transfer, is in writing and signed by the owner of the rights conveyed or such owner's duly authorized agent."

ASSIGNMENT AND PROTECTION OF RIGHTS 259

Section 205 of the Copyright Act provides for the recordation of transfers of copyright ownership (which is defined to include a "mortgage") and other documents pertaining to copyrights with the Copyright Office. Section 205(d) provides that, as between two conflicting transfers of the same property, the transfer executed first has priority if it is properly recorded

(i) within one month of its execution in the United States or within two months after its execution outside the United States or

(ii) at any time prior to the recordation in the appropriate manner of the later transfer; otherwise the later transfer prevails if recorded first in the proper manner and if taken in good faith, for valuable consideration[29] or on the basis of a binding agreement to pay royalties, and without notice of the earlier transfer.[30]

A "mortgage" of a copyright, application for registration of a copyright or other related property[31] must be filed with the U.S. Copyright Office.[32] It appears that the U.S. Copyright Office will only accept an assignment of a copyright by copyright registration number or by title.[33]

---

29. The term "valuable consideration" is not defined in the Copyright Act and therefore would probably be determined under state law.
30. A licensee may have rights in a copyright that will survive a foreclosure by a secured party of its security interest in the copyright. For example, § 205(e) of the Copyright Act provides that a nonexclusive license, whether recorded or not, prevails over a conflicting transfer of copyright ownership if the license is in writing and properly executed by or on behalf of the owner of the rights licensed and either (i) the license was taken before execution of the transfer or (ii) the license was taken in good faith before recordation of the transfer and without notice of it.
31. *See* text accompanying note 12, *supra*, for a description of property interests related to a copyright that may also be subject to the Copyright Act.
32. 37 C.F.R. § 201.4 contains requirements for the form of the filing and applicable fee.
33. 17 U.S.C. § 205(c). The court in *AEG Acquisition* raised but did not decide the question of whether recordation of a copyright mortgage is valid if it is recorded before the registration of the underlying copyright, although it noted that under analogous real property law such a filing "outside of the chain of title" could not be made. 127 B.R. at 41 n.8. The Copyright Act suggests that a filing is not effective to give notice to third parties unless a registration has been filed. *See* § 205(c) of the Copyright Act, 17 U.S.C. § 205(c). Regulations under the Patent Act and the Lanham Act contain a similar provision. 37 C.F.R. § 1.331(c) ("An instrument relating to a patent should identify the patent by number and date . . . an instrument relating to [an application] should identify the application by serial

2. Patents

While the Patent Act contains no specific provisions regulating security interests in patents, it provides that an assignment of an application for patent, patent or any interest therein must be made in writing, and also states that

> [a]n assignment, grant or conveyance shall be void as against any subsequent purchaser or mortgagee for a valuable consideration, without notice, unless it is recorded in the Patent and Trademark Office within three months from its date or prior to the date of such subsequent purchase or mortgage.[34]

Several approaches are available to filings with the Patent and Trademark Office. The secured party may file an absolute assignment of specified patents or applications by the debtor to the secured party with a license back to the debtor. This approach, however, may expose the secured party, as the owner of the patent, to infringement claims and other liability and may make the secured party (rather than the debtor) the only person with the right to sue for infringement. In order to avoid potential liability, instead of an absolute assignment the secured party instead will often file a security agreement or collateral assignment, although the Patent Act does not specifically provide for the filing of such a document and such document may therefore be rejected by the Patent and Trademark Office.[35] The Patent Act does refer to the filing of a mortgage on a patent, and the secured party can also file its security agreement with the title of "patent mortgage."

3. Trademarks

The Lanham Act provides for the filing of assignments of federally registered trademarks or trademark applications with the Patent and

---

cont.
       number . . . and date of filing . . . ."); 37 C.F.R. § 2.185 ("No assignment [of a trademark] will be recorded, except as may be ordered by the Commissioner, unless it has been executed and unless: (1) The certificate of registration is identified in the assignment by the certificate number . . . or . . . the application . . . is identified in the assignment by serial number . . . .").

34. 35 U.S.C. § 261.
35. 37 C.F.R. §§ 1.331 to 1.334 contain requirements for the form of the filing. 37 C.F.R. § 1.21 establishes the applicable fee.

Trademark Office.[36] The Lanham Act provides that "an assignment shall be void as against any subsequent purchaser for a valuable consideration without notice, unless it is recorded in the Patent and Trademark Office within three months after the date thereof or prior to such subsequent purchase."[37]

No provision is made under the Lanham Act for granting or perfecting a lien on a trademark or trademark application.

As with patents, there are alternative approaches to filings with the Patent and Trademark Office. The secured party may file an absolute assignment of the trademark from the debtor to the secured party with the Patent and Trademark Office,[38] with a license of the mark back to

36. "A registered mark or a mark for which application to register has been filed shall be assignable with the goodwill of the business in which the mark is used, or with that part of the goodwill of the business connected with the use of and symbolized by the mark . . . . Assignments shall be by instruments in writing duly executed. A separate record of assignments submitted for recording hereunder shall be maintained in the Patent and Trademark Office." 15 U.S.C. § 1060. *See* 37 C.F.R. §§ 2.171 and 2.185 to 2.187 for requirements applicable to assignments under the Lanham Act. The Lanham Act also provides that an application to register a mark prior to its commercial use cannot be assigned prior to filing with the Patent and Trademark Office of a verified statement of use of the mark, except to a successor to the applicant's business. 15 U.S.C. § 1060.

37. 15 U.S.C. § 1060.

38. A trademark can be validly assigned only in connection with the goodwill that is symbolized by the mark. An assignment of a mark without an accompanying transfer of associated goodwill is an "assignment in gross," which is invalid to transfer any rights in the mark. In order to protect a security interest in a trademark, the security agreement should state that the trademark or application is being assigned together with the goodwill of the business symbolized thereby, to avoid an assignment in gross that is not a valid assignment to the secured party (or does not permit the secured party to make a valid assignment of the mark to a purchaser at a foreclosure sale) and may invalidate the trademark. The Patent and Trademark Office might not accept an assignment that does not contain language indicating that there has been an assignment of goodwill, and even if it does it is not clear that such assignment would be effective. Also, merely including a reference to the goodwill associated with the trademark may not be sufficient, and the documentation should indicate that the secured party has been granted rights in more than just the trademark or application. *See Haymaker Sports, Inc. v. Turian*, 581 F.2d 257, 261 (C.C.P.A. 1978). The *Roman Cleanser* case suggests that an assignment of formulas and customer lists or machinery and equipment would be sufficient to validate an assignment of the trademark. 43 B.R. at 946-47, *aff'd*, 802 F.2d at 208-09.

To avoid an assignment in gross of a trademark upon default (since the default may be viewed as effecting an assignment of the trademark to the secured party), at the time an assignment to the secured party is recorded in the Patent and Trademark Office or when a trademark is transferred in connection with a

the debtor, although transferring ownership of the trademark may expose the secured party to liability as the owner of the trademark, including infringement liability. Also, the holder of a trademark is required to maintain quality control over the products or services on which a licensee uses the trademark, or the holder will be held to have abandoned the trademark. Exercising such control may be difficult for the secured party from a practical standpoint and may increase the risk of "lender liability" claims based on theories that the secured party is exercising control over the debtor.[39] More often, the secured party will file a collateral security agreement with the Patent and Trademark Office. The Patent and Trademark Office has issued policy statements indicating that it will accept for recordation documents that affect title to trademark registrations and applications other than assignments, although the recording thereof may not serve as constructive notice under the Lanham Act of the existence of an interest in the trademark registration or application.[40]

4. Mask Works

Section 903 of the Semiconductor Chip Protection Act contains provisions analogous to the Copyright Act. Filings under the Act are made with the Copyright Office.[41]

5. Technology Not Subject to Federal Law – Uniform Commercial Code Article 9

A security interest in collateral that is subject to Article 9 is perfected by filing a form called a "financing statement" in the appropriate states; for tangible personal property, taking possession of the property is also effective. UCC Section 9-103 provides that filings for intangible

cont.
    foreclosure sale, goodwill should be transferred to the secured party at the time the security interest is granted and to the purchaser at the foreclosure sale in connection with the sale.
39. "Lender liability" is a term used to refer to a variety of theories under which a lender may become liable to its borrower or to third parties with claims against its borrower (including tax, environmental and other government authorities). Many of these theories are premised on the lender's exercise of control over the business and operations of its borrower.
40. *See* TRADEMARK MANUAL OF EXAMINING PROCEDURE § 502.
41. 37 C.F.R. § 211.2 provides that 37 C.F.R. § 201.4 (which contains requirements for the form of filing and applicable fees for copyright mortgages) is applicable to filings made under the Semiconductor Chip Protection Act.

personal property are made in the state where the debtor has its principal place of business (or, if the debtor has no place of business, where the debtor resides)[42] and filings for tangible personal property are generally made in the state where the collateral is located.[43] Within the relevant state, the financing statement must be filed with the appropriate offices.[44] The filing generally is effective for five years and must be periodically renewed.[45] Additional filings are required if the debtor's location or the location of the collateral changes or if the debtor changes its name, identity or organizational structure.[46]

C. Documentation Issues

Both the security agreement and the financing statement must contain a description of the collateral. The description in the security agreement and the financing statement is sufficient if it "reasonably identifies" the collateral (*i.e.*, it makes possible the identification of the thing described).[47] In addition, the financing statement must contain a statement "indicating the types [*i.e.*, by UCC category, such as goods,

---

42. UCC § 9-103(3) provides that the law (including the conflict of laws rules) of the jurisdiction where the debtor is located governs the perfection (including where financing statements are to be filed) and the effect of perfection and nonperfection of the security interest in collateral of this type; a debtor is located at his place of business, if he has one, at his chief executive office if he has more than one place of business, and otherwise at his residence. If the debtor is located in a jurisdiction that is not part of the United States and which does not provide for perfection of the security interest by filing or recording in that jurisdiction, the law of the jurisdiction in the United States in which the debtor has its major executive offices in the United States governs the perfection and the effect of perfection or nonperfection of the security interest through filing. In the alternative, if the debtor is located in a jurisdiction that is not part of the United States and the collateral is accounts or general intangibles for money due or to become due, the security interest may be perfected by notification to the obligor on such account or general intangible.
43. UCC § 9-103(1) generally provides that perfection (including the jurisdiction where financing statements are to be filed) and the effect of perfection or nonperfection of a security interest in collateral of this type are governed by the law of the jurisdiction where the collateral is located.
44. UCC § 9-401 establishes the offices within a state where the financing statements are to be filed and UCC § 9-402 establishes the requirements for the content and execution of the financing statement. A filing fee and, in Maryland, Florida and Tennessee, significant additional recordation taxes, are applicable to the filing.
45. *See* UCC § 9-403.
46. *See* UCC §§ 9-103, 9-402(7).
47. *See* UCC § 9-110.

general intangibles or accounts], or describing the items, of collateral."[48] If a description of collateral does not meet the statutory requirement for identifying the collateral, the security interest may not be created or perfected. Problems are created by overly broad as well as overly narrow descriptions of collateral.

Courts have uniformly held that a general description of the collateral, such as "all personal property" or "all assets," does not reasonably identify the collateral. The secured party should use appropriate UCC categories (in the case of intellectual property, "general intangibles," "accounts" and "goods" will generally be the applicable categories) in its collateral description. Some courts have held that the term "general intangibles" is so broad that additional information regarding the general intangibles intended to be covered must be included in the collateral description for the description to be adequate. Therefore, when used, this term should be supplemented with an illustrative list of the types of property intended to be included in the collateral (such as copyrights, trademarks, trade names, service marks, patents, customer lists and source codes).

An overly narrow description of the collateral may be as harmful to the secured party as a description that is too generic. For example, referring to a specific edition of a computer program may not protect the secured party if an updated or improved edition is developed. Similarly, references to a computer program would not include the related user and technical documentation that the secured party would need to be able to license or sell rights to the program after a default by the debtor. The collateral description, therefore, should cover any records or documentation relating to the collateral and any other rights relating to the collateral (*e.g.*, warranty claims). The collateral description should also specifically refer to distribution agreements, royalty agreements and licenses of intellectual property by the debtor to its customers and distributors and the debtor's rights thereunder (including rights to payment) if such agreements, licenses, rights and payments are intended to be included in the secured party's collateral.

The collateral description should clearly include collateral acquired by the debtor after the date of the security agreement, if that is the intent of the parties. UCC Section 9-204 specifically permits a security interest in such "after-acquired property," but courts have almost uniformly required that express language to such effect appear in both the security agreement and in the financing statement.

---

48. *See* UCC § 9-402(1).

ASSIGNMENT AND PROTECTION OF RIGHTS 265

Many secured parties use a less detailed description of the collateral in their financing statement than appears in the security agreement. While this is legally permissible (since the financing statement description is only required to give third parties sufficient information to put them on notice of the need to make further inquiries), if collateral covered by the security agreement is not covered by the financing statement, the security interest in such collateral is not perfected. If the financing statement description of the collateral covers property that is not included in the security agreement description, a court may hold that there has been no grant of a security interest in that collateral (since the financing statement usually does not contain the language necessary to create a security interest) and the collateral will be limited to the narrower description in the security agreement. Therefore, the better practice is to use identical descriptions in the security agreement and the financing statement.

D. Covenants Protecting the Intellectual Property Rights Taken as Collateral

The secured party should consider including provisions in its security agreement that protect the value of its intellectual property collateral, such as the following:

- Unlike Article 9, which permits the original financing statement and security agreement to cover after-acquired property and does not require additional filings as new collateral comes into existence, the U.S. federal filing systems are set up for filings against specific items of intellectual property, registrations or applications, requiring a new filing whenever a new right that is subject to the federal laws is created. There should be covenants requiring prompt notice to the secured party of new trademarks, patents, copyrights and mask works (and registrations and applications for the same). A monthly compliance certificate is a good way to monitor whether new intellectual property is being created for which the secured party should make a federal filing to protect its interests.
- Since failure to use a trademark for any trademarked class of goods or services may result in loss of the trademark for those goods or services, there should be a covenant in the security

agreement requiring continuation of use of the trademark in connection with those goods or services.
- The debtor should be required to prepare and file renewals of trademark registrations at appropriate intervals; the secured party may have to file continuations as well, if it is on record in the Patent and Trademark Office as an assignee of the trademark.
- The secured party's approval of licenses of the technology should be required in order to prevent the debtor from granting such an extensive interest in the technology that the value of the intellectual property is diminished. For ordinary course of business licenses that are limited with respect to duration, territory, royalties and sublicensing rights, it may be sufficient if the secured party approves the form of license agreement (rather than each individual license).
- It most likely will be difficult for the secured party to obtain sufficient and current information for certain types of intellectual property, such as trade secrets, for such collateral to have any real value to the secured party. In addition, unless the debtor's employees successfully can be prohibited from disclosing trade secrets, customer lists and other similar information, this property has little practical value. Therefore, the secured party needs to have clear and complete information on trade secrets (include covenants in its security documentation requiring the debtor to keep the information up to date) and to develop other means (such as requiring periodic certifications from individuals employed by the debtor) of obtaining information.
- In order to maximize its protection against infringement and misuse, the secured party should consider requiring the debtor to obtain a patent for its trade secrets (to the extent they can be patented).

E. Remedies

In order to enhance its ability to foreclose on and dispose of collateral, and to maximize the value of the collateral to potential purchasers and licensees, the secured party should supplement the

ASSIGNMENT AND PROTECTION OF RIGHTS

remedies provided by Article 9[49] or other state laws[50] with the following provisions in its security agreement:

- The secured party specifically should be granted the right to license or exploit the technology, in the name of the debtor or otherwise, upon default.
- The secured party should have the right to enjoin the debtor from using or licensing the collateral; the value of collateral at a sale by the secured party after a default, or of a license of the collateral by the secured party to a third party after a default, may be diminished if the debtor continues to use or license the property.
- The secured party should have a power of attorney permitting it to convey or license the technology after a default. An absolute assignment of the intellectual property in the records of the Copyright Office and Patent and Trademark Office will also facilitate the secured party's ability to sell or license the intellectual property after a default. If these documents are not filed at the time the financing is provided to the debtor, the secured party should consider obtaining presigned copies to be filed at the time of a default by the debtor or obtaining a power of attorney from the debtor to make the filing. At a minimum, the secured party should insist on a contractual obligation by the debtor to undertake all such actions as are necessary or proper to assist the secured party in perfecting the secured party's security interest.
- The secured party should have an express acknowledgment from the debtor that delays in the disposition of the collateral may result in a decline in value of technology collateral or a loss of the rights to intellectual property collateral (*e.g.*, a delay by the secured party in selling or licensing a trademark after default may raise the issue of whether the trademark has been abandoned) and that for these reasons expeditious

---

49. Article 9 provides three basic remedies to a secured party. Under UCC § 9-502, the secured party may collect payments due to the debtor that are part of the collateral; under UCC § 9-504 the secured party may conduct a foreclosure sale or other disposition (including a lease or license) of the collateral (and, under specified circumstances, may purchase the collateral at the sale); and under UCC § 9-505 the secured party may, under specified circumstances, retain certain types of collateral in full satisfaction of the debtor's obligations.
50. Foreclosure of security interests in intellectual property is not governed by federal law. *See Republic Pictures Corp. v. Security-First National Bank*, 197 F.2d 767, 769-70 (9th Cir. 1952).

dispositions, even if they may not necessarily produce the highest possible price, will meet the requirement of Article 9 that dispositions of collateral by the secured party be commercially reasonable.

- The secured party should require that the debtor's key employees sign non-competition and non-disclosure agreements that have been approved by the secured party, and the secured party should have express rights to enforce these agreements (to protect the value of its collateral) and to assign such agreements to a purchaser of the collateral on foreclosure.

F. Source Code Escrow

If collateral includes computer software, the secured party should consider requiring the debtor to deliver a copy of the source code to the secured party or establish a source code escrow with a third party. Access to the source code will facilitate the secured party's ability to license the software, or fulfill maintenance, support and upgrade obligations to the debtor's customers so that the customers will continue to pay license fees for the software. The secured party should ensure that its copy of the source code is regularly updated for any modifications to the program by requiring the debtor to do so and securing inspection rights of the escrowed copy. If the debtor has established a source code escrow for the benefit of its customers, the secured party should review the extent of the rights and access to the source code given to the customers. Since the source code escrowed for customers is more likely to be updated regularly by the debtor, the secured party should obtain rights to the source code under this escrow arrangement.

In order to enhance the collectibility of receivables from the debtor's customers, the secured party should consider requiring that the license agreements between the debtor and its customer provide that the fees payable by the customer be for the maintenance of the source code escrow (in addition to any obligations of the debtor to maintain, support or upgrade the software) and be fully earned by reason of the escrow arrangement being made available for the benefit of the customer.

G. Due Diligence – Debtor's Rights in the Collateral

The debtor can only convey to the secured party the rights that the debtor has in the collateral. Therefore, the secured party should ascertain the debtor's rights in its technology and establish whether the debtor itself has a valid interest in the technology and in any important derivative works produced by a third party.

1. General

The first step is a search of the records of the Copyright Office and the Patent and Trademark Office to confirm the existence and record title to copyrights, copyright registrations, applications for copyright registration, patents, applications for patents, trademark registrations, applications for trademark registration, mask works and applications for mask work registration. In addition, the secured party should conduct other due diligence to determine whether other parties have rights in the intellectual property.

The secured party should review the development history of the technology to determine whether it was created by the debtor's employees or by independent contractors. (Rights to the copyright in a work are owned by the work's author, even if another party has paid for the work. One significant exception is where the work is created by an employee within the scope of employment, in which case it is a "work for hire" and the property of the employer.) The secured party also should review the debtor's license agreements to determine whether rights in derivative versions of the licensed property are granted to the debtor that would not otherwise belong to it. If the debtor does acquire rights in derivative works prepared by others, the collateral description should cover all derivative works and other variations or improvements to the collateral, not only by the debtor but also by third parties.

The risk to a secured party of failing to investigate the debtor's rights in its technology is illustrated in *In re C Tek Software, Inc.*[51] In *C Tek*, the debtor licensed software to a distributor but obtained no rights in modifications created by the distributor/licensee (and the modifications therefore remained the property of the distributor). When the debtor filed for bankruptcy, the bankruptcy court held that, because the debtor had no rights in the improvements to the software, the secured party only had a security interest in the original (and less marketable version) of the software and not in the valuable modifications.

2. Lien Searches

In order to determine whether the debtor has previously encumbered its rights to intellectual property and other assets, a lien search for

---

51. 127 B.R. 501, 507-08 (Bankr. D.N.H. 1991).

financing statements filed by other creditors and for tax and other liens should be made prior to taking a security interest in any personal property, including technology. For intellectual property and related receivables and other general intangibles and accounts, such a search should be made in the appropriate offices in the jurisdiction where the debtor has its principal place of business. For goods or other tangible personal property, the search should be made in the appropriate offices in the jurisdiction where the property is located. When copyrights, patents, trademarks or mask works are being taken as collateral, the applicable records of the Patent and Trademark Office (and, if the collateral includes state-registered trademarks, the applicable state trademark agency) and the Copyright Office also should be searched.

3. "Look-Back" Periods

The federal laws governing patents, copyrights, trademarks and mask works provide for significant periods, referred to as "look-back" periods, that make it difficult to determine the current state of the title to such intellectual property.[52] Although the secured party can require the debtor to represent that the debtor has good title to its property free of encumbrances, security interests and liens, this will not protect the secured party from fraud or errors by the debtor.

---

52. The Patent Act provides that an assignment, grant or conveyance is void as against any subsequent purchaser or mortgagee for a valuable consideration, without notice, unless it is recorded in the Patent and Trademark Office within three months from its date or at any time prior to the subsequent purchase or mortgage. 35 U.S.C. § 261.

The Copyright Act provides that as between two conflicting transfers of copyright ownership (which is defined to include a "mortgage"), the one executed first prevails if it is recorded in the Copyright Office within one month after its execution in the United States, within two months after its execution outside the United States or at any time prior to recordation in the Copyright Office of a later transfer. 17 U.S.C. § 205(d).

The Lanham Act provides that a trademark assignment is void against any subsequent purchaser for a valuable consideration without notice unless recorded in the Patent and Trademark Office within three months after the date thereof or prior to such subsequent purchase. 15 U.S.C. § 1060.

The Semiconductor Chip Protection Act provides for a three-month "look-back" period similar to those in the Patent Act and the Lanham Act.

H. Contractual Relationships

In addition to license and maintenance agreements and other contracts with its customers and distributors that generate receivables and revenues, the debtor will often have contracts that constitute a significant part of the value of its business, including supply and purchase agreements, distribution and franchise agreements and maintenance and licensing agreements for technology owned by others that the debtor uses in its business. The secured party may wish to include those agreements in its collateral to facilitate a sale of the debtor's business after a default, either because those contracts have independent value if sold, or because those contracts are necessary to meet obligations to the debtor's customers, and the ability to fulfill those obligations enhances the collectibility of existing receivables and permits the generation of new receivables.

The secured party must review these contracts for restrictions on assignment and, if possible, obtain any necessary consents. The secured party should also seek a right to receive notice of the debtor's default under the contracts and a right to cure the debtor's defaults. The review of the contracts should include a review for

- termination provisions,
- restrictions on assignment (if the contract does not expressly prohibit assignment then, unless it is a personal services contract, it will probably be assignable; UCC Section 9-318 permits valid assignment of payment rights even if the contract provides it is not assignable), and
- creditworthiness/insolvency risk of other parties to the contracts (which will affect collectibility of payments and certainty of performance).

II. CANADA

Like the United States, Canada has two systems of law applicable to establishing rights (including security interests) in intellectual property: national legislation governs copyrights and other types of intellectual property, while provincial laws govern security interests and commercial transactions dealing with intellectual property.

The Personal Property Security Act (which is similar to Article 9 of the U.S. Uniform Commercial Code)[53] which, has been adopted, with some variations, in six territories, is the provincial law generally applicable to security interests in personal property, including intangible personal property such as intellectual property. Common law rules and statutes are in effect in the Atlantic provinces and the Northwest Territory, and civil law governs in Quebec.

A security interest under the Personal Property Security Act (the "PPSA") will provide the secured party with the benefit of self-help remedies with respect to its collateral; in addition, the holder of a perfected security interest will have superior rights in an insolvency of the debtor.

The PPSA contains provisions relating to the attachment and perfection of security interests that are very similar to those under Article 9 of the UCC. The six jurisdictions that have adopted the PPSA provide central registries in each of such jurisdictions for filing of financing statements to perfect security interests in personal property, and have choice of law provision similar to those in Article 9 of the UCC for determining the jurisdiction whose law will govern (and where filings are to be made). In the five jurisdictions that have not adopted the PPSA and rely on common law, there is generally a variety of laws applicable to security interests in personal property as collateral and often no centralized system in such jurisdictions for recording the documents necessary to register the security interest. In Quebec, civil law principles govern security interests in personal property and must be analyzed to see how they can be extended to provide guidance with respect to intellectual property as collateral. In addition, the Special Corporate Powers Act in Quebec provides a mechanism for the creation of a security interest in personal property (including intellectual property) owned by a company.

The national Canadian laws relating to trademarks, copyrights, patents and industrial designs contain provisions relating to transfer or assignment that are similar to those in the U.S. federal laws regarding intellectual property and raise similar issues regarding whether (and to what extent) the federal laws pre-empt the PPSA or other provincial laws relating to security interests and, as a result, filing under both the national and provincial statutes are generally thought to be advisable for the protection of the secured party against purchasers of the intellectual property and other secured parties; in addition filing in more

---

53. The jurisdictions that have adopted the Personal Property Security Act are British Columbia, the Yukon Territory, Alberta, Saskatchewan, Manitoba and Ontario.

than one province may be advisable due to the absence of uniform choice of law provisions in the 12 provinces.

III. GERMANY

Given the unique and dominant role of the German banks in German commercial life, German debtor-creditor law invariably reflects, and should be understood in the context of, German bank practices. Security interests in intellectual property still are largely uncommon in Germany because banks, which are by far the largest and most frequent creditors and secured parties in Germany, are reluctant to use intangible assets such as intellectual property rights as collateral.

One reason for their reluctance is that the evaluation of a patent, utility model, know-how, copyright, design or software requires a level of expertise that banks usually do not possess. Even the debtor may not be able to predict the future development of the market and, in particular, the technical merits of the collateral itself. In some cases, however, the valuation of the technology may be based on license fees.

The second reason is that it is not possible, under German law, to verify whether the debtor has title to the collateral. The Patent Register, for example, does not show whether the registered person remains the owner of a patent, because the transfer of a patent does not require the registration of the new owner in the Patent Register. Moreover, there is neither a *bona fide* right protection with regard to intellectual property under German law nor an equivalent to the U.S. concept of "perfection." Therefore, a purported "secured" party always assumes the risk that the agreement providing it with rights to the collateral is void.

Finally, the exploitation of the collateral often causes severe problems for the secured party. Banks are neither familiar with specialized high-technology products or markets nor do they delve into the technical details of the collateral. Who, then, would buy sophisticated software from a bank, knowing that in the first event of malfunction, no maintenance or support could be obtained from either the bank or the defunct debtor?

Recently, however, there has been a discernible trend towards the grant of security interests in transferred technology. In particular, software and trademarks are being collateralized, following the amendment of Section 8 of the Trademark Act in 1992.[54] Prior to

---

54. Gesetz über die Erstreckung von gewerblichen Schutzrechten - Erstreckungsgesetz of April 23, 1992, BGB1 I, page 938, § 47 No. 3.

that amendment, a trademark assignment required that the business or the corresponding part of the business be transferred together with the trademark. Since this amendment, a trademark may be transferred separately from the underlying interest. The number of security interests taken in software is also increasing due to the amendment of the Copyright Act in 1993 and the growing prevalence and importance of software products.

The following discussion describes how to effectuate the transfer and assignment of intellectual property in Germany, and highlights certain provisions that should be included in the security agreement.

A. Applicable Legal Framework

1. Patents

A patent may be transferred pursuant to Section 15 of the Patent Act and Sections 398 and 413 of the German Civil Code.[55] In general, the transfer of patents requires no formalities. There are, however, some exceptions. Under Article 39 para. 1 and Article 44 para. 1 of the Community Patent Act,[56] as well as Article 72 of the European Patent Convention,[57] the transfer of a patent must be in writing as prescribed by law. The German Federal Supreme Court (*Bundesgerichtshof* – BGH) has held that these formal requirements are only fulfilled by a deed signed by each party to the security agreement.[58]

The transfer itself requires neither a registration in the Patent Register[59] nor the delivery of the patent deed.[60] However, the transferee of a European patent must be registered in the European Patent Register in order to secure the right to initiate proceedings against infringement of the patent by third parties.[61] Registration is recommended even with regard to German patents, because only the registered owner of a patent is entitled to correspond with the Patent

---

55. BÜRGERLICHES GESETZBUCH – BGB.
56. Übereinkommen über das europäische Patent für den Gemeinsamen Markt, December 15, 1975, as amended on December 21, 1989, BGBl 1991 II, pages 1361 *et seq.*
57. Übereinkommen über die Erteilung europäischer Patente, October 5, 1973, ABl 1979, page 3.
58. BGH NJW 1993, page 69.
59. BGH GRUR 1979, page 145.
60. RGZ 139, page 2.
61. Article 39 para. 2, Art. 44 para. 2 Community Patent Act.

Office and to dispose of the patent, and because there is an ongoing debate in German legal circles as to whether the non-registered owner of a patent is entitled to take judicial action against a third party. A written security agreement may be necessary pursuant to Section 34 of the German Anti-Cartel Act (*Gesetz gegen Wettbewerbsbeschränkungen* – GWB), if the transaction restrains competition.

2. Utility Models

The transfer of utility models is subject to the same laws as the transfer of patents.[62] The protection of utility models is, as a rule, limited to three years and may be extended to ten years under certain circumstances.[63]

3. Designs

The transfer of designs is subject to Section 3 of the Registered Designs Act[64] and Sections 398 and 413 of the BGB. There are no required formalities.[65] Registration is not necessary. The assignment is similar to the assignment of technical protection rights (patent and utility models). The protection under the Registered Designs Act is generally limited to five years, but may be extended to 20 years under certain circumstances.[66]

4. Trademarks

A trademark may be assigned under Section 8 para. 1 of the Trademark Act (*Warenzeichengesetz*) and Sections 398 and 413 of the BGB. As previously mentioned, since 1992, trademarks may be assigned separately from the business or the portion of the business to which the trademark relates.[67] While registration in the Trademark Register is not

---

62. § 22 Utility Model Act *(Gebrauchsmustergesetz)*, which is similar to § 15 Patent Act.
63. *Id.*
64. *Id.*
65. RGZ 153, page 1, 8; VON GAMM, GESCHMACKSMUSTERGESETZ, (2d ed. Munich 1989), 3, margin 15.
66. § 9 Registered Designs Act.
67. § 1 para. 1 Trademark Act, amended by the *Erstreckungsgesetz* of April 23, 1992, BGBl I, page 938, § 47 No. 3.

required,[68] it is strongly recommended because only the registered owner of a trademark may correspond with the Patent Office (Trademark Register) and, therefore, has the ability to dispose of the trademark. Moreover, it remains unclear whether the non-registered owner may take judicial action against a third party in case of infringement of the trademark.[69]

5. Copyrights

Pursuant to Section 29 of the Copyright Act,[70] a copyright itself cannot be transferred. However, the author may grant an exclusive right or a simple right of exploitation – a license – under Sections 34 and 35 of the Copyright Act. A simple non-exclusive license grants the transferee the right to use the protected work, but not to the exclusion of the author and other licensees. The license may be limited as to place, time or purpose. The owner of a simple non-exclusive license has no right to take legal action against copyright infringement by a third party. An exclusive right, on the other hand, grants the owner the right to use the copyright and exclude the author and all other third parties. At the same time, the exclusive licensee has the right to assign the license to third parties, provided that the author consents to the assignment.[71]

Under current German jurisprudence, it is unclear whether simple non-exclusive licenses may be subject to a security interest.[72] The transfer of an exclusive licensee, as a rule, requires the consent of the author. The same applies to the transfer of publishing rights.[73] The author's consent is not required if the license is transferred as part of a merger or if the work forms part of a transferred compilation. Since a business may not be subject to a security interest, only the latter exception is relevant in this context. Section 34 para. 5 of the Copyright Act provides that when the consent of the author is not required, whether by law or contract, the transferor and the transferee are jointly

---

68. BGH NJW 1968, 2188; BGH NJW 1971, page 1936.
69. Pietzker in GRUR 1973, page 561; BAUMBACH-HEFERMEHL, WARENZEICHENGESETZ, § 8, margin 34; Rogge in GRUR 1985, page 734, the latter with regard to a patent.
70. *Urheberrechtsgesetz.*
71. 35 para. 1 Copyright Act.
72. A leading opinion confirms that simple non-exclusive licenses may be transferred, SCHRICKER, URHEBERRECHT 34, margin 5 (1987); *but see* Hertin *in* FROMM-NORDEMANN, URHEBERRECHT 35, margin 1.
73. 28 Publishing Act *(Gesetz über das Verlagsrecht)* RGBl, 1901 page 217, as amended by BGBl 1965, I, 1294; BATTERT-MAUNZ, VERLAGSRECHT, 1984, page 28, margin 29.

and severally liable to the author for the fulfilment of the contract between the author and the transferor.

6. Licenses

In principle, the assignment of a license requires no formalities.[74] However, the license agreement must be in writing pursuant to Sections 34 and 20 of the Anti-Cartel Act, if the agreement triggers competition concerns. A registration in the Patent Register is not required,[75] but recommended. A simple non-exclusive license may not be transferred.[76] An exclusive license may only be transferred if the licensor consents to the transfer. Thus, the assignment of an exclusive license requires a tripartite transfer agreement between the original licensor, the licensee and the licensee's transferee.[77]

7. Software

Until mid-1993, the secured party had to determine whether the software program was protected by copyright law, which was only the case if the software program was an "individually distinctive creation." In order to eliminate this legal uncertainty, the Copyright Act was amended on June 9, 1993.[78] The amendment broadens the applicability of the Copyright Act with regard to software programs, and there is now a presumption of copyright protection for software programs. A party accepting software as collateral should be aware of the following consequences resulting from the copyright protection of software programs.

Under German law, it is not possible to transfer the ownership of copyright-protected software, although experience has shown that banks do not pay enough attention to this rule. Banks' security agreements are in many cases based on standard form contracts which provide that the software serves as collateral. Such a security agreement, however, is void. Only the floppy disk may be subject to a security

---

74. Ullmann *in* BENKARD, § 15 Patent Act, margin 44.
75. *Id.* margin 47.
76. BGHZ 62, pages 272, 276.
77. BGH NJW RR 1990, page 1251.
78. *Zweites Gesetz zur Änderung des Urheberrechtsgesetzes*, BGBl, page 910, which is based on the EU Directive concerning the protection of computer programs 91/250/EU, May 14, 1991, ABl EC No. I, 122, page 42.

interest, whereas the copyright on the software cannot be transferred.[79] However, except for the author, usually the computer programr,[80] or a licensee,[81] nobody, including the owner of the floppy disk, is entitled to exploit the software. The secured party owning the floppy disk would infringe upon the rights of the author or the licensee and, therefore, be liable for damages, if it used copies or otherwise exploited the program. Therefore, the security agreement must provide the secured party with a *license* to the software.

A license may be assigned under Section 33 paragraphs 2 and 3 of the Copyright Act and, therefore, be the subject of a security agreement.[82] However, pursuant to Section 34 para. 1 of the Copyright Act, the assignment of licenses requires that the author of the software consent to the transfer. The requirement of the author's consent may cause significant difficulties to the creditor, since the creditor is very often the last link in the following chain of license transfers:

- The author of the software grants a license to his employer (the software house) and agrees that the employer may grant the license to third parties.
- The employer grants the license to a distributor or as collateral to its bank or other creditors.
- The distributor grants a license to its customers or to its bank or other creditors.
- The bank or other creditors exploit the collateral by granting licenses.

As each of these transfers requires the consent of the software's author, the creditor must determine whether the author validly consented to each transfer. If, however, the author's employment contract grants licenses of newly created software to the author's employer, the author retains only the "empty," economically unimportant, right of exploitation and is deemed to have consented to all future transfers by the employer.[83]

In practice, the creditor may receive a license from the employer, which retains the right to use the software. For this reason, the security agreement should provide that the license is assigned subject to a "suspension." This condition is met if the creditor is entitled to exploit the collateral. In this case, the party furnishing security loses its right to

79. § 29 sentence 2 Copyright Act.
80. § 15 Copyright Act.
81. § 31 Copyright Act.
82. SCHRICKER, URHEBERRECHT, 34, margin 9.
83. Heidland *in* KTS 1990, page 183, 208.

exploit the software. All previously granted licenses remain valid, whereas subsequently granted licenses are void because licenses cannot be claimed by third parties pursuant to their *bona fide* acquisition of the license.

B. Documentation Issues

The following discussion, which uses a trademark as an example, sets forth the minimum provisions that should be included in a security agreement.

1. Definition of Collateral

The security agreement must contain a precise definition of the collateral. This means with regard to trademarks, that the trademark registration number should be specified together with the product for which the trademark has been registered. The secured debt must be specifically described and the contract should enumerate all conditions that must be met before the secured party is entitled to exploit the collateral.

2. Use by the Debtor

The contract should obligate the debtor to use the trademark. Otherwise, the trademark will be removed from the Trademark Roll after five years.[84] The parties should also provide for a minimum obligation of the debtor to advertise the trademark based on an agreed-upon advertising and marketing program.

3. Communication with the Patent Office

The debtor should have the right to be heard before the Patent Office because of the debtor's presumed familiarity with the collateral and the market. Moreover, the debtor should be required to monitor the market, in order to detect infringement of the trademark by third parties and to ensure that registration renewals are obtained on time.[85]

---

84. § 11 para. 1 No. 4 Trademark Act.
85. § 9 paras. 2 to 5 Trademark Act.

4. Third Party Infringement

Only the secured party should have the right to initiate legal proceedings against third parties infringing the trademark. The security agreement should, therefore, obligate the debtor to support the secured party with its expert knowledge and otherwise assist the secured party in prosecuting infringements. The debtor should bear the costs associated with such infringement actions.

5. Exploitation Rights

The security agreement should specify the conditions for the exploitation of the collateral. In particular, the secured party should be entitled to put the collateral up for private sale. Without such a clause, the secured party might not be able to comply with its duty to mitigate damage in case of the debtor's default.[86]

IV. RUSSIAN FEDERATION

The copyright regulations set forth in the Law On Copyright and Related Rights of September 23, 1992 are similar to the Law on Software and allow the proprietor of a copyright to transfer its economic rights in a copyright pursuant to a written agreement. The protection of patent rights is more strictly regulated and their use as collateral, therefore, subject to more rigorous requirements. The assignment of the patent for an invention, utility model or design is valid only when registered with the Russian Patent Department.[87] Patents for inventions are issued for 20 years. Patents for utility models are valid for five years and can be extended for an additional three years. The protection of design rights is available for an initial ten years and a subsequent five-year period.[88] The protection of inventions, utility models and designs deemed to be state secrets is subject to special legislation.[89] Similar rules are set forth in the Law On Trademarks and Service Marks. Trademarks can be registered with the Russian Patent Department. The protection is valid for ten years and can be repeatedly extended for subsequent ten-year periods.

---

86. BGH BB 1962, 663.
87. The Patent Law of Russia of September 23, 1992, art. 13.
88. Art. 3.
89. Patent Law, art. 3.

Significantly, any patent license or transfer agreement becomes valid only after registration with the Patent Department. The transfer of a trademark can be prohibited if it appears misleading in respect of the goods or their producer, which may present obstacles for using a trademark as a security.

V. CZECH REPUBLIC

Security interests in technology are virtually unknown in the Czech Republic. There is no case law and no legal literature on this subject.

A patent can be transferred pursuant to Section 15 of the Patent Act[90] by a written contract, which becomes effective *vis-à-vis* third parties upon registration with the Patent Register. A license to use a patent can be granted by written contract, which also becomes valid *vis-à-vis* third parties upon registration with the Patent Register.[91]

Under Czech law, there generally are two ways for proffering moveables, rights and claims as a security for credit. First, under Section 151 of the Civil Code, a lien can be created entitling the secured creditor to satisfy its claim by foreclosing on the collateral.[92] Only claims, not rights, can be pledged. As the patent right is by definition a right, it appears that patents cannot be pledged.

Second, under Section 553 of the Civil Code, the performance of an obligation may be secured by the transfer of the debtor's right to the creditor by written contract. Full ownership is transferred to the creditor, but automatically reverts to the debtor when the debtor fulfils its obligations. As the patent is transferable, it should be possible to pledge it as a security under Section 553 of the Civil Code. If the debtor does not fulfill its obligations, the creditor should be able to sell the patent to an unrelated third party.

Since patent *licenses* are claims, it should theoretically be possible to pledge them under Section 151h of the Civil Code. However, according to Section 11, para. 1 of the Patent Act, the owner of the patent has the exclusive right to grant licenses. It, therefore, appears that licenses cannot be pledged because, in case of foreclosure on the collateralized license, the rights of the owner would be infringed. For the same reason, it appears that an assignment of patent licenses under Section 553 of the Civil Code would not be possible.

---

90. Act No. 527/1990 Coll., as amended.
91. § 14 of the Patent Act.
92. §§ 151a to 151v of the Civil Code.

In general, the regulations regarding patents also apply to industrial models. An industrial model is deemed to be the external design of a product which is new and can be industrially applied.

Under the Copyright Act,[93] a copyright (which applies to software, since software cannot be patented in the Czech Republic) is not transferable. Every use of the work by third parties is subject to the prior consent of the author on a contractual basis. A pledge of copyright pursuant to Section 151h of the Civil Code is not possible because this section does not apply to rights. Similarly, a copyright transfer under Section 553 of the Civil Code is not possible because the copyright is not transferable.

Under the Trademark Act,[94] the owner of a trademark may assign its trademark or the right to use its trademark by written contract with the consent of the Czech Trademark Authority. This consent will be granted only if (i) the activities of the assignee cover all or at least part of the goods or services for which the mark had been registered and (ii) customers will not be misled by the assignment. Therefore, while a debtor should theoretically be able to pledge a trademark under Section 151h of the Civil Code (it is a right) and transfer it (with restrictions) under Section 553 of the Civil Code, pledging a trademark as a security is practically impossible, because the creditor to whom the trademark is pledged will not be able to sell it.

Royalty payment receivables may be pledged as a security without restrictions in the Czech Republic.

VI. THE NETHERLANDS

Security interests in intellectual property rights have been receiving increasing attention in the Netherlands[95] with the growing importance of intellectual property driven transactions.[96]

It is possible to pledge patents based on Article 40 of the Dutch Patent Act by means of a deed. However, the patent pledge can only be invoked against third parties if the pledge had previously been registered with the Dutch Patent Office. The creditor is required to have an address in The Hague. If it does not have such address, the address of

---

93. Act No. 35/1965 Coll., as amended.
94. Act No. 174/1988, as amended.
95. A special edition of the magazine BIJBLAD INDUSTRIELE EIGENDOM of December 1990 centered on securities and seizure.
96. *Cf.* A.A. Quaedvlieg *in* FINANCIERING EN AANSPRAKELIJKHEID, ZWOLLE 1994, p. 354.

the Dutch Patent Office will be considered the creditor's address. A patent application may also be pledged.[97] The Benelux Trademark Act is silent on the pledge of trademarks. Under current regulations, trademarks are to be pledged pursuant to the general rules of the Civil Code. As early as 1995, however, the possibility of pledging a trademark will be codified in the new Article 11C of the Benelux Trademark Act. Pledging of copyrights, design and trade name rights may be accomplished pursuant to the general rules in the Civil Code.

PART TWO – INSOLVENCY LAWS

A bankruptcy or insolvency of a transferee or transferor of technology can significantly and adversely affect the expectations and rights of the parties to a technology transfer. Frequently, rights to use or exploit technology can be terminated in an insolvency proceeding, leaving a party to a technology transfer without access to necessary technology and with a worthless claim for damages against the insolvent party. Similarly, the bankruptcy or insolvency of a debtor that has granted a security interest or similar interest in its property, including technology, as collateral can adversely affect the rights of the secured party. This Part discusses the effects of bankruptcy and insolvency laws on technology transfers and security interests in technology.

I. UNITED STATES

The United States Bankruptcy Code (the "Bankruptcy Code")[98] governs most insolvency proceedings in the United States and generally pre-empts state law.[99] Insolvency proceedings for most corporations,

---

97. *See* art. 2:236 § 2 Civil Code.
98. The Bankruptcy Code is codified as Title 11 of the U.S. Code, 11 U.S.C. § 101 *et seq.*
99. State laws provide procedures for creditors to seek the appointment of a receiver to administer the debtor's business and procedures for the debtor to deposit all of its assets with a receiver who will liquidate the assets and use the funds to pay creditors, but these are rarely used.

partnerships and other forms of business organizations, and for all individuals, are governed by the Bankruptcy Code.[100]

Under the Bankruptcy Code, the assets of the debtor,[101] which are referred to as the "bankruptcy estate," can be liquidated to repay the debtor's obligations, with the unpaid balance of the obligations being extinguished in most cases. Alternatively, the debtor can attempt to reorganize its affairs and repay its obligations, in most cases at a discount and over extended periods of time. The debtor can be responsible for its own bankruptcy proceeding, in which case it is referred to as a "debtor in possession," or the bankruptcy court can appoint an independent party referred to as a "trustee in bankruptcy" to manage the proceeding. The debtor in possession and the trustee in bankruptcy generally have the same powers and responsibilities in a bankruptcy proceeding, and for convenience will both be referred to in this discussion as the "bankruptcy trustee."

A. Invalidation of *Ipso Facto* Clauses (Bankruptcy Code Sections 365(e)(1) and 541(c)(1)(B))

Section 365(e)(1) invalidates *"ipso facto"* clauses – *i.e.,* contract clauses that attempt to terminate or modify a contract (or rights or obligations under a contract) after the commencement of a bankruptcy proceeding solely because of the insolvency of the debtor or the commencement of the bankruptcy proceeding. Similarly, Section 541(c)(1)(B) states that property of the debtor will become property of the bankruptcy estate regardless of any *ipso facto* clause in a contract relating to that property. Thus, many contract provisions that attempt to protect a party to a technology transfer upon a bankruptcy of the other party to the transfer – such as a provision requiring a sale of licensed technology to a licensee upon the bankruptcy of the licensor – will be ineffective.[102]

---

100. Because the Bankruptcy Code is most likely to be applicable to a party involved in a technology transfer, the discussion of U.S. laws applicable to insolvency will be limited to the Bankruptcy Code. The Bankruptcy Code is not applicable, however, to most financial institutions (which are subject to federal receivership and conservatorship laws or, in limited circumstances, state receivership laws) and insurance companies (which are subject to state receivership laws).
101. The Bankruptcy Code uses the term "debtor" to refer to the individual, entity or municipality with respect to which a proceeding has been commenced under the Bankruptcy Code.
102. Provisions that are tied to performance criteria, however, such as required minimum sales or minimum expenditures for development or marketing, are more likely to be upheld. The ability to exercise rights pursuant to such provisions will still be subject to the "automatic stay" under § 362 of the Bankruptcy Code, as described below.

B. Rejection, Assumption and Assignment of Executory Contracts, Including Special Provisions Relating to Intellectual Property Licenses (Bankruptcy Code Section 365)

If a contract is executory,[103] subject to limited exceptions, the bankruptcy trustee may seek bankruptcy court approval under Section 365 of the Bankruptcy Code to assume or reject the contract; if the contract is assumed the bankruptcy trustee generally has the power to assign the contract to a third party. The bankruptcy court will generally defer to the bankruptcy trustee's business judgment as to what is in the best interests of the debtor in deciding a motion to reject or accept a contract and to assign an accepted contract. Agreements relating to technology transfers frequently involve significant ongoing contractual obligations of both parties and will therefore be executory contracts for purposes of the Bankruptcy Code.

Rejection terminates the rights of the non-debtor party and the obligations of the debtor under the contract. For example, if a technology transfer agreement were an executory agreement and were rejected, the bankruptcy trustee could sell or relicense technology that is the subject of a rejected agreement to third parties and the transferee of the technology would lose its rights to continue to use or exploit the technology. Section 365(g) of the Bankruptcy Code provides that the rejection is treated as a breach of the contract by the debtor that occurred prior to the bankruptcy proceeding that entitles the non-debtor party to an unsecured claim for damages resulting from the breach.[104] Specific enforcement of the contract by the non-debtor party would generally not be available, even if such remedy would have been available in the absence of the bankruptcy proceeding.[105]

---

103. The Bankruptcy Code uses but does not define the concept of an executory contract. Most courts characterize an executory contract as one under which the obligations of both the debtor and the other party to the contract are so far unperformed that the failure of either to complete their performance would constitute a material breach excusing the performance of the other party, although some courts have adopted other tests.
104. Taking a security interest in the technology could create some economic incentive not to reject the contract if the contract provided that such damages would be a secured claim.
105. A mechanism that provides access to technology, such as a source code escrow, would not protect against rejection of the executory contract that created the right to use or exploit that technology. Similarly, taking a security interest in the technology to secure performance under the agreement will not prevent termination of the right to use or exploit the technology.

In order to assume an executory, the bankruptcy trustee must cure all existing defaults under the contract (other than those relating to financial condition of the debtor or commencement of its bankruptcy), provide compensation (or "adequate assurance" of compensation) for actual monetary losses incurred by the non-debtor party resulting from any defaults and provide "adequate assurance" of future performance of its obligations under the contract. The debtor can continue as a party to the assumed contract or can assign the contract to a third party; except for contracts to make loans or provide other financial accommodations to the debtor or contracts under which applicable non-bankruptcy law would excuse the non-debtor from accepting performance from or rendering performance to a party other than the debtor (*e.g.*, a personal services contract),[106] Section 365(c) and (f) of the Bankruptcy Code provides that all provisions in the contract and under applicable non-bankruptcy law that would otherwise prohibit, restrict or condition the assumption and assignment of the executory contract by the debtor or would terminate or permit the non-debtor to terminate the contract on such assignment or assumption are ineffective. As a condition to the assignment of the contract, the non-debtor party is entitled to receive adequate assurance of future performance from the prospective assignee; this adequate assurance will generally take the form of a presentation by the prospective assignee to the bankruptcy court regarding the prospective assignee's ability to perform the contract rather than specific commitments (financial or otherwise) to the non-debtor party to the contract. The assignment of the contract excuses the debtor, the bankruptcy estate and the bankruptcy trustee from liability for any breach occurring after the assignment of the contract. The non-debtor party may find itself accepting future performance from, and rendering future performance to, a party (either the debtor or an assignee) that is not qualified or does not have the resources to perform the contract[107] or that is a competitor.

Section 365(n) was added to the Bankruptcy Code in 1988 to clarify the rights of a licensee of certain types of technology pending the bankruptcy trustee's decision to assume or reject the license and to provide limited protections with respect to a licensee's right to continue to use technology if a license of that technology is rejected as an

---

106. Some courts have held technology contracts to be personal services contracts and therefore not assignable without the non-debtor party's consent. *See In re Alltech Plastics, Inc.*, 71 B.R. 686, 689 (W.D. Tenn. 1987); *Harris v. Emus Records Corp.*, 734 F.2d 1329, 1334 (9th Cir. 1984).

107. For example, the debtor may give adequate assurances of future performance that satisfy the bankruptcy court in connection with the assumption of the contract, but then be unable to retain key personnel or obtain other necessary technology to perform the contract because of its financial condition.

executory contract.[108] Section 365(n) applies only to executory licenses of intellectual property – not to assignments or other contractual relationships – and only in a bankruptcy of the licensor. Section 365(n) also limits the types of intellectual property licenses protected to those involving trade secrets, inventions, processes and designs protected under U.S. patent law, patent applications, plant varieties, works of authorship protected under U.S. copyright law (which would include software), and mask works protected under U.S. law.[109]

Section 365(n) provides that after commencement of the licensor's bankruptcy proceeding, but prior to assumption or rejection of the license, upon written request of the licensee, the bankruptcy trustee must either perform under the license or provide the licensed intellectual property to the licensee,[110] and the bankruptcy trustee may not interfere with the licensee's rights under the license or supplementary agreements to the licensed intellectual property, including any right to obtain such intellectual property from a third party, such as an escrow agent.

If the bankruptcy trustee assumes the license, it is treated the same as the assumption of any other executory contract, as described above.

Under Section 365(n), if the bankruptcy trustee rejects a license of intellectual property of a type covered by the section, then the licensee may elect

(i) to treat the license as terminated by the rejection, if by the terms of the license such a rejection would be a breach of contract that would entitle the licensee to treat the contract as terminated by its own terms, under applicable non-bankruptcy law or under an agreement made by the licensee with another person, and seek damages (which will be treated as an unsecured claim in the

---

108. § 365(n) permits the licensee to enforce exclusivity provisions in a license, which the licensee can use to protect its rights from the powers of the bankruptcy trustee to assume and assign the license and its rights to use, sell or lease property under § 363 of the Bankruptcy Code, as described below.
109. Bankruptcy Code § 101(56). As a result of the limitations in the definition of "intellectual property" for purposes of § 365(n), licenses of trademarks, trade names and service marks and of non-U.S. patents and copyrights are excluded from the protections provided to a licensee by § 365(n). A licensee may want to have separate licenses for technology that is not covered by § 365(n) to avoid an argument by the debtor that a license that covers property subject to § 365(n) and property that is not should not receive the benefits provided by the Section.
110. § 365(n) specifically provides the licensee with a right of access to the licensed technology (to the extent it is property covered by § 365(n)); however, a licensee should consider supplementing its statutory protections with a source code or other escrow arrangement for the technology.

bankruptcy and generally provide little practical compensation), or

(ii) to retain its rights under the license (including a right to enforce any exclusivity provision, but excluding any other right under applicable non-bankruptcy law to specific performance of the contract) and any agreement supplemental to the license (such as a source code or other escrow) as such rights existed *prior* to the commencement of the bankruptcy proceeding.

This limitation to rights existing prior to the commencement of the bankruptcy proceeding can have a significant adverse effect on the licensee if the licensed technology is of a type that is updated or supplemented periodically, or if the licensor is still developing the technology when the licensor's bankruptcy proceeding is commenced, since Section 365(n) will not provide the licensee with any rights to subsequent development of the technology by or on behalf of the licensor. If the licensee does not have the right to prepare derivative works under the license, the licensee may not be permitted to update, supplement or complete development of the technology so that it is useful. The licensee should reserve the right to adapt, modify and prepare derivative works based on the technology in the event of the licensor's failure to complete its obligations to develop the technology or to provide maintenance, support, updates or similar services. Even if the licensee has the legal right to update, supplement or complete the development of the technology, there will often be economic and practical impediments to do so, such as lack of technical expertise and the expense of doing so. In addition, the licensee may be unwilling to make the investment needed to update, supplement or develop the technology if it cannot recover those costs or if its right to enforce an exclusivity provision in the license may not protect it if the development of the technology is also continued or completed by the debtor.

The licensee may retain the rights under the license provided under Section 365(n) for the term provided in the license and any renewal period in the license. If the licensee chooses to retain its rights under the license, the licensee must provide the licensor with a written request for the continuation of the license; the licensee must make all royalty payments due under the contract and for the period of any extension; the licensee has no right to "setoff" any damages or other amounts due to the licensee from the debtor against royalties due under the license; and the licensee is deemed to waive any claim it may have due to the licensor's failure to perform its other obligations. If the licensee delivers the written request to retain its rights under the license, the licensor must provide the licensee with the intellectual property held by the licensor[111] and not interfere with the rights given to the licensee by the contract or any supplementary agreement, including any right to obtain the intellectual property from a third party, such as an escrow agent. The licensor cannot, however, be required to perform other obligations that it had under the license agreement, including any maintenance or development work, providing training or defending against third party infringement claims and pursuing infringers, and the licensee cannot sue for damages for failure to perform any such obligations. The licensee should therefore reserve the rights necessary to be able to develop and maintain the technology, and to defend against and pursue infringement claims if the licensor fails to do so, although as noted above the licensee's practical protections from retaining such rights may be limited.

In drafting a license agreement, in order to limit its obligations to payment for the technology and rights that it will be permitted to retain under Section 365(n), a licensee should consider requiring that the agreement for the use of technology and related royalty payments be separate from agreements for the licensor to provide services, such as upgrades and maintenance. It may also be in the licensee's interest to allocate royalty payments between the types of technology covered by Section 365(n) and other types of technology. In addition, allocations could be set that create economic disincentives for the bankruptcy trustee to reject the license (for example, by allocating a higher proportion of payments to provision of services and less to royalties for technology covered by Section 365(n), so that there is an incentive to assume the contract and perform the services).

If the licensee elects to treat the rejected contract as terminated, it is treated the same as any other rejection of an executory contract, as described above.

C. Right of Bankruptcy Trustee to Use, Sell or Lease Property (Bankruptcy Code Section 363)

Section 363 of the Bankruptcy Code provides that the bankruptcy trustee can use, sell or lease property of the debtor, including the debtor's technology, in the ordinary course of business without the approval of the bankruptcy court and can use, sell or lease such

---

111. If the intellectual property to be provided under the license includes obligations to provide information or technical support other than in written form, the licensee may receive little practical benefit from this provision.

property outside the ordinary course of business with court approval.[112] The court can authorize the use, sale or lease of the property even if the debtor entered into agreements that would prohibit such actions (subject to the limited protections for licenses of technology under Section 365(n) described above). Any party that has an interest in property so used, sold or leased or proposed to be so used, sold or leased may apply to the bankruptcy court for an order under Section 363(e) of the Bankruptcy Code prohibiting or conditioning such use, sale or lease as necessary to provide "adequate protection" for such interest. Section 361 of the Bankruptcy Code provides that "adequate protection" of a person's interest in property may be provided by requiring the bankruptcy trustee to make a cash payment or periodic cash payments to the extent that the use, sale or lease under Section 363 results in a decrease in value of such person's interest in such property, providing to such person an additional or replacement lien to the extent that such sale, use or lease results in a decrease in the value of such person's interest in such property or granting such other relief as will result in the realization by such person of the "indubitable equivalent" of such person's interest in such property; most of this language was drafted with the protection of a secured party, rather than a licensee or licensor of technology, in mind. Adequate protection can take any form that the bankruptcy court (which has significant discretion in this area) believes will protect the non-debtor party's interest and generally is tangible in nature (such as the provision of a letter of credit or a lien on other property).

Section 363(f) of the Bankruptcy Code gives the bankruptcy trustee the power to sell property of the debtor free and clear of any interest in such property, including a security interest or the interests of a licensee, if

(i) applicable non-bankruptcy law permits sale of such property free and clear of such interest,
(ii) the owner of such interest consents,
(iii) such interest is a lien and the price at which such property is sold is greater than the aggregate value of all liens on such property,
(iv) such interest is in *bona fide* dispute, or

112. § 363(l) of the Bankruptcy Code provides that the bankruptcy trustee can use, sell or lease property of the debtor under § 363, or as part of the plan to reorganize the debtor's business, notwithstanding any provision in a contract, lease or applicable law that is conditioned on the insolvency or financial condition of the debtor or on the commencement of the debtor's bankruptcy proceeding (*i.e.,* an *ipso facto* provision) and that effects (or gives an option to effect) a forfeiture, modification or termination of the debtor's interest in such property.

(v) such person could be compelled, in a legal or equitable proceeding, to accept a money satisfaction of such interest.

The bankruptcy courts have construed this provision broadly to permit the bankruptcy trustee to dispose of property in order to satisfy claims against the debtor.

Section 363(h) of the Bankruptcy Code permits the bankruptcy trustee to sell both the debtor's interest and the interest of any co-owners in property in which the debtor had at the time of commencement of the bankruptcy proceeding an undivided interest as a tenant in common, joint tenant or tenant by the entirety if

(i) partition in kind of such property among the bankruptcy trustee and such co-owners is impracticable;
(ii) sale of the debtor's undivided interest in such property would realize significantly less for the bankruptcy estate than sale of such property free of the interests of such co-owners;
(iii) the benefit to the bankruptcy estate of a sale of such property free of the interests of co-owners outweighs the detriment, if any, to such co-owners; and
(iv) such property is not used in the production, transmission, or distribution, for sale, of electric energy or of natural or synthetic gas for heat, light or power.

Section 363(i) of the Bankruptcy Code gives the co-owners of the property the right to purchase such property at the price at which such sale is to be consummated. If the co-owners do not exercise this right, they will receive their proportionate share of the proceeds of the sale (after deduction of costs and expenses of the sale) pursuant to Section 363(j) of the Bankruptcy Code. Therefore, if two parties have established an arrangement to own and develop technology together, the bankruptcy of one of those parties could result in the co-owner's loss of its rights to the property or the need for the co-owner to obtain the funds to purchase the debtor's interest in the technology.[113]

D. Automatic Stay (Bankruptcy Code Section 362)

Under Section 362 of the Bankruptcy Code, upon the filing of a bankruptcy proceeding an "automatic stay" is imposed that prohibits the pursuit of most actions against the debtor. The stay is applicable to

---

113. A similar issue could arise where two parties form a joint venture to develop or exploit technology, since either of the parties could place the joint venture into bankruptcy.

all individuals and entities and to most actions relating to the debtor and its property, including the commencement or continuation of a judicial, administrative or other action or proceeding against the debtor, any act to obtain possession, or exercise control over, the debtor's property, any act to terminate an agreement with the debtor, or to create, perfect or enforce any lien against the debtor's property, and any act to collect, assess or recover a claim against the debtor that arose before the filing of the bankruptcy proceeding. The purpose of the stay is to maintain the *status quo* and give the bankruptcy trustee and creditors the opportunity to assess the debtor's condition and prospects and the creditors' positions in order to permit orderly administration of the bankruptcy estate and maximize the value realized in a liquidation or enhance the prospects for a successful reorganization and continued operation of the debtor's business.

The stay will generally prohibit the exercise of remedies (including termination for default) that are provided in the agreements with the debtor or under applicable law, without a hearing before and approval from the bankruptcy court. For example, the stay would prevent a lawsuit to recover unpaid license fees or royalties or the termination of a license agreement for failure of the licensee to make payments or of the licensor to provide required maintenance or upgrades.

E. Avoiding Powers of the Bankruptcy Trustee (Bankruptcy Code Sections 544, 547 and 548)

The bankruptcy trustee has broad powers to "avoid" (*i.e.*, set aside) transfers of property or an interest in property of the debtor made by the debtor prior to the commencement of the bankruptcy proceeding. The termination of the debtor's rights under a contract may constitute a transfer for purposes of these powers. The avoidance of the transfer results in the return of the property to the debtor.

Under Section 544(a) of the Bankruptcy Code, the bankruptcy trustee is given the rights and powers of the holder of a judicial lien on all property of the debtor. If under applicable law the holder of such a lien has priority over a transferee of technology, then the transferee's rights can be avoided by the bankruptcy trustee and the property or interest in property returned to the debtor.

Transfers of property or an interest in property of the debtor may be set aside under Section 547 of the Bankruptcy Code as "preferential transfers," even though all appropriate measures have been taken to perfect the transfer against third parties. For a transfer to constitute a preferential transfer that can be avoided, it must

ASSIGNMENT AND PROTECTION OF RIGHTS 293

  (i) be to or for the benefit of a creditor,[114]
  (ii) be made on account of an antecedent obligation,
  (iii) be made while the transferor is insolvent,
  (iv) be made 90 days or less before bankruptcy (one year or less if the transferee is an "insider" of the debtor), and
  (v) enable the transferee to receive more than it would have received if the debtor's assets were liquidated. For example, transfers of technology made by a financially troubled company during the specified period to satisfy a pre-existing obligation of the debtor, such as a transfer of rights to a derivative work in satisfaction of overdue license fees or royalties, are subject to avoidance.

Under Section 548 of the Bankruptcy Code, the bankruptcy trustee may avoid a transfer of property or an interest in property of the debtor made one year or less before the debtor's bankruptcy if the transfer either

  (i) was made with actual intent to hinder, delay or defraud creditors or
  (ii) was made, without regard to intent, for less than reasonably equivalent value and the transferor was, at the time of the transfer, insolvent, had unreasonably small capital or was unable to pay its obligations as they became due, or was rendered so by the transfer.

For example, purchases or licenses of technology at less than a fair price from a financially troubled company made during the relevant period would be subject to avoidance under this "fraudulent conveyance" provision.[115]

---

114. The Bankruptcy Code uses the term "creditor" to refer to any person that has a claim against the debtor that arose at the time of or before the commencement of the debtor's bankruptcy proceeding; this term includes the holder of a right to payment (whether or not such right is reduced to judgment, liquidated or unliquidated, fixed, contingent, matured, unmatured, disputed, undisputed, legal, equitable, secured or unsecured) or right to an equitable remedy for breach of performance if such breach gives rise to a right to payment.
115. Similar provisions appear in state fraudulent transfer and fraudulent conveyance laws, which often provide time periods significantly longer than the one-year period under the Bankruptcy Code for which transactions may be challenged and avoided. Under § 544(b) of the Bankruptcy Code, the bankruptcy trustee may use these state law provisions in a bankruptcy proceeding. In addition, creditors can invoke these state laws even if no proceeding under the Bankruptcy Code is pending.

F. Bankruptcy Code Provisions Affecting Security Interests

Generally the rights of a secured party to its collateral are honored in a bankruptcy proceeding of the debtor. There are situations, however, where the Bankruptcy Code can limit or invalidate the rights of a secured party.

1. Preferential Transfers (Bankruptcy Code Section 547)

Unperfected security interests (or security interests that were not perfected more than 90 days, or in cases where an insider is benefited more than one year, prior to bankruptcy) can often be "avoided" as a preferential transfer (*i.e.,* such security interest will be rendered unenforceable against the debtor and third parties) in the debtor's bankruptcy proceeding by the bankruptcy trustee, effectively reducing the secured party to the status of a general creditor. Payments by the debtor of obligations secured by a security interest that has been avoided may be recaptured from the secured party.

2. Avoiding Powers (Bankruptcy Code Section 544)

The bankruptcy trustee, under the "strong arm clause" of Section 544(a) of the Bankruptcy Code, has every right and power state law confers upon the holder of a lien obtained by legal or equitable proceeding. A lien creditor generally takes priority over unperfected security interests.[116]

3. Fraudulent Transfers (Bankruptcy Code Section 548)

If a security interest is granted within one year prior to bankruptcy with actual intent to hinder, delay or defraud creditors of the debtor or for less than fair consideration and at the time of the transfer the debtor was insolvent, had unreasonably small capital or was unable to pay its

---

116. *See, e.g.,* UCC § 9-301(1)(b) ("an unperfected security interest is subordinate to the rights of a person who becomes a lien creditor before the security interest is perfected"); *Peregrine,* 116 B.R. at 205-06 (trustee in bankruptcy, with the powers of a judicial lien creditor, has priority under Copyright Act over unperfected security interest in copyright).

debts as they became due, or was rendered so by the transaction, the bankruptcy trustee can avoid the security interest.[117] The existence of a fraudulent transfer is frequently alleged where a subsidiary grants a security interest in its assets to secure the obligations of its parent corporation or a corporation grants such a security interest to secure the obligations of its stockholders.[118]

4. Cut-Off of Security Interests (Bankruptcy Code Section 552)

Section 552 of the Bankruptcy Code provides that property acquired by the debtor after the commencement of the bankruptcy proceeding is not subject to a lien resulting from any security agreement entered into before the commencement of the proceeding except to the extent of proceeds, products, offspring, rents or profits of collateral that existed prior to commencement of the bankruptcy proceeding. It is possible that the bankruptcy courts would find that payments under a license of technology were not "proceeds" of the technology that would be protected under Section 552, since proceeds are defined in Section 9-306 of the UCC as "whatever is received upon the sale, exchange, collection or other disposition of collateral or proceeds" and a license may not constitute a transfer of sufficient rights to constitute a disposition that creates proceeds.

5. Sale of Property Free of Liens (Bankruptcy Code Section 363(f))

Section 363(f) of the Bankruptcy Code gives the bankruptcy trustee the power to sell property of the debtor free and clear of any interest in such property, including a lien on such property.

6. Automatic Stay (Bankruptcy Code Section 362)

The automatic stay effectively prevents a secured party from taking any action to perfect a security interest, liquidate collateral or collect or enforce the obligations due to the secured party from the debtor until the bankruptcy court grants permission, which can result in significant delays.

---

117. *See supra*, note 115, regarding similar powers under state fraudulent transfer and fraudulent conveyance laws.
118. For example, in the acquisition of a corporation the acquiror may borrow the funds to finance the purchase of the corporation and cause the acquired company to give the lender a security interest in the acquired company's assets to secure the loan.

II. GERMANY

The effects of German bankruptcy law on technology transfers vary considerably with the type of intellectual property right involved. One must, therefore, look to the interaction between the bankruptcy laws and the laws governing the intellectual property rights that are the subject of the bankruptcy proceedings.[119]

A. Patents

1. German Patents

Under Section 1 para. 1 of the German Bankruptcy Act, bankruptcy proceedings apply to all assets which belong to the bankrupt at the time proceedings are initiated to the extent they are subject to attachment and execution. This is limited, however, by Section 1 para. 4 of the Bankruptcy Act, which provides that items that are not attachable do not form part of the bankrupt's estate.

Under Sections 857 para. 1 and 851 para.1 of the German Code of Civil Procedure, rights are attachable if they are transferable. Under Section 14 para. 1 of the Patent Act, a patent may be assigned with or without restrictions. Therefore, a patent right is attachable and may be deemed part of the bankrupt's estate. If the patent is sold and assigned in a technology transfer, the transferee is considered the legal holder of the patent. If the legal holder is declared bankrupt, the patent will form part of the bankrupt's estate.

Under Section 6 para. 1 of the Bankruptcy Act, the bankrupt is not entitled to dispose of its property once bankruptcy proceedings are initiated. After adjudication of the bankruptcy proceedings, the receiver has the power to manage and dispose of the property in any manner within the framework of the receiver's legal obligations. Thus, the receiver is entitled to sell patents privately or exchange or sell them by auction. The receiver may also carry on operations and use the patents

---

119. Patents are governed by the Patent Act of December 16, 1980 (the "Patent Act"); utility models by the Utility Model Act of August 28, 1986 (the "Utility Model Act"); employee inventions by the Act on Employees' Inventions of July 25, 1957 (the "Act on Employees' Inventions"); designs by the Act Concerning Copyright in Designs of January 11, 1976 (the "Design Act"); trademarks by the Trademark Act of January 2, 1968 (the "Trademark Act"); and copyrights are governed by the Act Dealing With Copyright and Related Rights of September 9, 1965 (the "Copyright Act").

for the estate's account. Significantly, the receiver also is entitled to grant licenses for the patents.

2. Foreign Patents

In the international technology transfer context, it frequently is necessary to determine whether a German court may attach foreign patents belonging to a German citizen or entity or, in the reverse case, whether a foreign court may attach a German patent which belongs to a citizen or entity of a foreign country. The Federal Supreme Court (*Bundesgerichtshof* – BGH) has held that the foreign assets of the German bankrupt belong to the estate of the German bankrupt, if the holder of those assets becomes bankrupt in Germany.[120] This also applies to foreign patents. Thus, a creditor in bankruptcy who has obtained an executed foreign judgment or decree must restore the attached assets under the rules of undue enrichment. The reverse case is presented when a foreign court is asked to attach a German patent which belongs to a citizen of a foreign country. This issue has been discussed by German legal scholars for many years. The controversy was settled by the Federal Supreme Court in 1985, when it held that the adjudication of bankruptcy in a foreign country includes the German assets of the debtor, so that the patents belong to the foreign debtor's estate.[121]

3. European Union Patents

Under Article 41 para. 1 of the Agreement Concerning Patents for the Common Market, a European patent is governed by the bankruptcy proceedings of the country which first adjudicated the proceedings, irrespective of where the patent was granted or the bankrupt has its legal seat.

B. Utility Models

Section 22 of the Utility Model Act concerning the assignment of the protective right is identical to Section 15 of the Patent Act. Therefore, the procedure with regard to utility models follows the patent regime.

---

120. BGHZ 88, pages 147, 150.
121. BGHZ 95, page 257.

C. Licenses

To the extent a license is attachable, it forms part of the bankrupt's estate. Attachability depends on whether the license can be assigned, which, in turn, is determined by the nature of the license agreement. A non-exclusive license is not assignable and, therefore, unattachable. The prevalent view in German legal circles is that a license is analogous to a lease. Therefore, Section 19 of the Bankruptcy Act applies. This section provides that the receiver (on behalf of the bankrupt licensee) as well as the licensor may terminate the license agreement. If the license agreement remains effective, the receiver is obligated to pay royalties.[122] The receiver may not in any other way dispose of the non-exclusive license such as, for example, by way of transfer or sublicensing. In the event of the licensor's bankruptcy, the license agreement, in principle, remains effective pursuant to Section 21 of the Bankruptcy Act. However, the receiver (on behalf of the licensor) may refuse to fulfill the licensor's obligations under the license agreement pursuant to Section 17 of the Bankruptcy Act, if the license was not granted before the adjudication of the bankruptcy.

In contrast to the non-exclusive license, the exclusive license is contractually assignable and, therefore, attachable. Thus, an exclusive license forms part of the licensee's bankrupt estate. If, however, the license agreement itself provides that the exclusive license is not assignable, the exclusive license is treated as a non-exclusive license.

D. Employee Inventions

Whereas so-called "free" inventions are treated like patents or utility models, service inventions – which are made by an employee during employment and are substantially based on the know-how of the employer – are governed by the Act on Employees' Inventions. Under Section 6 of that Act, the employer may receive a limited or unlimited right to use the service invention. If bankruptcy proceedings are initiated against the employer, the employee has a right of pre-emption with regard to unlimited service inventions, provided that the receiver of the bankrupt's estate disposes of the service inventions without the business or the corresponding part of the business. Limited service inventions are treated as a simple non-exclusive license.[123]

---

122. § 59 para. 1 No. 2 Bankruptcy Act (*i.e.,* a direct or preferred debt of the bankruptcy estate).
123. Bartenbach-Volz, Gesetz über Arbeitnehmererfindungen, (2d ed. 1990), § 27, margin 12.

E. Trade Secrets and Know-How

Trade secrets and know-how form part of the bankrupt's estate, provided that their owner exploits the trade secret or know-how or takes appropriate steps to do so. The receiver may license or otherwise dispose of trade secrets and know-how. If there is a pending application for a patent with regard to trade secrets or know-how, the receiver is entitled to exploit such patent rights.

F. Designs

Under Section 3 of the Design Act, designs are assignable and, therefore, attachable. Designs form part of the bankrupt's estate upon registration or exploitation by the author.[124]

G. Trademarks

In case of a transferee's bankruptcy, the trademark belongs to the bankrupt's estate. The receiver is entitled to dispose of the trademark, prosecute trademark infringements and sue for damages. However, if the trademark contains the family name of the bankrupt, any transfer of the trademark is subject to the bankrupt's consent.

H. Copyrights

Under Section 29 sentence 2 of the Copyright Act, a copyright may not be conveyed, in whole or in part (except in the case of a testamentary disposition or the settlement of an estate). Therefore, the copyright itself is not attachable and does not form part of the bankrupt's estate. However, the author is entitled to grant licenses to the copyright.[125] The right to grant licenses is attachable and, consequently, forms part of the bankrupt estate, provided that the author consents pursuant to Section 113 of the Copyright Act.[126] If the author is entitled to license fees or if the author has a claim for damages with regard to the infringement of the copyright before the adjudication of bankruptcy proceedings, then those claims will form part of the bankrupt's estate. If the receiver asserts these claims, no prior consent of

---

124. KUHN-UHLENBRUCK, KONKURSORDNUNG, § 1, margin 66.
125. § 31 Copyright Act.
126. GOTTWALD, INSOLVENZRECHTSHANDBUCH, 1990, § 26, margin 45.

the author is required. Provided that an exclusive or non-exclusive license had been granted by the author before the adjudication of bankruptcy, the receiver may proceed as described in Section C above.

In principle, these rules also apply to software. However, Section 69b of the Copyright Act contains a special provision with regard to employee inventions (see Section D above) under which the employer is exclusively entitled to exercise all exploitation rights with regard to the software, if the software is created by an employee in the course of the employee's duties or following the employer's instructions. Although the employee remains the author of the work, the employer becomes the holder of the copyright. Therefore, the exploitation rights of the software form part of the employer's estate.

Section 36 of the Publishing Act contains specific provisions applicable to publishing contracts in case of the publisher's bankruptcy. If the bankruptcy proceedings are adjudicated before the publisher starts to reproduce the work, the author is entitled to withdraw from the contract, whereas under Section 17 of the Bankruptcy Act, only the receiver would have a right of withdrawal. If the author is not entitled to withdrawal because the reproduction of the work had already begun, the receiver may insist on the fulfilment of the publishing contract. The author's right to compensation then becomes a preferred claim. The receiver may also choose not to perform the contract. If so, the author's right to fulfilment of the contract becomes a claim for damages, which is considered an ordinary debt in bankruptcy proceedings.

III. FRANCE

The protection of the transferor's rights in technology in the event of the transferee's bankruptcy is governed by Law No. 85-98 of January 25, 1985, as amended by Law No. 94-475 of June 10, 1994, enforceable as of October 1, 1994 ("Law No. 85-98"). This law reflects paramount public policy and cannot be escaped by the parties' contractual selection of non-French law.[127] It is applicable to all transfers of technology, including transfers of patents, know-how and software.

In the case of the transferee's bankruptcy, the rights of the transferor may be jeopardized when the technology is licensed or assigned. Significantly, the transferor is not authorized to terminate a license

---

127. *See* Chapter Six, Part I.

agreement because the licensee becomes bankrupt.[128] Instead, the transferor must file a formal request with the official receiver appointed by the court. If this request remains unanswered for more than one month, the transferor may terminate the agreement. If the official receiver elects to keep the agreement in force, the transferor must accept the receiver's decision, although the transferor's rights will be protected, as the receiver must comply with all contractual provisions, including payment of royalties due to the transferor. Thus, the receiver may elect to keep the agreement in force only if it is in a position to comply with all of the agreement's provisions.

If the technology is assigned, there is obviously no difficulty if the transferee is declared bankrupt after the consideration for the technology had been fully tendered. There, nevertheless, remains the risk that the receiver will authorize one of the transferor's competitors to exploit the technology transferred to the licensee. By contrast, when the transferee is declared bankrupt before the transfer price is fully paid, the creditor transferor must then officially declare its rights to the so-called *représentant des créanciers*, appointed by the court. Such declaration should be made within two months from the publication of the bankruptcy in the official newspapers.

IV. CZECH REPUBLIC

The Czech Bankruptcy Act is very new and, thus far, there has been virtually no experience with its application.[129] Bankruptcy proceedings will apply to the property that belonged to the debtor on the day the bankruptcy order was issued, and to any property acquired in the course of the bankruptcy proceedings, including salaries, wages and other similar income. The bankrupt's assets do not, however, include property which cannot be made subject to execution (enforcement) of the court's order. Execution is possible in assignable property rights which do not constitute rights personally attaching to the debtor.

Patents may be assigned and sold and are not subject to execution under special regulations. As they are fully transferable, they are not deemed to be personally attaching rights. Therefore, if a patent owner becomes bankrupt, the patent will be included in the bankrupt's estate and may be sold by the executor. *Mutatis mutandis*, the same is true

128. Art. 37, para. 5 of Law No. 85-98 of January 26, 1985, as amended by Law No. 94-475 of June 10, 1994.
129. Act No. 328/1991 Coll., as amended.

for patent licenses. However, a transfer of a license is only valid with the consent of the owner of the patent. If the bankrupt owner licensed the patent to a third party, the executor is free to act, subject only to the license agreement. If the licensee, in turn, sublicenses the patent, that sublicense cannot be disposed of, because its disposition would violate the rights of the patent owner. In general, the same rules apply to industrial models.

As copyrights are not transferable, they are not included in the bankrupt's estate. A trademark, or right to the use of a trademark, is only transferable with the consent of the Czech Trademark Authority, which will only be granted if the trademark is used for similar goods or services. Since trademarks may be assigned (subject to restrictions) or sold, are not subject to execution under special regulations, and do not seem to attach personally, they become part of the bankrupt's estate. However, as a practical matter, the receiver will find it difficult to assign them.

Claims to royalty payments are monetary claims and in general become part of the bankrupt's estate. However, subject to exceptions applicable to preferential claims, only one-fifth of an author's royalties are subject to attachment.

V. THE NETHERLANDS

The more general subject of intellectual property rights in bankruptcy has not received much attention in Dutch law, let alone the rights of the transferor in the event of the transferee's bankruptcy. Dutch law currently only regulates copyrights in relation to bankruptcy. Bankruptcy generally constitutes a seizure of the entire assets of the debtor as of the moment it is declared bankrupt, as well as a seizure of what the debtor acquires during the bankruptcy. Copyright, however, does not fall within the bankrupt's estate, unless the copyright can be seized.[130] A copyright cannot be seized if it belongs to the author and the work has not yet been published or if the copyright was assigned by legacy.[131] Therefore, if the author of a work becomes bankrupt, the copyright in its work will not become part of the bankrupt's estate. That is not to say, however, that the fruits of the exploitation of the copyright will not fall within the bankrupt's estate.[132] By contrast, if the author of a work

---

130. Art. 21 of 1 Bankruptcy Law.
131. Art. 2 § 3 Copyright Act.
132. SPOOR/VERKADE, AUTEURSRECHT, Deventer 1993, p. 349.

assigns the copyright, and the assignee becomes bankrupt, then the copyright will be included in the bankrupt's estate. Other intellectual property rights should become part of the bankrupt estate without restrictions.

VI. SPAIN

The transferor's rights in technology in the event of the transferee's bankruptcy in Spain are related both to the law of industrial and intellectual property and to bankruptcy law. The proceeding established in the Civil Code (the so-called *"concurso de acreedores"*), which applies when a natural person, who is not an entrepreneur, becomes bankrupt, must be distinguished from the two proceedings regulated by the commercial law: the bankruptcy (*quiebra*), regulated by the Code of Commerce, and the temporary receivership (*suspension de pagos*), whose purpose is to solve a crisis situation by an agreement between the debtor and its creditors. Unfortunately, these laws are dated, and there are significant gaps in Spanish bankruptcy regulation. While this discussion focuses on strict bankruptcy proceedings, most of it should also apply to temporary receiverships.

Intellectual property rights such as patents, utility models and trademarks, may be legally transferred in Spain. Therefore, they may also be attached and executed, *i.e.,* sold by the judge in a public auction in a bankruptcy proceeding. The principal of ancillarity, according to which rights may only be assigned together with all other assets of the undertaking, does not apply. These rights may be transferred, attached and executed separately from the underlying business subject to two exceptions. First, Article 54 of the Patent Act only allows the transfer of the right of prior use on a patented invention together with the underlying business. Second, Article 79 of the Trademark Act only permits assignment of the commercial name together with the business. A copyright may not be sold under Spanish law. Only exploitation rights in the copyright may be assigned, *i.e.,* transferred in exchange for royalties or otherwise licensed.

Article 878 of the Commercial Code voids all transfers of assets of the bankrupt's estate that take effect prior to the commencement of the bankruptcy proceedings and after the date on which the bankruptcy is given retroactive effect. That date is fixed by a judge. Immediately after the bankruptcy is declared, the receiver may sell the bankrupt's assets in order to satisfy creditors. The bankrupt's estate includes all of the bankrupt's assets regardless of where the assets are or have been obtained, so that assets located in a foreign country are included in the bankrupt's estate. There is a minimum price below which the receiver cannot sell the assets, however. This minimum price is set by the deputy (*comisario*) of the judge in the liquidation of the estate. For purposes of setting that price, intellectual property rights are considered commercial assets.

With respect to most licenses, unless there is a contractual provision to the contrary, both the licensor and the licensee are allowed to terminate the contract when the other party is declared bankrupt if the receiver of the bankrupt party decides to maintain the contract in effect. The fees generated after commencement of the bankruptcy proceedings will be credited to the bankrupt's estate with preference given to other previous debts. License agreements cannot be transferred to other persons by the licensee or the receiver without the consent of the intellectual property rights' owner.

Under the Intellectual Property Act, a copyright cannot be sold. However, the exploitation rights pertaining to the copyright can be assigned or licensed. The granting and the assignment of a license must be in writing. An assignment does not have to be registered in the Intellectual Property Registry in order to be valid. However, when registered, the contract holds a presumption of existence as shown by the registry records. In principle, the bankruptcy of the author or the owner of a copyright does not affect the copyright licensing agreement. In case of bankruptcy of the licensee, the outstanding licensing fees constitute a privileged credit against the estate of the licensee, and their payment ranks in priority with salaries owed by the licensee.

Licensed copyrights can only be attached and assigned in a licensee's bankruptcy proceeding if the author consented to such new assignment or license. The author's consent is not necessary, however, when copyright exploitation rights are attached and assigned as part of the licensee's global business undertaking.

Chapter Six

Applicable Law and Resolution of Technology Transfer Disputes

Pierre Lenoir and Nathalie Meyer Fabre
Jeantet & Associés, Paris

Ralph A. Taylor, Jr. and Harry Rubin
Shaw, Pittman, Potts & Trowbridge, Washington, D.C.

Only too often the placement of choice of law and dispute resolution provisions in a contract – right at the end just before the signature lines – betrays the parties' failure to appreciate the importance of those provisions for the implementation and enforcement of their contractual relationship. This Chapter discusses the choice of law and dispute resolution considerations that are most salient to technology transfers. Although careful and thoughtful drafting of choice of law and dispute resolution clauses cannot eliminate all problems that may arise, it can and should substantially minimize uncertainty.

I. APPLICABLE LAW

The selection of the law applicable to technology transfer transactions is as important for the formation and performance of the contract as it is for the resolution of any disputes that may arise under it. Throughout the performance of the contract, certainty as to which law applies will enable the parties to determine their rights, obligations, and legal maneuvring room when the contract is silent or ambiguous with respect to particular issues. Clarity as to which body of law applies is critical in the event of a dispute, because disputes are resolved not only on the basis of the relevant facts and terms of the contract but also in accordance with general principles of applicable law.

In many jurisdictions, especially those in Europe, certain agreements, such as employment and agency contracts, are subject to special rules of law. The determination of the law governing technology transfer agreements generally is not based on such idiosyncratic rules. Therefore, this discussion will largely track the general principles governing the determination of applicable law in international contracts.

A. Determination of Applicable Law

Several legal systems may concurrently govern an international contract. These include the laws of each party's domicile or principal place of business; the laws of the jurisdiction where the contract is performed or has a substantial effect; the law of supranational regimes, such as the rules and regulations of the European Union (EU) and North American Free Trade Agreement (NAFTA); and international law as set forth in treaties and conventions. In the overwhelming majority of jurisdictions, the parties are free to select the applicable law, subject to certain important limitations discussed below.

1. Failure to Designate Express Choice of Law

Parties frequently fail to choose, whether expressly or implicitly, the applicable law, for a number of reasons: the importance of doing so eluded them; they were unable to reach agreement; or they simply assumed that a certain law would apply. Absent an express choice by the parties, most modern legal systems provide that the applicable law will be that of the jurisdiction to which the contract is most closely related. This determination is made by various methods. Although in the majority of cases all methods frequently lead to similar results, this is not always the case. Thus, the failure to designate applicable law may produce significant unexpected and adverse consequences.

For example, should doubt arise regarding the validity of the contract or certain clauses, or should, in the course of performance, a question arise as to which the contract provides no clear answer, it will be necessary to seek guidance from the applicable legal system. This, in turn, will require the parties to predict which law will be applied. Predictability is made even more difficult if the contract fails to specify how and where disputes are to be resolved, because courts in different jurisdictions will apply different choice and conflicts of law rules to determine the applicable law.

The uncertainty of choice of law is particularly hazardous when the task of determining the applicable law is relegated to arbitrators.

Indeed, when the parties have not imposed their mutual will on the arbitrators, the latter can apply any conflicts of law rules.[1] The arbitrators could even skip the conflict rules altogether and directly determine the proper applicable law, or settle the dispute in accordance with such "rules of law" – possibly of non-national origin – as they may deem appropriate.[2] By contrast, a national court will determine the applicable law by applying its jurisdiction's conflict of law rules, as modified by bilateral or multilateral treaties or supranational regimes.

a. The Rome Convention

European parties, parties contracting with Europeans, or parties whose contract will be performed in Europe should pay particular attention to the **EEC Convention on the Law Applicable to Contractual Obligation**, which was signed in Rome on June 19, 1980, and became effective on April 1, 1991 (the "Rome Convention").[3] The Rome Convention includes uniform choice of law rules entirely replacing those previously effective in the contracting states. Because courts in the contracting states will apply the law in accordance with the Rome Convention, contesting parties from such nations will face less uncertainty before a court than before arbitrators. Nevertheless, in the absence of the parties' express choice of law, the rules of the Rome Convention afford the courts considerable latitude in determining the applicable law.

For example, the Rome Convention provides that in the absence of the choice of law by the parties, "the contract shall be governed by the

---

1. *See* Rules of Arbitration of the International Chamber of Commerce, art. 13.3.
2. *See* art. 1496 of the **French** New Code of Civil Procedure, or art. 1054(2) of the **Dutch** Code of Civil Procedure.
3. 1980 O.J. (L 266) 1 [hereinafter Rome Convention]. The Rome Convention is binding in **Belgium, Denmark, France, Germany, Greece, Ireland, Italy, Luxembourg, the Netherlands,** and the **United Kingdom** with respect to certain contracts. On the Rome Convention, *see, inter alia,* Mario Giuliano & Paul Lagarde, Council Report on the Convention on the Law Applicable to Contractual Obligations, 1980 O.J. (C 282) 1; CONTRACT CONFLICTS, THE EEC CONVENTION ON THE LAW APPLICABLE TO CONTRACTUAL OBLIGATIONS: A COMPARATIVE STUDY (P.M. North ed., 1982); G.R. Delaume, *The European Convention on the Law Applicable to Contractual Obligations. Why a Convention?*, 22 VA. J. INT'L L. 105 (1981); A.L. Diamond, *Harmonization of Private International Law Relating to Contractual Obligations,* REC. COURS LA HAYE, IV, t. 199, 233-312 (1986); J. Foyer, *Entrée en Vigueur de la Convention de Rome du 19 Juin 1980 sur la Loi Applicable aux Obligations Contractuelles,* JDI 601 (1991); H. Gaudemet-Tallon, *Le Nouveau Droit International Privé Européen des Contrats,* RTD EUR. 215 (1981); A.J. Jaffey, *The English Proper Law Doctrine and the EEC*

law of the country with which it is most closely connected.[4] This formula is similar to the method developed by many legal systems, which seek to identify the transaction's center of gravity to determine the proper applicable law. The Rome Convention attempts to simplify the search for the applicable law and render it more predictable by specifying that the contract is presumed to be most closely connected to the country where the party responsible for the most characteristic performance of the contract resides or has its principal place of business. The "characteristic performer" in a technology transfer contract frequently is the transferor. As a general rule, therefore, in the absence of the parties' applicable law election, it is the law of the country in which the transferor has its principal place of business that will govern the contract.

The Rome Convention, however, concedes that the presumption based on the "characteristic performance" may be unworkable,[5] particularly when the parties' respective performances both appear equally "characteristic" of the contract. This would be the case, for example, when the transferee is required not only to pay for the technology, but also to perform activities that are "characteristic" of the contract, such as to use the technology in a specified manner, supply raw materials, or make available its technical expertise, production facilities, or marketing network.

The presumption based on "characteristic performance" under the Rome Convention also is rebuttable. It will be disregarded altogether "if it appears from the circumstances as a whole that the contract is more closely connected with another country."[6] Therefore, if a technology transfer is negotiated and concluded in the transferee's country and many features of the contract, such as transfer of know-how, technical assistance, or supply of equipment, are to be performed there as well, a court may find that the contract is more closely related to the transferee's country, especially if the transferor subcontracts part of its performance.

---

cont.

Convention, 33 INT'L & COMP. L.Q. 531 (1984); P. Lagarde, *Le Nouveau Droit International Privé des Contrats Aprés L'Entrée en Vigueur de la Convention de Rome du 19 Juin 1980*, REV. CRIT. DIP 287 (1991); O. LANDO, *The EEC Convention on the Law Applicable to Contractual Obligations*, 24 COMMON MKT. L. REV. 159, 159-214 (1987).

4. Rome Convention, *supra* note 3, art. 4.1.
5. *Id.* art. 4.5.
6. *Id.*

b. General Choice of Law Principles

Absent an agreement or treaty on which law applies, a forum court will typically follow its own choice of law principles. Those principles, which may vary from country to country (and, in the United States, from state to state), may dictate application of the forum state's or nation's law or the law of another state or nation.

In the **United States**, factors relevant to the choice of applicable law may include the needs of the international system – comity among nations; the relevant policies of the forum; the relevant general policies and interests of other interested nations and states in the determination of a particular issue; the protection of the parties' justified expectations; the policies underlying the particular field of law; achieving certainty, predictability, and uniformity of results; and the ease of determining and applying the law to be chosen.[7]

In an action based on breach of contract, courts in the United States typically apply the law of the state or country that has the most significant relationship to the transaction and the parties with respect to the factors described above. The courts will look at where the contract was made; where it was negotiated; where it is to be performed; the location of the subject matter of the contract; and the domicile, residence, nationality, place of incorporation, and place of business of the parties.[8] If the place of negotiation and the place of performance are in the same country or state, the local law of that country or state typically will be applied.

Nevertheless, application of these principles in specific cases is often unpredictable. Generally, but not always, a contract for the sale of goods will be governed by the law of the state where the goods are to be delivered.[9] Similarly, contracts for the provision of services generally will be governed by the law of the state or country where the services, or a majority of the services, will be performed.

In the United States, a choice of law provision typically applies to the substantive law of the chosen nation or state, not its procedural law. Thus, a court in the United States typically applies its own rules on how the litigation is to be conducted, even when it applies the substantive law of another state or nation.

Statutes of limitations pose a special problem. Generally, statutes of limitations are perceived as procedural, so an action may not be brought in a forum if that forum's applicable statute of limitations would bar the action. Conversely, even if the law of another state or nation would bar

---

7. RESTATEMENT (SECOND) OF CONFLICTS § 6 (1971).
8. *Id.* § 188.
9. *But see* discussion on U.N. Convention on Contracts for the International Sale of Goods, *infra*.

the action, the action may proceed in the chosen forum so long as it is not barred by the forum's statute of limitations.[10] Exceptions exist, however, when the forum has a statute that "borrows" the statute of limitations of another state or where the applicable substantive law itself bars the right (as opposed to the remedy) after a certain time has passed. Thus, if the substantive law of the chosen state or nation creates a legal right and provides that any action to enforce that right must be brought within a particular time period, the forum state will apply that time period rather than the forum's own statute of limitations.

As the foregoing shows, relegating the determination of applicable law to a court or arbitral tribunal necessarily, therefore, requires the assumption of varying degrees of risk and, correspondingly, generates uncertainty.

2. Express Choice of Law

The parties' express identification of the applicable law in the contract will materially enhance predictability of outcome in the construction, interpretation and enforcement of the contract. Moreover, the freedom to choose the applicable law permits the parties to subject their relations to the legal system they deem most suitable for the transaction or that they otherwise find more advantageous or convenient.

The parties will leave the least room for uncertainty if they expressly state their choice of law in a specific clause in their contract. The choice of law clause should be carefully drafted so as to leave no room for ambiguity. The choice of law clause should be separate from the clause setting forth the dispute resolution mechanisms and procedures because the applicable law is conceptually distinct and plays an ongoing role, even in the absence of a dispute. In addition, this will minimise any possible confusion between the substantive law and the procedure governing dispute resolution.

In theory, the parties may select the applicable law after the conclusion of the contract, or in the rare case, wish to modify their original choice, by means of a written amendment, particularly on the occasion of a dispute. The parties' ability to agree on the applicable law, however, may be substantially compromised after a dispute arises, so parties should not rely on the availability of this option.[11]

---

10. *See generally* RESTATEMENT (SECOND) OF CONFLICTS § 142 (1971).
11. Under the **Rome Convention,** a late choice is valid provided it does not prejudice the formal validity of the contract or adversely affect the rights of third parties. Rome Convention, *supra* note 3, art. 3.2.

The parties may choose the applicable law based on its relationship to the transaction, *e.g.,* because it corresponds to one or both parties' place of business; the jurisdiction where the contract was concluded; or where a significant portion of the contract will be performed. In the technology transfer context, it often is advisable to select the same applicable law that governs the intellectual property rights embodying the transferred technology.

Although there usually is a nexus between the chosen law and the transaction or the parties, certain jurisdictions will recognize the parties' choice even if the selected law has little or no relationship to the contract.[12] Most jurisdictions do, however, require that the parties' choice not be designed to escape the application of the mandatory laws of the country where the contract is to be performed.[13] Parties selecting a law of a jurisdiction whose relationship with the parties or the transaction is tenuous, therefore, should verify with local counsel whether the selected jurisdiction, as well as other jurisdictions where the other party may seek to enforce the contract, will respect the parties' choice.

The parties do not have to state the reasons for their choice of law, and their decision may be dictated by considerations varying greatly in nature and importance. The choice of a particular law is sometimes rooted in "political" reasons. The desire to apply an impartial law could lead to the selection of the law of a "neutral" jurisdiction, where neither party is domiciled. On the other hand, the dominant party could well insist on the selection of a law that it deems favorable. Finally, significant practical reasons may militate in favor of designating a system of law with which the parties or their counsel are familiar; one that is easily accessible, reliable, or particularly well developed in certain areas of the law, such as that of Delaware law in the case of U.S. corporate law; or which corresponds to the language of the contract or the law of the forum that is contractually designated for dispute resolution.

The choice of each legal system will have different advantages and drawbacks. For example, although in a transaction between an Italian and American party, the best developed corporate law may be that of Delaware, it may only be accessible to the Italian party at great expense. The parties will invariably have to evaluate the trade-offs presented by

12. The **Rome Convention**, for example, requires no connection between the chosen law and the contract. The **State of New York** permits parties to choose New York law as the governing law for any contract, agreement or undertaking involving at least $250,000 U.S. regardless of whether the contract, agreement or undertaking "bears a reasonable relation" to New York. N.Y. GEN. OBLIG. LAW § 5-1401 (Consol. 1994).
13. *See* Section I.B.1.

the different choice of law options based on their priorities. In choosing the applicable law, however, the parties should above all be guided by what the legal consequences would be if either party were to enforce the contract under the laws of the contemplated jurisdiction.

If the contracting parties want the law of the **United States** to apply, they must be very specific. Unlike other nations, there is no single law of the United States and no general federal common law. Rather, each of the 50 states and the District of Columbia has its own substantive law, which may vary dramatically from state to state. Accordingly, a choice of law provision should specify a specific state whose law is to be applied. A choice that merely provides for application of "the law of the United States" is grossly insufficient.

a. Non-national Law

Parties frequently contemplate excluding the application of all national legal systems and resort solely, for instance, to "general principles of law" or to "international commercial practices." Significantly, under most legal regimes – including, in particular, the one established by the **Rome Convention** – the foregoing would not constitute a valid choice of law. In addition, should a court be called upon to settle a dispute relating to the contract, it would first seek to determine the national legal system applicable to the contract. The court would then give effect to the application of the non-national "rules" only to the *limited* extent that the national legal system determined by the court to govern the contracts would sanction it. Whether the parties' choice would be respected, therefore, would depend entirely on the applicable national legal system, which is what parties selecting non-national laws seek to avoid in the first place.

In contrast, when the parties also agree to refer their disputes to arbitration, the arbitrators – who are required above all to respect the will of the parties – may apply the non-national rules chosen by the parties. Their arbitral award should be recognized and enforceable, at least in jurisdictions where the nature of the rules applied by the arbitral tribunal is not ordinarily scrutinized.[14] The parties should, nevertheless, avoid using non-national laws, unless there is no alternative. The selection of non-national rules is risky and its consequences marred by uncertainty. These "rules" essentially consist of vague and difficult to

---

14. Thus, in **France,** *see* in the latest instance: Paris Court of Appeals, July 13, 1989, Clunet 1990.430, note Goldman; REV. CRIT. DR. INT. PR. 1990.305, note Oppetit; Rev. Arb. 1990.663, note Lagarde. In that case, it was held that the arbitrators complied with their terms of reference by deciding that the most appropriate law was *lex mercatoria*.

ascertain principles and practices that are specific to particular industries and invariably lack sufficient substance to provide any meaningful guidance.

b. *International Regimes*

The parties must ascertain whether they wish to invite or exclude the applicability of relevant international conventions or treaties. Of particular relevance to the transfer of technology across borders is **The United Nations Convention on Contracts for the International Sale of Goods** (CISG), which took effect in many countries on January 1, 1988, and since has been adopted by several others, including the **United States**.[15] Generally, the CISG governs sales of goods between parties doing business in countries that have adopted the CISG. Technology companies should be familiar with the CISG because it is likely to affect their international contracts.

Under the CISG, "goods" include both tangible and moveable items. Thus, it is clear that the CISG does not apply to intellectual property, such as copyrights and trademarks, but does apply to tangible items, such as computer hardware.[16] Whether the CISG applies to computer software is less clear. On one hand, the value of software arguably lies in its intellectual property. On the other hand, software is manifested physically in source code and tangibly fixed on a diskette or other media. Recently, commentators have opined that computer software (particularly mass-marketed software) should be considered "goods" for purposes of the CISG. Thus, transactions involving either the sale of software or licensing of software (which is analogous to a sale) very well may be covered by the CISG.

The CISG also applies to certain mixed contracts involving *both* goods and services. If the "preponderant" part of the obligations of the party supplying the goods consists of the supply of labor or other services, the CISG will not apply, unless the parties agree otherwise. If,

---

15. As of October 31, 1994, the following countries had either ratified, accepted, approved, or acceded to the CISG: **Argentina, Australia, Austria, Belarus, Bosnia and Herzegovina, Bulgaria, Canada, Chile, China, Czech Republic, Denmark, Ecuador, Egypt, Estonia, Finland, France, Georgia, Germany, Ghana, Guinea, Hungary, Iraq, Italy, Lesotho, Mexico, Republic of Moldova, Netherlands, New Zealand, Norway, Poland, Romania, Russian Federation, Singapore, Slovakia, Slovenia, Spain, Sweden, Switzerland, Syrian Arab Republic, Uganda, Ukraine, United States of America, Venezuela, Yugoslavia** and **Zambia**.
16. Lea Ann P. Stone, *Implications of the United Nations Convention for the International Sale of Goods*, TECHNOLOGY LAW NOTES (Shaw, Pittman, Potts & Trowbridge), Summer 1992, at 4.

on the other hand, the services supplied are merely *incidental* to the sold goods, the contract will be subject to the CISG. The CISG generally will apply to contracts for manufactured goods unless the purchaser of the goods supplies a substantial part of the materials required for their manufacture or production.

The CISG only will govern a transaction of contract parties whose places of business are located in different countries. Significantly, the determination of where a party's place of business is located for purposes of the CISG depends neither on the party's nationality nor on the transaction's civil or commercial character. If a party has more than one place of business, the place of business most closely related to the contract and its performance is considered in evaluating whether the CISG applies. However, the CISG specifies that it will apply only if both parties' businesses are located in countries that have adopted the CISG, *or* rules of private international law lead to the application of the law of a country that is party to the CISG.[17] Consequently, the CISG will apply when a party doing business in the United States is involved only if the other contracting party has its place of business in a country that is a party to the CISG. That the parties have their places of business in different countries must be apparent either from the contract, or from dealings between or information disclosed by the parties prior to the conclusion of the contract.

It is critical to remember that the CISG applies *automatically* to transactions meeting the above criteria. Parties may, however, contractually agree to exclude application of part or all of the CISG, but should draft the exclusion carefully to ensure application of the desired law. For example, if the parties wish to subject the agreement to the California version of the Uniform Commercial Code (UCC), a statement that the "laws of California shall apply" is not sufficient to exclude the CISG. The CISG would supersede California's state law because the United States is a party to the CISG. A very specific provision, such as "[t]he UCC as adopted in the State of California shall govern this contract, and the parties expressly agree that the CISG shall not apply" should enable the parties to achieve the desired result.

The CISG resembles the UCC in many respects, and both legal schemes endorse the parties' freedom to vary their obligations by contract. Nevertheless, their differences may be important to technology companies operating under purchase and sale order transactions or

---

17. In its ratification of the CISG, the **United States** declared that it would not be bound by the latter provision.

primarily oral contracts, because there are several major differences between the two legal schemes relating to acceptance, oral agreement and assurances for performance.[18]

The UCC provisions also provide a contracting party, particularly a buyer, with greater freedom to protect its interests during periods of uncertain performance by the other party, as well as greater certainty as to when a contract may be considered repudiated. Consequently, a party may wish to select the UCC as the applicable law, or alternatively, to include the language of the UCC assurance provision in a contract otherwise governed by the CISG.

Although in many cases, especially those involving single deal transactions based on well-documented and detailed written agreements, it may make little practical difference whether the CISG, the UCC or another major commercial legal system applies, the parties should verify the existence of any such differences and contemplate their

---

18. *Acceptance*: The UCC provides that, as between merchants, a contract will exist if the parties agree on major terms (*e.g.,* quantity, description, and the like), regardless of any differences in "boilerplate" language on purchase or sale forms. The CISG requires that a valid acceptance be a mirror image of the offer. Consequently, if the boilerplate language of purchase and sale forms differs in a transaction governed by the CISG, then no contract exists.

Oral Agreements: The UCC generally provides that contracts for U.S.$500.00 or more are not enforceable unless embodied in a sufficient writing signed by the party against whom enforcement is sought. The CISG provides that no writing is necessary, and that contracts may be proven by any means, including the testimony of witnesses. Due to several exceptions to the UCC rule, the two provisions may not be as different as they first appear. Nevertheless, companies that do not which to be bound before a written contract is signed should state expressly in preliminary correspondence and discussions that no contract exists or is binding until it is embodied in a signed writing.

Adequate Assurances of Performance: The UCC allows either party to demand, in writing, adequate assurance of the other party's due performance of its obligations if reasonable grounds for insecurity regarding performance exist. The party requesting assurance may suspend its performance until it receives such assurance, as long as suspension is commercially reasonable. If adequate assurance is not received within a reasonable time, not exceeding 30 days, the requesting party may consider the contract repudiated. Under the CISG, a party may suspend its performance under a contract if it is apparent the other party will not perform a substantial part of its obligations as a result of (a) a serious deficiency in the other party's ability to perform or creditworthiness, or (b) the other party's conduct in preparing to perform or performing the contract. Before suspension, the party desiring to suspend performance must give notice to the other party, and must continue its performance. The concerned party has no right to demand such assurance under the CISG, unlike under the UCC. If it becomes "clear" before the date of performance that the other party will commit a fundamental breach of the contract, a party may declare the contract "avoided." *See* Stone, *supra* note 16.

consequences for the implementation of the transaction as well as any potentially ensuing disputes.

c. *Severability*

Recent attention has focused on the parties' ability to divide their contract into several parts and subject each to a different law. The **Rome Convention**, for example, allows the parties to "select the law applicable to the whole or a part only of the contract," which suggests that each part of the contract may be subjected to a different governing law. Experience shows, however, that only a set of rights and obligations that are logically severable from *other* elements of a complex contractual transaction should be subjected to different laws. Thus, the parties could subject the supply of equipment, the transfer of the associated know-how, and their technical assistance obligations to different laws. This option should be used with extreme care, however, and only when dictated by overwhelming reasons. In practice, subjecting various aspects of the same transaction to different legal systems inevitably invites a host of complex practical and legal problems.

3. Implied Choice of Law

In the absence of an express choice of law, effect is generally given to the implied choice of the parties, so long as that implicit choice is readily discernible. Under the **Rome Convention**, the choice "must be expressed or demonstrated with reasonable certainty by the terms of the contract or the circumstances of the case." Thus, utilization of a standard contract popular in a certain jurisdiction, or including in the contract references to the laws of a particular country or a clause whereby the parties consent to the jurisdiction of the courts of a given country, could, without contrary evidence or contract language, support the conclusion that the parties, by implication, selected the law of the country in question. When the parties enter into several contracts relating to a single transaction or a series of transactions, it may also be inferred, absent other evidence, that the law expressly chosen in one contract (*e.g.*, joint venture agreement) also governs the other contracts (*e.g.*, license agreement).

When no express choice is made, it often is difficult to predict whether a court, or arbitral tribunal, will sufficiently discern the parties' implicit intention to its satisfaction, so as to designate the law the parties "implicitly intended" to apply. Therefore, if the parties do agree on the law to which they intend to subject their contract, they should express their intention clearly and unambiguously in the contract and not rely on the implicit choice of law.

B. Limitations on the Freedom to Select the Applicable Law

The law of the contract – whether it is expressly designated by the parties, implicitly inferred from the contract and other evidence, or derived from an objective nexus between the contract and a particular country – ordinarily will govern most aspects of the agreement. Some contract related matters, however, exceed the scope of contractual law. And, even within the bounds of contract law, certain superseding laws will apply notwithstanding the parties' choice of law.

The parties cannot contract out of the application of two categories of laws:

(i) *superseding* public policy laws of other jurisdictions that will apply to the performance of the contract or the rights of the parties, if one party were to attempt to enforce the contract under the laws of any such other jurisdiction; and

(ii) the *mandatory* laws of the jurisdiction whose law was selected, which will apply notwithstanding the parties' contractual provisions, notably to ensure that none of those provisions violates the mandatory provisions.

Mandatory rules are principally encountered in connection with conditions governing the formation of the contract (*e.g.,* does the chosen law require that the price be determined or determinable in order for the contract to be valid?); contractual limitations of liability (*e.g.,* to what extent and under what conditions does the selected law permit the transferor contractually to escape statutory obligations, liabilities or warranties?);[19] and damages payable in the event of non-performance (*e.g.,* does the chosen law permit the court to reduce or increase agreed damages or penalties and, if so, to what extent?).

Contractual clauses that are inconsistent with superseding provisions may be partially unenforceable, void, or, even invalidate the entire contract, if the irregularity affects an essential element of the agreement. Mandatory provisions generally only modify the relevant contract language, but do not nullify the entire agreement.

The parties should also be mindful of the potential application of extra-contractual or supplementary provisions. Issues that altogether fall outside the scope of contractual law are likely to be resolved in accordance with the laws of the jurisdiction where the issue arose, which may not necessarily be the law selected by the parties. Contractual matters that are not adequately addressed by the parties may be

---

19. *See also* Chapter Three, Sections VII and VIII.

resolved by supplementary provisions of the applicable law designated by the parties.

1. Superseding Public Policy Laws

Most jurisdictions have enacted laws that are said to rise to the level of public policy. These laws will override the parties' choice of law. In **France**, these rules are called *"lois de police."* They are said to be "internationally peremptory" because they are intended to apply to all contracts, even if the contracts are governed by other legal systems.[20]

Certain aspects of international technology transfers routinely trigger the application of public policy rules, and the public policy laws of different countries frequently are inconsistent as they are not designed to achieve the same objectives. The objectives differ, in particular, according to whether the country in question is a net exporter or importer of technology.

In industrialized market economies, the policing of technology transfers is primarily aimed at protecting free competition by preventing restrictive trade practices, and technology export restrictions are an important foreign policy tool rooted in national security considerations.[21] In developing countries, technology transfer controls are mainly designed to ensure that the contemplated transfer is desirable from those countries' macroeconomic perspective. The stringency of the control measures varies, however, quite significantly from one country to another, often depending on each country's technological development.

a. Competition Law

As discussed in considerable detail in Chapters Two and Three, technology transfer contracts often trigger competition concerns. Competition laws apply irrespective of the law governing the relations between the parties to the contract, whenever performance of the contract has, or is likely to have, an adverse effect on competition in the relevant market.

---

20. *See, e.g.,* **Rome Convention,** *supra* note 4, art. 7.
21. As a result of the political changes and economic reforms adopted in most Eastern European countries, their technology transfer control policies will now reflect objectives and methodologies that are similar to those of other industrialized countries. *See also* Chapter Two, Section II.B.3 and 9, and Chapter Three, Section V.

The compulsory application of competition rules to technology transfer transactions is especially troublesome because the purpose of competition regulation – ensuring competition – inherently conflicts with the technology owners' rights to protect and exploit their technology as they see fit. In an integrated market, such as the one established by the EU, this conflict is compounded by inconsistencies between the member states' national laws, which are designed – still, on an essentially territorial basis – to protect proprietary rights of technology owners, and EU law, which strives to promote free competition and free movement of goods within the EU.

EU authorities responsible for implementing competition law have endeavored to reconcile those conflicting objectives.[22] The European Court of Justice has affirmed that EU law recognizes the prerogatives granted by the local legislation of EU member states to intellectual property rights' owners only in so far as they fall within their specific subject matter[23] or are designed to guarantee the essential function of those rights.[24] These principles have been applied in numerous Commission decisions.[25]

The complexity and potentially significant impact of competition laws mandate that parties to technology transfers pay close attention – irrespective of their choice of law – to the competition laws effective in

---

22. *See* B. Goldman, A. Lyon-Caen & L. Vogel, DROIT COMMUNAUTAIRE EUROPÉEN 665 (Dalloz, 5th ed., 1994); E. Gavalda & G. Parleani, *Traité de Droit Communautaire des Affaires,* LITEC, 665 (1992); S. WEATHERILL & P. BEAUMONT, EC LAW: THE ESSENTIAL GUIDE TO THE LEGAL WORKINGS OF THE EUROPEAN COMMUNITY 726 (1993).
23. Case 78/70, *Deutsche Gramaphon GmbH v. Metro-SB-Grossmärkte GmbH,* E.C.R. 487 (1971); Case 15/74, *Centrafarm v. Sterling Drug,* E.C.R. 1147 (1974).
24. Case 102/77, *Hoffman-La Roche v. Centrafarm,* E.C.R. 1139 (1978).
25. Based on the experience acquired in applying Articles 85 and 86 of the Treaty of Rome to technology transfer contracts, moreover, the Commission has issued two Regulations adopting block-exemptions respectively for patent and know-how licensing agreements: Commission Regulation 2349/84 of July 23, 1984 on the Application of Article 85(3) to Certain Categories of Patent Licensing Agreements, 1984 O.J. (L 219) 15 and Commission Regulation No. 556/89 of November 30, 1988 on the Application of Article 85(3) of the Treaty to Certain Categories of Know-How Licensing Agreements, 1989 O.J. (L 61) 1. Both Regulations were amended by Commission Regulation No. 151/93 of December 23, 1992 Amending Regulations 417/85, 418/85, 2349/84 and 556/89 on the Application of Article 85(3) of the Treaty to Certain Categories of Specialization Agreements, Research and Development Agreements, Patent Licensing Agreements and Know-How Licensing Agreements, 1993 O.J. (L 21) 8. The EC Commission issued recently a draft of a new regulation, the purpose of which is to merge Regulations Nos. 2349/84 and 556/89. *See also* Chapter Two, Section I.C.1 and Chapter Three, Section V.

those markets in which performance of their contract might produce anticompetitive effects. This is particularly true for parties to contracts likely to affect competition in the EU or the United States.

b. Trade Regulation

Many countries have enacted export or import controls. These apply irrespective of the parties' choice of law and may determine the validity or enforceability of technology transfer contracts.

Export limitations frequently are imposed in order to prevent technology transfers that might adversely affect the foreign policy, security or strategic interest of the exporting country.[26] A particularly striking illustration of export restrictions rooted in foreign policy objectives are economic sanctions, such as the national or EU measures implementing the United Nations embargo of Iraq following the invasion of Kuwait. These measures[27] apply to all activities subject to the embargo, notwithstanding any contracts previously made.

High technology, which often may be put to "dual use" (*i.e.*, it may be used for both civil and military purposes), is the main target of such restrictions. These are usually implemented through an intricate system of export licenses and are enforced by specialized governmental authorities.[28]

In the 1970s, a number of developing countries enacted legislation subjecting all technology *imports* to prior governmental approval. The members of the Andean Group **(Bolivia, Colombia, Ecuador, Peru, Venezuela)** have enunciated common technology transfer policies illustrative of the desire of developing countries to control transferred technology. Prior approval procedures of technology transfers – originally designed to control currency outflows – have been instituted in a number of countries in order to prevent foreign transferors from imposing on domestic transferees contractual restrictions not deemed in the importing countries' interest and as a means of ensuring that the contemplated transfer be consistent with the recipient country's

---

26. In the **United States**, such measures are taken under the Export Administration Act of 1979, 50 U.S.C. § 2404. In **France**, the last notice of the government concerning the products and technologies submitted to a control of their final destination has been issued on January 24, 1992.
27. Within the **EU**: EC Council Regulation No. 2340/90 of August 8, 1990, 1990 O.J. (L 213) and No. 3155/90 of October 29, 1990, 1990 O.J. (L 304). In the **United States**: Executive orders issued by President Bush – Exec. Order No. 12,724, 55 Fed. Reg. 33,089 (1990) (Iraq); Exec. Order No. 12,725, 55 Fed. Reg. 33,091 (1990) (Kuwait).
28. *See* export control discussion in Chapter Two, Section II.B.9.

APPLICABLE LAW AND RESOLUTION OF DISPUTES 321

industrial development policy and its capacity to assimilate technology.[29]

In reviewing technology transfer agreements for registration and approval, the competent authority will examine the legal, economic and technical aspects of the agreement in light of national technology transfer policies. The reviewing authority will seek to ensure, on the one hand, that the contract include no provision deemed to constitute an unfair trade practice such as, for example,

(i) provisions that limit the transferee's right to export goods manufactured under the license or, frequently, re-export licensed goods to third countries;
(ii) provisions that restrict the transferor's right to use the technology after expiration or termination of the agreement;
(iii) "tying" clauses which unreasonably require the transferee to purchase products, raw materials, equipment, or services from the transferor; or
(iv) provisions that restrict the transferee's right to compete with the transferor after the expiration of the agreement.[30]

The examining governmental authority will also seek to ensure that certain provisions are incorporated in the contract, such as royalty limitations; a provision fixing the term of the agreement for a period not exceeding a specified maximum number of years; and a full description of the technology transfer process. The governmental authority may even require (*e.g.*, under the laws of the **Philippines** and the former **Brazilian** technology transfer regulations) that the entire contract be governed by the national law of the transferee's country and that this country be the venue of any arbitration proceedings between the parties, or even that its courts be accorded exclusive jurisdiction over any dispute arising out of the contract.

Such restrictions and requirements are in some countries rigidly applied to all technology transfer agreements, but in other countries (*e.g.*, **India, South Korea**) they rather constitute guidelines for the evaluation of agreements by the approving authority. In several countries state intervention is also designed to regulate and control capital outflows and profit reparation (*e.g.*, **Argentina**).[31] The most recent trend in many nations with sufficiently developed industrial

---

29. A Draft International Code of Conduct on the Transfer of Technology has been developed by an UNCTAD Group of experts. For an exhaustive bibliography, *see* UNCTAD Doc. TD/B/C.6/INF.2/Rev. 7 (Jan. 29, 1991).
30. *See* Chapter Three, Sections I, V, XI and XII.
31. *See* Chapter Two, Section II.B.5.

capacity and ability to assimilate foreign technology is to encourage technology transfers by alleviating previously imposed restrictions.[32]

In its Decision No. 291, the Commission of the **Cartagena Agreement** (Andean Pact) has modified the former rules and provided national bodies with discretionary approval rights for technology agreements even if those include certain prohibited restrictive clauses. Some countries (*e.g.*, **Colombia**) have instituted an automatic approval procedure for technology transfer agreements which comply with all applicable standard requirements.

The enforcement mechanisms used to ensure compliance with technology transfer laws vary. The failure to ask for, or receive, approval of the contemplated agreement will often result in a prohibition on the transfer of fees and royalties out of the country or in the loss of tax exemptions. It may also result in the agreement being rendered unenforceable, and many countries impose stiff fines and criminal penalties for violation of international trade controls, particularly export control laws.

2. Application of Supplementary and Extra-Contractual Laws

Subject to the application of superseding or mandatory laws, contractual law ordinarily will govern all aspects related to the agreement, including conditions of formation; consequences and scope of nullity; performance of contractual obligations; and consequences of breach. Certain aspects of technology transfer transactions, however, may be deemed outside the scope of contractual law. Under many legal systems, the legal capacity of the parties is governed by the law of their nationality or the law of their domicile.[33] Whether the party signing the contract has the authority to bind the entity on whose behalf it is ostensibly signing the contract ordinarily is determined by the law governing the source of the signatory's representative authority (*e.g.*, in the case of a corporate entity, the law of incorporation; in the case of an agent, the law governing the contract between principal and agent).

Under the **Rome Convention**, a contract is formally valid when it satisfies the formal requirements of either the law of the contract, or the law of the country where it was concluded.[34] Technology transfer contracts are not subject to any different rules in this respect. Significantly, however, disputes arising in connection with technology

---

32. *E.g.*, **Brazilian** INPI Res. No. 22 of February 1994.
33. *But see* Rome Convention, *supra* note 4, art. 11, which sets forth an exception to the *lex patriae* in favor of the *lex loci contractus*.
34. *Id.* art. 9.

transfers are not always of a contractual nature. Non-contractual disputes will be resolved under the law that is rendered applicable based on the legal issue in question, not the law of the contract.

Therefore, when a dispute relates directly to intellectual property rights, such as when it calls into question the very existence, validity or scope of those rights, the matter is excluded from the law of the contract and falls within the law – and the jurisdiction of the courts – of the country that accorded protection to the intellectual property rights in question.[35]

Technology transfer transactions may give rise to disputes based on tort or other delictual theories, such as the disclosure of a trade secret during negotiations, fraud, or unfair competition. According to widely accepted doctrine, such disputes will be governed by the law of the place of wrong, the *lex loci delicti*.

The parties should also pay attention to the *supplementary* provisions of the chosen law, particularly when the contract is silent on particular issues. Supplementary provisions apply in the absence of contractual clauses expressly derogating from applicable (non-mandatory) laws. They complement the contract by supplying provisions not specified by the parties. For example, if the contract contains no details on warranties – which is a substantial deficiency to be avoided by parties to technology transfers – the parties should consult their chosen governing law in order to ascertain what, if any, implied warranties that law will impose.[36]

II. DISPUTE RESOLUTION IN INTERNATIONAL TECHNOLOGY TRANSACTIONS

A carefully drafted technology transfer agreement will minimize the likelihood of disputes between the parties, but no amount of care will guarantee that a dispute will never arise. This section discusses the most common methods for resolving contractual disputes and offers contracting parties several options when drafting technology transfer agreements and proceeding with dispute resolution.

---

35. BATIFFOL & LAGARDE, TRAITÉ DE DROIT INTERNATIONAL PRIVÉ, T.2., Paris, LGDJ 198 (1993); AUDIT, *Droit International Privé*, Paris, ECONOMICA, 600 (1993); DICEY & MORRIS, THE CONFLICTS OF LAWS 960 (1987).
36. *See* Chapter Three, Section VII concerning the implied warranties of the Uniform Commercial Code in the **United States**.

The two primary methods of dispute resolution are arbitration and litigation. Neither method is perfect, but each has its own benefits that should be considered when the contract is being negotiated and drafted. Although it may be awkward to consider and discuss dispute resolution procedures in the course of negotiating what both parties hope will be a mutually profitable and amicable contractual relationship, the failure to do so may produce significant adverse and unpredictable consequences.

A. Litigation

Absent a contractual agreement to provide for some alternative means of dispute resolution, the primary – and perhaps only – available method of dispute resolution is litigation in a national court of law.[37] Litigation, as the term is used here, is conducted through public proceedings in a government provided court, subject to specific and often complex rules of procedure and evidence. For example, in the **United States**, trials of civil cases in the federal courts are governed by various statutory provisions and lengthy rules of civil procedure, applicable generally in all federal trial courts nationwide. These rules are supplemented by local rules of civil procedure applicable to specific federal courts in each state or federal district. In addition, there are federal rules of evidence applicable to trials in all federal courts. Appeals from trial court decisions are governed by separate rules of appellate procedure, which are also supplemented by the local rules of each of the federal appellate courts. Similarly, each of the 50 states and the District of Columbia has its own judicial system and its own set of statutes, rules, and procedures. Although there is a trend for the states to follow the federal rules of procedure in civil cases, vast differences remain among the states and between the states and the federal system.

1. The Litigation Forum

Litigation may be conducted in any court that has proper jurisdiction – that is, the power to decide the case. Jurisdiction typically has two parts: subject matter jurisdiction and jurisdiction over the parties. Subject matter jurisdiction is based on the nature of the controversy presented to the court. Thus, the federal courts in the **United States** are courts of limited jurisdiction empowered to hear only certain types of

---

37. It is possible for parties to agree to arbitration or some other means of dispute resolution after a dispute has arisen, but it is often too late at that time for the parties to be able to agree to any litigation alternatives.

cases. These include cases arising under the U.S. Constitution, laws or treaties of the United States, and controversies between citizens of a state and citizens or subjects of a foreign state or country where the matter in controversy exceeds the sum or value of U.S. $50,000.[38]

State courts in the United States are regarded as courts of general jurisdiction and consider almost any controversy, although within a state court system there may be both courts of general jurisdiction and limited jurisdiction. To complicate matters further, the jurisdiction of a federal court may be concurrent with a state court, meaning that a plaintiff could initially choose to bring a lawsuit in either a federal or state court.

Personal jurisdiction relates to the power of the court over the individual or entity before it. A plaintiff consents to personal jurisdiction merely by filing a lawsuit in the particular forum, but a defendant must have certain "minimum contacts" with the forum before jurisdiction over him is proper.[39]

Parties may contractually agree that personal jurisdiction will be permitted in one or more courts. Thus, if a court otherwise has subject matter jurisdiction, parties to a dispute or potential dispute may consent to suit in that court even if the court might otherwise not have personal jurisdiction over the parties. Nevertheless, generally, but not always, a forum state requires some connection between it and the parties before it will permit private litigants to use its limited judicial resources to resolve private disputes. In some cases, however, that connection may be quite limited. For example, in **New York State**, parties may agree to the choice of New York as a forum provided they have agreed that New York law governs the contract, agreement, or undertaking at issue and that the amount in controversy is not less than U.S. $1,000,000.[40] Absent such statute, or other connection that the court will deem

---

38. 28 U.S.C. §§ 1331, 1332.
39. In the **United States**, the minimum contacts requirement is mandated by the U.S. Constitution. *International Shoe Co. v. Washington,* 326 U.S. 310 (1945). In an effort to define what contacts are sufficient, most states have enacted so-called "long-arm" statutes that describe in broad terms contacts sufficient to give the courts personal jurisdiction over an out-of-state defendant. *See, e.g.,* MD. CODE ANN., CTS. & JUD. PROC. § 6-103 (1989 & Supp. 1992) (granting personal jurisdiction over, among others, persons or entities that transact business or perform any character of work or services in Maryland; contract to supply goods or services in the State; or have an interest in, use, or possess real property in the State).
40. N.Y. GEN. OBLIG. LAW § 5-1402 (Consol. 1994).

sufficient, the court may refuse to honor the parties' choice. **California, Delaware, Florida,** and **Ohio** have similar, but not identical, statutes.[41]

Often, there will be more than one forum that will have personal and subject matter jurisdiction to resolve a dispute. For example, a contract between a U.S. company and a French company might be enforceable in the courts of either France or the United States. Within the United States, the dispute might be enforceable in one or more state or federal courts. Absent an agreement limiting the available choices, generally a plaintiff may select the forum that it perceives as most favorable or convenient or perhaps least favorable or convenient to the defendant. Once the plaintiff has chosen, the defendant's options to obtain a different forum are severely limited.[42] For this reason, parties to an international technology transfer agreement should give serious consideration to narrowing the available forums by agreeing to one or a few possible forums for resolving any dispute that may arise.

For many years, courts in the United States and elsewhere declined to enforce forum selection clauses on the grounds that they were contrary to public policy. In 1972, however, the United States Supreme Court held that such clauses are enforceable unless the contract clause is unreasonable and unjust, or is invalid for such reasons as fraud or overreaching.[43] A party desiring to challenge a forum selection clause generally has a heavy burden of proof.

The parties' selection[44] of a litigation forum may be determined by several factors: these include the perceived neutrality of the forum; its perceived expertise in technology transfer issues; the speed by which the case will proceed to trial;[45] the court's rules of procedure; the willingness

---

41. CAL. CIV. PROC. CODE § 410.40 (Deering 1994); DEL. CODE ANN. tit. 6, § 2708 (1993); FLA. STAT. § 685.102 (1993); OHIO REV. CODE ANN. § 2307.39 (Baldwin 1994).
42. For example, courts in the **United States** recognize the doctrine of *forum non conveniens,* which permits a court to transfer the case, upon a proper showing by defendant, to a forum more convenient to the parties and witnesses. For federal courts, the doctrine is codified in 28 U.S.C. § 1404. Nevertheless, there generally is a strong presumption in favor of plaintiff's choice.
43. *M/S Bremen v. Zapata Off-Shore Co.,* 407 U.S. 1 (1972); *See also Carnival Cruise Lines, Inc. v. Shute,* 499 U.S. 585 (1991).
44. As noted, if the parties have not contractually agreed to a forum, the plaintiff will make the initial choice when it files suit. Although a plaintiff may consider the factors described here, it will weigh them in the manner that best suits its own purposes.
45. The speed of the judicial process varies dramatically from court to court and jurisdiction to jurisdiction. In some courts, a case may go to trial five months or sooner after suit was filed; in other courts, with crowded dockets and less aggressive case management procedures, years may pass between the filing of the complaint and the commencement of trial.

of a court to grant summary judgment;[46] the location of the parties' assets;[47] the convenience of the parties; the convenience of the witnesses; and the choice of applicable law. Not all of the factors identified may apply in every case, and the importance of each factor will vary with the circumstances. It nevertheless is dangerous to agree to a forum without at least reviewing all relevant factors.[48]

Convenience of the parties and witnesses and the choice of applicable law are often the most frequently considered factors in forum selection agreements. Thus, in a contract between a French entity and an English entity, governed by English law, the parties might decide that any dispute will be heard only in a court in England.

Nevertheless, different courts have different rules of practice and procedure that must often be considered. For example, the courts of any state in the United States that has adopted the Uniform Commercial Code might interpret a dispute governed by the UCC in a similar manner. Different state courts, however, have different rules of procedure and practice that may affect how the case is prepared and tried, what evidence is considered, how appeals are taken, and how a judgment may be enforced.

In addition, different forums will apply their own statutes of limitations in many types of cases. For example, in the United States each state has its own statutes of limitations, which require that a lawsuit be brought within a certain period of time after an alleged tort or breach of contract has occurred. The limitation periods vary from state to state and depend on the nature of the cause of action (for example, tort or contract). Thus, absent a forum selection clause, a plaintiff that has, for whatever reason, delayed in filing suit after an alleged breach of contract has occurred might select a forum that has a longer statute of limitations to avoid having its action barred.

Further complications arise when, as is often the case in litigation between **U.S. and foreign entities**, the litigation is specified or permitted to occur in a United States federal court. Civil disputes tried in federal

---

46. In the **United States**, all federal courts and most state courts are empowered to grant summary judgment on any claim as to which there is "no genuine issue as to any material fact" and on which a party is entitled to judgment as a matter of law. *See, e.g.,* FED. R. CIV. P. 56. Because the material facts are not in dispute, the only issues to be resolved are legal issues, which the court may decide without a trial. In practice, however, some courts are more willing to grant summary judgment than others.
47. *See* Enforcement of Judgments, *infra.*
48. Of course, the selected forum may be chosen on the basis of one party's superior bargaining power and not on the basis of consideration of which forum is best for both parties.

court are subject to the federal rules of civil trial and pretrial procedure. Generally, however, there is no federal "common law," so in contract disputes eligible to be heard in federal court, absent a choice of law agreement, the court will apply the substantive law of the state in which the federal court sits.[49] Thus, a federal court sitting in the State of New York would apply New York substantive law while a federal court sitting in Delaware would apply Delaware law.

In selecting a forum, the parties must be careful to ensure that the agreed-upon forum is in fact available to both parties. This requires knowledge of the selected forum's law. For example, a recent decision of the United States Court of Appeals for the Fourth Circuit illustrates that courts will enforce forum selection clauses even when doing so may produce a result not intended by one or both parties.

The case,[50] involved a contract between an Indian medical institute (the "Institute") and a U.S. entity that sold the Institute a piece of expensive medical equipment. The contract provided that "no suit in regard to any matter whatsoever arising under or by virtue of this Agreement shall be instituted in any court save a court of competent jurisdiction at Hyderabad [India] . . . ." When the machine failed to operate, the Institute filed suit against the U.S. seller in a federal court in Maryland. The U.S. company sought to dismiss the case asserting that the contract provided that the exclusive forum would be in India. The Institute argued that the Indian court did not have jurisdiction over the U.S. company and that, therefore, the Institute could not sue in India. The court rejected the Institute's argument and dismissed the case, even though doing so effectively left the Institute without *any* forum in which to enforce the contract. The court observed that the Institute, as an Indian organization, should be charged with knowledge of the legal implications of the forum selection clause and should have known that it would have been unable to sue the U.S. entity in India.

To minimize the risk of obtaining results such as this, a forum selection clause should be accompanied by an express agreement by both parties that they consent to suit in the selected forum and waive any and all objections based on lack of jurisdiction. In addition, it may be wise to include an alternative, "fail safe" forum, in the event the primary forum nevertheless is unavailable for any reason.

Parties to a forum selection clause should also consider how a court, even one to whose jurisdiction the parties consented, first obtains the power to exercise the jurisdiction. In the **United States**, a court generally

---

49. *Erie Railroad Co. v. Tompkins,* 304 U.S. 64 (1938).
50. *Nizam's Institute of Medical Sciences v. Exchange Technologies, Inc.,* No. 93-2196, 1994 U.S. App. LEXIS 16552 (July 5, 1994).

cannot exercise its otherwise proper jurisdiction until the defendant has been formally served with the initial suit papers. This is called "service of process," and traditionally requires the personal delivery of suit papers and a formal summons on the defendant. Although the modern trend in the **United States** is to permit substitutes for personal service, such as service by mail, certain formalities remain that can render service of process difficult.[51] It is therefore often advisable, in connection with a forum selection clause, to specify a method by which service of process shall be made, or designate a person or entity within the forum's jurisdiction that is irrevocably appointed to accept service on behalf of the party. The parties should also consider providing in the contract that they consent to and irrevocably waive any objections to service of process.

2. The Pretrial and Trial Process

In the **United States** and some other countries (such as the **United Kingdom**), once a lawsuit is filed, the parties are permitted to obtain from each other and from third parties documents and facts relevant to the dispute. The courts are empowered to compel compliance by recalcitrant parties. The process is called "discovery," and it can be detailed, expensive, intrusive, and time-consuming. In many cases, however, it provides the only means for a party to obtain evidence to prove or defend its case. In addition, discovery may disclose information that facilitates an out of court settlement.

Typical discovery rights include the right of each party to compel the other to produce documents and potential evidence relevant to the dispute, to answer written interrogatories seeking information about the issues, and to provide oral testimony, under oath, of witnesses and those who may generally have knowledge of the facts of the dispute. The scope of permissible discovery is quite broad. In the **United States**, a party typically may obtain discovery

> regarding any matter, not privileged, which is relevant to the subject matter involved in the pending action... including the existence, description, nature, custody, condition, and location of any books, documents,[52] or other tangible things and the identity and location of

---

51. *See* FED. R. CIV. P. 4. Subdivision (f) of that rule is intended to give effect to the Hague Convention on the Service Abroad of Judicial and Extrajudicial Documents.
52. Documents include writings, drawings, graphs, checks, photographs, phone records, and other data compilations, including disks, and magnetically or electronically encoded information. *See, e.g.,* FED. R. CIV. P. 34(a); FED. R. EVID. 1001.

persons having knowledge of any discoverable matter. The information sought need not be admissible if the kind of information sought appears reasonably calculated to lead to the discovery of admissible evidence.[53]

Under this broad standard a party may probe deeply into its opponent's business, financial records, confidential internal memoranda, electronic files, technical information and the like, even if the parties are competitors. Safeguards and limitations do exist, and much has been written about the need to curb abuses of discovery. Nevertheless, any party to a technology transfer agreement in which litigation is a possible means of dispute resolution should be aware of the discovery process and its implications.

Once discovery is completed, the trial itself may either be before a judge or a jury. In the United States, the right to a trial by jury is constitutionally guaranteed. It can, however, be waived by agreement or by failure of a party timely to demand a jury trial in accordance with the rules of court. If either party to a technology transfer agreement feels that a jury trial of any dispute under that agreement would be inappropriate (because of the technical complexity of the matter, perceived local bias, language difficulties, or any number of other subjective reasons), the agreement should contain a provision clearly and explicitly waiving the right to trial by jury by both parties.

In addition, if not addressed elsewhere in the contract, an agreement permitting litigation should provide a method of awarding attorneys' fees and costs. Absent such an agreement, in the **United Kingdom**, for example, the prevailing party typically recovers its attorneys' fees and costs. In contrast, in the **United States**, rarely is the prevailing party awarded fees and costs; rather, regardless of who wins, each party generally bears its own fees and costs.[54] If the parties desire to change this result, they must do so by agreement.

3. Enforcement of Judgments

Unfortunately for plaintiffs, the award of a judgment in plaintiff's favor is not necessarily the end of the litigation road. The defendant may, for example, take one or more appeals. Moreover, regardless of any appeals, unless the defendant voluntarily complies with the judgment, it will be necessary for the plaintiff to take steps to enforce it. If the defendant has assets in the forum state or country, this may be

---

53. FED. R. CIV. P. 26(b)(1).
54. This of course produces an entire set of incentives, disincentives and other competing considerations relevant to deciding whether to designate the United States as the dispute resolution forum.

relatively easy. For example, in the **United States**, a judgment constitutes a lien on the real property of the judgment debtor located within the court's jurisdiction.[55] A judgment creditor can use legal process to foreclose on this lien. Similarly, a judgment creditor can, subject to a number of exceptions, attach the bank accounts and personal assets of the judgment debtor in the forum state's jurisdiction. Both the states and the U.S. federal government also have procedures for registering and enforcing a judgment entered in one state or federal district in other states and districts where a defendant may have assets.[56]

The situation may be quite different, however, if a party desires to enforce a judgment in a country other than the one in which the judgment was entered. In many instances, the enforcement of a foreign judgment is governed by treaty or international convention. For example, in **Europe**, the Brussels Convention of 1968[57] and the Lugano Convention 1988[58] generally allow a judgment entered in a signatory state to be enforced in any other signatory state in accordance with the procedures set forth in these Conventions.[59]

If no convention or treaty applies, a judgment creditor seeking to enforce a judgment in a foreign country typically must file a separate lawsuit in that foreign country, which is governed by the foreign court's own rules of law. For example, the enforcement of a foreign judgment in the **United States** is governed by the laws of the 50 states and the District of Columbia. Generally, the courts in the **United States** will recognize judgments entered in a foreign nation if the foreign court had jurisdiction; if there has been an opportunity for a full and fair trial; and the judgment was not procured by fraud.[60] Any entity seeking to enforce a foreign judgment in the United States, therefore, must *prove*, among other things, that the foreign court had jurisdiction; that a full and fair trial was held under a system of impartial administration of justice without any prejudice in the court or system of laws; and that the judgment is not tainted by fraud.

The enforceability abroad of any judgment rendered in the United States depends on the law and policy of the foreign jurisdiction in which the party seeks enforcement of the judgment. The principles for enforcement of a United States judgment abroad generally are similar,

---

55. 28 U.S.C. § 1962.
56. *See, e.g.,* 28 U.S.C. § 1963.
57. *See* Stephen Cromie & Graeme Russel, *Enforcing Judgments: The International Perspective*, PLC, Sept. 1994, at 16.
58. *Id.* at 17.
59. The United States is not a signatory to either Convention.
60. *See Hilton v. Guyot*, 159 U.S. 113 (1895); RESTATEMENT (SECOND) OF CONFLICTS § 98 (1971).

but not identical to those applicable in the United States. Most other jurisdictions require proof of jurisdiction, finality of judgment, the absence of fraud, and the absence of any public policy grounds for not recognizing the judgment. Exceptions and variations, however, abound. For example, the courts in **Canada** generally do not recognize jurisdiction based on "long-arm" statutes. The courts in **Germany** also appear wary of long-arm jurisdiction. Under German law, a German defendant must have actually appeared in the original suit, been personally served in the foreign state, or been served in Germany with German judicial assistance.[61] Many jurisdictions (*e.g.,* **Germany, Mexico, Japan**) also require some form of reciprocity for enforcement. In still other jurisdictions, the **Netherlands** for example, a foreign judgment will be recognized and enforced only pursuant to a treaty. Thus, if a judgment is entered in a country, such as the United States, that has no treaty with the Netherlands, the dispute must be litigated again in the Netherlands.

There are too many variations to pronounce any general rule. Accordingly, the parties to a technology transfer agreement must pay careful attention to the laws of any jurisdiction in which a judgment would be enforced before agreeing to any particular forum for litigation.[62]

Due to the potential difficulties of enforcing a foreign judgment, in selecting a dispute resolution forum, the parties should consider where the parties have assets that could be reached to satisfy the judgment. If the parties agree that the most reasonable forum is one in which one of the parties has no assets, they should consider including a provision requiring that party to provide a performance bond, letter of credit, or some other collateral that would be available to satisfy any judgment entered against that party with respect to the contract.

B. Arbitration

Arbitration is a nonjudicial method of private dispute resolution. It tends to be the prevailing method of dispute resolution in technology transfer agreements.[63] Arbitration is consensual, meaning that it will be

---

61. *See generally* Ved P. Nanda & David K. Pansius, LITIGATION OF INTERNATIONAL DISPUTES IN U.S. COURTS § 12.07 (1990).
62. *Id.*
63. There are numerous treatises on the subject of arbitration, and it is presumed that most entities involved in international technology transactions have some familiarity with the arbitration procedure. Accordingly, this section will only address some of the more important issues associated with arbitration as a dispute resolution mechanism.

used only if both parties have consented, either in the technology transfer agreement that is the subject of the dispute or by separate agreement executed after the dispute arises. Arbitration is perceived to offer several advantages over traditional litigation: in practice, these assumptions may or may not prove to be true. The perceived advantages of arbitration over litigation are that it may be faster than litigation; it may be less expensive; and decisions will be fairer and more commercially reasonable (because the arbitrators, unlike judges, are often expert in the subject matter of the dispute). In addition, the arbitrators are involved with the case from the very beginning. In contrast, in litigation, different judges may be assigned to the case at different phases of the proceeding. Indeed, the judge who actually hears the trial of the case may not be assigned until the day of the trial.

On the other hand, litigation is backed by the full powers of the courts, which can compel the attendance of witnesses and enforce any judgment or order entered in the proceeding. In arbitration, the exercise of such powers may be more cumbersome. In addition, arbitrators may not have the power to issue preliminary or provisional relief such as a temporary restraining order. Moreover, in most court systems, a party has the right to seek correction of any legal errors committed by the trial court through one or more appeals to higher courts. Appeals of arbitration awards are often severely limited. Thus, an arbitrator could make serious errors of law or fact and the decision would nevertheless be final and non-reviewable.

For these reasons, arbitration is not well suited to resolving huge "bet the company" disputes that turn on difficult legal issues such as the validity of a patent or trademark. The underlying principles may have implications far beyond the immediate dispute and may affect a company's position in the market or even its very survival.

Arbitration is generally perceived as being faster than litigation, although that perception is not necessarily always correct. Even if arbitration is faster, the parties must consider whether speed is what they want and whether they are willing to tolerate a less than perfectly just decision in the interest of speed. A fast arbitration may produce a compromise that ends the dispute, but not necessarily in accordance with the law or the intent of the parties. Many parties to technology transactions cannot afford to allow difficult disputes to last months or years because the longer the dispute lasts, the more poisoned the parties' relationship can become. Moreover, while the parties spend years litigating, the technology may become dated or competitors may move in. In such instances, the parties may be willing to accept the imperfections of arbitration. On the other hand, if establishing a principle is more important than speed, arbitration may be less desirable.

Courts were once reluctant to enforce arbitration clauses, because they ousted courts of jurisdiction and were perceived to deprive the parties of certain fundamental rights. That view has now changed, and in the **United States,** the federal government and a substantial number of states have enacted statutes that recognize and encourage the arbitration of disputes.[64] These statutes also provide mechanisms for enforcement of arbitration awards and facilitation of arbitration proceedings.[65]

Arbitrations typically are conducted under much less formal rules than court litigation. The rules of evidence often are relaxed, and the proceedings generally are more informal than a court proceeding. In addition, unlike a court proceeding, an arbitration is private and need not be subjected to scrutiny by competitors or the press. Confidentiality may be especially important in intellectual property disputes, and in disputes where the inner workings of a company may be probed and offered into evidence.

Under the rules of many arbitration organizations, no provision is made for discovery.[66] Although this may produce a cost benefit, before selecting arbitration, a party should carefully consider the nature of any dispute that may arise and whether the party would need to obtain evidence from its opponent in order to prove its case. In some cases, for example, where the claim may involve false accounting under a software license agreement, extensive discovery may be necessary and arbitration may not be the best form of dispute resolution. In other situations, a party might favor arbitration because the lack of discovery may favor that party. For example, a transferor that has already received some or all of the payment due from the transferee may have less to gain from allowing discovery; any dispute is likely to relate to the transferor's conduct, and the transferor may benefit from the inability of the transferee to obtain discovery concerning their conduct.

Even where the balance of other factors tips in favor of arbitration, the parties should consider whether to provide in the contractual arbitration clause a provision that discovery will be permitted. Moreover, even if discovery is not foreclosed by agreement or rule, the parties should consider whether to limit the scope of permissible discovery. Such limits could relate to both the methods of discovery

---

64. *See, e.g.,* U.S. Arbitration Act, 9 U.S.C. § 1 (1988).
65. *See, e.g., id.* §§ 7, 9.
66. *See, e.g.,* American Arbitration Association International Arbitration Rules; International Chamber of Commerce Rules of Conciliation and Arbitration.

available (for example, depositions, document requests, written interrogatories) and the breadth of matters that may be the subject of discovery requests. Absent such agreement, the permissibility and scope of any discovery often is left solely to the discretion of the arbitrator.[67]

In deciding on arbitration, the parties should also consider which arbitration tribunal will conduct the arbitration; the place of the arbitration; the number of arbitrators; the enforceability of the arbitration award; the language in which the arbitration will be conducted; the award of costs; and the availability of preliminary or provisional remedies pending an arbitration decision.

Of course, choice of law should also be considered.[68] For example, an arbitration clause should explicitly state that the validity, construction, interpretation, and performance of the contract shall be governed solely and exclusively by the laws of the chosen country – or, in the case of the United States, the chosen state – without reference to conflicts of law principles. If any law is to be excluded, for example, the United Nations Convention on Contracts of the International Sale of Goods or the law of any other country, the exclusion should also be stated explicitly.

There are a number of available arbitration tribunals, and each has its own rules of arbitration. These include the American Arbitration Association, the International Chamber of Commerce, the Japanese Commercial Arbitration Association, the London Court of Arbitration, and the Arbitration Institute for the Stockholm Chamber of Commerce (particularly for disputes involving Russian parties). Accordingly, before selecting a tribunal, the parties should satisfy themselves that the tribunal's rules are consistent with the parties' expectations and needs. Although no tribunal need be designated, failure to do so requires the parties to be much more explicit in describing how the arbitration will be conducted. This, of course, increases the possibility that an important issue will be overlooked. In contrast, the designation of a particular tribunal will automatically make that tribunal's rules of procedure applicable to the arbitration, unless the parties agree to specific modifications.

An important matter for the parties to determine is the number of arbitrators. An arbitration will be far less expensive if only a single arbitrator is selected. Nevertheless, parties frequently are reluctant to leave the resolution of important matters in the hands of a single arbitrator. Accordingly, arbitration agreements typically provide for three, or sometimes more, arbitrators.

---

67. *See, e.g.,* U.S. Arbitration Act, *supra* note 64, § 7.
68. *See* Section I.

When three arbitrators are to be appointed, the usual procedure is for each party to nominate an arbitrator and for the two arbitrators who are appointed to appoint a third arbitrator. It is common that all three arbitrators are to be neutral and impartial.[69] The parties may, however, provide that the party appointed arbitrators will be advocates for the position of the party appointing them. Partisan or biased arbitrators, however, may not be permitted under the statutes or rules of one or more jurisdictions or tribunals.[70]

The parties may also want to specify the qualifications of arbitrators to be appointed. For example, in a three-person arbitration panel, it may be desirable to require that at least one arbitrator be a lawyer. The parties may also wish to specify that the arbitrators be fluent in the relevant language and have some experience in the business and expertise in the technology that are the subject of the technology transfer agreement.

The place of arbitration is important, not only for the convenience of the parties, but also because it may establish the law that governs the arbitration. Even if the parties specify the substantive law that governs the dispute, the law of the place of arbitration may affect, among other things, the manner in which the arbitration is conducted, the appointment, removal, and replacement of arbitrators, and the form of the arbitration award.

An arbitration clause may designate different places of arbitration, depending on which party institutes the arbitration. Such provision may alleviate problems associated with enforcing any award if the place of arbitration is where the respondent's assets are located. Such a provision may also promote negotiation prior to arbitration, if each place selected is otherwise somewhat inconvenient for the party that must initiate arbitration in that place.

Because arbitration is consensual, the parties must be careful to specify which contractual disputes may be decided by arbitration. Generally, the parties will want to draft the clause expansively to avoid loopholes that will permit a party to delay the proceeding by arguing that certain aspects of the dispute are not subject to arbitration. Thus, for example, a clause should typically provide that arbitration will apply to all disputes of any nature whatsoever arising out of, or relating in any way to, the contract or breach thereof. By contrast, the parties may wish to limit the breadth of the arbitration clause if they are engaged in a number of related transactions, some of which they may not want to subject to arbitration. Any narrowing, however, invites dispute over

---

69. *See, e.g.,* American Arbitration Association International Rules, art. 7.
70. *See, e.g.,* I.C.C. Rules, art. 2(8); U.S. Arbitration Act, *supra* note 64, § 10.

whether a particular provision or breach is or is not subject to arbitration, so the language must be carefully chosen. The parties should also specify who resolves questions concerning the scope of the arbitration clause. Unless the parties provide that the arbitrator makes those determinations, it could be decided by a court; this of course could introduce delay, expense and considerable uncertainty into the process.

Another important issue to address is how the arbitrators will apportion attorney's fees and costs associated with arbitration. Absent an agreement of the parties, the arbitrators determine how to apportion these costs, which include the fees and expenses of the arbitrators, the cost of the tribunal, the cost of experts, and attorney's fees. It is not uncommon for arbitrators to equally apportion some or all of these costs. If the parties desire that fees and costs be awarded to the prevailing party or on some other basis, they should so state in their agreement.

Notwithstanding the desire of the parties to make arbitration the exclusive method of dispute resolution, there may be occasions where an arbitration remedy will be inadequate. As noted, arbitrators do not have the full powers of the courts and may not be able to provide certain remedies. For example, a court has the power preliminarily to enjoin a party from engaging in certain conduct if that conduct would irreparably injure or threaten to injure the opposing party irreparably. An arbitrator may not have a similar power. Accordingly, the parties should consider including a provision in the arbitration clause that provides that notwithstanding the agreement that arbitration is the exclusive remedy, nothing in the agreement will prevent either party from seeking preliminary injunctive relief from a court of competent jurisdiction in aid of pending or anticipated arbitration. Injunctive relief is particularly critical to protect against unauthorized disclosure or use of proprietary or confidential information. In the technology transfer or intellectual property contexts, therefore, injunctive relief exceptions usually are included as a matter of course.

1. Enforcement

Surprisingly, the enforcement of an arbitration award may actually be easier than the enforcement of a court judgment. The **U.N. Convention on the Recognition and Enforcement of Foreign Arbitral Awards**,[71] also known as the "New York Convention" (the "Convention"), sets out the procedure for the recognition and enforcement of arbitral awards. Most of the world's trading nations

---

71. 21 U.S.T. 2517, T.I.A.S. No. 6997, 330 U.N.T.S. 38.

are party to this Convention. The Convention provides for both the recognition and enforcement of arbitration awards, provided the party seeking recognition and enforcement establishes the award and the arbitration agreement under which it was made. The Convention provides that recognition and enforcement of the award may be refused only under limited circumstances, for example when the party against whom the award is invoked was not given proper notice or when the award did not fall within the terms of the submission to arbitration. The Convention, however, does not explicitly provide for appeals to the courts to correct legal errors.[72]

To facilitate enforcement, the agreement should include a specific provision stating that a judgment of a court shall be entered and enforced in any court of competent jurisdiction over the parties or their assets upon the award made pursuant to the arbitration. Indeed, such a provision is explicitly required by the terms of the United States Arbitration Act.[73]

C. Other Alternative Dispute Resolution Mechanisms

As disputes among parties to technology transfers grow ever more technical and the burdens and delays of litigation or arbitration increase, Alternative Dispute Resolution (ADR) may be an attractive option.[74] ADR is gaining increasing popularity in the United States and elsewhere. ADR mechanisms include simple negotiation, mediation, conciliation, mini-trials, summary jury trials, and many others. These methods are available as alternatives or adjuncts to litigation or arbitration. In contrast to arbitration and litigation, ADR typically does not result in a final, binding, and enforceable award.

Mediation usually involves a neutral and respected third party listening to each party's position, sometimes with both parties and sometimes individually, and attempting to bring the parties together to achieve a settlement of the dispute themselves. Conciliation is a similar process, but a conciliator typically proposes what he believes is a fair solution after having heard from both parties and having weighed their respective positions.

Another form of ADR, which is gaining increased acceptance in the United States, is the "mini-trial." Although the format varies, typically each party presents an argument and summary of the evidence it is

---

72. The U.S. Arbitration Act similarly limits the grounds on which an arbitration award can be overturned. 9 U.S.C. §§ 1.
73. *Id.* § 9.
74. As used here, ADR excludes arbitration.

prepared to prove to a neutral adviser or panel. The panel may include a representative from the senior management of each party. Alternatively, a senior manager from each company may be compelled to attend and observe the mini-trial. In either instance, the purpose is to ensure that the business persons see and hear the relative strengths and weaknesses of one another's case so that they are better able to make a rational decision as to whether to settle or litigate. At the end of the mini-trial, the adviser or panel issues an advisory decision that will further inform the parties of how a neutral entity views the dispute.

A summary jury trial is very similar to a mini-trial, except that the advisory decision makers are a panel of impartial jurors, who are instructed to follow applicable law. Although the jurors typically are debriefed following the verdict, the process may be more legalistic and less proactive than mini-trials.

Although mini-trials and summary jury trials may be effective in bringing about a settlement, they may be time-consuming and require costly preparation. In addition, if a party is skeptical about whether those techniques will result in settlement, the party may hold back evidence or arguments and thus undermine the effectiveness of the procedure. On the other hand, if the parties are wholly forthcoming and settlement does not result, the opposing party is likely to be much better educated about the opponent's position than it otherwise would be.

Although ADR may be agreed to in advance of an arising dispute, more often the parties first consider ADR after a dispute occurs and before they commit themselves to litigation or arbitration. Not addressing ADR in the contract has advantages and disadvantages. Some disputes are better suited to ADR than others and until a dispute arises, it may be difficult to determine whether ADR would be useful or would simply increase cost and delay. On the other hand, a contractual obligation to use ADR before litigation or arbitration may promote compromise and settlement without resort to more formal procedures. It may also be easier for the parties to agree to an ADR mechanism, and the mediator or neutral advisers to be employed, at the time the parties are negotiating their contract and before any dispute arises.

Whenever the parties consent to ADR, either before or after a dispute arises, there should be a written agreement that defines the ADR process and identifies, at least generally, the type of ADR mediator to be employed.

As noted in prior sections, statutes of limitations typically require that a litigation or arbitration be begun within a certain time period. The running of this limitation generally will not be tolled while the parties pursue ADR. Thus, unless the parties are diligent, it is possible that a party may lose its right to a formal adjudication of the dispute because of delay caused by ADR. Accordingly, any ADR agreement should specify a time period within which ADR must be concluded. Alternatively, or in addition, the agreement should provide that the running of any applicable statute of limitations will be tolled during the pendency of ADR.

Many ADR agreements, especially those incorporated in the basic contract between the parties, provide that the parties will "in good faith" attempt to resolve amicably any dispute by ADR prior to litigation or arbitration. Certainly, ADR must be conducted in good faith if it is to be successful. A party must be careful, however, not to include in an ADR clause additional[75] or poorly defined contractual obligations that its adversary may later argue were also breached. Accordingly, whether or not the term "good faith" is explicitly used, any ADR agreement should provide that either party may terminate the ADR at any time in its sole discretion (especially if negotiation, mediation or conciliation is the chosen method); that in agreeing to ADR, each party is free to act in its own self-interest; and that neither party is bound to reach any agreement or compromise in the ADR. The parties should further agree that all ADR procedures will be strictly confidential and that the parties agree not to use the willingness to engage in ADR or any statements made during ADR against the other party.

There are many forms of ADR, and the options may be limited only by the creativity of the parties. For any form of ADR to be successful, however, the parties must have confidence in the neutral entity assisting them. They must be willing to compromise and must enter into the process in good faith and not with a hidden desire to delay or gain some other advantage.

---

75. Particularly perilous in this context are the expressions "best efforts" (when dealing with the **United States**) or "best endeavors" (when dealing with the **United Kingdom**). These have the effect of imposing an extremely high standard of legal obligation on the parties.

Chapter Seven

Convergence of Technologies and Complex Transfer Structures

Trevor W. Nagel
Shaw, Pittman, Potts & Trowbridge, Washington, D.C.

Mark M. Turner
Denton Hall, London[1]

The transfer of technology has become both increasingly global and complex over the past decade. Rapid technological advancement generally and the growing demand for international information technology (IT) capability in particular have made it difficult for the corporate world to keep abreast of cutting-edge technologies; for governments to maintain and promote rational regulatory systems that enhance rather than hinder technological advances; and for legal systems to sort through what often is a quagmire of intellectual property rights and interests.

The convergence of technologies, especially in the areas of telecommunications, IT and entertainment, is exemplified by the fast emerging world of multi-media products. For example, a technology which was originally developed for the storage of digitized computer records, the CD-ROM, is now being used to spearhead the growth of new entertainment media. It has proven to have unexpectedly wide applications as a carrier of digitized text, graphics, sound, films, and other works now at a time when one of the main drawbacks of the technology, slower access times than a floppy disk, has been overcome with double, triple and even quadruple speed CD-ROM drives on the market.

---

1. The authors wish to thank Linda Kordziel from Shaw, Pittman, Potts & Trowbridge's Washington, D.C. office for her assistance in preparing this Chapter.

Two related themes emerge from the increasing convergence of technologies and technological advancement: complexity and uncertainty. On the one hand, the technologies themselves, and the decisions associated with selecting appropriate technologies and structuring their transfer, are becoming increasingly complex. On the other hand, these complex technology transfers involve decisions in a world of uncertainty with respect to the future development and uses of the technology and the determination of the price and performance standards that should be expected from the technology. In a world of rapid technological advancement, today's technologies can be outdated and rendered obsolete, thereby leaving a business with the unenviable choice of either writing off a large investment in outmoded technology or suffering a competitive disadvantage in the marketplace. This situation is particularly acute with respect to IT, which has ceased to be merely a non-core support function and now increasingly constitutes an integral part of the delivery of the core competence of the organization. To take an example from the banking industry, the proliferation and acceptance of automatic teller machines (ATMs) has fundamentally changed the way in which customers select and interact with retail banks. Such changes will continue and even accelerate. Imagine the impact on retail banking of the implementation of a successful home banking system through interactive TV.

This Chapter examines how to cope with and exploit the uncertainty associated with complex technology transfers to achieve the business objectives of the parties. Because of the significant substantive ramifications of the structure selected for effecting technology transfers, this Chapter's particular focus is on how to structure, negotiate and draft arrangements which anticipate uncertainty in technological development.

Section I outlines several ways to structure complex technology transfers and proffers three short case studies: incubators in Israel, the European Union and United States approaches to cooperative research ventures, and the outsourcing of IT functions for strategic purposes. The first two case studies illustrate the transfer of technology in its early research stage, while the third case study exemplifies the transfer of technology applications and technology in its later stage of development. Section II posits that uncertainty in technology transfers is often a "double-edged sword." Although uncertainty may result in many technological, business and legal problems for the parties, it may also produce unanticipated technological developments which may be financially rewarding if properly exploited. This Section also explores ways in which the parties can anticipate and deal with unexpected research applications and markets for technology.

Section III discusses mechanisms for monitoring uncertainty in complex technology transfers, and specifically by whom and how technology transfers should be administered through the life of the transaction. Section IV examines the unwinding of complex technology transfer structures and, especially, the termination and restructuring issues which need to be considered by the parties when initially consummating the transaction. The concluding Section revisits briefly some of the legal and practical themes of complex technology transfers.

I. STRUCTURING UNCERTAINTY IN COMPLEX TECHNOLOGY TRANSFERS

A. Types of Collaboration

In addition to the basic transfer structures described in detail in Chapter Two, there are several types of collaboration that are particularly suitable for complex technological alliances. Although the structure used in any particular case will be dictated by business objectives, it is possible to identify broad categories of relationships which are common across different technologies and industries.

1. Contract Research

This is the loosest form of alliance, with the research entity usually playing a passive role in the overall direction of the project. The research entity is often asked to solve a particular technical problem without being involved in other areas of research and technology development. This type of relationship tends to be conducted on an arm's length basis, with the research entity receiving payment on a fixed fee or per day basis, without assuming any of the risks or rewards of the project. For the commercial entity, the key advantage of contract research is that it provides access to specialist expertise, which the commercial entity does not possess, to solve a particular problem. For instance, a pharmaceutical company may need help in devising a delivery system for a new drug.

The most important issues in this type of relationship for the commercial entity concern confidentiality of the research and ownership of the results. As a general principle, the commercial entity will treat the contract deliverables as "works for hire" and expect to own the results of research it has funded outright, possibly with a non-exclusive license back to the research entity for its business. A sensitive issue is whether the research entity can use the results for work commissioned by a competitor in the same field. Often a suitable compromise (particularly where an academic research institution is involved) is for the research entity to use the results as "background intellectual property rights," or, in other words, general knowledge derived from the research. In return, the research entity may agree not to be involved in a project in the same field for a period of time such as three years. Another approach is for the parties to agree that any "residual knowledge" – knowledge retained "in the heads" of those associated with the project – is available for use and exploitation by either party, provided that this knowledge does not infringe on any specific intellectual property rights belonging to a particular party.

2. Industrial Sponsorship

This type of collaboration usually involves a corporation funding basic research in a particular field over a period of time at one or more academic or non-profit research institutions. There may also be a commitment by the corporation to supply equipment, raw materials or personnel. In exchange, the corporation may get advance notice of results of the research or exclusive access to them, exclusive exploitation rights in a particular field, a share of royalties from any exploitation or any combination of these. This type of collaboration is most suited to long-term pure research, where the outcome is uncertain and the timing is not determinative. One of the main intangible benefits to the corporation from industrial sponsorships is that it can expose its own staff to work at the leading edge of research. The inclusion of provisions in the agreement for the interchange of personnel, joint seminars and so on are particularly significant in this context. The corporation also has an opportunity to influence the direction of basic research in the chosen area. Similar issues to those described in the Contract Research subsection above frequently arise in regards to the exploitation of the results of the research.

3. Industrial Collaboration

Collaborative research between businesses is becoming increasingly popular as research and development costs continue to escalate, research agendas demand more specialization, and industries become increasingly technology driven. Moreover, industrial collaboration can improve efficiency and cut product development times. The electronics industry is now dotted with cooperative research ventures. One example is the Power PC microchip design produced by Motorola, Apple and IBM,[2] which are strong competitors in other areas. This example highlights one of the main commercial disadvantages of industrial collaboration, namely the danger of assisting an actual or potential competitor in solving its own problems. Thus, industrial collaboration should be very carefully planned to restrict its impact to particular areas of research and development.

4. Case Study: Cooperative Research Ventures

In an increasingly competitive world marketplace, technology businesses face a number of economic realities. First, the costs of developing a new technology and bringing it to the marketplace may exceed available resources. Second, the economics of high-technology manufacturing has changed because of consumer demands and shorter product life cycles. Third, technology businesses must quickly develop and implement production strategies because competition may limit to no more than six months or a year the exclusivity resulting from being first to market. Many high-technology businesses are thus turning to cooperative research ventures to assist them in establishing, maintaining and promoting their competitive edge in a particular industry or market.[3] The advantages of this cooperative structure are that it may reduce the costs of developing new technologies; share the risks associated with research and development; avoid duplication in research initiatives; and acquire better and quicker access to new technological developments, markets and inexpensive sources for production and marketing of research results.[4]

The disadvantage of a cooperative research venture is that it may violate antitrust laws.[5] Close cooperation between competitors provides an inherent temptation to collude in a horizontal cartel or other anticompetitive business behaviors. Alternatively, the potential oligopolistic market power of several large businesses in a cooperative research venture could be abused to create barriers for other entities striving to enter a particular technology. Both the **European Union** and

---

2. *See, e.g.,* Steve Lohr, *In Pursuit of Computing's Holy Grail*, N.Y. TIMES, May 23, 1993.
3. *See generally* Michelle K. Lee & Mavis K. Lee, *High Technology Consortia: A Panacea for America's Technological Competitiveness Problems?*, 6 HIGH TECH. L.J. 335-362 (1991).
4. *Id.* at 340. *See* Chapter Two, Section II.A.3.
5. *See generally* Chapter Two, Section II.B.3.

the **United States** have attempted to balance the economic advantages and potential anticompetitive practices of cooperative research ventures by regulating these complex technology structures. The different approaches of each are outlined briefly below.

a. European Union and EFTA

The treatment of cooperative research ventures under the laws of the European Union varies dramatically depending on whether the venture is categorized as "concentrative" or "cooperative." The assessment is often very difficult to make in practice, but EU law provides the following guidance:[6]

(i) A joint venture will be regarded as concentrative if it performs, on a permanent basis, all the functions of an autonomous economic entity, and does not give rise to the coordination of the competitive behavior of the parties among themselves or between themselves and the joint venture.[7]

(ii) A joint venture will be regarded as cooperative where its object or effect is the coordination of certain competitive behavior of the parties which otherwise remain independent.

Concentrative joint ventures are considered under the EU Merger Control Regulation.[8] Concentrations above a certain financial threshold (the "Community Dimension")[9] are generally dealt with by the European Commission's Merger Task Force (part of its Competition Directorate), while concentrations below this threshold generally fall within the exclusive competence of the national competition authorities

---

6. Commission Notice regarding concentrative and cooperative operations under Council Regulation 4064/89 of 21 December 1989 on the control of concentrations between undertakings, 1990 O.J. (C 203) 10. *See generally* Chapter Two, Section II.B.3.
7. Council Regulation 4064/89, art. 3(2), 1989 O.J. (L 395).
8. Council Regulation 4064/89, 1989 O.J. (L 395) 1.
9. A concentration will have a Community Dimension where the following cumulative test is met: the combined aggregate worldwide turnover of all the parties concerned exceeds ECU 5,000 million, and the aggregate EEA-wide turnover of at least two of the parties concerned exceeds ECU 250 million, unless each of the parties concerned achieves more than two-thirds of its aggregate EEA-wide turnover within one and the same member state. *Id.* at art. 1(2). A concentration having a Community Dimension must not be put into effect until three weeks after it has been notified to the European Commission or the EFTA Surveillance Authority. *Id.* at art. 7(1). Such concentrations must be notified within one week of the conclusion of the Agreement (which is the date of signature as opposed to the fulfilment of any conditions precedent), the announcement of a public bid or the acquisition of a controlling interest, whichever is the earlier. *Id.* at art. 4(1). Fines may be imposed for breach of the above requirements.

in each member state. Cooperative joint ventures are considered by the European Commission's general competition authorities under Article 85 of the Treaty of Rome.

Article 85(1) of the Treaty of Rome prohibits any agreements which may affect trade between member states and which have the object or effect of preventing, restricting or distorting competition in the Common Market. Such agreements will be automatically void and unenforceable unless granted an individual exemption by the European Commission under Article 85(3). An exemption will be granted when, broadly, the benefit of an agreement to consumers and to technical and economic progress outweighs any anticompetitive effect. As an alternative, the European Commission may grant "negative clearance" whereby the agreement in question falls outside the ambit of Article 85(1) altogether. Notification for exemption or negative clearance generally protects against fines being imposed by the European Commission from the date of notification which may otherwise be up to ten per cent of the total worldwide turnover of the parties concerned. Any third parties adversely affected by the operation of an agreement in breach of Article 85(1) may also claim damages in their respective national courts.

Generally, the European Commission has taken a favorable attitude to cooperative research ventures. Its criteria for assessing technological and other joint ventures have been published in some detail.[10] It should be noted that parallel provisions to the EU competition rules also apply in the six EFTA countries. In this respect, both the European Commission and the EFTA Surveillance Authority have jurisdiction, with rules governing how the jurisdiction is allocated between these two bodies.

The Commission has produced a number of "block exemption" Regulations, which exempt certain agreements by category, thus obviating the need for individual exemptions under Article 85(3). The most significant of these for cooperative research ventures is Council Regulation 418/85, which came into force on March 1, 1985, and which exempts research and development joint ventures meeting certain requirements. The Regulation, which will continue in force until December 31, 1997, applies to joint research and development products, joint exploitation of the results of research and development of products, and joint research and development of products which

---

10. Commission Notice Concerning the Assessment of Co-operative Joint Ventures pursuant to Article 85 of the EEC Treaty, 1993 O.J. (C 43) 2. Similar guidelines were adopted by the EFTA Surveillance Authority on 6 April 1994, 1994 O.J. (L 186) 57.

otherwise would violate Article 85(1). Research and development of products or processes is defined as including the acquisition of technical knowledge, the conducting of theoretical analysis and experimentation, technical testing of products or processes, the establishing of the necessary facilities and the obtaining of intellectual property rights and results.[11] The exemption only applies if the agreement provides that the work in question will be carried out within a definitive program, that the results are accessible to all parties, and that any party is free to exploit the results independently.[12]

The exemption does not apply to agreements between competing manufacturers of existing products, which first, could be improved or replaced by the contract products and second, when the agreement is executed, represent collectively over 20 per cent of the market for such products, either within the EU or within a substantial part of it. If the technological collaboration involves joint distribution, this threshold is reduced to ten per cent.[13]

The exemption lists certain provisions which must be included in the agreement without the loss of the block exemption protection (known as "White List" provisions).[14] One example is that a party may not carry out independent research work or create third party agreements within the ambit of the contract program during its term.[15] The block exemption also sets out a number of provisions which are not permitted in an agreement (known as "Black List" provisions).[16] For example, the parties may not be restricted from carrying out independent research and development in a different field or in the same field after termination of the joint program.[17] In addition, the block exemptions set out certain provisions which the parties may include in the contract but are not mandatory (known as "Grey List" provisions).[18] For example, the parties may be required to communicate patented or non-patented technical knowledge necessary for the exploitation of the results of the research and development program.[19]

Protection under the Block Exemption will last for the duration of the research and development program plus five years, provided that the

---

11. Council Regulation 418/85, art. 1, 1985 O.J. (L 53).
12. *Id.* at art. 2.
13. *Id.* at art. 3(2).
14. *Id.* at art. 4.
15. *Id.* at art. 4(1)(a).
16. *Id.* at art. 6.
17. *Id.* at art. 6(a).
18. *Id.* at art. 5.
19. *Id.* at art. 5(a).

parties involved are not competing manufacturers and that the results are to be jointly exploited.[20] If, on the other hand, the parties are competing manufacturers, the five-year protection will only apply provided the parties' combined production is under the 20 per cent market share threshold.[21] At the end of the five-year exploitation period, provided the 20 per cent threshold is not exceeded, the exemption will continue indefinitely.[22] There is, however, some flexibility regarding the 20 per cent market share threshold. The exemption will continue to apply if the parties' market share does not exceed 22 per cent for any two successive fiscal years.[23] Once the relevant market share is exceeded, the exemption will cease six months after the end of that fiscal year in which the excess share of the market occurred.[24]

The block exemption also details an opposition procedure[25] whereby agreements which contain provisions falling beyond the White and Grey Lists, but not within the Black List, can be notified to the European Commission and can be considered exempt if the Commission does not make an opposition to the provisions within six months. This is an important procedure as cooperative research ventures are generally so *sui generis* that key provisions frequently fall between the "Lists."

b. United States

The treatment of cooperative research ventures under U.S. law is more straightforward. In order to promote research and development, Congress enacted the National Cooperative Research Act of 1984 (the "1984 Act").[26] The 1984 Act clarified the application of antitrust laws with respect to joint research and development ventures. The 1984 Act, however, protected only joint research and development ventures and

---

20. *Id.* at art. 3(1).
21. *Id.* at art. 3(2).
22. *Id.* at art. 3(3).
23. *Id.* at art. 3(4).
24. *Id.* at art. 3(5).
25. *Id.* at art. 7.
26. 15 U.S.C. §§ 4301-4305 (1988). *See* H.R. CONF. REP. NO. 1044, 98th Cong., 2d Sess. 1 (1984), *reprinted in* 1984 U.S.C.C.A.N. 3131.

did not encompass production joint ventures.[27] Thus, Congress enacted the National Cooperative Production Amendments of 1993 to extend the provisions of the 1984 Act to production joint ventures and amended the short title of the 1984 Act to the National Cooperative Research and Production Act of 1993 (the "Act").[28] The purpose of the 1993 Amendments is "to promote innovation, facilitate trade, and strengthen the competitiveness of the United States in world markets . . . ."[29] Congress found that:

(i) technological innovation and its profitable commercialization are important for the United States to compete in world markets;
(ii) cooperative arrangements among nonaffiliated corporations are often essential for successful technological innovation; and
(iii) the antitrust laws may have been mistakenly perceived to inhibit procompetitive cooperative arrangements.[30]

The Act defines "joint venture" as any group of activities by two or more persons for the purpose of

> theoretical analysis, experimentation, or systematic study of phenomena or observable facts . . . development or testing of basic engineering techniques . . . experimental production and testing of models . . . production of a product, process, or service . . . [or] testing in connection with the production of a product, process, or service.[31]

The term "joint venture" also covers activities necessary to develop a technology for commercialization, such as "the establishment and operation of facilities for the conducting of the venture, conducting the venture on a protected and proprietary basis, and prosecuting applications for patents and granting of licenses for the results of the venture."[32]

The Act requires any party to a joint venture to make certain filings in order to invoke its protections for the collaboration. Acting on behalf of the joint venture, the party must file with the U.S. Attorney General and the Federal Trade Commission a written notification disclosing the identities of the parties to the venture and the nature and objectives of

---

27. For an article criticizing the 1984 Act as "not going far enough" in protecting strategic collaborations, *see* Thomas M. Jorde & David J. Teece, *Innovation, Cooperation and Antitrust*, 4 HIGH TECH. L.J. 1, 50-54 (1989).
28. 15 U.S.C. §§ 4301-4306 (Supp. V 1993).
29. *See* 15 U.S.C. § 4301.
30. *See id.*
31. 15 U.S.C. § 4301(a)(6).
32. 15 U.S.C. § 4301(a).

the venture.[33] If a purpose of the joint venture is the production of a product, process, or service, the written notification must also disclose the identity and nationality of any person who is a party to the venture or who controls any party to the venture.[34]

In general, the Act provides three benefits to joint ventures whose activities fall within its guidelines and who have duly filed a written notification of their activities in accordance with the Act. First, the Act states that properly structured joint ventures will not be deemed to infringe antitrust laws on a *per se* basis, but shall be judged under a rule of reason.[35] The rule of reason requires the court to take into account all relevant factors affecting competition, including the effects on competition in properly defined, relevant research, development, product, process, and service markets.[36] For the purpose of determining a properly defined relevant market, worldwide capacity is considered to the extent that it may be appropriate in the circumstances.[37] In other words, the rule of reason requires courts to undertake a detailed analysis of the anticompetitive effects of the defendants' activities and thus places a higher burden on antitrust plaintiffs than the *per se* rule (which enables courts to make rather arbitrary judgments about the anticompetitive effects of the proscribed activity).[38] This is in sharp contrast to the rather arbitrary market share limits under EU competition law. Second, the Act further discourages antitrust suits against joint ventures by awarding costs, including reasonable attorneys' fees, to substantially prevailing defendants if the suit or the plaintiffs' conduct during the litigation was "frivolous, unreasonable, without foundation, or in bad faith."[39] Finally, the Act states that violators of federal or state antitrust laws will only be responsible for "actual damages."[40] This provision relieves antitrust defendants involved in joint ventures from the treble damages that generally apply in antitrust suits if their disclosed activities are found to be anticompetitive. However, a production joint venture seeking the protection of the "de-trebling damages provision" of the Act is required to locate its principal production facilities in the U.S. or its territories, and the parties to the joint venture and those in control of the parties

---

33. 15 U.S.C. § 4305(a).
34. *Id.*
35. 15 U.S.C. § 4302. *See also* Chapter Two, Section II.B.3.
36. 15 U.S.C. § 4302.
37. *Id.*
38. *See* Chapter Two, Section II.B.3.
39. 15 U.S.C. § 4304.
40. 15 U.S.C. § 4303.

must be either a U.S. person or a foreign person from a country whose law accords antitrust treatment no less favorable to U.S. persons than to such country's domestic persons with respect to participation in production joint ventures.[41]

5. Governmental Support

The effect of incentives offered by national or local government for particular types of collaboration should not be underestimated. These incentives can take the form of tax incentives, grants and funding from strategic research foundations, and more subtle measures such as industrial policy initiatives. Traditionally, this type of collaboration has been aimed at basic research rather than product development, but increasingly governments are seeking to maximize the commercial opportunities through academic research, thereby supporting near market research and product development. In addition to the financial benefits which participation in this type of collaboration may bring, there are frequently other intangible, but important, political benefits.

In **Israel**, for instance, the government has sponsored an innovative program of *"incubators"* attached to research institutes. Basic research is centered on seven universities, including leading institutions such as the Weitzman Institute and Tel Aviv University, which have all set up commercial entities to exploit their innovations. Incubators are the subject of the Case Study below. Some have also set up science parks. In **South Korea**, the government has announced a long-term Highly Advanced National Program under which the government and industry will contribute U.S.$46 billion over nine years to research and development in 14 industrial sectors.[42] **Australia** has introduced a variety of initiatives, including the creation of over 50 "cooperative research centers," which are federally funded research programs drawn up between industry and academic institutions.[43] In the **European Union**, approximately ECU 2.47 billion were committed in 1992 to support EU research. It is clear that this large-scale financial backing will be an important factor in the success of the "European Technology Community."[44] The European Commission has now implemented a

---

41. 15 U.S.C. § 4306.
42. Government of South Korea, Highly Advanced National [Han] Project (Apr. 1992).
43. The Office of the Chief Scientist, Australia, CRCs in Brief (June 1993).
44. Court of Auditors Annual Report 1992, 1993 O.J. (C 309).

"Fourth Framework Program,"[45] running from 1994 to 1998, for the funding of EU research projects. This fourth in the series of Community funding programs focuses upon, among other things, information, communication, and industrial technologies. In addition to the above, there are a number of other EU programs, for example, the Strategic Program for Innovation and Technology Transfer (SPRINT).[46] SPRINT has a budget of ECU 121 million and provides funding towards project costs, supporting areas relating to innovation management, networks of experts and technological promotional activities, such as conferences and exhibitions.

6. Case Study: Incubators in Israel

The Israeli Office of the Chief Scientist of the Ministry of Industry and Trade (the OCS) currently supports 28 incubators sponsoring approximately 250 projects.[47] These incubators provide facilities and administrative services to the projects. The projects are usually research and development-oriented and are undertaken by businesses possessing technological blueprints, but lacking the resources or business experience to develop them. The incubators allow the projects to develop technological ideas, while attracting commercial investors and strategic partners. Once a project is self-sustaining and ready for commercial investors or strategic partners, the project leaves the incubator.

In general, incubators can be classified as either independent incubators or incubators with non-governmental industrial or financial support.[48] An independent incubator is an independent legal entity, such as an association or a non-profit corporation. Representatives from the local industries, the business sector and research institutes contribute professionally to the promotion of the incubator. A project sponsored by an independent incubator must meet several conditions:

(i) the project must be incorporated and managed as a separate business;

---

45. Decision No. 1110/94 of the European Parliament and of the Council of 26 April 1994 concerning the Fourth Framework Program of the European Community's activities in the field of research and technological development and demonstration (1994–1998), 1994 O.J. (L 126).
46. Council Decision 89/286, 1989 O.J. (L 112), amended by Council Decision 94/5, 1994 O.J. (L 6).
47. *See* Barry Levenfeld, Business Opportunities in Israel – Intellectual Property 24-28 (June, 1994) (Yigal Arnon & Co., on file with Shaw, Pittman, Potts & Trowbridge).
48. *Id.* at 24.

(ii) at least 50 per cent of the project's employees must be new immigrants to Israel;
(iii) the project must have non-governmental support in addition to that provided by the OCS; and
(iv) ownership in the project in its initial state must be allocated as follows – at least 50 per cent to the owner of the idea or entrepreneur, at least ten per cent to the employees, and up to 40 per cent to the incubator and any investors of supplementary funds.[49]

The OCS gives financial support for the operation of the independent incubator and the projects located in the incubator.[50] A successful project is required to contribute to a special fund established by the OCS in an amount equal to two per cent of the proceeds received from its sales, and to pay the state royalties of three per cent of the proceeds of sales of the developed projects, until the total amount of the grant is returned.[51]

The OCS also provides limited support in certain cases for incubators with non-governmental industrial or financial support. The governmental support available to these incubator projects may include a grant of 66 per cent of approved research and development costs, a market feasibility study by the OCS, or a grant of 50 per cent of costs for a private market feasibility study.[52] Moreover, a separate entity is set up to conduct each project, and the entrepreneurs are allocated a share of at least 26 per cent in the ownership of the entity.[53]

The Har Hozvim Technological Entrepreneurship Centre (HiTEC) is one example of a successful incubator with industrial and financial support.[54] HiTEC is operated by an association of eight high-technology corporations and receives financial support from the members of that association and the OCS. HiTEC currently has nine approved projects and has created a total of 42 high-technology jobs. HiTEC provides introductions, experts, access to laboratories, libraries and procurement facilities, and assists in seeking strategic partners and commercial investors for its projects.

Incubators raise similar intellectual property concerns as in any complex high-technology structure. Despite the support given by the incubator, many projects often fail to protect their intellectual property rights adequately. Moreover, a potential purchaser of the technology

---

49. *Id.* at 25-26.
50. *Id.* at 26.
51. *Id.*
52. *Id.* at 27.
53. *Id.*
54. *Id.*

being developed in an incubator does not have the opportunity to influence the direction of the basic research of a project. However, a potential purchaser who can evaluate the economic prospects of a project may obtain rights and interests in a new technology at a relatively low cost.

7. Strategic Outsourcing

The prior examples of structuring complex technology transfers involve the early stages of technology. Strategic outsourcing is an example of a complex technology transfer structure which tends to implicate technology development towards the end of its research cycle, namely its applications. Many businesses whose operations, services, and products are heavily technology dependent, such as banks and other financial institutions, hospitals, and companies involved in the communications, hospitality and travel industries, must make critical choices when selecting key technological applications. For example, it is important for many banks and financial institutions to have sophisticated credit card processing technology and for hotels or airlines to have state-of-the-art global reservation systems. For these businesses, it is not the transfer of technology *per se*, but rather the transfer of technological *applications* which are critical for maintaining a competitive edge.

Many of these corporations have concluded that it is advantageous to transfer responsibility for selecting and running key IT functions to IT specialists; these corporations have decided to "outsource" critical IT functions such as data centers, local area networks and wide area networks to a third party service provider or outsourcing vendor.[55] The major outsourcing vendors offering a broad range of services on a global basis across a variety of industries include EDS, ISSC (IBM's service corporation) and CSC. There are also a large number of niche "players" catering to specialized industry groups.

Whereas many "traditional" outsourcings were undertaken purely for economic reasons – to remove certain IT assets off the books of the corporation and to have its IT functions operated more efficiently by an outsourcing vendor – some corporations have taken the outsourcing route for strategic reasons, because the outsourcing vendor may be

---

55. *See* Trevor W. Nagel & Michael T. Murphy, Avoiding Pitfalls in Outsourcing (paper presented at "Computer Law and Business in the New Europe and Beyond," a conference organized by International Federation of Computer Law Associations, The Computer Law Association, Inc., and Society for Computers and Law, Bath, England, June 16-17, 1994) (on file with Shaw, Pittman, Potts & Trowbridge).

better equipped to assess the IT needs of the corporation and to evaluate the current and anticipated IT applications relating to rapidly evolving industries.[56] In other words, many technology end-user corporations consider the outsourcing vendor to be better situated to select "winners" among technology applications than the corporation itself, thereby enabling the corporation to dedicate its limited resources to its core competence. Tasks such as the design, installation and support of domestic and international telecommunication networks, can be ideal candidates for strategic outsourcing. Also, strategic outsourcing can be used as a means of upgrading outmoded technology and often involves the outsourcing vendor undertaking software development work or otherwise "fine tuning" the technological applications for the corporation. Because strategic outsourcing focuses on the applications of technology and related services, it raises a number of different issues than the complex technology structures discussed above, such as the pricing of services, service level performance and the transfer of technological applications from the vendor to the corporation upon the expiration or termination of the service contract.

8. Case Study: Certain Practical Issues in Structuring a Strategic Outsourcing

Although simple in concept, the outsourcing of IT functions to an outsourcing vendor is an exceedingly complex transaction to price, structure and negotiate. These transactions often involve substantial fees, in some cases one or more billion U.S. dollars, for the provision of a wide range of IT applications and services over a seven to ten-year period. The agreements recording the outsourcing are often long and complex. The basic agreement can be 75–200 pages with many more pages of technical appendices. Six to 18 months typically elapse from the initial decision to outsource until the execution of the definitive agreement.

Because of the unique fashion in which any large bank or airline conducts business, there is no simple market mechanism for determining the applicable price for the IT functions and applications provided by the outsourcing vendor. Thus, the only way a corporation can be assured that it is receiving the best price for the transaction is to structure a *bidding process* between several viable outsourcing vendors. This is usually undertaken by the corporation issuing a comprehensive "request for proposal" to interested outsourcing vendors and then

---

56. *Id.* at 2-3.

comparing responses.[57] The maintenance of competition between viable vendors via this process is essential for the corporation's ability to optimize its leverage throughout the negotiation of the transaction.

A corporation should consider two key factors in maintaining a viable bidding process between vendors. First, although soliciting bids from a large number of vendors may increase competition, more bidders may considerably drain key resources within the corporation, as it is necessary to consider and evaluate complex proposals from each bidder. In addition, each bidder may decide to engage key corporate personnel in an ongoing dialogue relating to its proposed outsourcing solution. Thus, the more bidders, the more time consumed and the more expensive are the transaction costs associated with the strategic outsourcing. Corporations must find a balance between the number of bidders necessary to sustain competition, on the one hand, and limiting the number of bidders to a short list so as to make the process manageable for the key corporate personnel who, by nature of their positions, have other major ongoing commitments in the corporation, on the other hand. Second, strategic outsourcing generally anticipates the application and transfer of new technologies and technological development. Different bidders may adopt varying approaches toward these technological developments and propose the implementation of different applications. In order to evaluate charges for "apples and apples" rather than "apples and oranges," it is necessary at some point in the price negotiation for the corporation to lead the short list vendors to a preferred technological solution. Although many corporations initially deem it advantageous to examine a wide range of possible technological solutions to their IT problems, in practice it is difficult to compare the pricing of heterogeneous proposals.

There are several other key facets to negotiating a strategic outsourcing. It is necessary to determine the precise scope of the contracts and functions to be included in the transaction.[58] Generally, the outsourcing vendor will provide those services and applications that are within the scope for the negotiated price, but will want to charge additional fees for functions or services determined to be outside the scope. It is critical that both the corporation and the outsourcing vendor understand what is within the scope of the services, otherwise there will be constant price haggling between the parties for the duration of the agreement. On a related point, many outsourcing vendors will contend

---

57. *Id.* at 6-8.
58. For a discussion of the importance of determining the scope of a transaction in the banking industry, *see* Harry H. Glasspiegel & Robert E. Zahler, *Scoping the Data-Processing Contract*, AM. BANKER, Nov. 1, 1989.

that they should be the exclusive provider of any new services or technological applications to the corporation. The corporation should attempt to negotiate the right to seek from any viable vendor new services and applications which are outside the scope of the contract. Without this right, the corporation will have lost its competitive leverage and could be subject to premium pricing for new services and technology applications.

Another important pricing issue relates to "windfall" profits that an outsourcing vendor may obtain as the result of an unanticipated development in the technology being provided by the outsourcer. Given the rapid advancement in technology, it is quite possible that there will be a significant technological improvement that could result in the vendor being able to provide an application to the corporation in the later years of the contract at a substantially lower cost than was anticipated at the time of execution. It is inequitable for the outsourcing vendor to be the sole beneficiary of this unanticipated development in technology. Thus, corporations are advised to negotiate a clause stating that any windfall benefits resulting from unanticipated technological advancements shall be shared equitably between the parties, commensurate with the pricing structure of the contract.

Also key to the negotiation of an outsourcing arrangement are the performance standards to be met by the outsourcing vendor.[59] In addition to potentially running a corporation's IT functions more efficiently and being better situated to make strategic decisions concerning future technology and applications, an outsourcing vendor should also be equipped to extract better performance from existing technologies than the corporation. To that end, the outsourcing arrangement should anticipate the application of state-of-the-art technology and increased performance standards approaching, if not achieving, the world's best practice in the industry. Because performance standards should enhance the business objectives of the corporation, the outsourcing vendor should be provided with incentives to perform according to a reward and credit system relating to its achieved performance. Also, as technology improves, the performance standards and their corresponding reward and credit criteria should be adjusted appropriately. In certain circumstances, high performance standards may also create a pricing issue, as the vendor may need to use more expensive technology or supplementary applications to achieve the stipulated performance standards. Thus, performance and pricing should be viewed as interdependent issues.

---

59. *See* Nagel & Murphy, *supra* note 55, at 15-16.

Many corporations may be unsure of their strategic direction and business objectives for the duration of a long-term outsourcing arrangement. Consequently, most corporations may find it necessary to secure the right to terminate the outsourcing arrangement for convenience in the event that it no longer supports their business objectives or strategic purposes.[60] Moreover, it is often difficult in these complex technological arrangements to terminate an outsourcing vendor for fault as the relationship between the parties is so inherently entwined that it will be difficult to attribute any problem solely or predominately to the actions or omissions of the outsourcing vendor. Thus, termination for convenience may be the only means of terminating a less than optimally performing outsourcing vendor. Outsourcing vendors resist termination for convenience because they frequently are required to make substantial initial investments in technology to implement the outsourcing arrangement and assert that it takes a substantial period of time to return a fair margin on that initial investment. The reasonable resolution to this negotiation is often that a corporation will agree to pay a premium for a termination for convenience. This premium should be based on the unreturned profits on the initial investment of the outsourcing vendor plus the reasonable rate of return that the vendor would have expected for the services and applications to be provided for the remainder of the term of the outsourcing arrangement. Thus, the premium for a termination for convenience should *decline* over the term of the outsourcing arrangement.

Finally, as a practical matter, the vendor's cooperation is critical for achieving a smooth transfer of the services and technological applications back to the corporation or to another vendor upon termination of the outsourcing arrangement.[61] For this reason, the outsourcing vendor should be contractually obliged to give the corporation (and any replacement vendor) transition assistance in arranging and effecting the transfer, regardless of the reasons for the termination of the arrangement. This assistance should begin before the actual termination date in recognition of the need for a lengthy transition process and should continue for some time after the outsourcing arrangement terminates to ensure that the technological applications can be migrated with minimal disruption to the corporation's business activities. The outsourcing arrangement, finally, should stipulate the charges that the corporation must pay the outsourcing vendor for this assistance.

---

60. *Id.* at 20.
61. *Id.* at 20-22.

B. Selection of Partners

After a party has duly considered the principal types of complex technology transfer transactions,[62] it needs to consider the factors for selecting an appropriate partner for those arrangements. The available partners fall into several distinct groups.

1. University or Research Institutes

These tend to be suitable for medium- or long-term basic research where time constraints are less important. They are invariably cheaper than most viable commercial alternatives and the quality of their work tends to be first rate.

2. Competitors

A competitor will have the necessary knowledge, design and manufacturing expertise required, but it is unlikely that a party will wish to give its competitor any concrete advantage which it does not obtain for itself. In addition, the competition laws of many jurisdictions will prohibit or limit the scope of cooperation between competitors.[63] In practice the most likely form of collaboration will be for medium to long-term basic research or, alternatively, for producing products with industry-wide applications, such as operating software or microprocessors for computers. Another interesting example is the strategic outsourcing of reservation systems among competitors in the hospitality and travel industry. In this industry where margins are often low and a state-of-the-art reservation system is critical to booking business, airlines with sophisticated and effective reservations systems, for example, have outsourced this IT application to their competitors on the basis that the margins to be obtained from transferring this technology to competitors exceed any decline in margins through lost sales to these competitors.

3. Other Industries

The problems caused by the involvement of competitors are greatly reduced if the strategic partner is a business from a complementary industry. For example, a textile corporation may form an alliance to develop a new thread with a specialist chemical corporation experienced

---

62. *See* Chapter Two.
63. *See* earlier discussion in Section I.A.3, Chapter Two, Section II.B.3 and Chapter Three, Section II.

in producing artificial fiber. This kind of strategic alliance is becoming very common among businesses entering the new multi-media markets. Alliances between businesses in the computer, telecommunications, film, cable TV, and other industries are intended to provide the participants with complementary technologies, marketing and production skills and content drawn from markets which traditionally have been considered independent. A word of caution is in order, however. With the rapid convergence of technologies that is taking place in the IT and other industries, complementary industry partners may become competitors by the end of a long-term strategic alliance.

4. Nationality

The country of origin of the potential strategic partner should be carefully considered. For some projects, particularly those supported by governments and quasi-governmental organizations, a local partner will be desirable if not essential. A local partner may also prove invaluable in analyzing local markets for the products of the alliance or identifying and evaluating distributors and sales agents. Some countries, such as **Brazil,** have local content rules which can only be satisfied by involving a local partner in research and manufacture.[64] A local partner may also provide access to financial benefits from national or local government.[65]

Often the purpose and scope of the collaboration will determine the selection of partners and the parties would be well advised to include contractual provisions ensuring the ability to change the makeup of the collaborative team at different stages of the project. The local collaborative model, at the basic research stage, for instance, might include a small team involving one or two academic institutions and complementary businesses. As product development progresses, the academic participants may drop out and be replaced by foreign corporations with more relevant product experience, which are better placed to develop and customize the products for local markets and ultimately market and service the finished technology.

One limiting factor in the selection of collaborators is the optimal number of partners. In order to ensure maximum cooperation and exchange of information and ideas in a cooperative research venture, for example, it is rarely beneficial to have more than four active participants at any one stage. Also, the larger the number of active participants, the tighter the management structure should be, including clear reporting

---

64. *See* Chapter Two, Section II.B.7.
65. *See* Chapter Two, Sections II.A.18 and II.B.7.

lines and a small management team in operational control of the project.

C. Financing Issues

In complex strategic alliances, one party frequently finances at least part of the work done by others. This gives rise to a number of issues, the key ones being:

1. Monitoring Expenditures

Clear budgets should be established for collaborative expenditures and monitored on a monthly basis. Regular written reports on the financial progress of the project and estimates of future expenditures should be made at least quarterly. The funding party should have the right to audit expenditures at regular intervals.

2. Payment Against Milestones

It is normal practice to stipulate that funds may be drawn down against the achievement of specific objectives as the work progresses. However, although this is the only effective control that the funding party can exert over expenditures, it is often difficult in practice to structure a set of applicable objective milestones for the term of a project.

3. Unforeseen Additional Expenditure

The funding party will not want to commit itself to meeting additional expenses for project cost overruns. However, without an assurance that any additional costs will be covered, there is no guarantee that the research and development will be completed. A number of options are available for dealing with this sensitive issue. One is to obtain a commitment by the funding party to meet cost overruns in exchange for reimbursement on a priority basis from the fees, royalties or other revenues generated by the project. Another is for all or some of the parties to cover cost overruns in equal shares, and if a party is unable to meet its share of cost overruns, there will be a corresponding decline in its proportionate interest in the venture.

In addition to these general issues, there will usually be specific requirements if government funds are used or if a government agency is one of the collaborators.[66]

D. Implementing the Collaboration

After having selected the partners and funding the venture, the parties should structure the different elements of the collaboration so that the contributed resources are applied efficiently. The key issues to be addressed in most alliances are the following.

1. Research Facilities

The parties should decide whether the research or development will be performed at one or more of the parties' existing facilities or at new facilities. The cost of a new facility usually outweighs the cost of upgrading existing facilities, but other factors affect this decision, such as the availability of financial incentives, ease of access to local markets and that proximity itself may result in the "host" party obtaining inordinate control over the direction and activities of the collaboration. Whichever course is chosen, the ownership of the new or enhanced facility will have to be settled. This can be difficult to resolve, particularly if the party operating the facility did not entirely fund it. Options to be considered include leasing the facility to the other parties, using a share of royalties or other revenues to fund the cost of the site, or selling the site (or a share in it) to the other parties on termination of the collaboration. The possibility of subletting parts of the facility to the parties or others also should be contemplated.

2. Equipment

There is usually more flexibility in arrangements regarding equipment than there is with facilities. Major capital items can be purchased and made available to the parties in a variety of ways, including outright sale, lease or hire and contribution in kind. As with facilities, the possibility of leasing machines or equipment to the parties or others should be considered.

---

66. *See, e.g.,* Section I.A.4.a. of this Chapter regarding research funding from the European Union.

3. Support Services

The parties in a strategic alliance will frequently have to supply support services such as accounting, marketing and prototype manufacture, particularly in the early stages of a collaboration. It is important to identify the best party to supply each service, rather than leaving it to the one with the local presence or the deepest pockets. In addition, the marginal cost of these services to the party supplying them may be small, but the value to the alliance can be significant, so it is important to reflect this in the arrangement. One way of achieving this is to charge out these services on a fee paying basis to be recouped from revenues.

4. Personnel and Management Resources

A complex strategic alliance raises many personnel and management issues. A number of these are considered in Section III below in the context of cultural factors and monitoring change.[67] In implementing a collaboration, it is critical to consider the optimum management structure for the alliance.[68] This usually involves a strong day-to-day leadership for the alliance and either using executives on long-term secondment from the parties or specially recruited managers. The selected management structure should be complemented by a clear sense of strategic direction and involvement by the parties. Labor law issues arise both in the context of secondment arrangements between the parties and the alliance and the terms of employment of specially recruited executives, as well as in the provisions of the collaboration agreement governing the day-to-day management and determination of the strategic direction of the operation.

At the operational level, the parties may also need to decide whether scientists, production staff and others are to be recruited directly by the alliance or seconded from the parties. In the early stages of an alliance, secondment is usually the only option, but later it may be appropriate for the alliance to employ staff directly to increase their identification with the project and shift the full overhead cost of the employees to the collaboration.

---

67. *See* Chapter Two, Sections II.A.8 and 9.
68. *See* Chapter Two, Section II.A.16.

5. Background Intellectual Property Rights

Technological strategic alliances generally use the existing intellectual property owned or licensed by one or more of the parties. In addition, the work done by the collaboration is likely to yield substantial new intellectual property rights. The typical arm's length license of background intellectual property rights may therefore be inappropriate, and special attention must be given to issues such as the scope of use of the rights by the alliance, rights of termination for the licensor and use of the rights following termination of the alliance.

II. STRUCTURING UNCERTAINTY IN COMPLEX TECHNOLOGY TRANSFERS

A. Building Uncertainty into the Collaboration

The collaboration should include procedures and mechanisms not only for coping with unanticipated technological developments, but also for capitalizing on and exploiting these opportunities. Because of the ever-increasing speed of technological change and the consequent reduction in acceptable research and development time-lags and product life-cycles, the collaboration should not be a static arrangement, but rather a robust and organic long-term alliance. The collaboration should not be made redundant by technological change but rather anticipate and, if possible, capitalize on unforeseen developments. Unexpected developments may have a positive impact upon the collaboration. Some well-known examples of research and development projects with unexpected benefits are the following.

1. Minoxidil

This drug, developed by Upjohn in the 1970s for easing high blood pressure, has been shown to promote hair growth, and research has been conducted to establish whether it can be used to cure baldness.[69]

---

69. *See, e.g.,*, Lee Smith, *Hair-Raising Happenings at Upjohn*, FORTUNE, Apr. 6, 1981, at 67.

2. Aspirin

This drug has been widely available for most of this century as a painkiller and is routinely used for the relief of fever and inflammation. In 1988, a new study showed that aspirin is also effective in the prevention of heart attacks and is now widely used to help prevent second and subsequent heart attacks and related conditions. Research is also under way in three other areas where aspirin may prove useful, namely the prevention of pregnancy toxemia, bowel cancer and dementia.[70]

3. Computer Imaging Sperm Selection

A software tool which was originally developed in the United Kingdom to monitor traffic flows has been adapted to identify and color code the sperm most likely to fertilize an egg.[71] In 1994, the first baby was born as a result of using this fertility treatment.

The unexpected opportunity may also be a new geographic market or customer market for the alliance's planned products.

The agreement governing the alliance should recognize the possibility of the occurrence and impact of unexpected technological change and provide a mechanism to deal with this phenomenon. First, the agreement should resolve how to monitor technology changes and identify opportunities for the parties, as discussed in Section III below. Second, the agreement should be sufficiently flexible to allow for the exploitation of new opportunities. This issue is discussed in the remaining paragraphs of this Section.

B. Ownership of Research Results

The parties must adopt an ownership structure which makes it easy to exploit research results and related intellectual property rights. Most forms of joint ownership are, therefore, inappropriate because they usually require all the joint owners to execute a license or other agreement concerning the intellectual property rights. If more than one party desires to stay actively involved in the exploitation of the intellectual property rights, then one solution is to create a new legal

---

70. *See, e.g., Aspirin Tied to a Lower Cancer Risk*, N.Y. TIMES, August 17, 1994, at C8; European Aspirin Foundation, Aspirin: The Amazing Story Today (Nov. 1993) (unpublished manuscript, on file with Denton Hall).
71. *See, e.g.,* Charlene Laino, *Newest Fertilization Tool for Couples – a Computer*, CHI. SUN TIMES, July 26, 1994, at 22.

entity to exploit the rights. Alternatively, if one party is to do most of the exploitation, it might be appropriate for it to license another party with an interest in a particular field of application on an exclusive basis.

Some parties will have special ownership requirements. For instance, many governmental bodies will be legally or politically unable to assign their rights to a foreign corporation. In these circumstances, an arrangement for the foreign corporation to hold the rights in trust or to exploit them as an agent may be appropriate. Charities participating in research projects may want to fulfill their charitable aims, for instance, by stipulating that a new crop variety should be made available at concessionary rates to developing countries. Academic institutions will want to report research results in journals and at academic conferences as soon as possible, especially if they are unexpected, because dissemination of information is an integral part of the open pedagogical philosophy of universities and the reputation of the academics involved depends on publication. In these circumstances, the other parties may be able to delay publication or excise some of the particularly sensitive elements from the article, but not prevent publication altogether. Many reputable research institutions will refuse to accept industry sponsored research grants if the rights of publication of research results in academic journals are fettered by restrictions other than a short delay for the industry sponsor to comment on the material to be submitted for publication. Often, the research institution will not be compelled to take the industry sponsor's comments into account, but will only agree to give them due consideration.

C. Exploitation of Unexpected Results

Within the collaboration, the parties should seek the right to exploit individually any unexpected collaboration results. In most circumstances this right will be granted on a non-exclusive royalty free basis, which will alleviate, for example, problems under EU competition law.

Outside the collaboration, in most cases it is best to entrust one of the parties with the exploitation of the intellectual property rights to allow for a coherent marketing strategy. The other parties may in any event have little interest in exploiting these rights, particularly if they are not commercial concerns. A variety of means can be employed to make sure that the rights are being properly exploited by one of the parties. These include stipulating an annual payment to the other parties by the exploiting party; performance targets for the exploiting party (either financial ones, such as sales or royalty income, or milestones such as product approval or the completion of clinical trials); and regular performance audits by one or more of the other parties or outside consultants.

D. Unexpected Territorial Opportunities

While it is easy to extend existing arrangements to new territories, it may not always be appropriate. Another party or, perhaps, a new local partner may be in a better position to exploit the intellectual property rights in a new territory. This issue should always be considered before extending the existing arrangements into a new territory. The legal and tax consequences of adding a new territory must also be considered.[72]

E. Non-competition Clauses and Conflicts of Interest

An unexpected opportunity can give rise to serious conflicts of interest if the new development affects the existing product portfolio of one of the parties. That party may be left with the unenviable option of disposing of its interest in the collaboration or selling the conflicting product business. This problem can be exacerbated if the collaboration agreement contains a non-competition clause generally focusing on the business of the alliance, rather than specific activities. If that business changes unexpectedly, the existing businesses of the parties may be caught by this type of clause. On the other hand, a non-competition clause focusing on specific activities may prove useless if the business of the alliance changes radically as a result of an unexpected technological development.

III. MONITORING UNCERTAINTY IN COMPLEX TECHNOLOGY TRANSFERS

Parties often couch complex technology transfers in terms of "strategic alliances" and "partnerships." These terms imply that the parties have common goals and interests and also tend to emphasize the need for trust between the parties. Trust and commonality of purpose are essential elements of any long-term complex technology transfer, but they should be supplemented by clearly defined contractual rights and

---

72. *See generally* Chapters Two, Three and Four.

obligations. To take a cooperative research venture, for example, there is often a direct conflict between one party's profit motive and the research needs of the other parties. At such times, the "trust me, I am your partner" approach rings hollow and the other parties need the support of well-drafted contractual rights to ensure equitable treatment.[73]

To a great extent, the challenge for parties in a complex technology transfer is to build a relationship which translates generally conceived business objectives into specific rights and obligations that are capable of objective evaluation and enforcement. The parties should not regard this process as a pre-emptory strike in anticipation of future disputes and impasse. Rather, the parties should approach these issues as an exploration of whether they have mutually consistent and attainable expectations beyond just broad common business objectives before they undertake significant and, often irreversible, commercial commitments. Moreover, shortcuts in this process may defer important issues to a time when much more is at stake and one or more of the parties is no longer disposed towards compromise. In a strategic outsourcing, for example, the corporation is typically at a disadvantage in these circumstances because, in the absence of contractual provisions, there is little leverage to force the outsourcing vendor to compromise when the outsourcing is in the implementation phase. While it is impossible to anticipate everything that could happen during the course of a long-term complex technology transfer, the contract should address and monitor the uncertainty that could arise in at least the following areas.

A. Cultural Differences Between the Parties

It is important not to underestimate the differences between parties from very different "cultural" backgrounds.[74] For example, a small entrepreneurial software company which has developed data compression technology may enter into a strategic alliance with a large established telecommunications company in order to develop a high density multi-media product. This type of arrangement often brings to the fore a large number of corporate culture differences. These include different technology backgrounds, managerial styles, operational procedures, and corporate environments resulting from the sheer size differential of the two organizations. In the small entrepreneurial

---

73. *See generally* Chapter Three.
74. These differences are most obvious where the parties are from different countries or industries, but can also arise within the same industry. *See* Chapter Two, Sections II.A.9, 13, and 14.

corporation, the software engineers may have a considerable level of executive contact and guidance on a daily basis and expect to escalate research issues quickly up a relatively short corporate ladder. By contrast, those accustomed to the large telecommunications conglomerate, may tolerate a far more bureaucratic, procedure-intensive style of operation. Moreover, the key executives of the smaller software company may be surprised to find that they have virtually no day-to-day contact with the senior executives of the telecommunications company with whom they initially discussed the collaboration. In fact, in many large telecommunications companies, once a letter of intent has been signed between the parties, senior executives tend to hand over the negotiation of the contract and the administration of the technology transfer to middle management such as contract negotiators, project directors and attorneys. Executives from the smaller software company may often find that this "hand over" results in them having lost all leverage relating to positions discussed but not included in the terms of the letter of intent. As a general rule, the smaller corporation, which often is receiving substantial financial assistance from the large corporation as part of the complex technology transfer, will have its optimal bargaining power *before* the signing of a letter of intent and should attempt to settle and record all key issues relating to the structure of the technology transfer at this initial stage.

Both parties should bear in mind that the operating styles and characteristics of different types of organizations may cause major problems over the period of a long-term arrangement and should recognize the importance of instituting mechanisms and management procedures to respond to the resultant uncertainty during technological development. Common solutions to this problem include periodic meetings of senior executives to evaluate the direction of the complex technology transfer and the inclusion of dispute escalation clauses in the contract. These clauses set out procedures by which disputes between the parties can be escalated in parallel up the corporate ladder of each party.

B. Monitoring Technological Development

In order to manage the uncertainty associated with many complex technology transfers, the parties must be able to monitor technological development. This will provide a number of benefits, including an appreciation of the body of joint knowledge created by the venture and an early identification of marketable technology. The key is to ensure that the technology is being monitored at various levels by appropriate personnel. Whereas day-to-day research development should be monitored by technical personnel, periodic and frequent evaluations of the development of the research should be performed by more senior executives with a broader perspective on the strategic aspects of the project. The parties should also provide incentives for technicians and engineers to report to strategic development personnel any abnormal changes in the technology transfer as soon as possible after detection and to cooperate on an ongoing basis in an intellectual property protection plan to determine the nature of the intellectual property that has been created and whether the related intellectual property rights are appropriately protected.[75] For example, a patent detection, protection and requisition program is an essential part of any biotechnology collaboration. Moreover, the monitoring process ideally should vary with different tiers of the relationship. Whereas key executives may be involved in periodic strategic meetings, the day-to-day operations may be reported via status reports approved by project directors.

C. Monitoring the Exploitation of the Technology

Where possible, the parties need to establish objective quantitative goals for the exploitation of the technology in various regions or jurisdictions. A procedure should be developed by marketing personnel responsible for determining the appropriate quantitative and qualitative performance standards.[76]

D. Establishing Management Controls

By means of sufficient management controls, each party should ensure that it is protected as the relationship evolves in response to unforeseen events. The contract should cover at least three areas of management control.

1. Key Personnel

In a cooperative research venture or strategic outsourcing, one party may want key personnel assigned to the project by another party to possess the necessary skills and experience to perform at the required level. That party may wish to ensure that these personnel are not

---

75. *See* Chapter One.
76. *See* Chapter Three, Section IX.B.

reassigned to other projects at a time that would severely impair the implementation of the transaction. Thus, a party may want the contractual right to approve in advance any key personnel assigned to the project and to require other parties to remove unacceptable personnel. The contract may also stipulate procedures for reassigning key personnel to other projects.

2. Control Over Functionality

One party to a complex technology transfer should not be permitted to change the functionality of the technology or applications without the other parties' prior approval. Any changes to functionality in a complex technology transfer should be subject to the mutual approval of all parties.

3. Control Over the Method of Performance

Frequently, a party to a complex technology transfer may take the position that the methods used to transfer technology are not the other party's concern as long as the deliverables are generated in accordance with the contract and applicable performance standards. While there is some merit to this position, in many circumstances, such as a strategic outsourcing, the customer may have a legitimate interest in retaining a degree of control over how the technology transfer or services relating to the technology application are performed. There are two basic reasons for this. First, if the methods used by one party are not compatible with the other parties' existing work practice and procedures, the latter parties' business objectives may not be fully realized. Second, a party may want to ensure that the technology being developed or transferred is consistent with its strategic plan, particularly if the party has or intends to make a substantial investment in software development or some other technology beyond the scope of the collaboration. In general, however, the more control one party seeks over the technology used to perform the transfer or services, the less control the other party will have over its factors of production, and thus its costs.[77]

The foregoing underscores that the more complex the relationship between the parties, the more sophisticated is the approach required for the effective management of the collaboration. To maximize benefits, the parties need to undertake regular reviews of the scope of the

---

77. *See* Chapter Two, Section II.A.16.

relationship to establish whether changes need to be made in the administration of the venture. It is often helpful to test the progress of the relationship against a general statement of the principles of the collaboration, although these general goals may also change over time. If the managerial mechanisms are flexible and capable of evolving, the venture has a much better chance of long-term success.

IV. UNWINDING COMPLEX TECHNOLOGY TRANSFERS

A. Term of the Agreement and Renewal

Strategic technological alliances are invariably long term and intended to last for three to five years or even longer.[78] Many strategic outsourcing agreements have ten-year terms. The initial term of the agreement must give sufficient time for the project to mature and for each party to recover its investment. On the other hand, technological obsolescence and the fact that the rights involved will often expire impose upper limits on the initial term of any alliance. Although the term may be renewable, it is rare for an alliance to contemplate an initial term that exceeds ten to 15 years.[79]

The agreement may of course be terminated before the end of the term for the usual events of default, such as serious breach, insolvency, project failure or change of control of one of the parties. Due to the long-term nature of complex strategic alliances, termination should only be considered as a very last resort; the balance may be in favor of restructuring rather than terminating the arrangement. To deal with the possibility of breach or non-performance, it is very important to take a specific approach to structuring creative remedies and incentives to encourage performance.[80] A hierarchy of sanctions can be created to match the seriousness of the breach. These include the following.

1. Limiting Access to Information

This can be an effective remedy for certain types of non-compliance,

---

78. *See* Chapter Two, Section II.A.11.
79. There are also limits on the term of alliances imposed by EU competition law. *See* the discussion in Section I.A.4.a. of this Chapter and Council Regulation 418/85, art. 3, 1985 O.J. (L 53).
80. *See generally* Chapter Two, Section B.10 and Chapter Three.

such as failure to make staff or support services available. In the early stages of a project research results, product designs and marketing plans may be the most valuable asset of the alliance.

2. Grant of Rights

The grant of licenses to use or exploit intellectual property rights derived from the project can be delayed or suspended. This type of sanction is only suitable for serious breaches in most circumstances. Sometimes an intermediate sanction is to reduce exclusive rights to non-exclusive status. The non-breaching party should, however, always consider this option cautiously as the non-exclusive rights retained by the breaching party may dampen the enthusiasm of any third party considering joining the collaboration.

3. Financial Compensation

The payment by the defaulting party to the other parties for the cost of the default can be appropriate if the loss is readily quantifiable. For instance, failure to pay funds can result in payment of the cost of obtaining the funds elsewhere. This amount can be deducted from royalties or other amounts due to the defaulting party, accruing interest in the meantime. The same principle could be applied to a failure to supply equipment, raw materials or personnel. A variety of options relating to the restriction or elimination of a party's equity shares in the venture is also an effective sanction in certain circumstances.[81]

In addition, while dispute resolution is addressed in greater detail in Chapter Six, for the purpose of this discussion, it should be noted that it is usually impossible for a strategic alliance to resort to the courts without destroying the relationship between the parties. This means that detailed dispute resolution procedures should be included in the agreement, covering escalation to a senior level in the organizations concerned. If this fails, the issue may be referred to an independent expert, if it is a technical dispute, or to some form of alternative dispute resolution or binding arbitration if it is a commercial issue.

---

81. *See* Chapter Two, Section II.B.10.

B. Unwinding the Collaboration

Although the parties may be reluctant to discuss this topic in detail at the start of the project, it is important to provide for what happens to the various components of the alliance on its termination.[82] Many of the issues referred to in Section II.B of Chapter Two and Chapter Three also will be relevant on termination of the alliance. Additional issues include the following.

1. Allocation of Use and Ownership

If the collaboration has been successful, substantial and valuable intellectual property will have been created. The division of ownership and licenses in effect while the alliance operates may not be appropriate on termination. If that is the case, the options discussed in Chapter Two, Section II.B.10 should be considered.[83] In addition, ownership and use can be separated, so that for instance an academic institution may retain a non-exclusive license to use the intellectual property rights for its own non-profit research.

2. Contracts with Outsiders

There will also be a network of contracts with the parties and others for supplying goods and services, licensing intellectual property and so on. These contracts will have to be terminated, assigned or renegotiated. To put the parties in the best position, all contracts on behalf of the alliance should be structured to be freely assignable to the individual parties without consent being required.[84]

3. Personnel

Secondment contracts for the supply of personnel to the alliance by one of the parties will usually terminate if the alliance terminates. There will still be the question of what happens to staff especially hired by the alliance. One party may agree to take responsibility for the costs of terminating their employment in return for obtaining the first opportunity to offer them new jobs with its own organization. It may

---

82. *See generally* Chapter Three, Section XII.
83. *See also* Chapter Three, Section IV.
84. *But see* Chapter Three, Section V.H.

also be appropriate to limit one party from poaching the staff of another for a period of time, which can be accomplished by the inclusion of appropriate non-solicitation provisions.[85]

4. Non-competition Obligations

If one or more of the parties acquires all of the technology created as a result of the collaboration, it may be appropriate to impose a non-competition obligation on the other parties to preserve the value of these assets. However, there are restrictions in many jurisdictions on the enforceability of this type of clause.[86]

V. THE CHALLENGE OF COMPLEX TECHNOLOGY TRANSFER

This Chapter has examined some of the difficulties involved in structuring sophisticated technology transfers. One difficulty is the complexity of these transactions on many levels. Different issues arise depending on whether the technology is in its early research stage, as in the cases of incubators and cooperative research ventures, or in its later development stage, as in the case of strategic outsourcing of technology applications. Moreover, the technologies themselves are often complex because of rapid scientific advancements and convergence with other technologies.

Another difficulty in structuring a sophisticated technology transfer is uncertainty. Uncertainty is an integral part of all long-term, complex arrangements and may sometimes lead to unanticipated results that are advantageous for all parties. From a strategic perspective, the relationship should be sufficiently flexible to accommodate changing circumstances and parties should adopt procedures that maximize their capacity to monitor and evaluate uncertainty throughout the life of a complex technology transfer. This result is enhanced by clearly and rigorously defining the scope of the technology transfer and, correspondingly, identifying the rights that are being transferred and the rights that are not being transferred early in the negotiation of any complex technology transfer.[87] In other words, the parties should avoid

---

85. *See* Chapter Three, Sections XI and XII.
86. *See* Chapter Three, Section XI.
87. *See* Chapter Three.

the common pitfall of failing to appreciate the dimensions and complexity of the established relationship.

Thus, properly structuring a technology transfer requires the parties to contemplate the advantages, drawbacks and implications of various technology transfer structures.[88] Compounding the parties' difficulties is that current legal structures and intellectual property right regimes are increasingly challenged by the evolution of technology to the point where, perhaps, they might prove inadequate to respond to future trends and developments.[89] The advancements in complex technologies and resultant difficulties in structuring transactions and categorizing intellectual property rights is as challenging to the legal profession as it is to the business and technology communities.

---

88. *See* Chapter Two.
89. Several commentators have argued that copyright law has inherent limitations straining its application to certain emerging technologies or information industry products. *See, e.g.,* Trevor W. Nagel, *Software Development: The Limits of Existing Legal Protection,* 9 HARV. INT'L REV. 46-48 (Feb./Mar. 1987); Virginia R. Lyons, *Carrying Copyright Too Far: The Inadequacy of the Current System of Protection for Computer Programs,* 12 HASTINGS COMM. & ENT. L.J. 81, 93 (1989); Mark M. Turner, *Generality Mars EC Software Draft,* FIN. TIMES (London), May 31, 1990, at 10. For general discussions supporting the antithesis that copyright is a sufficiently flexible and robust intellectual property right to cope with emerging forms of IT, *see* Arthur R. Miller, *Copyright Protection for Computer Programs, Databases, and Computer-Generated Works: Is Anything New Since CONTU?,* 106 HARV. L. REV. 978, 1015-22 (1993); Jane C. Ginsburg, *Creation and Commercial Value: Copyright Protection of Works of Information,* 90 COLUM. L. REV. 1865, 1893-1897 (1990). The U.S. government's Information Infrastructure Task Force recently issued a "Green Paper" proposing that existing copyright laws with minor amendments would sufficiently protect intellectual property on the "Information Superhighway." *See generally* Report of the Working Group on Intellectual Property Rights, Intellectual Property and the National Information Infrastructure (July, 1994) (preliminary draft).

Appendix One

The Editor and Contributing Author

Harry Rubin has been coordinating the activities of the international practice group of Shaw, Pittman, Potts & Trowbridge out of the firm's Washington, D.C. office since 1990.

His practice focuses on international transactions, including transnational joint ventures and strategic alliances, structuring and advising on complex high technology transfers, and intellectual property management licensing and distribution, with primary emphasis on the computer hardware and software, electronics, telecommunications, transportation, energy, publishing and on-line service industries. He frequently advises on transactions and competitive bidding in the European Union, Eastern Europe, Asia, and the Middle East.

He received his B.A. degree, *magna cum laude*, in Government from Harvard University in 1985 and was elected to *Phi Beta Kappa*. He received John Harvard and Harvard College honorary scholarships for academic achievement of the highest distinction and the Center for Middle Eastern Studies research award. He received his J.D. degree from Columbia Law School in 1988, where he was associate editor of the *Columbia Journal of Transnational Law* and was named International Fellow of Columbia University. He also received the Certificate of Achievement in International and Foreign Law of Columbia's Parker School of Foreign and Comparative Law and the Milton B. Conford Prize in Jurisprudence.

Mr. Rubin has published numerous articles on corporate and international business law, intellectual property, and technology transfer topics. He is a frequent speaker in the United States and other countries on international technology transfers and international transactions and has co-chaired and organized conferences for the International Bar Association and the American Conference Institute on those subjects.

A native of Munich, Germany, Mr. Rubin immigrated to Israel in 1972. From 1978 to 1981, he served in the External Relations Department, Directorate of Military Intelligence of the Israel Defense Forces. He has been living in the United States since 1981. Mr. Rubin is fluent in German, French, English, and Hebrew.

Appendix Two

The Contributing Authors

Thomas E. Crocker is of counsel to Shaw, Pittman, Potts & Trowbridge. Mr. Crocker worked for over five years as a Foreign Service Officer with the U.S. Department of State. He served as Staff Assistant to the Under Secretary of State for Security Assistance, Science and Technology, as a Political Officer at the American Embassy in Lisbon and as Spanish Desk Officer. Mr. Crocker was actively involved in numerous technology transfer and munitions control issues and Spanish base negotiations and accession to NATO. Mr. Crocker has been with Shaw Pittman since 1983 and has specialized in international banking and trade issues. During this time, Mr. Crocker has represented European and Japanese banks on regulatory issues, as well as a wide variety of domestic and foreign companies in their dealings with the U.S. Departments of Commerce, Defense and State, the Office of the U.S. Trade Representative, the White House and Congress. Mr. Crocker speaks regularly and has published articles on current issues and developments in the international banking, trade and politico-military areas. He is a graduate of Princeton University (A.B. 1971 *Cum Laude*) and Columbia University School of Law (J.D. 1974). Mr. Crocker speaks Portuguese, French and Spanish.

D. Kevin Dolan is a partner in the Washington, D.C. office of Weil, Gotshal & Manges, where he advises clients based both in the United States and abroad on international and U.S. tax matters. His areas of specialty include international mergers and acquisitions, debt capitalization, internal restructurings, intangibles' licensing, research and development cost sharing arrangements, transfer pricing, U.S. real estate investment, foreign currency transaction, and financial products, as well as a range of foreign tax credit and deferral provisions relevant to U.S. multinationals. His practice encompasses both planning/transactional matters and controversy matters, including transfer pricing and debt-equity characterization. From 1986 to 1989, Mr. Dolan served at the Internal Revenue Service as its first Associate Chief Counsel (International), where he was responsible for all regulatory, private ruling, and litigation matters within the Internal Revenue Service in the international tax area, including certain Competent Authority responsibilities under U.S. tax treaties. Earlier in his career,

Mr. Dolan was a member of the Office of International Tax Counsel of the U.S. Treasury Department, and the Office of Chief Counsel of the Internal Revenue Service. Mr. Dolan publishes and lectures frequently on international tax law and has completed a soon to be published, multi-volume treatise on the international tax aspects of international mergers and acquisitions. He holds an undergraduate degree from the University of Virginia and his J.D. from the University of Michigan.

Daniela P. Feldhausen is a member of the international and high-technology practice groups at Shaw, Pittman, Potts & Trowbridge. After graduating *magna cum laude* from the undergraduate program at University of California at Berkeley's Business School in 1987, she worked in investment banking for Deutsche Bank in Frankfurt, Germany. Two years later, she returned to the United States to study law at the University of California at Berkeley's Boalt Hall School of Law. While at Boalt, she interned at the law firm then known as Westrick & Eckholdt, now Bruckhaus, Westrick, Stegemann, in Frankfurt Germany. She specializes in domestic and international license agreements, as well as financings and general corporate work for high technology companies. She is fluent in German and English.

Dr. Klaus Günther is a partner in the Cologne office of Oppenhoff & Rädler. His practice encompasses commercial, corporate, banking and arbitration matters. He also advises on intellectual property licensing and related matters. Dr. Günther was admitted to the Bar in 1970 after studying at the Universities of Munich and Cologne. He received an LL.M. degree from the University of California at Berkeley's Boalt Hall School of Law in 1967 and his J.D. in 1971. Dr. Günther has published numerous articles and contributed to a number of books on commercial transactions, agency, and banking matters. He is President of the German-American Lawyers Association and Country Chairman of the Committee for International Sales of the International Bar Association. He is fluent in English, German and French.

Deborah Ishihara has worked for Clifford Chance since 1990, variously involved in intellectual property, commercial and international banking work. She is now a lawyer in the media, computer and communications group where she specializes in intellectual property, computer law and telecommunications. She has experience in patent infringement litigation and has represented clients on trademark infringement and counterfeiting matters.

Kevin McMahon is a partner in the New York office of Weil, Gotshal & Manges. He is a graduate of the University of Pennsylvania in electrical engineering, received his law degree from Georgetown University and is a registered patent attorney. He has had over 25 years of experience in patent and intellectual property law, both in corporate practice as chief patent counsel of a major international corporation and in private practice. His major areas of practice include Patent Office litigation, transactional matters and counselling in diverse technology areas. He has served as a member of the Patent Law Committee of the Association of the Bar of the City of New York.

Pierre Lenoir has been a partner in the Paris office of Jeantet & Associés since 1978 and heads its intellectual property department. He received his legal education from the University of Paris and the University of Nanterre. Mr. Lenoir has been a member of the Paris Bar since 1972, and is a member of the French group's executive committee of the International Association for the Protection of Intellectual Property.

Nathalie Meyer Fabre is an attorney in the Paris office of Jeantet & Associés. She received her law degree from the University of Paris. She has been a member of the Paris Bar and associated with the firm since 1989. Ms. Meyer Fabre specializes in private international law and arbitration.

Christopher Millard (LL.B. 1980, University of Sheffield; M.A. 1982, University of Toronto; LL.M. 1983, University of Toronto) is a partner in the media, computer and communications group at Clifford Chance in London. His practice focuses on intellectual property rights in software and data, hardware and software procurement and distribution agreements, outsourcing transactions, data protection, telecommunications regulation, and communications contracts. As a Senior Visiting Fellow of the University of London, he teaches LL.M. courses in information technology law and telecommunications law. He is currently Joint Chairman of the Society for Computers and Law and

President of the International Federation of Computer Law Associations.

Trevor W. Nagel is a partner in Shaw, Pittman, Potts, and Trowbridge's high technology and international practice groups. His practice focuses on the telecommunications and computer hardware and software industries, with primary emphasis on domestic and international outsourcing. He has B.A. and LL.B. degrees from the University of Adelaide in South Australia, an LL.M. from the University of Chicago and an S.J.D. from Harvard Law School. He is admitted as a Barrister in the Supreme Court of New South Wales and the High Court of Australia and is a member of the Massachusetts Bar. A member of several professional organizations in the high-technology field, he is a frequent speaker and author on technology-related topics.

Mark Owen is a Solicitor of the Supreme Court of England and Wales and a member of the California Bar. He is employed by Clifford Chance in London where he specializes in intellectual property and information technology law. He has also worked in the Palo Alto, California office of Brown & Bain where he was involved in high-technology litigation relating to intellectual property rights in computer software and hardware.

Lynn A. Soukup, a partner in Shaw, Pittman, Potts and Trowbridge's corporate department, concentrates in the areas of commercial finance, asset-backed securities and asset sales and acquisitions. Ms. Soukup has represented both lenders and borrowers in commercial lending transactions, loan modifications and workouts involving a variety of industries and credit facilities. Ms. Soukup frequently works with the technology, bankruptcy, workout, real estate and banking practice groups of the firm on matters relating to secured transactions and intellectual property collateral. Her work in the asset-backed securities area has involved the representation of financial institutions and corporations in the issuance of pass-through certificates, medium-term notes and commercial paper backed by credit card receivables, home equity lines, government leases and car loans. Ms. Soukup has also represented a variety of issuers, including financial institutions and holding companies, in public and private debt and equity offerings. Ms. Soukup was awarded her B.A. degree, *magna cum laude*, in Economics from Bucknell University in 1978 and her J.D., *magna cum laude*, from the Georgetown University Law Center in 1981.

Ralph A. Taylor, Jr. is a partner in the litigation department of Shaw, Pittman, Potts & Trowbridge, and is on the editorial board of the firm's *Technology Law Notes* Newsletter. His practice includes arbitration and complex litigation matters before a variety of courts and tribunals for a wide range of clients, including technology vendors and licensors. Mr. Taylor received a B.S.E. degree (with honors in electrical engineering) from Princeton University in 1970. He received his J.D. degree from the University of Virginia in 1975, where he was awarded the Order of the Coif and was a Notes Editor of the *Virginia Law Review*. He is a member of the American Bar Association Section of Litigation and its Computer Litigation Committee. He is also an Associate Editor of *Litigation News*.

Mark Turner is a partner and the head of the technology group at Denton Hall in London. Throughout his career he has advised on a wide range of commercial and intellectual property issues for technology clients, primarily in the information technology, biotechnology, publishing, and retail industries. Over the last three years he has become increasingly involved in advising on multimedia and has acted for content providers, producers and distributors. Mr. Turner read law at University College, Oxford, as an Exhibitioner and qualified as a Solicitor in 1983. He is general editor of the book *Practical Intellectual Property*, co-author of the Chapter on the licensing of intellectual property rights in Butterworth's *Encyclopedia of Competition Law* and a correspondent for *Computer Law and Security Report*. He is currently working on a book on multimedia law and practice.

Michael Walsh is an associate in the Washington, D.C. office of Weil, Gotshal & Manges, where he specializes in international and corporate tax law. Mr. Walsh received a B.A. degree from Yale University (1989) and his J.D. degree from Harvard Law School (1993).

Constantine J. Zepos is a member of the corporate and international practice groups at Shaw, Pittman, Potts & Trowbridge. He received his B.A. degree *magna cum laude* in Economics from Connecticut College in 1989 and was elected to *Phi Beta Kappa*. He received his J.D. and

M.B.A. degrees from Duke University in 1993. At law school, he served as Senior Staff Editor of the *Duke Journal of Comparative & International Law*. A native of Athens, Greece, Mr. Zepos is fluent in Greek, English, and French.

Index

Agency
  competition law, 118-119
  European Union Directives, 77-78
Agent
  commercial, European Union Directive, 77-78
  independent contractor, 73
  technology transfer via, 72-73
  transferor, power to bind, 73
Andean Group
  common technology transfer policies, 320-322
Applicable law. *See also* Choice of law
  failure to designate,
    consequences of, 306-310
    validity of contract, doubts as to, 306
Arbitration
  advantages of, 333
  appeals, 333
  choice of law, 306-307, 312, 335
  considerations, 335
  contractual disputes to be decided by, 336-337
  discovery, 334
  enforcement of awards, 337-338
  enforcement of clauses, 334
  fees and costs, 337
  nature of, 332-333
  number of arbitrators, 335-336
  place of, 336
  remedy, inadequacy of, 337
  speed of, 333
  tribunals, 335
Argentina
  distribution agreements, duration of, 211
  full patent protection, lacking, 166
  joint ventures, 88
  licenses,
    parties, relationship of, 217
    technology, approval of, 156-157
  technology transfer,
    alliances for, 79
    legal issues, 110
    royalty payments, 128

Argentina *contd*
  product liability law, 134
Australia
  cooperative research, 352
  motor vehicle local content requirement, 137
  product liability law, 134

Belgium
  licenses, duration and renewal, 212
Brazil
  joint ventures, 88-89
  technology licenses, approval of, 157
  technology transfer,
    alliances for, 80
    legal issues, 110
    royalty payments, 128

Canada
  enforcement of judgments, 332
  joint ventures, 89
  license, non-competition provisions, 209
  product liability law, 135
  security interests, 271-273
  technology transfer,
    alliances for, 80
    royalty payments, 127-128
  transfer or assignment of rights, statutory provisions, 272
China
  copyright law, 30-31
  designs, protection of, 38
  intellectual property laws, poor enforcement of, 166
  joint ventures, 95-96
    Chinese resources, using, 137
  licenses,
    assignment, 187
    confidentiality provisions, 192
    duration and renewal, 212
    grant-back, 188
    laws and regulations, warranty for conformity to, 196

China *contd*
  maintenance and training
    arrangements, 207
  post-termination rights and
    obligations, 216
  remedies, 200
  revenues, payment of, 202
  termination, reasons for, 214
  territorial restrictions, 176
  tying, 186
  patent law, 21-22
  technology licenses, approval of, 157-158
  technology transfer,
    legal issues, 110-111
    royalty payments, 130
  trade secrets, protection of, 8
  trademark law, 44-45
  Unfair Competition Law, 8
Choice of law
  arbitration, for, 335
  arbitrators, determination by, 306-307
  characteristic performance, 308
  degrees of risk, assumption of, 310
  determination of, 306
  express,
    advantages and disadvantages, 311
    clause in agreement, by, 310
    international regimes, 313-316
    mandatory laws, escaping, 311
    non-national law, 312
    predictability of outcome,
      enhancing, 310
    reasons for, 311
    severability, 316
    transaction, relationship to, 311
  general principles, 309-310
  implied, 316
  importance of, 305
  jurisdiction to which most closely related, 306
  limitations on freedom of,
    competition laws, application of, 318-320
    extra-contractual provisions, potential application of, 317, 322-323
    mandatory laws, not superseding, 317

Choice of law *contd*
    public policy laws, superseding, 318-322
    supplementary provisions, potential application of, 317, 322-323
    trade regulation, application of, 320-322
  modification of, 310
  Rome Convention, 307-308, 312
  supranational regimes, 306
  U.N. Convention on Contracts for the International Sale of Goods, 313-316. *See also* U.N. Convention on Contracts for the International Sale of Goods
  United States, of, 309, 312
Collaboration
  agreement, term of, 373
  breach of agreement,
    access to information, limiting, 373-374
    financial compensation, 374
    sanctions, 373
  conflicts of interest, 368
  contract research, 343-344
  cooperative research ventures,
    disadvantage of, 345
    European Union and EFTA, in, 346-349
    reasons for, 345
    United States, in, 349-352
  cultural differences, 369-370
  exploitation of technology, exploiting, 371
  financing, 362
  governmental support, 352-355
  implementing,
    background intellectual property rights, 365
    equipment, 363
    personnel and management resources, 364
    research facilities, 363
    support services, 364
  industrial, 344-345
  industrial sponsorship, 344
  management controls,
    functionality, over, 372
    key personnel, 371-372

INDEX

Collaboration *contd*
  method of performance, over, 372-373
  non-competition clauses, 368
  ownership of research results, 366-367
  partners, selection of,
    competitors, 360
    limiting factors, 361
    nationality, 361
    other industries, from, 360-361
    research institutes, 360
    university, 360
  purpose and scope of, 361
  strategic outsourcing, 355-359
  technological development, monitoring, 370-371
  uncertainty,
    building in, 365-366
    monitoring, 368-373
  unexpected developments,
    aspirin, 366
    computer imaging sperm selection, 366
    exploitation of, 367
    Minoxidil, 365
    positive impact of, 365
    territorial opportunities, 368
  unwinding,
    allocation of use and ownership, 375
    non-competition obligations, 376
    outsiders, contracts with, 375
    personnel, 375
Competition law
  choice of law, not superseded by, 318-320
  confidential information and know-how, transfer of, 7
  European Union, of, 113-119
  licensing, relating to,
    approval under, 161
    Israel, in, 165
    Japan, in, 164
    Korea, in, 164
    TRIPs Agreement, 161
    United States, in, 163
  supranational regimes, 113-119
  triggering, 113
  United States, in, 119-126

Computer software
  copyright protection, 26
  trademark protection, 39-40
Confidential information
  advantages of, 4
  Coca Cola formulation, 4
  competition law, consideration of, 7
  confidentiality agreements,
    advantages of, 5
    contents of, 6
    drafting, 6
  disadvantages of, 4-5
  ephemeral nature of protection, 4
  idea, control of, 4
  illegal disclosure of, 5
  information not being, 6
  international agreements, 7
  misappropriation, action for, 5
  potential customer or ally, disclosure to, 5
  protection of, 3
  return to owner, 6
  supranational protection regimes, 7
  trade secrets. *See* Trade secrets
Consumer electronics
  transfer by direct sale and assignment, 70
Convergence of technologies
  collaboration. *See* Collaboration
  complexity, 342
  multi-media products, 341
  uncertainty, 342
Cooperative research, 345-352
  European Union, in, 346-349
  United States, in, 349-352
Copyright
  advantages of, 28
  automatically arising, 11
  Berne Convention, 29
  China, law in, 30-31
  computer software, protection of, 26
  disadvantages of, 28-29
  duration of, 28
  employee, work by, 27
  European Union initiatives, 29
  France, law in, 31-32
  Japan, law in, 32
  meaning, 26-28
  Mexico, law in, 32-33

Copyright *contd*
  NAFTA provisions, 30
  owner, 27
  registration not dependent on, 27
  similar work, creation of, 28-29
  supranational regimes, 29-30
  technology field, in, 26
  United Kingdom, law in, 33
  United States, law in, 34
  Universal Copyright Convention, 29
  valuation, 51
Corporation
  joint venture as, 84-85
Czech Republic
  bankruptcy, transfer of rights on, 301-302
  joint ventures, 89-90
  licenses,
    assignment, 187
    duration and renewal, 213
    fee, payment of, 217
    laws and regulations, warranty for conformity to, 197
    ownership under, 171
  security interests, 281-282

Designs
  Berne Convention, 35
  China, law in, 38
  European Union,
    proposed Harmonization Directive, 36
    proposed registration, 37
  France, law in, 38
  GATT TRIPs, 38
  Hague Union, 35-36
  Japan, law in, 39
  meaning, 35
  Mexico, law in, 39
  NAFTA provisions, 38
  Paris Convention, 35
  protection,
    civil law countries, in, 35
    common law countries, in, 35
  supranational regimes, 35-38
  United Kingdom, law in, 39
  United States, law in, 39

Disputes, resolution of
  Alternative Dispute Resolution, 338-340
  applicable law. *See* Applicable law; Choice of law
  arbitration,
    advantages of, 333
    appeals, 333
    choice of law, 335
    considerations, 335
    contractual disputes to be decided by, 336-337
    discovery, 334
    enforcement of awards, 337-338
    enforcement of clauses, 334
    fees and costs, 337
    nature of, 332-333
    number of arbitrators, 335-336
    place of, 336
    remedy, inadequacy of, 337
    speed of, 333
    tribunals, 335
  drafting agreements, 323
  litigation,
    conduct of, 324
    discovery, 329-330
    enforcement of judgments, 330-332
    forum, 324-329
    powers of court, backed by, 333
    pretrial process, 329-330
    trial process, 330
  mediation, 338
  mini-trial, 338-339
  primary methods of, 324
  summary jury trial, 339
Distributor
  meaning, 73
  prices, setting, 74
  technology transfer via, 73-74

Egypt
  employee's invention, ownership of, 172
European Economic Interest Grouping
  joint venture, as, 86
European Union
  audiovisual and telecommunications industries, problems in, 167
  Community Trademark, 41-42, 48-50

INDEX

European Union *contd*
  competition law,
    abuse of dominant position, 161
    agency agreements, 118-119
    agreements subject to, 155
    application of, 119
    black list provisions, 155
    block exemptions, 155, 162, 347
    choice of law, not superseded by, 319
    cooperative research ventures, effect on, 347
    distribution agreements, 116-117
    exclusive distribution agreements, block exemption, 117, 163
    exclusive purchasing agreements, block exemption, 117
    exclusivity, 178-179
    franchising agreements, block exemption, 118
    grey list provisions, 155
    joint ventures, 114-116
    know-how licenses, 161-162
    licensing terms and practices, 161-163
    Merger Control Regulation, 115-116
    mergers and acquisitions, 116
    minimum performance requirements, exemption of, 204
    non-competition provisions, prohibition of, 208
    notifications, 154-156
    patent block exemption, 161
    primary sources of, 113-114
    research and development joint ventures block exemption, 347-349
    royalty payments, provisions on, 205-206
    territorial restrictions, 173-174
    unregistered licenses, avoiding, 154
    white list provisions, 155
  cooperative research ventures, treatment of, 346-349
  copyright initiatives, 29
  designs,
    proposed Harmonization Directive, 36
    proposed registration, 37

European Union *contd*
  draft regulation on technology transfers, 155-156
  export controls, elimination of, 140
  joint ventures,
    EU enterprise, treated as, 137-138
  licenses,
    duration and renewal, 211
    grant-back, 188
    most favored nations clause, 218
    no-challenge clauses, 189
    post-termination rights and obligations, 215-216
    resale price maintenance, 184
    subsequent transfer, conditions for, 183
    tying and quality control, 186
  local content of goods, 136
  patents, consideration of competition law, 25
  product liability directive, 131-132
  software licenses, 181
  technology transfer, royalty payments, 129
Export controls
  choice of law, not superseded by, 320-322
  COCOM, under, 139
  European Union, in, 140
  France, in, 147-148
  Germany, in, 147
  Italy, in, 147
  Japan, in, 147-148
  licenses, provisions of, 218
  multilateral nonproliferation regimes, under, 140
  NAFTA, within, 141
  supranational regimes, 140-141
  technology transfers, application to, 139
  United Kingdom, in, 147
  United States, in, 141-147

France
  bankruptcy, transfer of rights on, 300-301
  copyright law, 31-32
  designs, protection of, 38
  export controls, 147-148

France *contd*
  Intellectual Property Code, 8
  joint ventures, 91-93
  licenses,
    exclusivity, 179
    laws and regulations, warranty for conformity to, 197
    ownership under, 170
  patent law, 22
  technology licenses, approval of, 159-160
  technology transfer,
    alliances for, 82
    legal issues, 112
  trade secrets, protection of, 8
  trademark law, 45
Franchising
  agreements, block exemption, 118
  commercial vehicles, 74
  complete package of technology and rights, transfer of, 74
  criteria, relationship between, 77
  defining terminology, 76
  foreign markets, in, 74
  high-technology transfer, 74
  Hong Kong, in, 81
  Hungary, in, 83
  joint ventures, 74
  Korea, in, 81-82
  sub-franchising, 76

GATT
  confidential information, protection of, 7
  designs, protection of, 38
  TRIPs Agreement,
    designs, protection of, 38
    licensing terms and practices under, 161
Germany
  copyright,
    bankruptcy, on, 299-300
    transfer of, 276-277
  debtor-creditor law, 273
  designs,
    attachability, 299
    transfer of, 275
  enforcement of judgments, 332
  export controls, 147

Germany *contd*
  insolvency. *See* Insolvency
  joint ventures, 93-94
  know-how,
    bankruptcy law, effect of, 299
  license,
    assignment of, 277
    attachability, 298
  patents,
    bankruptcy law, effect of, 296-297
    employee inventions, 298
    transfer of, 274-275
  security interests. *See* Security interests
  software, transfer of ownership, 277-279
  technology transfer,
    alliances for, 82
    legal issues, 112
  trade secrets,
    bankruptcy law, effect of, 299
  trademarks,
    bankruptcy, ownership on, 299
    transfer of, 275-276
  utility models,
    bankruptcy law, effect of, 297
    transfer of, 275

Hong Kong
  franchising, 81
Hungary
  franchising, 83
  joint ventures, 91
  technology transfer, royalty payments, 129

India
  intellectual property laws, poor protection from, 167
  joint ventures, 94-95
  licenses,
    duration and renewal, 213
    revenues, payment of, 203
    subsequent transfer, conditions for, 183
    territorial restrictions, 176
    tying, 186
  product liability law, 135
  technology licenses, approval of, 160

INDEX

India *contd*
  technology transfers, legal issues, 111
Incubators
  Israel, in, 352, 353-355
Industrial sponsorship
  collaboration, as, 344
Insolvency
  Czech Republic, in, 301-302
  France, transfer of rights in, 300-301
  Germany, in,
    copyright, treatment of, 299-300
    designs, attachability, 299
    employee inventions, treatment of, 298
    licenses, attachability, 298
    patents, effect on, 296-297
    trade secrets and know-how, treatment of, 299
    trademarks, ownership of, 299
    utility models, effect on, 297
  Netherlands, in, 302-303
  Spain, in, 303-304
  technology rights, termination of, 283
  United States, in,
    automatic stay, 291-292, 295
    avoiding powers of trustee, 292-294
    Bankruptcy Code, 283-284
    bankruptcy estate, liquidation of, 284
    cut off of security interests, 295
    executory contracts, rejection, assumption and assignment of, 285-289
    fraudulent transfers, 294
    ipso facto clauses, invalidation of, 284
    preferential transfers, 294-295
    property, bankruptcy trustee's right to use, sell or lease, 289-291
    sale of property free from liens, 295
    security interests, provisions affecting, 294-295
    technology licensee, rights of, 286-289
    transfers of property, avoiding, 292-293
Intellectual property rights
  comparative table, 54

Intellectual property rights *contd*
  confidential information. *See* Confidential information
  contractual allocation, 153
  convention adoptions, 58-67
  copyright. *See* Copyright
  enforcement of, 2
  identification and ongoing protection of, 52
  intangible character of, 1
  international dimensions, 53
  obtaining, means of, 50
  patents. *See* Patents
  protection of, 1
  reputation of business, relating to, 2
  technology, embodied in, 1
  trademarks. *See* Trademarks
  trade secrets. *See* Trade secrets
  transferees, practical issues for, 50-52
  types of, 2
  valuation, 51
  value, loss of, 1
  worldwide system, lack of, 1-2
Inventions
  exploitation of, 3
  patents. *See* Patents
Israel
  competition law,
    licensing, relating to, 165
  distribution agreements, duration of, 213
  licenses,
    non-competition provisions, 210
    remedies, 201
    territorial restrictions, 177
    use restrictions, 183
Italy
  export controls, 147
  joint ventures, 94
  licenses, duration and renewal, 212
  technology transfer,
    alliances for, 83
    legal issues, 113

Japan
  competition law,
    licensing, relating to, 164
  copyright law, 32
  copyright, ownership of, 169

Japan *contd*
  designs, protection of, 39
  export controls, 147-148
  intellectual property laws, poor enforcement of, 167
  joint ventures, 95
  licenses,
    confidentiality provisions, 192-193
    grant-back, 188
    laws and regulations, warranty for conformity to, 196
    non-competition provisions, 209
    remedies, 201
    resale price maintenance, 185
    royalty structure, 206
    termination, reasons for, 214
    territorial restrictions, 176
    tying, 186
    use restrictions, 182
  patent law, 22-24
  product liability law, 135
  technology licenses, approval of, 158-159
  technology transfer,
    alliances for, 80-81
    legal issues, 111
    royalty payments, 129
  trade secrets, protection of, 8-9
  trademark law, 45-46
  trademark registration, ownership of rights to, 169
  Unfair Competition Prevention Law, 8

Joint ventures
  Argentina, in, 88
  Brazil, in, 88-89
  business cultures, 101
  Canada, in, 89
  capital, 98
  China, in, 95-96
  competitive environment, 104
  concentrative, 115, 346
  control of operations, 108
  cooperative, 346
  corporation, as, 84-85
  cost differentials, expenses and financing, 99-100
  Czech and Slovak Republics, in, 89-90
  development structures, 230

Joint ventures *contd*
  equity investment, 127
  equity ownership, 108
  EU enterprise, treated as, 137-138
  European Union competition law, 114-116
  exit mechanisms, 148-151
  France, in, 91-93
  franchising vehicle, as, 74
  Germany, in, 93-94
  goals, 103-104
  Hungary, in, 91
  India, in, 94-95
  Italy, in, 94
  Japan, in, 95
  know-how, 97
  Korea, in, 96
  local content,
    China, in, 137
    requirement of, 135
  managerial control, 104-105
  market access, 98
  market size, 99
  materials and supplies, 99
  meaning, 83-84
  Merger Control Regulation, 115-116
  nature of technology, 105-106
  ownership of technology, 106
  partnership, as, 85-86
  personnel, 100-101
  political environment, 106
  proprietary information, 102-103
  research and development, 97
  risk, allocation of, 99
  Russia, in, 90
  separate entity, or, 83-84
  strategy, 103
  Taiwan, in, 96
  technology, 97
  term, 102
  time constraints, 101-102
  U.S. National Cooperative Research Act, 349-352
  United States, in, 87-88
    acquisitions, 123-124
    antitrust law, 121-124
    statutory provisions, 122
  United States party, with,

INDEX

Joint ventures *contd*
    domestic or foreign partnership, 243-247
    sale or license of technology, 242
    special considerations, 240
    technology, contribution of, 241
    U.S partnership with foreign subsidiary, use of, 245-247
    U.S. partner's foreign subsidiary, use of, 244-245
Judgments
    enforcement of, 330-332

Korea
    competition law,
        licensing, relating to, 164
    intellectual property laws, poor enforcement of, 167
    joint ventures, 96
    licenses,
        confidentiality provisions, 193
        duration and renewal, 212
        grant-back, 189
        laws and regulations, warranty for conformity to, 197
        ownership under, 170
        post-termination rights and obligations, 216
        revenues, payment of, 202-203
        tying, 186
        use restrictions, 182
    product liability law, 134
    technology licenses, approval of, 159
    technology transfer,
        alliances for, 81-82
        legal issues, 111
        royalty payments, 129

Licenses
    agreement,
        assignment, 187
        confidentiality, safeguarding, 190-193
        cross license, 188-189
        exclusivity, 177-179
        export controls, 218
        fee, payment of, 217
        grant-back, 188-189
        maintenance and training arrangements, 207

Licenses *contd*
    most favored nations clause, 218
    no-challenge clauses, 189-190
    non-competition provisions, 208-210
    parties, relationship of, 217
    purpose, specifying, 172
    quality control, 185-186
    remedies, 198-201
    resale price maintenance, 184-185
    revenues, provision for, 201-207
    "Shrink-wrap", 180, 183
    subsequent transfer, conditions for, 183
    term and termination, 210-216
    territorial restrictions, 172-177
    tying, 185-186
    use restrictions, 179-183
    warranties and disclaimers, 194-198
    allocation of rights, 166
    competition law,
        approval under, 161
        European Union, of, 161-163
        Israel, in, 165
        Japan, in, 164
        Korea, in, 164
        supranational regimes, 161-163
        TRIPs Agreement, 161
        United States, in, 163-164
    confidentiality provisions,
        China, in, 192
        exceptions, 191-192
        importance of, 190
        Japan, in, 192-193
        Korea, in, 193
        procedures, 191
        reciprocity, 191-192
        scope, 190-191
    duration and renewal,
        Argentina, in, 211
        Belgium, in, 212
        certainty of, 210
        China, in, 212
        Czech and Slovak Republics, in, 213
        developing countries, in, 210
        India, in, 213
        Israel, in, 213
        Italy, in, 212

Licenses *contd*
  Korea, in, 212
  Mexico, in, 211-212
  Nigeria, in, 213
  patents, expiry of, 210
  Philippines, in, 212
  supranational regimes, 211
  Taiwan, in, 212
  European Union, notification to, 154-156
  exclusivity,
    advantages and disadvantages of, 177-178
    France, in, 179
    specification of, 177
    supranational regimes, 178-179
  Germany, in,
    assignment of, 277
    attachability, 298
  government approvals,
    Argentina, in, 156-157
    Brazil, in, 157
    China, in, 157-158
    France, in, 159-160
    India, in, 160
    Japan, in, 158-159
    Korea, in, 159
    Mexico, in, 157
    Nigeria, in, 160
    Philippines, in, 159
    requirement of, 154
    responsibility for obtaining, 154
    Russia, in, 160
    supranational regimes, 154-156
    United States, in, 156
  grant, delay or suspension of, 374
  laws and regulations, conformity to,
    China, in, 196
    Czech and Slovak Republics, in, 197
    France, in, 197
    Japan, in, 196
    Korea, in, 197
    Mexico, in, 196
    Nigeria, in, 197
    United States, in, 195-196
    warranty of, 195

Licenses *contd*
  non-competition provisions,
    Canada, in, 209
    European Union, in, 208
    importance of, 208
    Israel, in, 210
    Japan, in, 209
    supranational regimes, 208
    United States, in, 208-209
  ownership under,
    contractual rights, use of, 167
    Czech and Slovak Republics, in, 171
    Egypt, in, 172
    France, in, 170
    Japan, in, 169
    Korea, in, 170
    Mexico, in, 168
    particular countries, reputation of, 166
    Philippines, in, 170
    Russia, in, 171
    Taiwan, in, 170
    target country, laws of, 168
    United States, in, 168
  post-termination rights and obligations, 215-216
  remedies,
    categories of, 198
    China, in, 200
    contractual, 199
    damages, 198
    indemnity, 198-199
    injunctive relief, 198
    Israel, in, 201
    Japan, in, 201
    limitation of liability, 199
    supranational regimes, 200
    United Kingdom, in, 201
    United States, in, 200
  restrictions, imposition of, 153
  revenues, payment of,
    audit right, 206
    China, in, 202
    forms of, 202-204
    India, in, 203
    Korea, in, 202-203
    mechanism for, 201
    Mexico, in, 202

INDEX

Licenses *contd*
   minimum performance
     requirements, 204
   Nigeria, in, 203
   Poland, in, 203
   records, 206
   royalty structure, 205-206
   shrink-wrap, 180
   taxation. *See* Taxation
   technology, listing details of, 165-166
   termination, reasons for, 213-215
   territorial restrictions,
     agreement, in, 172-173
     China, in, 176
     European Union, in, 173-174
     India, in, 176
     Israel, in, 177
     Japan, in, 176
     Nigeria, in, 176
     Philippines, in, 176
     Poland, in, 176
     supranational regimes, 173-174
     Taiwan, in, 176
     United States, in, 175
   trademarks, responsibility for, 167
   use restrictions,
     details of, 179
     Israel, in, 183
     Japan, in, 182
     Korea, in, 182
     software license, in, 180
     specific, 179-180
     supranational regimes, 180-181
     United States, in, 181-182
   warranties,
     contentious topic, as, 194
     laws and regulations, conformity to, 195-198
     non-infringement, 194-195
     performance, 195
     use, operation and results, 195
   use of term, 72

Mergers and acquisitions
   competition law, 116
     United States, in, 124
   technology transfers through, 70, 96-97

Mexico
   copyright law, 32-33
   designs, protection of, 39
   employee's inventions, ownership of, 168
   licenses,
     assignment, 187
     duration and renewal, 211-212
     laws and regulations, warranty for conformity to, 196
     post-termination rights and obligations, 216
     revenues, payment of, 202
   patent law, 24
   technology licenses, approval of, 157
   technology transfer,
     alliances for, 80
     legal issues, 110
     royalty payments, 128
   trade secrets, protection of, 9
   trademark law, 46
Multi-media products
   development of, 341
Muslim countries
   licenses, grant-back, 189

NAFTA
   breach of license, remedies for, 200
   confidential information, protection of, 7
   copyright provisions, 30
   designs, protection of, 38
   export controls, 140-141
   local content of goods, 136
   patent protection, 21
   trade barriers, effect on, 138-139
   trademark provisions, 44

Netherlands
   bankruptcy, transfer of rights on, 302-303
   enforcement of judgments, 332
   security interests, 282-283
New Zealand
   product liability law, 135
Nigeria
   licenses,
     duration and renewal, 213
     grant-back, 189

Nigeria *contd*
    laws and regulations, warranty for
      conformity to, 197
    revenues, payment of, 203
    territorial restrictions, 176
    tying, 186
  technology licenses, approval of, 160
Norway
  cost sharing arrangements, 229

Outsourcing
  practical issues in structuring,
    356-359
  strategic, 355-359

Partnership
  joint venture as, 85-86
Patents
  advantages of, 14
  alternatives to, 16
  application for, 11, 13, 15-16
  biotechnology inventions, 21
  China, law in, 21-22
  Community Patent Convention, 18-19
  comparative table, 55
  compulsory license, 15
  disadvantages of, 14-15
  duration of, 12
  ethical issues, 14
  European Patent Convention, 17
  European Union countries, in, 25
  expense of, 14-15
  exploitation, monopoly right for, 14
  France, law in, 22
  grant of, 20
  immoral inventions, 14
  invention, protection of, 4
  inventions for which granted, 13
  Japan, law in, 22-24
  maximum protection, obtaining, 16
  meaning, 12-14
  Mexico, law in, 24
  Patent Co-operation Treaty, 16-17
  petty, 16
  pharmaceutical,
    duration, 12
    Supplementary Protection
      Certificates, 19-20
  prior art, 13

Patents *contd*
  protection of, 12
  renewal fees, 15
  specification, 15
  supranational regimes, 16-21
  unified system, lack of, 13
  Untied Kingdom, in, 14, 24-25
  United States, in, 13-14, 25-26
  utility models, 16
Philippines
  licenses,
    duration and renewal, 212
    grant-back, 188
    no-challenge clauses, 190
    ownership under, 170
    post-termination rights and
      obligations, 216
    royalty structure, 206
    territorial restrictions, 176
  technology licenses, approval of, 159
Poland
  licenses,
    resale price maintenance, 185
    revenues, payment of, 203
    territorial restrictions, 176
  technology transfer,
    royalty payments, 129
    legal issues, 112
Product liability
  Australia, law in, 134
  Canada, law in, 135
  claims, 131
  European Union Directive, 131-132
  India, law in, 135
  Japan, law in, 135
  Korea, law in, 134
  limitation of, 130-131
  New Zealand, law in, 135
  supranational regimes, 131-132
  Turkey, law in, 135
  United States, law in, 132-134

Regional trading blocks
  European Union, 137-138
  NAFTA, 138-139
  proliferation of, 137
  supranational regimes, 137-139
Representative
  technology transfer via, 74

INDEX

Resale price maintenance
  licenses, control in, 184-185
Reverse engineering
  design, obtaining, 3
Rome Convention
  choice of law, 307-308
    express, 312
    implied, 316
  formal validity under, 322-323
  severability of contract, 316
Russia
  copyright regulations, 280
  joint ventures, 90
  licenses,
    ownership under, 171
    resale price maintenance, 185
  security interests, 280-281
  technology licenses, approval of, 160
  technology transfer, royalty
    payments, 129

Secured transactions
  arrangements for, 252
  security interests. *See* Security
    interests
Security interests
  Canada, in, 271-273
  Czech Republic, in, 281-282
  Germany, in,
    applicable legal framework, 274-279
    collateral, definition of, 279
    copyrights, transfer of, 276-277
    debtor, use by, 279
    designs, transfer of, 275
    documentation, 279-280
    evaluation of intellectual property,
      273
    exploitation of capital, 273
    exploitation rights, 280
    licenses, assignment of, 277
    Patent Office, communication with,
      279
    patents, transfer of, 274-275
    software, in, 274
    software, protection of, 277-279
    third party infringement, 280
    title to collateral, verification of,
      273
    trademarks, transfer of, 275-276

Security interests *contd*
  trend towards grant of, 273
  utility models, transfer of, 275
  Netherlands, in, 282-283
  Russian Federation, in, 280-281
  United States, in,
    applicable legal framework, 253-257
    automatic stay of action, 295
    avoiding powers of bankruptcy
      trustee, 294
    Bankruptcy Code provisions
      affecting, 294-295
    collateral,
      debtor's rights in, 268-270
      description of, 263-265
    contractual relationships, 271
    copyright, in, 255, 258-259
    creation and perfection of, 257-263
    cut off, 295
    debtor's rights, investigation of, 269
    default provisions, 267
    documentation, 263-265
    due diligence, 268-270
    effect of, 252-253
    intellectual property rights,
      covenants protecting, 265-266
    lien searches, 269-270
    lien, 252
    "look-back" periods, 270
    masks works, in, 257, 262
    meaning, 252
    non-competition and non-
      disclosure agreements, 268
    patents, in, 256, 260
    personal property, in, 253-254
    preferential transfers, 294-295
    remedies, 266-268
    sale of property free from liens, 295
    security instrument and financing
      agreement, description in, 263-264
    source code escrow, 268
    State law, 254
    technology not subject to federal
      law, 262-263
    title, search as to, 269
    trademarks, in, 256-257, 260-262
Semiconductor chips
  topographical rights, 39
Slovak Republic

Security interests *contd*
  joint ventures, 89-90
  licenses,
    assignment, 187
    duration and renewal, 213
    fee, payment of, 217
    laws and regulations, warranty for conformity to, 197
    ownership under, 171
Software, 26, 27, 28, 29, 30, 51, 144, 194, 226, 268
  copyright protection in Mexico, 33
  copyright protection in United States, 34
  EU Software Directive, 181
  Germany, 277-279
  license, 180, 207
Spain
  bankruptcy, transfer of rights on, 303-304

Taiwan
  author, person being, 170
  joint ventures, 96
  licenses,
    duration and renewal, 212
    territorial restrictions, 176
  technology transfer, royalty payments, 129
Taxation
  capital contributions to, 226-227
  cross licenses, 225-226
  development structures,
    ad hoc arrangements, 228
    contract research and licensing arrangements, 228-229
    cost sharing, 229-230
    joint venture arrangements, 230
    partnerships, 230-231
  distributions, 227
  foreign multinational groups, arrangements within,
    cost sharing arrangements, 234-236
    research and licensing contracts, 231-234
  license and sale distinguished,
    amount and timing of income recognized, 224
    differing treatment of, 221

Taxation *contd*
    foreign tax credit, treatment of, 224
    imputed income rules, application of, 224
    instalment sale treatment, 222
    law articulating, 221
    passive foreign investment corporation, foreign corporation as, 224
    related parties, royalties from, 223
    royalty or capital gain, 222
    source rules, 222
    transferor, status of, 223
    US safe harbors, 221
  like-kind exchanges, 225-226
  rollover treatment, 226
  stock, transfers for, 226-227
  technology income, of, 219
  transfer forms, consequences of, 220
  U.S. multinational groups, arrangements within,
    contract research, 236-238
    cost sharing, 239-240
  United States party, joint ventures with,
    domestic or foreign partnership, 243-247
    sale or license of technology, 242
    special considerations, 240
    technology, contribution of, 241
    U.S partnership with foreign subsidiary, use of, 245-247
    U.S. partner's foreign subsidiary, use of, 244-245
Technology
  broad meaning of, 2
  inherent value, protection of, 2
Technology income
  affiliate receiving, deciding, 219
  taxation. *See* Taxation
Technology transfers
  basic forms of, 70
  business factors in selecting structure for,
    business cultures, 101
    capital, 98
    competitive environment, 104
    cost differentials, expenses and financing, 99-100

INDEX

Technology transfers *contd*
  goals, 103-104
  know-how, 97
  managerial control, 104-105
  market access, 98
  market size, 98-99
  materials and supplies, 99
  nature of technology, 105-106
  personnel, 100-101
  political environment, 106
  proprietary information, 102-103
  relationships between, 107
  research and development, 97
  risk, allocation of, 99
  strategy, 103
  technology, 97
  term, 102
  time constraints, 101-102
business objectives, 69
competition between parties, 126
competition law. *See* Competition law
complex,
  challenge of, 376-377
  unwinding, 373-376
contractual alliances, 70
  agents, via, 72-73
  Argentina, in, 79-80
  Brazil, in, 80
  Canada, in, 80
  competition law, 116-119
  contractual partner, products made available to end-users by, 72
  distributors, via, 73-74
  European Union Directives, 77-78
  France, in, 82
  franchising, 74-77
  Germany, in, 82
  Hong Kong, in, 81
  Hungary, in, 83
  Italy, in, 83
  Japan, in, 80-81
  Korea, in, 81-82
  Mexico, in, 80
  representatives, via, 74
  supranational regimes, 77-78
  United States law, 124-126
  United States, in, 78-79
development structures,
  ad hoc arrangements, 228

Technology transfers *contd*
  contract research and licensing arrangements, 228-229
  cost sharing, 229-230
  joint venture arrangements, 230
  partnerships, 230-231
direct end-use licensing, 71
direct sale and assignment,
  consumer electronics, for, 70
  products and technology distinguished, 70
  reasons for, 71
  restrictions, inconsistent with imposition of, 153
  transferor, loss of control by, 70
draft regulation, 155-156
exit mechanisms, 148-151
export controls. *See* Export controls
forms of, 220
joint ventures. *See* Joint ventures
legal factors in selecting structure for,
  Argentina, in, 110
  Brazil, in, 110
  China, in, 110-111
  control of operations, 108
  equity ownership, 108
  France, in, 112
  Germany, in, 112
  India, in, 111
  Italy, in, 113
  Japan, in, 111
  Korea, in, 111
  Mexico, in, 110
  ownership of technology, 106
  Poland, in, 112
  United Kingdom, in, 112
  United States, in, 109
licensing. *See* Licenses
local content,
  China, in, 137
  European Union, in, 136
  NAFTA, under, 136
  requirement of, 135
  supranational regimes, 136
  United States, in, 137
maximal protection, securing, 69
merger and acquisition, through, 70, 96-97
  competition law, 116

Technology transfers *contd*
  payment for,
    Argentina, in, 128
    Brazil, in, 128
    Canada, in, 127-128
    China, in, 130
    European Union, in, 129
    generally, 127
    Hungary, in, 129
    Japan, in, 129
    Korea, in, 129
    Mexico, in, 128
    Poland, in, 129
    Russia, in, 129
    Taiwan, in, 129
    Thailand, in, 130
    United States, in, 127-128
  product liability. *See* Product liability
  retention of rights, 251
  secured transactions. *See* Secured transactions; Security interests
  strategic alliances, 70-77. *See* also contractual alliances, *above*
  suitable structure, deciding on, 69, 152
  translation of documents, 168
Thailand
  technology transfer, royalty payments, 130
Trade secrets
  disclosure, prevention of, 7
  protection of,
    China, in, 8
    France, in, 8
    Japan, in, 8-9
    Mexico, in, 9
    United Kingdom, in, 9-10
    United States, in, 10-11
Trademarks
  China, law in, 44-45
  comparative table, 56-57
  computer software field, in, 39-40
  deciding which to register, 48-50
  European Union Community Trademark, 41-42, 48-50
  form of, 40
  France, law in, 45
  Japan, law in, 45-46
  large number of countries, registration in, 49

Trademarks *contd*
  Madrid Arrangement, 42-44
  Madrid Protocol, 43-44, 48-50
  meaning, 40
  Mexico, law in, 46
  NAFTA, provisions of, 44
  particular goods or services, registered for, 41
  responsibility for obtaining, 167
  rights in, 40
  separate national applications, filing, 48-49
  several countries, protection in through one action, 49-50
  small number of countries, registration in, 49
  supranational regimes, 41-44
  United Kingdom, law in, 46-47
  United States, law in, 47
  use of, 39
Turkey
  product liability law, 135

U.N. Convention on Contracts for the International Sale of Goods
  application of, 313
  automatic application of, 314
  different countries, application where parties based in, 314
  goods, meaning, 313
  mixed contracts, application to, 313
  UCC, resembling, 314
Uniform Commercial Code
  CISG resembling, 314
  freedom to protect interests under, 315
United Kingdom
  designs, protection of, 39
  export controls, 147
  licenses, remedies, 201
  patent law, 24-25
  patent system, 14
  technology transfers, legal issues, 112
  trade secrets, protection of, 9-10
  trademark law, 46-47
  United States, law in, 33
United States
  antitrust law,
    Clayton Act, 120

INDEX

United States *contd*
    contractual alliances, 124-126
    joint ventures, 121-124
    licensing, relating to, 163-164
    mergers and acquisitions, 124
    Robinson-Patman Act, 120
    Sherman Act, 120
    statutory provisions, 119
    territorial restrictions, 175
    violations of, 120
  arbitration clauses, enforcement of, 334
  choice of law of, 309, 312
  cooperative research ventures, treatment of, 349-352
  copyright,
    law, 34
    mortgage of, 259
    ownership of, 168
      transfer of, 258-259
    security interest in, 255
    works for hire, 27
  designs, protection of, 39
  export controls,
    Distribution License, 143
    dual-use, 141-147
    embargoed countries, 146
    Enhanced Pollution Control Initiative, 144
    Export Administration Regulations, 141-144
    export, definition, 141-142
    extraterritorial application, 143
    International Traffic in Arms regulations, 144-146
    liberalization, 142
    licenses, 141
    nuclear-related goods and technical data, 146
  insolvency. *See* Insolvency
  joint ventures, 87-88
    acquisitions, 123-124
    antitrust law, 121-124
    statutory provisions, 122
  licenses,
    laws and regulations, warranty for conformity to, 195-196

United States *contd*
    non-competition provisions, 208-209
    ownership under, 168
    remedies, 200
    resale price maintenance, 184
    use restrictions, 181-182
  litigation,
    conduct of, 324
    enforcement of judgments, 331
    forum, 324-329
    pretrial process, 329-330
    trial process, 330
  mask works,
    ownership, transfer of, 262
    protection of, 39
    security interest in, 257
  patents,
    assignment of application, 260
    law, 25-26
    mortgage of, 260
    security interest in, 256
    system, 13-14
  product liability law, 132-134
  public procurement contracts, 137
  security interests. *See* Security interests
  technology licenses, approval of, 156
  technology transfer,
    alliances for, 78-79
    legal issues, 109
    royalty payments, 127-128
  trade secrets, protection of, 10-11
  trademarks,
    assignment, 260-262
    law, 47
    lien, 261
    security interest in, 256-257

Warranties
  licenses, in,
    contentious topic, as, 194
    laws and regulations, conformity to, 195-198
    non-infringement, 194-195
    performance, 195
    use, operation and results, 195